WAYS OF LYING

WAYS OF LYING

Dissimulation, Persecution, and
Conformity in Early Modern Europe

Perez Zagorin

Harvard University Press
Cambridge, Massachusetts
London, England
1990

Copyright © 1990 by the President and Fellows of Harvard College
All rights reserved
Printed in the United States of America
10   9   8   7   6   5   4   3   2   1

This book is printed on acid-free paper, and its binding materials
have been chosen for strength and durability.

Library of Congress Cataloging-in-Publication Data

Zagorin, Perez.
  Ways of lying : dissimulation, persecution, and conformity in
early modern Europe / Perez Zagorin.
      p.   cm.
  ISBN 0-674-94834-3 (alk. paper)
  1. Truthfulness and falsehood—History—16th century.
  2. Truthfulness and falsehood—History—17th century.
  3. Persecution—Europe—History—16th century. 4. Persecution—
  Europe—History—17th century. 5. Reformation. 6. Counter-
  Reformation—Europe. 7. Europe—Church history—16th century.
  8. Europe—Church history—17th century. I. Title. II. Title:
  Dissimulation, persecution, and conformity in early modern Europe.
  BR1608.E8Z34   1990   89-77600
  177'.3—dc20   CIP

Preface

The use of speech and writing to deceive instead of inform and to convey falsehood rather than truth may seem like a perversion; yet it falls, as the simplest reflection makes clear, within the normal function of language. In verbal language humans gained an evolutionary privilege denied to all other animals. As a result, they also acquired the privilege of being able to lie. Stendhal stated a truism when he remarked, in *The Red and the Black,* that "speech has been given to man to hide his thoughts." Since the faculty of lying is coterminous with language itself, we cannot doubt that human beings have always told lies, not only to others, but likewise, paradoxically, to themselves. But if lying in this sense remains a universal possibility in any sort of human existence, it may sometimes also appear as a historically and socially determined phenomenon in those communities and societies in which pressures for religious or political conformity have impelled dissident individuals or groups to lie and dissemble in self-protection. In all societies, rulers and governments also lie, of course. I am not speaking of them, however, but of their subjects and citizens who turn to dissimulation to escape persecution. There have been innumerable instances of this sort in the twentieth century, most notably in countries under the sway of fascist or communist dictatorships or other forms of despotism. But even largely democratic countries provide examples. From the 1930s to the 1950s, many people in the United States were faced with dilemmas of truthtelling because of congressional inquisitions into their political beliefs and affiliations. One of those investigated during that period was the German communist poet and playwright Bertolt Brecht, who spent part of his wartime exile in Hollywood and was called before the House of Representatives' Un-American Activities Committee on

30 October 1947 along with other noted Hollywood writers. A sympathetic biographer, J. K. Lyon, has described his testimony as "a polite exercise in cunning and duplicity." Brecht used equivocation to skew and withhold the truth, although when asked the central question whether he had ever been a member of the Communist party, he denied it. The next day he left the United States for good, eventually to live in East Germany, where he was treated as an honored cultural figure. As a self-styled revolutionary, Brecht's political deceit and the many moral ambiguities which marked his career are partially explained by some lines from his play *The Measure Taken* (1930):

> What meanness would you not commit, to
> Stamp out meanness?
> If, at last, you could change the world, what
> Would you think yourself too good for?

In subsequent disagreements with the East German authorities he acted in the same way. When some of his works were criticized for formalism or lack of positiveness, he complied by making slight changes in performance while leaving their published version unaltered. Throughout his life, Brecht employed cunning and dissimulation in dealing with political authority.

Dissimulation with a similar purpose of averting repression, though in far different historical circumstances, forms the subject matter of this book. The lives and ideas of nonconformists, dissenters, rebels, and heterodox thinkers and how they have coped with oppressive powers have been among my abiding preoccupations as a historian. My interest in the present subject was awakened when I became familiar with John Calvin's polemics against Nicodemism, a form of religious dissimulation, while writing *Rebels and Rulers*. In that study of revolution in early modern Europe I was pursuing the problem of religious and political commitment: How did rebels in the early modern states arm themselves morally and ideologically to resist divinely appointed kings? Calvin's tracts made me aware of the Reformation Protestants who, far from openly committing themselves to the new faith, dissembled their beliefs by a feigned conformity to Catholicism. Later on, as I perceived many other notable manifestations of dissimulation, I resolved to investigate the whole subject. This book is the result.

Since the 1950s, the social, political, religious, cultural, and intellectual history of sixteenth- and seventeenth-century Europe has been revitalized through a vast variety of studies. Investigations of social groups, classes, and structures, of demography and family, religion and mentalities, political institutions and ideas, science, popular culture, the transmission of intellectual traditions, and the role of hermeticism and the occult in philosophy have yielded a rich harvest that has fundamentally transformed our understanding of early modern civilization. In this book I have attempted to contribute a further dimension to the knowledge of early modern Europe by giving an account of the place the theory and practice of dissimulation occupied in the religion and culture of the age. Historians of the sixteenth and seventeenth centuries have largely neglected this subject. With a few exceptions they have failed to recognize its existence or have remained unaware of its scope and ramifications. The following chapters show, however, that the legitimation and practice of dissimulation were major factors in the lives of religious bodies, intellectuals, philosophers, and men of letters.

Many institutions and individuals have provided invaluable support in the preparation of this book. In 1983 a Guggenheim Fellowship enabled me to make a substantial start on the research. During the academic year 1983–84, I also enjoyed the support of the Andrew Mellon Foundation and a fellowship from the National Endowment for the Humanities under Grant FC 20029. Of exceptional importance was a fellowship in 1983–84 at the Center for Advanced Study in the Behavioral Sciences, which provided an ideal physical and intellectual environment in which to work. I am most grateful to Dr. Gardner Lindzey, the former Director of the Behavioral Sciences Center, and his capable staff for their assistance during the period I spent there.

I also owe warm thanks to the following friends, colleagues, and scholars for their aid, suggestions, and criticisms: Alfredo Alvar Ezquerra; Peter Bietenholz; John D'Amico, a former student whose tragically premature death cut short a brilliant career in Renaissance studies; Daniel Field; Steven Horwitz; Tina Isaacs; Abraham Karp; Donald Kelley; Dean Kernan; Karen Kupperman; Frederick Locke; John Marshall; Werner Packull; Joseph Pérez; Edward Peters; Joseph Scalzo; Ella Schwartz; Paul Seaver; Johann Sommerville; Brian Tierney; and Richard Westfall.

I am grateful to a number of libraries and their staffs for their cooperation and the use of their collections: first and foremost, Rush Rhees Library of the University of Rochester and Mrs. Eva Syrkin and her colleagues in the Interlibrary Loan Department; Colgate Rochester Divinity School Library; Olin Library, Cornell University; Butler Library, Columbia University; Union Theological Seminary Library and McAlpin Collection; Beinecke Library and Sterling Memorial Library, Yale University; Houghton, Widener, Harvard Law School, and Andover Divinity School libraries, Harvard University; Crosby Library, Gonzaga University, and its librarian, Robert L. Burr; Robbins Library of Canon Law and Bancroft Library, University of California at Berkeley; Stanford University Library; library of the University of California at Los Angeles; British Library, London; Bibliothèque Mazarine, Paris; Bibliothèque Protestante, Paris; Bibliothèque Municipale, Bordeaux; the library of the Institut d'Etudes Ibériques et Ibero-Américaines, University of Bordeaux; Bibliothèque Inguimbertine, Carpentras; Bibliothèque Municipale, Toulouse; Biblioteca Nacional, Madrid.

Finally, I wish to express what is inexpressible, my boundless obligation to my wife, Honoré Sharrer. Her life as a painter and mine as a historian have always been united in the closest bonds of love and amity. Without her support, neither this nor any other work I have done would have been possible.

Contents

1. Dissimulation in Historical Context   1
2. Sources   15
3. The Marranos and Crypto-Judaism   38
4. Calvin and Nicodemism   63
5. Nicodemism in Italy   83
6. Nicodemism: Controversialists, Sectarians, Familists   100
7. Nicodemism and Catholic Recusancy in England   131
8. Casuistry, Mental Reservation, and Dr. Navarrus   153
9. England and the Controversy over Mental Reservation   186
10. Casuistry and Dissimulation in English Protestantism   221
11. Occultism and Dissimulation   255
12. Libertinism, Unbelief, and the Dissimulation of Philosophers   289

Index   331

Nescit vivere qui nescit dissimulare.
—Sixteenth-century maxim

. . . for a long time I have not said what I believed,
nor do I ever believe what I say, and if indeed
sometimes I do happen to tell the truth, I hide it
among so many lies that it is hard to find.
—Machiavelli to Francesco Guicciardini, 17 May 1521

. . . To beguile the time,
Look like the time; bear welcome in your eye,
Your hand, your tongue. Look like th' innocent flower,
But be the serpent under 't.
—Shakespeare, *Macbeth,* I.5.65–68

. . . car la dissimulation est de plus notable qualitez
de ce siècle.
—Montaigne, "De Dementir," *Essais*

CHAPTER 1

Dissimulation in Historical Context

The phenomenon of dissimulation is as widespread as the world and as old as nature itself. Not only is it common in every kind of human relationship, but through the operation of natural selection many plant and other animal species have evolved devices of dissimulation (which evolutionary biologists call deception or mimicry) so as to improve their chances of getting food and of surviving against natural enemies. Dissimulation and its correlative, simulation, to deceive predators is observable in adaptations such as that of insects that resemble the excrement of birds, snails, and other insects; caterpillars whose curious swaying movements feign the swinging fragment of a twig; and beetles and moths indistinguishable from the bark of the trees in which they live. To frighten off attackers, some flies have developed an astonishing resemblance to the more formidable bees and wasps, while the harmless green snake imitates the poisonous variety when cornered and, like the adder, poises itself to strike. A number of good-tasting swallowtail butterflies protect themselves by simulating their kindred species of the unpalatable variety, and certain squirrels similarly mimic repellent-tasting tree shrews. Some tropical bugs deceive by imitating seeds, thorns, or the cocoon of a foul-tasting moth. Many plants and flowers use deceptions of color or odor to lure the insects that pollinate them. An especially well-known instance of deception is the brood-parasitism of the cuckoo. This bird introduces its single egg into the nests of certain other birds, which, on account of its resemblance, cannot distinguish it from their own eggs. When the newborn cuckoo hatches, it ejects the other eggs or fledglings from the nest, thus getting rid of all competitors for food from its hosts.[1]

All these examples of dissimulation are merely the product of a blind natural selection in the struggle for existence. In the human domain, by profound contrast, dissimulation is the result of both conscious choice and an intention to deceive. Yet dissimulation may be thought to occur so constantly in human intercourse that it cannot conceivably possess any historical dimension or significance. An anthropologist of Spanish village life has remarked, for example, that "the Andalusians are the most accomplished liars I have ever encountered, for it requires training and intelligence to distinguish rapidly when truth is owed and when it is to be concealed, and to acquire conscious control over facial expression is an ability which takes practice from childhood."[2] This talent for dissimulation, which the writer attributes rightly or wrongly to the Andalusians, may be a cultural trait and part of their mores, but it apparently has no particular historical character. Should not dissimulation then be considered as merely one of those permanent aspects of human nature, as universal, say, as aggression or the sex drive?

Although this inference may be true in a general sense, a fundamental distinction must be made between the dissimulation common to all human affairs and the practice of dissimulation as it has been rationalized and justified by theologians, casuists, philosophers, and political theorists. The first kind, which comprises the infinity of cases in which people lie and deceive for any number of possible reasons, such as fear, self-interest, gain, vanity, or unwillingness to inflict harm or pain, is simply a response to recurrent everyday situations and does not belong to the domain of history at all. The second kind, however, is a distinct and profoundly important historical phenomenon that is especially related to politics and, even more, to the persecution by states and churches of heretical and minority religious bodies and heterodox and dangerous ideas. In the case of those who are victims of either religious or intellectual intolerance, dissimulation is also associated with clandestinity, the maintenance of an underground existence, and esotericism. In this second form, it

[1] See Wolfgang Wickler, *Mimicry in Plants and Animals* (New York: McGraw-Hill, 1968); and D. Owen, *Camouflage and Mimicry* (Chicago: University of Chicago Press, 1980).

[2] Julian A. Pitt-Rivers, *The People of the Sierra,* 2d ed. (Chicago: University of Chicago Press, 1971), p. xvi.

played a major role in the religious and intellectual life of Western Europe in the sixteenth and seventeenth centuries, not to speak of its antecedents in the Middle Ages and its persistence to a certain extent during the Enlightenment. Moreover, as such it possessed ramifications and interconnections that have hardly been recognized, much less explored by historians. This sort of dissimulation was often employed and defended by its practitioners on the basis of doctrines which derived from a tradition of discussion and exempla going back to the Bible itself, and which included the writings of classical and Christian philosophers, theologians, canonists, and other thinkers.

Although the term *dissimulation* occurs somewhat more commonly in the literature than *simulation,* the two are simply different sides of the same coin. In the Latin from which they derive, both have virtually identical meanings. *Dissimulatio* signified dissembling, feigning, concealing, or keeping secret. *Simulatio* also meant feigning or a falsely assumed appearance, deceit, hypocrisy, pretense, or insincerity. The two words might therefore be used interchangeably, each denoting deception with the further possible connotation of lying. For precision's sake, however, we can also say that in a strict sense dissimulation is pretending not to be what one actually is, whereas simulation is pretending to be what one actually is not.

An interesting case of dissimulation for religious reasons is provided by a historical instance lying far afield from European civilization that nevertheless serves well to illustrate its character.

The Shi'ites, an important schismatic sect of Islam originating in the seventh and eighth centuries and whose principal centers became Persia (Iran) and Iraq, have been frequently subjected to persecution by the orthodox majority of Sunni Muslims. They hold that the heirs of Ali, Muhammad's son-in-law and fourth caliph, whose line was dispossessed after his death, are the only legitimate heads and leaders of the faithful. Accordingly, they trace a series of rightful successors to Ali, the Imams, whom they regard as supernatural beings with divine attributes or even as the incarnation of God. Of these, the twelfth Imam, who disappeared in the ninth century, is believed to have concealed himself until the end of time. Shi'ites therefore await the redemptive return of this hidden Imam, who lives a sinless existence as ruler of the world and who comforts and aids his followers even in his concealment. Shi'ism justifies these beliefs by the claim that besides the exoteric interpretation of the Koran, there exists an esoteric interpretation containing a secret knowledge that Muhammad confided to Ali and he in turn to his heir.[3]

One of the most notable features of Shi'ite teaching is *taqiyah,* which has been described as "a doctrine of legitimate dissimulation."[4] According to a leading theologian of the sect, its members "are well known for their practice of *taqiyah.* In case of danger they dissimulate their religion and hide their particular religious rites and ritual practices from their opponents." He explains that the doctrine is grounded in the Koran, which bids believers to guard themselves against unbelievers (III, 28), and states that those who do not believe in Allah, "save him who is forced thereto and is still content with Faith," will suffer the wrath of Allah (XVI, 106). The latter verse is said to have been revealed concerning Ammar ibn Yasir, who was imprisoned and tortured by infidels and forced to conform to idolatry, but having escaped and fled to Muhammad at Medina in distress and penitence, was told by the prophet that he had not fallen from the faith and had done his duty. Another Koranic verse cited for *taqiyah* declares: "Whether ye conceal what is in your hearts or reveal it, Allah knows it" (III, 27).[5]

The same authority also explains that *taqiyah* may be used when there is fear of danger that cannot be fought or resisted. In such cases resistance would not be brave and courageous but rash and foolhardy. The practice is accordingly permitted if there is danger to the life of one's self or family, danger to the honor or virtue of one's wife or other female family members, or danger of loss of property to an extent resulting in destitution or inability to maintain one's self or family.[6] Another writer cites an instance in which Abu Kasim, a tenth-century representative of the hidden Imam, used *taqiyah* in speaking of religion with influential Sunnis: he appeared to agree with them but deceived them by using equivocation, which he later laughed about as

[3] Gustave von Grunebaum, *Medieval Islam,* 2d ed. (Chicago: University of Chicago Press, 1961), pp. 186–193; Hamilton A. Gibb, *Mohammedanism: An Historical Survey,* 2d ed. (Oxford: Oxford University Press, 1953), pp. 120–126; Dwight M. Donaldson, *The Shi'ite Religion* (London: Luzac, 1933).

[4] Donaldson, *The Shi'ite Religion,* p. 195; see also Mary Bateson, " 'The Figure of Tinsel': A Study of Hypocrisy and Pessimism in Iranian Culture," *Daedalus,* 108, no. 3 (1979).

[5] Allamah Tabataba'i, *Shi'ite Islam* (London: Allen & Unwin, 1975), pp. 223–225; von Grunebaum, *Medieval Islam,* p. 191.

[6] Tabatab'i, *Shi'ite Islam,* pp. 223–225. Shi'ism also exalts martyrdom, but only when essential for the defense of religion.

a good joke. "During the long periods of Sunnite supremacy," it is pointed out, "the Shi'ite theologians had been driven to cover" and so "took refuge in dissimulation." Shi'ite pilgrims at Medina, if not allowed to stand and pray in the place recommended by the Imams, could use *taqiyah* and pray "after the manner of the Sunnites."⁷

As will be seen in the following chapters, this doctrine of dissimulation within a branch of Islam parallels doctrines held by believers in the Christian religion.

The topic of dissimulation has figured chiefly and most widely in Western thought in moral theology and philosophy. Analyses of the dilemmas of the human conscience, human conduct, and the virtues, vices, and sins must confront the problem of lying. Here the essential issue has always been whether dissimulation, that is, lying and deception, is ever justifiable. The question has been examined by many religious and secular thinkers from antiquity to the present, including Augustine, Aquinas, and Kant.⁸ In *On Lying (De Mendacio), Against Lying (Contra Mendacium)*, and other works, Augustine condemned all lying on any grounds as sinful and evil, although he did not consider every type of lie equally culpable. In the eighteenth century Kant condemned lying even more rigorously, if possible.⁹ Augustine's treatment of dissimulation was so acute and comprehensive that it largely

⁷ Donaldson, *The Shi'ite Religion*, pp. 253–254, 291.

⁸ A summary of some of the highlights in the discussion of lying by moral philosophers is given in Sissela Bok, *Lying: Moral Choice in Public and Private Life* (New York: Vintage Books, 1978). The appendix includes a selection of opinions from Augustine, Aquinas, Bacon, Grotius, Kant, and others. Bok deals with the related problem of secrecy in *Secrets: On the Ethics of Concealment and Revelation* (New York: Pantheon, 1982). The article, "Mensonge," in *Dictionnaire de théologie catholique*, ed. A. Vacant, E. Mangenot, and E. Amann, 18 vols. (Paris: Letouzey, 1930–1972), contains a good survey of the treatment of lying by Catholic and other thinkers. Julius A. Dorszynski, *Catholic Teaching about the Morality of Lying* (Washington, D.C.: Catholic University Press, 1948), presents a brief review of Catholic thought on the subject. Exceptionally useful is Gregor Müller's *Die Wahrhaftigkeitspflicht und die Problematik der Lüge* (Freiburg: Herder, 1962), which contains extracts on the problem of lying from a great number of authors from the patristic period to the twentieth century, as well as a systematic discussion of the question.

⁹ Immanuel Kant, "On a Supposed Right to Lie from Benevolent Motives," in *The Critique of Practical Reason and Other Writings in Moral Philosophy*, ed. Lewis White Beck (Chicago: University of Chicago Press, 1949). Bok, *Lying*, pp. 39–41 and passim, discusses Kant's view.

defined the terms of all subsequent discussion in Catholic philosophy. The topic was pursued by a succession of medieval writers, including Thomas Aquinas in his *Summa Theologiae*. In the sixteenth century it underwent great enlargement by Catholic theologians and casuists. Drawing on biblical, patristic, and other sources, they elaborated a rationale or theory of dissimulation involving devices such as equivocation and mental reservation and sanctioning various practices of deceit as licit and justifiable in certain circumstances. This major development gave dissimulation an unprecedented importance and explains why Pascal made it one of the targets of his celebrated attack on Jesuit casuistry in his *Provincial Letters*.

The theme of dissimulation has also figured notably in the literature on politics and statecraft. Here it is related to the well-known theory of reason-of-state as an aspect of the problem of preserving and increasing the state's or ruler's power, without regard to morality if necessary.[10] Machiavelli's famous chapter 18 of *The Prince* (1513), "In What Way Princes Should Keep Faith," has been rightly regarded as a classic endorsement of deception for reasons of state. The ruler is to imitate the *astuzia* or cunning of the fox and to violate his promise whenever it suits his interests. Because most men are bad and do not observe faith, the prince is not obliged to keep faith with them. But the prince must know how to disguise his faithlessness and should therefore learn to be a "great feigner and dissembler" *(gran simulatore e dissimulatore)*.[11]

Of course, Machiavellianism was by no means the only conception of politics in which the theme of dissimulation became a commonplace. In his *Annals* of imperial Rome, the historian Tacitus bitingly presented dissimulation as the emperor Tiberius' foremost trait: even during his years in exile at Rhodes before he assumed power, he thought of nothing but dissimulation and his secret lusts *(aliud quam . . . simulationem et secretas libidines)*. Moreover, Tiberius reckoned dissimulation highest among his own virtues *(nullam . . . ex virtutibus suis quam dissimulationem dilegebat)*. Even when he was dying, according to Tacitus, Tiberius' power of dissimulation did not leave him.[12]

[10] See Friedrich Meinecke, *Machiavellism: The Doctrine of Raison d'Etat and Its Place in Modern History* (London: Routledge & Kegan Paul, 1957).

[11] *Il principe,* 1513, ed. A. L. Burd (Oxford, 1891), p. 304.

[12] *Annals,* ed. and trans. A. J. Church and W. J. Broadribb (London, 1882), 1.4, 4.71, 6.50; see also Ronald Syme, *Tacitus,* 2 vols. (Oxford: Clarendon Press, 1958), vol. 1, chap. 32.

Tacitus' penetrating observations on the rulers of Rome won the admiration of Machiavelli's contemporary, the politician and historian Francesco Guicciardini, who praised Tacitus for exposing the thoughts of tyrants and teaching men living under a tyranny how to comport themselves. Guicciardini likewise regarded dissimulation in politics as unavoidable.[13] In the later sixteenth and the seventeenth centuries, following the great Dutch scholar Justus Lipsius' 1574 edition of Tacitus' works, the Roman historian was used no less than Machiavelli as a guide to reason-of-state. In cold-eyed scrutiny or in despairing judgment of the ambition of princes, Tacitism's distinguished adherents commented on the role of dissimulation in the government of states.[14] Thus, in Spain in the seventeenth century numerous political theorists drew on both Tacitus and Machiavelli to weigh the legitimacy of rulers' use of *dissimulación* and *simulación*.[15]

In the past as well as the present, politics has seemed to many the domain of dissimulation par excellence. Writers have deplored not only the mendacity of rulers and governments but also the deceitfulness of politicians in general. In the social world of the early modern kingdoms, *courtier* became a byword for dishonesty and faithlessness. In opposition to an established literary genre that delineated the virtues of the ideal courtier, there emerged another portraying the courtier as a person without truth or morals, a flatterer and sycophant of those in power, and an adept in the Machiavellian art of deceit. One of the most popular and influential works on courtiership was Baldassare Castiglione's *The Book of the Courtier* (1528), a dialogue expounding the qualities appropriate to the perfect courtier. Despite its neoplatonic refinement, as a practical manual for success in courts Castiglione's charming book did not exclude a faculty for dissimulation from its image of the courtly ideal. One of its main themes was that of *sprezzatura,* of which an inadequate English

[13] Francesco Guicciardini, *Ricordi,* ed. Ninian Thompson (New York: S. F. Vanni, 1949), 1st ser., nos. 45–46, 78–79.

[14] See Meinecke, *Machiavellism,* p. 25 and chap. 3; Arnaldo Momigliano, "The First Political Commentary on Tacitus," *Essays in Ancient and Modern Historiography* (Middletown, Conn.: Wesleyan University Press, 1977); Kenneth Schellhase, *Tacitus in Renaissance Political Thought* (Chicago: University of Chicago Press, 1976), chaps. 1, 4–6. Lipsius himself was an exponent of dissimulation; see below, Chapter 6.

[15] J. A. Fernández-Santamaria, "The Question of Political Deceit," in *Reason of State and Statecraft in Spanish Political Thought 1595–1640* (Lanham, Md.: University Press of America, 1983), cites many interesting texts dealing with dissimulation.

equivalent is "nonchalance," the art or pose of masking artifice by seeming to do everything effortlessly. This was related to another quality, *grazia* or grace, which likewise contributed to the impression the courtier strove to make. Because these and other notions implied feigning or dissembling, overlapping even with a Machiavellian *astuzia,* some contemporaries found Castiglione's recommended flexibility, adaptability, and role playing scarcely distinguishable from deviousness, falsehood, and duplicity. They saw hypocrisy as a necessary connotation of his conception of the courtly life, since the attributes needed to gain the favor of princes depended on a readiness to sacrifice personal integrity in favor of conformity and dissembling.[16] Dissimulation also figured in other well-known handbooks for courtiers and worldly men, such as the Spanish Jesuit Balthazar Gracián's *Manual of the Art of Discretion* (1653). Gracián counseled his readers "to think with the few and speak with the many" and to "conceal your purpose" because "the most practical wisdom consists in dissimulation."[17] As the courts of princes were commonly thought to be breeding grounds for such practices, it was no wonder that the maxim *Nescit vivere qui nescit dissimulare*—"He who does not know how to dissimulate does not know how to live"—was frequently applied to courtiers by political observers.

Both the theory of reason-of-state and early modern attitudes to courtiership are significant aspects of the subject of dissimulation that have been widely discussed by historians. What matters to us here, however, is not the dissimulation of rulers, governments, or politicians, but that of their subjects who resorted to it as a refuge

[16] Baldassare Castiglione, *Il libro del cortegiano,* in *Opere di Baldassare Castiglione, Giovanni Della Casa, Benvenuto Cellini,* ed. Carlo Cordié (Milan: Ricciardi Editore, n.d.), bk. 1, chaps. 26–28. See Giovanni Macchia, "La scuola della dissimulazione," in *Il paradiso della ragione,* 2d ed. (Bari: Laterza, 1964); G. Ferroni, " 'Sprezzatura' e Simulazione," in *La corte e il "Cortegiano,"* ed. Carlo Ossola, 2 vols. (Rome: Bulzoni, 1980), vol. 1; Pauline M. Smith, *The Anti-Courtier Trend in Sixteenth-Century French Literature* (Geneva: Droz, 1966); Daniel Javitch, *Poetry and Courtliness in Renaissance England* (Princeton: Princeton University Press, 1978), chap. 2; Perez Zagorin, *Rebels and Rulers,* 2 vols. (Cambridge: Cambridge University Press, 1982), 2:103–105.

[17] Balthazar Gracián, *Oraculo manual y arte de prudencia,* ed. L. Walton with an introduction and parallel English text as *A Manual of the Art of Discretion* (New York: William Salloch, 1953), pp. 59, 81, 121. The 1684 French translation was titled *L'homme de cour.* Gracián as a reason-of-state theorist is discussed by Fernández-Santamaría, *Reason of State,* pp. 294–296.

from the repressive power of states and churches. Its essence under the pressure for conformity in a persecuting society finds a recent illustration in an exiled sociologist's account of the situation in her homeland: "In Cuba you participate or you become suspect. And they ostracize and jail the suspect. Therefore, many people engage in dissimulation. They live one life in public and another life in private. And to that life they admit very few people because it is a big risk."[18] What is pictured here is dissimulation as a defensive response to the danger of persecution by a contemporary communist regime. Our concern in the following chapters is the same phenomenon as manifested in the sixteenth and seventeenth centuries.

Yet another context in which dissimulation has been discussed is the history of premodern philosophy, particularly political theory. The importance assigned to dissimulation in this connection is particularly associated with the late Leo Strauss's distinctive method of reading texts. According to Strauss, before the liberal era of free expression writers who held subversive views were compelled to convey them by means of subterfuge in order to deceive both persecutors and the common reader. This technique of dissimulation, the result of persecution, gave rise to a peculiar type of literature "in which the truth about all crucial things is presented exclusively between the lines. That literature is addressed, not to all readers, but to trustworthy and intelligent readers only." The distinction between an edifying, popular meaning accessible to any reader and a hidden philosophic meaning expressed between the lines for the instruction of the few was necessary if a writer wanted to escape harm for stating unpleasant and unpopular truths.[19]

Strauss suggested several ways of comprehending or decoding the esoteric content of such writings but admitted that "reading between the lines" is difficult and runs into problems of evidence.[20] What he failed to acknowledge are the errors and abuses to which this method is liable. Starting with the assumption of an author's intention to convey a hidden message, the Straussian interpreter tortures and manipulates the text to produce a result guaranteed in advance. In this way Strauss himself offered a highly implausible interpretation of Locke's political

---

[18] Silvia Pedraza-Bailey, "Cuba: Reflections on a Revolution," *Dissent,* 30, no. 4 (1983), 510.

[19] Leo Strauss, *Persecution and the Art of Writing* (Glencoe: Free Press, 1952), pp. 25, 35–36.

[20] Ibid., pp. 26–32.

ideas, claiming to prove that Locke had no belief in natural law and was really a Hobbesian, despite the weight of evidence to the contrary.[21] Strauss's disciples have been guilty of similar distortions through their tendentious misreadings pretending to lay bare the subversive meanings allegedly concealed in certain texts.[22]

That a philosopher might strive to dissimulate his thoughts and profess orthodoxy while intending to communicate a covert heterodox meaning is, in principle, unexceptionable. The caution displayed by Locke and Descartes in publishing their ideas is well known, and there are numerous authors who distinguished between outward profession and inner conviction. In the same connection, a leading student of Hobbes has raised the possibility that the apparently contradictory treatment of certain questions in his political philosophy may have been due to his having two doctrines, an esoteric one for the initiated and an exoteric one for the ordinary reader.[23] In the early eighteenth century the English freethinker John Toland spoke from his own experience when he declared that persecution caused authors to become "supple in their conduct," "reserv'd in opening their minds about most things," and "ambiguous in their expressions." "To what sneaking equivocations," he commented, "to what wretched shifts and subterfuges, are men of excellent endowments forc'd to have recourse thro human frailty, merely to escape disgrace or starving."[24]

The fact that fear of persecution could influence writers to disguise their ideas does not, however, license the Straussian method of reading. The dissimulation ascribed to a particular author must be proved or at least shown to be highly probable in light of all the evidence, not merely assumed. Moreover, the text must be treated with scruple and

[21] Leo Strauss, *Natural Right and History* (Chicago: University of Chicago Press, 1953), pp. 202–250.

[22] For critiques of the Straussian method of reading and its results, see Hans Aarsleff, "Some Observations on Recent Locke Scholarship," in *John Locke: Problems and Perspectives,* ed. John W. Yolton (Cambridge: Cambridge University Press, 1969), pp. 218–219, 264–270; Charles H. Monson, Jr., "Locke's Political Theory and Its Interpreters," in *Locke and Berkeley* ed. Charles Martin and David M. Armstrong (Garden City, N.Y.: Doubleday, 1968); Myles Burnyeat, "Sphinx without a Secret," *New York Review of Books,* May 30, 1985, pp. 30–36.

[23] Michael Oakeshott, *Hobbes on Civil Association* (Berkeley: University of California Press, 1975), p. 118. The boldness of Hobbes's ideas on religion and other subjects persuades me of the implausibility of this suggestion; see below, Chapter 12.

[24] John Toland, *Tetradymus* (London, 1720), p. vii; see below, Chapter 12.

caution, not wrested and strained to yield a preconceived conclusion. Even if no final judgment as to whether or not it harbors an esoteric meaning should be possible, at least the distortions that so easily result from the Straussian type of scholarship will have been avoided.

Considering the emphasis that Strauss laid on the deceptions employed by philosophers to convey their thoughts, it is surprising that he never discussed those constellations of ideas in early modern Europe which explicitly sanctioned the use of dissimulation. Thus, among thinkers in the occultist tradition, that curious amalgam of hermetic and neoplatonist philosophy, astrology, alchemy, cabala, and magic which lay at the threshold of the scientific revolution and included Marsilio Ficino, Agrippa, Paracelsus, John Dee, and diverse others, esotericism was a guiding principle. It was a common notion among them, one, paradoxically, proclaimed openly in their writings, that they dealt in a mysterious higher knowledge that must be kept secret from the vulgar and reserved exclusively to the initiated. Francis Bacon, who was knowledgeable in this tradition, referred to its esotericism as the "enigmatical method," which was designed, he explained, "to remove the vulgar capacities from being admitted to the secrets of knowledges, and to reserve them to selected auditors, or wits of such sharpness as can pierce the veil." Although he deplored the frauds and impostures to which esotericism could give rise, he spoke approvingly of "the discretion anciently observed . . . of publishing in a manner whereby it shall not be to the capacity nor taste of all," but adapted, rather, to win the minds of those fit to receive such knowledge while excluding others who might misuse it.[25]

Like the thinkers of the occultist school, the French libertine philosophers of the early seventeenth century, who were suspected of religious unbelief, emphasized the necessity of dissimulation and reserve both for reasons of safety and for keeping dangerous thoughts from the multitude.

Esotericism, the conception of a secret knowledge to be revealed only to an elite and harmful if communicated to the masses, thus intrinsically implied a doctrine of dissimulation. The following chapters accordingly include an account of this doctrine and of some of the thinkers concerned with the kind of knowledge that caused them to resort to it.

[25] Francis Bacon, *The Advancement of Learning,* ed. W. A. Wright (Oxford: Clarendon Press, 1900), pp. 171–172; *Valerius Terminus, Works,* 2 vols. (Boston, n.d.), 1:71.

Finally, dissimulation appears as a central feature of practically all forms of religious dissidence in the early modern era. The few historians who have perceived its importance in this connection, however, have tended to identify it exclusively with only one of its manifestations, the phenomenon known as Nicodemism. This term derives from "Nicodemites," the name the reformer John Calvin gave the crypto-Protestants and members of underground churches in Catholic lands who betrayed their faith by conforming outwardly to Catholic rites. Its origin lay in the gospel of John, which depicts the Pharisee Nicodemus as a believer in Christ who from fear of the Jews concealed his faith and came to hear Jesus only secretly by night (John 3:1–2). Historians have accordingly come to designate as Nicodemism the dissimulation used in self-protection by various sorts of Protestants and sectarians during the Reformation and Counter-Reformation.

A religiously motivated dissimulation, in recent years Nicodemism has been most closely studied by two Italian scholars, the late Delio Cantimori and Carlo Ginzburg, whose researches have contributed greatly to an understanding of its character. Cantimori dealt principally with the Italian evangelicals, heretics, and reformers who were attracted or converted to Protestantism but dissimulated their beliefs by rationalizing their continued conformity to the Catholic church. Ginzburg examined Nicodemism outside Italy as well and discussed a number of European writers engaged on either side of the controversy concerning the licitness of religious dissimulation. He also claimed to have discovered the specific origin and first statement of the principle of religious dissimulation in a treatise by Otto Brunfels, a Strasbourg Protestant.[26]

Valuable as their work has been, by limiting the problem of dissimulation exclusively to Nicodemism these two historians failed to comprehend it in its full scope and background. In the first place, they indicate little or no awareness that the issue of dissimulation long antedated the sixteenth century in discussions by Christian moral philosophers from an early time in the history of the church. In this discussion, moreover, which was carried on continuously from classical antiquity through the Middle Ages, the text in John concerning Nicodemus was of far less importance than other scriptural examples. Had Ginzburg taken into consideration this body of literature, he

---

[26] Cantimori's main contribution to the history of Nicodemism is *Eretici italiani del cinquecento* (1939; repr., Florence: Sansoni, 1967); Carlo Ginzburg, *Il Nicodemismo. Simulazione e dissimulazione nell'Europa del '500* (Turin: Einaudi, 1970).

could not have fallen into the error of ascribing the original rationale for Nicodemism to Otto Brunfels.[27]

In the second place, during the sixteenth century itself there were significant manifestations and justifications of religious dissimulation outside the boundaries of Protestantism. A case in point was the practice of English Catholics under Elizabeth I and James I of attending the services of the Protestant state church as required by law. Attempts to justify this type of dissimulation as well as other expressions of Catholic conformity to the Protestant establishment provoked major debates among English Catholics. With the help of continental casuists, English Jesuits also propounded doctrines and devices of dissimulation which they defended as permissible, and these too became highly controversial. Such examples demonstrate how misleading it is to identify religious dissimulation entirely with Nicodemism. Because of this limitation of vision, historians of Nicodemism and of the English Catholics have failed to recognize the ground common to both in regard to the theory and practice of dissimulation.

Another case perhaps even more important than English Catholicism is that of the Spanish Marranos and crypto-Judaism. The mass conversions of Spanish Jews dating from the end of the fourteenth century, followed by their expulsion from Spain in 1492, created in Spain a body of New Christians or *conversos* consisting of former Jews and their descendants who were distinguished from Old Christians by their background. Subjected to various legal and social disabilities, *conversos* were suspected of secret fidelity to Judaism and therefore disparagingly referred to as Marranos, meaning "pigs" or "unclean." The exposure and punishment of secret Judaizers was the main motive for the establishment of the Spanish Inquisition in 1478. A parallel forcible conversion and subsequent expulsion of Jews occurred in Portugal during the fifteenth and sixteenth centuries.

This brief survey should make it clear that dissimulation was a significant reality in the culture of sixteenth- and seventeenth-century Europe. The widespread existence of doctrines authorizing dissimulation sheds a profound new light upon the mentality of the age.

[27] See below, Chapter 4; see also the valuable critical survey by Albano Biondi, "La giustificazione della simulazione nel cinquecento," in *Eresia e riforma nell'Italia del cinquecento* (De Kalb: Northern Illinois University Press, 1974).

The phenomenon of dissimulation rationalized by doctrine was so extensive that it was like a submerged continent in the religious, intellectual, and social life of early modern Europe. Parts of this continent, as well as its general outlines and larger features, have remained uncharted until now. Indeed, their scale and complexity are beyond the power of one historian to compass. In surveying this continent, the following chapters will examine not only manifestations of clandestinity and deceitful conformity among religious communities but also the writings of many Catholics and Protestants concerned with the guidance of conscience and therefore with the question of dissimulation in reference to oaths and religious and political tests. One of the difficulties of this task is the fact that dissimulation is by its nature often elusive and very hard to prove. In addition, it is sometimes impossible to distinguish between deliberate deception and a decision simply to remain silent on the part of those whose beliefs were at variance with the official creed of a persecuting society. Often, moreover, we can see dissemblers and hear their voices only through the descriptions of their persecutors and adversaries. Yet of their existence and the arguments they used to justify themselves there can be no doubt.

CHAPTER 2

Sources

The theory of dissimulation with its legitimation of deception in given circumstances was based almost entirely on biblical precedents or examples and on subsequent comments and discussion concerning these examples. Some scriptural texts were cited so frequently that they became virtual commonplaces in the consideration of dissimulation and lying. Furthermore, depending on the purpose or situation, certain texts would fit the case better than others. Thus, the justification for deceiving authorities or judges during an official interrogation or legal trial presented a somewhat different problem from that of rationalizing one's pretended conformity to a religion or church that one actually rejected as idolatrous or heretical. This chapter surveys the scriptural texts and discussions of dissimulation by patristic and later Christian thinkers that are essential to an understanding of the doctrine of dissimulation as it was developed in the sixteenth and seventeenth centuries.

Perhaps the most important text directly and explicitly concerned with dissimulation to be found in the Bible, and most certainly in the New Testament, is Galatians 2:11-14. This passage provided a major point of departure for Augustine's later discussion of lying.[1]

Paul's letter to the Galatians dealt with a fundamental problem in

---

[1] Albano Biondi ably discusses the significance of Galatians in "La giustificazione della simulazione nel cinquecento," in *Eresia e riforma nell'Italia del cinquecento* (De Kalb: Northern Illinois University Press, 1974). Carlo Ginzburg, *Il Nicodemismo. Simulazione e dissimulazione religiosa nell'Europa del '500* (Turin: Einaudi, 1970,), pp. 74, 76, mentions the letter in passing but ignores its crucial importance, as does Delio Cantimori, *Eretici italiani del cinquecento* (Florence: Sansoni, 1967).

the early history of Christianity: the relationship between Jewish and Gentile converts and whether believers who received the faith of Christ were bound by the ordinances of the Jewish law. Paul insisted that those who are justified by their faith in Christ are freed from their bondage to the law. Galatians 2:11–14 recounts his rebuke to Peter at Antioch for Judaizing, that is, for conforming to the Jewish law and wanting Gentile converts to do the same, thereby dissembling his convictions.

According to Paul's account, Peter had ceased to observe the law and thus used to eat with Gentiles. Upon the arrival of certain Jewish Christians from Jerusalem, however, he was fearful of their disapproval and therefore withdrew himself from the Gentile converts. Other Jewish converts who were present likewise "dissembled with him," and even Paul's companion Barnabas "was carried away with their dissimulation."[2] Thereupon Paul publicly reprehended Peter for his dissimulation in not walking uprightly in the truth of the gospel, saying to him, "If thou, being a Jew, livest after the manner of the Gentiles, and not as do the Jews, why compellest thou the Gentiles to live as do the Jews?"

The point at issue in this episode is clear. Peter had learned to abandon the prohibition against eating with the impure by which many Jewish Christians still felt themselves bound.[3] Having relinquished his scruples against living as non-Jews did, he nonetheless hypocritically separated himself from the Gentile Christians on this occasion and was therefore guilty of dissimulation.[4]

Of the patristic commentaries on Galatians, Jerome's, written around 387, was the most important, and his interpretation of the incident of Peter's dissimulation led to a serious disagreement with Augustine.[5]

According to Jerome, Paul's rebuke to Peter was merely feigned, having been prearranged between the two apostles for the benefit of both Jewish and Gentile converts. Thus each of them dissimulated. Peter, although he had previously eaten with the Gentiles, went from

---

[2] The Authorized Version's "dissimulation," renders *hypokrisis* in the original Greek text, translated as *simulatio* in the Vulgate. All biblical references and quotations in this volume are from the 1611 Authorized Version unless otherwise stated.

[3] See esp. Acts 10:27, 11:3.

[4] In dealing with this text, I have used the commentary by Joseph B. Lightfoot, *Saint Paul's Epistle to the Galatians,* 10th ed. (London: Macmillan, 1902).

[5] Ibid, pp. 232–233.

them lest the Jewish converts be lost to the faith of Christ; and Paul "with the same art" simulated his public reproof of Peter, not to accuse him but to correct those for whose sake "he had dissimulated" *(simulaverat)* so that the pride of the Jews and the desperation of the Gentiles should be taken away. What else, Jerome asked, should Peter and Paul, pillars of the church, have done amidst the disagreement of Jews and Gentiles? By their "feigned quarrel" *(simulata contentio),* however, they kept peace among believers and maintained the church's faith in concord between them.

Jerome pointed out, furthermore, that Paul himself made use of dissimulation on the occasions when he observed Jewish rites, as in Acts 16:3 and 18:8, and when he declared that "Unto the Jews I became as a Jew" in order to gain the Jews (1 Corinthians 9:20), and also said, "Give none offence, neither to the Jews, nor to the Gentiles, nor to the church of God" (1 Cor. 10:22). The examples of Jehu, king of Israel, who feigned worship of the idol Baal in order to kill its priests (2 Kings 10:18–28), and of David, who pretended madness (1 Samuel 21:12–13), also taught, Jerome contended, that "dissimulation may sometimes be accepted as useful" *(utilem vero simulationem et assumendam tempore).* Nor was it any wonder, he observed, that just men would dissimulate for their own and others' salvation, seeing that "our Lord himself who was without sin . . . used dissimulation in taking on sinful flesh so that he might take on for us the justice of God."

Jerome concluded his remarks on this episode with the comment that if anyone was displeased with his interpretation showing both that Peter did not sin and that Paul did not rebuke an apostle greater than himself, then that person should explain by what reasoning Paul could have reprehended Peter for something he had done himself.[6]

Jerome not only held, therefore, that both Paul and Peter dissimulated; he likewise justified and approved their doing so. It was this opinion that provoked the protest of Augustine. His commentary on Galatians, though not referring to Jerome, briefly denied that Paul fell into dissimulation and explained that he had properly reprimanded Peter for his conduct.[7] But in several letters to Jerome between 395 and 405 he strongly expressed his dissent from the latter's view of the critical episode in Galatians.

[6] *Commentariorum in Epistolam ad Galatas Tres Libri,* in *Patrologiae Latinae Cursus Completus,* ed. Jacques Migne, 221 vols. (Paris, 1844–1855), 26: cols. 363–367 (cited hereafter as *PLCC*).

[7] *Epistolae ad Galatas Expositionis Liber Unus, PLCC,* 35: cols. 2113–14.

In the first letter Augustine stated that he had read Jerome's commentary, including the part where he excused Peter from "pernicious dissimulation" *(perniciosa simulatio)*. He regretted, he said, that Jerome should defend lying. It was also extremely dangerous, he continued,

> to admit that anything in the Sacred Books should be a lie; that is that the men who have ... written the Scriptures for us should have lied in their books. It is quite another question whether good men should ever lie, and still another whether a writer of the Holy Scriptures ought to lie—but no, this is not another question—it is no question at all. If we once admit in that supreme authority even one helpful lie [*officioso mendacio*], nothing will be left of these books, because whenever anyone finds something difficult to practice or hard to believe, he will follow this same most dangerous precedent and explain it as the idea or practice of a lying author.

He went on to deny that Paul dissimulated in rebuking Peter and to stress the constant care with which Paul safeguarded the truth. With all his strength, Augustine declared, he wished to show "that all those proofs which are offered in support of the usefulness of lying ought to be understood as teaching the necessity of truth everywhere." Jerome himself would come to see that scripture is undermined, leaving anyone to believe or disbelieve what he likes, "if once the opinion has been established that the men through whose ministry the scriptures have come down to us could be guilty of lying."[8]

In a letter written about two years later Augustine again expressed his dissatisfaction with Jerome's interpretation of Paul's reproof of Peter and reaffirmed his belief that if the validity of helpful lies were ever admitted in the scriptures, their authority would be destroyed and it would become impossible to use them to condemn deliberate deceit. He explained Paul's famous saying in 1 Corinthians 9:20 that he became as a Jew to the Jews as having been spoken "through mercy and compassion, not deceit and dissimulation" *(non simulatione fallaciae)*. Paul did not condemn Jewish practices as dangerous to the conscience provided men did not put their hope of salvation in them, because he knew that salvation comes only from Christ. Paul therefore did not rebuke Peter for observing Jewish practices, but for pretending

[8] *Epistolae, PLCC,* 33: cols. 112–113. I have used the English translation with a few slight changes in Augustine, *Letters,* trans. Wilfred Parsons, 5 vols. (Washington, D.C.: Catholic University Press, 1951–1956), 1:93–98. The term *officioso mendacio,* which the English translation renders as "polite lie," means in this context a helpful lie, one serviceable in a good cause.

that they were necessary for salvation after the coming of the Lord. Although Peter knew that they were unnecessary, he dissimulated for fear of "them who were of the circumcision." For this sin he was justly corrected, and Paul only stated the truth. Augustine ended by begging Jerome to rectify his exposition of this matter.[9]

Jerome responded to Augustine's criticisms, defending himself and his view of the Galatians episode, in a letter written around 404.[10] He pointed out, as he had in his commentary, that his own interpretation followed that of Origen. Peter, he said, knew very well that the Jews were freed from the law, but was constrained to dissimulate at Antioch lest the Jews, of whom he was the apostle, separate themselves from the Christian faith. Paul, on the other hand, who condemned Peter for dissimulating, did the same thing himself when for fear of the Jews he made the Gentile Timothy undergo circumcision (Acts 16:3) and also performed other Jewish rites in order not to scandalize the Jews who believed in Christ. Since both Peter and Paul "feigned" (*fixerint*) observance of the Jewish law, "with what face, therefore, with what audacity could Paul rebuke in another the fault he himself had committed?" Yet neither of them was guilty of lying, and the two merely allowed an honest dispensation, thus demonstrating their prudence as apostles.

In engaging the great question of obedience to Jewish law by either Jewish or Gentile converts to Christianity, Jerome condemned all such observance. On this point he differed somewhat from Augustine, who had defended Paul's compliance with Jewish practices as done for charitable reasons and as permissible as long as not deemed necessary for salvation. Peter, Jerome asserted, "only pretended to observe the law, but Paul, that reprehender of Peter, audaciously observed it as legal." He reiterated his conclusion that both apostles "for fear of the Jews who were believers observed . . . or rather simulated observing" the Jewish law. He asked Augustine, furthermore, not to think that he favored lying or was a "magistrum mendacii,"; he was the disciple of the Christ who said, "I am the way, the life, and the truth."

A reply from Augustine the following year was apparently the last in this acrimonious correspondence between the two church fathers over the meaning of the controverted passages in Galatians.[11] It

---

[9] *Epistolae, PLCC*, 33: cols. 154–158; *Letters*, 1:172–179.
[10] Jerome's letter is printed in Augustine, *Epistolae, PLCC*, 33: cols. 251–263; and in Jerome, *Epistolae, PLCC*, 22: cols. 916–931.
[11] *Epistolae, PLCC*, 33: cols. 275–291; *Letters*, 1:390–420.

renewed the attack on Jerome's claim that the scriptures permitted
dissimulation and also included an extensive discussion of the relationship of the law to the gospel and the apostles' attitude toward
Jewish rites. But on the matter of lying, Augustine maintained that
if it was better to believe that Paul wrote falsely rather than that
Peter acted wrongly, then let it also be said, though an abhorrent
saying, that it would be better to believe that the gospel lies rather
than that Christ was denied by Peter; or that the Old Testament lies
rather than that David, a great prophet so eminently chosen by God,
had committed adultery by seducing another man's wife and was
guilty of murder by killing her husband.[12] Having delivered this
strong rhetorical rebuttal, Augustine affirmed that he would rather
learn from scripture that men are truly corrected, approved, or condemned than have his trust in it undermined because he feared to
believe that the conduct of certain excellent and praiseworthy persons is sometimes deserving of blame. On this ground he rejected as
strongly as before Jerome's opinion that Paul blamed Peter for something he had done himself. If Peter did rightly, then Paul lied in
rebuking him. But if Paul spoke the truth, then Peter did what he
should not have done. And, Augustine repeated, he did not believe
that Paul lied. He added the observation, picked up by later writers,
that Peter received his rebuke with a meek and holy humiliation as
done for his good. Because the apostle did not refuse correction even
from his inferiors when he left the path of righteousness, he set a
precious and holy example to posterity.

Apart from his letters to Jerome, Augustine addressed the subject of
lying in several other works. He touched on it briefly in his *Enchiridion,*
a treatise on faith, hope, and charity;[13] and most fully and notably in the
two treatises *On Lying* (ca. 395) and *Against Lying,* (ca. 420). In these,
besides discussing Galatians and other scriptural precedents alleged for
dissimulation, he looked at the problem of lying in a broader perspective. These magisterial examinations of the diverse aspects of lying
exerted a profound influence on all later theologians and canonists.

In *On Lying,* and again in *Against Lying,* Augustine defined a lie as
"a false statement made with the intention to deceive" *(enuntiationem*

---

[12] The references are to Matt. 26:69–26:75 and 2 Sam. 11:2–11:27.

[13] *Enchiridion (PLCC,* 40: cols. 240–242) deals with deception and lying; see the
translation by B. M. Peebles Augustine, *Writings,* 8 vols. (1947; repr., Washington
D.C.: Catholic University Press, 1966), vol. 4, chap. 6.

falsam cum voluntate fallendi).[14] This definition became classic and was
to be repeated by innumerable authors. While stressing the intention
to deceive as the hallmark of the lie, Augustine also characterized it as
speech that is contrary to what is in the mind. Hence the liar is a
person "who holds one opinion in his mind and . . . gives expression
to another through words or any other outward manifestation."[15]
The conception of the lie as a speech *contra mentem,* which occupied a
subordinate place in Augustine's treatment, was to be given much
greater prominence and emphasis by casuists of the sixteenth century.

In *On Lying* Augustine divided the different kinds of lies into eight
categories and analyzed them with much ingenuity. In reviewing many
of the typical situations and causes thought to make lying and false
witness defensible, he argued that a lie is not admissible in any of them.
Whether the excuse is to preserve someone's safety or chastity or even
to save a life, the lie remains a sin. To the man who was asked to betray
the whereabouts of an innocent person, Augustine's advice was not to
give false witness but rather to answer, "I know where he is but will
never disclose it," no matter what the cost of such an action.[16]

Besides cases taken from common life, Augustine noted scriptural
examples of apparent dissimulation cited by defenders of the usefulness or necessity of deception. Some of them were to reappear repeatedly in the discussions of subsequent writers. Among the better
known were Jacob's pretense to Isaac that he was the latter's firstborn
son, Esau (Genesis 27:19); and the Egyptian midwives' lying to Pharaoh with God's approval in order to save the Hebrew children
(Exodus 1:17–20).[17]

The judgment of Augustine in these and other instances was that
the Old Testament provides no precedents to justify lies. He therefore
either explained them away or interpreted them as metaphorical
expressions rather than as falsehoods. Likewise, he declared of the
New Testament that Jesus used figurative language and that it con-

[14] *De Mendacio, PLCC,* 40: col. 491; in *Contra Mendacio* the definition is formulated as "a false meaning [*significatio*] told with the intention to deceive"; ibid.,
col. 537. I have used the English translation with a few slight changes in Augustine, *Treatises on Various Subjects,* trans. M. S. Muldowney and H. B. Jaffee (Washington D.C.: Catholic University Press, 1952). For Augustine's definition of the
lie, pp. 60, 160.

[15] *Treatises,* p. 55.

[16] Ibid., p. 86.

[17] Ibid., p. 60.

tained nothing "which would sanction the telling of a lie." Hence the dissimulation of Peter and Barnabas is not only mentioned in Galatians, but is reproved and corrected.[18] Augustine often emphasized that the scriptures should not be read literally; "all things in the gospel . . . which, to the ignorant, seem to be lies, are figurative in signification." It is in this sense that Paul's words "I am made all things to all men" (1 Cor. 9:22) must be understood. They do not mean that Paul resorted to lies, but that by sympathy and charity he wrought conversion. Contrary to later writers who claimed biblical support for dissimulation, in *On Lying* Augustine categorically concluded that "when all aspects of the problem of lying have been considered, it is clear that the testimony of Holy Scripture advises that one should never lie at all, since no examples of lies, deserving of imitation, are found in . . . the deeds of the saints."[19]

Against Lying covered part of the same ground, but with a somewhat different focus, owing to its having been written in connection with the Priscillianist heresy. The latter grew up around the figure of Priscillian, bishop of Avila, who was executed in 385 by imperial decree, apparently the first and only heretic in antiquity to suffer death from the secular arm. He and his disciples were accused of Manichaeanism and of engaging in black arts and sexual orgies. They were reported to harbor a secret doctrine that they felt free in conscience to conceal from the unworthy by dissimulation and lying. Hostile evidence claimed that they paid no regard to truth and would say one thing in public and another in private.[20] It was these practices that caused the later apologists for religious dissimulation to be likened to the Priscillianists by their opponents. A correspondent in Spain had sent Augustine an account of a Priscillianist work that invoked scriptural precedents to justify the dissimulation of religious beliefs to enemies and unfit persons. The correspondent himself held, moreover, that one need not deal truthfully with heretics and might use deceit to detect them. It was the issues posed by the Priscillianist defense of lying that called forth Augustine's reflections on this occasion.

Against Lying restated Augustine's repudiation of the lie, particularly in matters of religion. He condemned equally the dissimulation of religious belief and any sort of deception to discover heretics or their

[18] Ibid., pp. 62–63.
[19] Ibid., p. 107.
[20] Henry Chadwick, *Priscillian of Avila. The Occult and the Charismatic in the Early Church* (Oxford: Clarendon Press, 1976), chap. 1.

doctrines. Though acknowledging that some lies are more culpable than others and that the reason for or intention of an action makes a difference, he declared that things such as lying, "which are clearly sins, ought not to be done under any pretext of a good reason, for any supposedly good end, with any seeming good intention."[21]

Among the arguments he countered was the distinction between heart and tongue, which was to be widely used by later theorists of dissimulation. The Priscillianists held that "what is true must be kept in the heart, but that it is no sin to utter what is false with the tongue to strangers." Augustine observed that this opinion dishonored the martyrs and altogether removed the possibility of holy martyrdom. But in any case he rejected the distinction: "Did not almost all those who disowned Christ in the presence of their persecutors keep in their hearts what they believed about him? Yet for not making with the mouth profession of faith unto salvation they perished, except such as repented and lived again." Likewise, when Peter denied Christ, he did not have the same thing in his heart as on his tongue; although he lied in his denial, he kept the truth within. "Why then," Augustine asked, "did he weep bitterly for having disowned him with his tongue, if it sufficed unto salvation to believe in his heart?" To speak truth in the heart, he emphasized, could not mean that one may tell a lie with the tongue.[22]

Reviewing some scriptural examples the Priscillianists advanced to excuse lying, Augustine mentioned Abraham's pretense that his wife Sarah was his sister (Gen. 12:11–13), Jacob's pretense to be Esau (Gen. 27:19), the Egyptian midwives' deception of Pharaoh (Exod. 1:17–20), David's feigning of madness (1 Sam. 21:13), and Jesus' pretense to his disciples on the road to Emmaus that he would go further (Luke 24:28). He also alluded to cases of metaphor, as when Christ is called a rock (1 Cor. 10:4) and a lion (Revelation 5:5).[23]

Wherever the scripture seemed to present a plain instance of dissimulation, Augustine's rule was to stigmatize it. Thus he again endorsed Paul's reproof of Peter in Galatians and defended him from the charge of conforming to Jewish practices in any deceptive way. Of the Egyptian midwives, he argued that God rewarded them for their good deed of mercy, not for their bad deed of deception, and perhaps pardoned the latter because of the former.[24]

[21] *Treatises*, p. 143.
[22] Ibid., pp. 127, 128, 139–140.
[23] Ibid., pp. 151–154, 160–161.
[24] Ibid., pp. 158, 165–166.

He also allowed that it was justifiable to conceal the truth and that this was not the same as lying, an important point that became standard in later treatments of the subject. "Although everyone who lies wants to conceal the truth," he noted, "not everyone who conceals the truth lies. Generally, we conceal the truth not by lying but by keeping quiet." He applied this principle to Christ, who never spoke falsehood but held back many truths; and to Abraham, who never said Sarah was not his wife but merely concealed it; and, as she was also his brother's daughter, he could properly call her his sister.[25]

In most instances, however, Augustine contended that apparent cases of dissimulation in the scriptures are really prophetic, mystical, or figurative statements conveying a truth if rightly understood: "It is not a lie when signs signifying one thing are put for another to serve the understanding of a truth." In this way he explained Jacob's pretense to be the firstborn Esau as signifying the coming of Christ and the church, and interpreted Jesus' telling his disciples he would go further as a mystery signifying the fulfillment of redemption.[26]

Augustine revealed his humanity when confronting the dilemmas that cause people to plead the necessity of lies. Of such difficulties, as in the case of the patient who may die if told of the death of his only son, he admitted:

> because we are human and live among humans, I confess that I am not among those who are no longer troubled by the problem of doing a lesser evil to avoid a greater. Often in human affairs my human feeling overcomes me and I am unable to resist . . . [and] am moved by these arguments more powerfully than wisely.

But he thrust such considerations aside, he declared, when he contemplated the intellectual beauty of Christ, who is truth itself. And he warned as well that to permit lies in these cases that had troubled him would enable the evil of lying to grow little by little until the mass of lies turned into a plague.[27]

Other church fathers, such as Clement of Alexandria, Origen, and John Chrysostom, made an exception for situations in which the truth

[25] Ibid., pp. 151–152.

[26] Ibid.

[27] Ibid., pp. 171–172. In the quoted passage, I have translated "compensativa peccata" (*PLCC,* 40: col. 543) as "doing a lesser evil to avoid a greater," in accord with Peter R. Brown, *Augustine of Hippo* (Berkeley: University of California Press, 1975), p. 274.

could be harmful to the one who told it or to others. In these cases they believed that lying was permissible and might even be a necessity to avoid grave consequences.[28] Augustine, on the contrary, though sensitive to such problems, consistently refused to countenance lying for any reason. So far as the future was concerned, however, it was less his comprehensive condemnation of the lie than his discussion of scriptural precedents and his close analysis of lying and dissimulation that exercised the deepest influence.

Another essential text on dissimulation was contained in Pope Gregory the Great's *Moralia* (ca. 500), a commentary on the book of Job which was one of the most important works of doctrinal and moral instruction in medieval culture. Commenting on the rebuke administered to Job by one of his interlocutors for declaring that his righteousness was greater than God's (Job 35:2), Gregory noted that every reader understands that Job did not really say this. Rather, Job examined his life and, believing that he was scourged by God to wash away his sins, was confident that he would come to victory because he found no guilt in himself for which he deserved to be smitten. What, then, was Job's sin, Gregory asked, if he spoke words that unknowingly agreed with God's secret judgment concerning himself? And "what harm is there," he continued, "if in the judgment of men our words differ superficially from the rectitude of truth when in the heart they are in accord with it?" From this reflection he laid down a conclusion distinguishing heart from word and inner state from its outward expression: "the ears of men judge our words as they sound outwardly, but the divine judgment hears them as they are uttered from within. Among men the heart is judged by the words; with God the words are judged by the heart."[29]

This statement is known from the opening words of the Latin text as "Humanae aures." It later acquired a far-reaching juristic import through its incorporation in the great mid-twelfth-century compilation of the canon law, Gratian's *Decretum.* By its attempt to synthesize

---

[28] The article "Mensonge," in *Dictionnaire de théologie catholique,* ed. A. Vacant, E. Mangenot, and E. Amann, 18 vols. (Paris, Letouzey, 1930–1972), surveys some of the church fathers' views.

[29] *Moralium Libri, sive Expositio in Librum B. Job,* bk. 26, chap. 10 *(PLCC,* 76: col. 357). The Latin text runs: "Humanae aures verba nostra talia judicant qualia foris sonant; divina vero judicia talia ea audiunt qualia ex intimis proferuntur. Apud homines cor ex verbis, apud Deum vero verba pensantur ex corde."

and harmonize the law of the church, this work achieved an immeasurable significance in the legal and moral life of Catholic civilization. It became the first part of the codification of canon law, the *Corpus Iuris Canonici,* and was used by students and glossed or discussed in treatises by jurists for centuries.

Gratian's treatment of lying and dissimulation in the *Decretum* fills nearly thirty columns of the modern edition and proceeds from a group of five questions concerning oaths and perjury by clerics. The texts and dicta that follow cover a wide variety of issues and contain many pronouncements from scripture, church fathers, popes, councils, and other sources. One of the main glosses on the *Decretum,* the *Glossa Ordinaria,* written by Johannes Teutonicus at the beginning of the thirteenth century, added marginal comments that were incorporated in many of the manuscript copies and early printed editions. The part of the *Decretum* devoted to lying therefore provided a virtual thesaurus of the subject for later canonists and theologians.[30]

The chapter "Humanae aures" forms part of this collection. Just preceding it is a chapter citing a saying of Augustine that it is perjury to swear falsely even on a stone, for although the stone does not hear one speaking, God does and punishes the deceit. "Humanae aures" follows under the rubric "To God our words come not from the mouth but from the heart." The passage as I have quoted it above from Gregory's *Moralia* is then cited, after which Gratian adds: "Certainly he is one that knows who explains from the words of another his will and intention; for he ought not to consider the words but rather the will and intention, because the intention should not serve the words, but the words the intention."[31] This is one of the statements, with its key citation from the *Moralia,* that casuists in the sixteenth century were to put to use to provide a new latitude for dissimulation.

Among authorities Gratian referred most frequently to Augustine.

[30] *Decretum . . . Gratiani, Corpus Iuris Canonici,* ed. E. Richter and Emil A. Friedberg, 2d ed., 2 vols. (1879; repr., Graz: Akademische Druck U. Verlagsanstalt, 1959), vol. 1, pt. 2, causa xxii, deals with lying. On the work of Gratian and its importance, see Johann von Schulte, *Die Geschichte der Quellen und Literatur des Canonischen Rechts von Gratian bis auf Gegenwart,* 3 vols. (Stuttgart, 1875–1880), vol. 1, bk. 1; Stephan Kuttner, *Gratian and the Schools of Law 1140–1234* (London: Variorum Reprints, 1983).

[31] *Decretum,* pt. 2, causa xxii, q. v, c. xi 1: col. 885): "Certe noverit ille, qui intentionem et voluntatem alterius variis verbis explicat, quia non debet aliquis verba considerare, sed voluntatem et intentionem, quia non debet intentio verbis deservire, sed verba intentioni."

Besides much else he cited the latter's definition of a lie as "a false *significatio* made with the intention to deceive" and his eightfold classification of lies. In another chapter stating that a spiritual man ought not to lie even to save a life, he quoted Augustine's remark that "it is one thing to lie and another to hide the truth," and that someone who does not wish to betray another to certain death should be ready to conceal the truth rather than tell a falsehood, lest he kill his own soul to save another's body.[32]

From Jerome's commentary on Galatians, Gratian took the opinion that "dissimulation may sometimes be accepted as useful," as well as the scriptural precedents Jerome used to support his position, including those of Jehu, David, and Christ himself. Gratian's dictum on this text was that some lies are venial and others damnable. He proceeded to question whether Augustine was right to hold that one should not lie to save a life. In this connection he cited the case of Abraham, who for their common safety asked his wife Sarah to say that she was his sister. He concluded with Augustine, however, that Abraham did not lie but sought to conceal the truth by silence, and, moreover, that Sarah could be correctly called his sister because she was his brother's daughter.[33]

Elsewhere Gratian also mentioned the examples of the Egyptian midwives who lied to save the Hebrew children and Jacob's pretense to be his firstborn brother Esau. Of the first case he said that the midwives were rewarded by God for their piety and punished for their lie. His dictum on the second excused Jacob from lying for the reason that he was first by right though not by birth.[34] He added, however, that many things were permitted in the Old Testament which were no longer licit, and cited from Gregory's *Moralia* another pronouncement that examples from the Old Testament must not be used to sanction lying.[35]

An equally famous work contemporaneous with Gratian's *Decretum* which included a consideration of lying was Peter Lombard's *Sen-*

[32] Ibid., q. ii, c. v, viii, xiv (cols. 868, 869, 871).

[33] Ibid., c. xxi, xxii (cols. 873–874). On Jerome's justification of dissimulation the *Glossa Ordinaria* comments that it is an argument that "deceit against an enemy is good"; *Decretum Divi Gratiani Universi Iuris Canonici . . . cum Glossis . . .* (Lyons, 1554), p. 825.

[34] *Decretum,* pt. 2, causa xxii, q. ii, c. xx, xxii (1: col. 873). In pt. 1 Gratian states that the canonical scriptures contain no lies: distinctio ix, c. v. (col. 17).

[35] Ibid., causa xxii, q. ii, c. xviii, xix (col. 872).

tences. This treatise became the standard theological textbook in the universities of medieval Europe and the subject of a legion of commentators. In the third book of the *Sentences,* Peter took up lying in relation to the precepts of the Decalogue and the commandment against bearing false witness. Generally, his discussion closely followed that of Augustine. In defining the lie, he linked the intention to deceive with speaking contrary to what is in the mind. Thus, "to lie," he declared, "is to speak against that which one knows in one's mind." Therefore, all who lie speak falsely because they speak against what they know, "that is, with the will of deceiving." Similarly, to speak against one's mind with the attestation of an oath was perjury. In one place he defined perjury as speaking falsely by swearing with the intention to deceive.[36]

The era of Gratian's *Decretum* and Peter Lombard's *Sentences* witnessed not only a great development of legal science but also the emergence of the universities and the efflorescence of scholastic theology and philosophy. Of subsequent medieval thinkers who discussed lying and dissimulation, Thomas Aquinas, who created one of the great philosophical systems of the thirteenth century, was probably the medieval Christian philosopher most cited by the canonists, casuists, and moral theologians of Catholic Europe in the sixteenth century.

In his commentaries on Paul's letters, Aquinas dealt concisely with the episode of dissimulation in Galatians. He explained that Peter in Judaizing sinned venially from human weakness and that Paul's public rebuke was just and proper. Summarizing the "no small controversy" between Jerome and Augustine, Aquinas judged Augustine's the better argument and endorsed his belief that the scriptures did not authorize any falsehood.[37]

In his *Summa Theologiae* Aquinas included a systematic treatment of the problems connected with lying. This vast theological synthesis also encompassed the moral domain and examined assorted questions concerning oaths, perjury, lying, deception, and hypocrisy. Its scope and

---

[36] *Sententiarum Libri Quatuor*, bk. 3, distinctiones xxxviii–xxxix (*PLCC*, 192: cols. 833–834, 836). The text of Peter's definition runs: "Mentire vero est loqui contra hoc quod animo sentit . . . Omnis ergo qui loquitur mendacium mentitur, quia loquitur contra quod animo sentit, id est, voluntate fallendi."

[37] *Super Epistolas S. Pauli Lectura*, ed. P. Raffaele Cai, 2 vols. (Turin: Marietti, 1953), 1:583–584.

detail made it an imposing guide to the resolution of a wide range of moral complications involved in the Christian imperative of truth-telling.

Though rejecting the lie as strongly as Augustine, Aquinas entered more closely into practical difficulties and applications and provided for further distinctions and qualifications. A number of the questions he considered dealt with legal procedure and the conduct of defendants, witnesses, lawyers, and judges. Thus, he stated that an accused person was obliged to tell the truth about evidence and was guilty of mortal sin if he lied or remained silent. He ruled out, however, any obligation to self-incrimination and added the significant proviso that a defendant questioned by a judge "contrary to law" *(non . . . secundum ordinem legis)* need not answer; and, although he must not lie, he might resort to an appeal or "some other licit subterfuge" *(aliter licite subterfugere)*.[38]

Aquinas emphasized that an accused might not commit perjury or use fraud or deceit, which are the same as lying, even in self-defense. But he also pointed out, in words that echoed the *Decretum,* that "it is one thing to be silent about the truth and another to tell a falsehood." The first was permissible in certain circumstances, because one was not obliged to admit the whole truth but only the part a judge could legally inquire about when proceeding on a well-founded rumor, clear evidence, or partial proof of a crime. An accused might therefore defend himself by concealing the truth he had no obligation to admit. This was not trickery, "but rather prudent evasion" *(sed magis prudenter evadere)*. He further concluded that "a wise man does not conceal himself by trickery but through prudence" *(sapiens non abscondit se calumniose, sed prudenter)*.[39]

In discussing oaths, Aquinas touched on an important consideration that apologists for dissimulation three centuries later were greatly to expand. He stated that when the intention of one who swore an oath was not the same as that of the person to whom he swore, and the difference was a result of deceit, then the oath must be kept in the sense in which the latter intended or understood it. If the swearer did

---

[38] *Summa Theologiae,* ed. Dominican Fathers with Latin text and English translation, 60 vols. (London: Blackfriars, 1964–1976), 2a2ae, q. 69, arts. 1, 2 (38:117–119). In quoting from this edition I have occasionally slightly modified the translation.

[39] Ibid., art. 2 (pp. 119–121).

not use deceit, however, then the oath obliged him only in accord with his own intention. In support of this judgment, Aquinas adduced the text of Gregory's "Humanae aures."[40]

When he dealt specifically with the vice of lying, Aquinas repeated and enlarged on Augustine's definition. Besides emphasizing the will and intention to deceive, his analysis highlighted the formal character of the lie as speech contrary to what is in the mind. An indication of this, he observed, was that "the term *mendacium* derives from its being speech *contra mentem.*" He also cited Augustine's classification of lies and considered another division of the lie into the "helpful, humorous, and malicious" *(officiosum, jocosum, perniciosum).*[41] In determining whether every lie is sinful, he used scriptural examples mostly familiar from earlier writers: the Egyptian midwives, Abraham and Sarah, Jacob and Esau; and also the pious Judith, who lied in order to slay Holofernes and was commended for it (Judith 15).[42]

With respect to such instances, Aquinas affirmed that what was inherently evil could not become good or licit, and that lying was inherently evil on account of its disordered objective: "words by their nature being signs of thought, it is contrary to their nature and out of order for anyone to signify by words other than he thinks." This was a topic that would also engage later writers who designed a rationale for dissimulation. Aquinas therefore held with Augustine that every lie was sinful and denied that anywhere in the gospels or canonical scriptures was falsehood ever asserted or sanctioned. He resolved the scriptural cases, as Augustine had done, mainly on the principle that what seemed like a lie must be interpreted as said figuratively and prophetically. Thus he claimed that Jacob's pretense to be Esau had a mystical sense as a prophecy that a younger people, the Gentiles, would take the place of the firstborn, the Jews.[43]

Aquinas barred lying even to prevent injury or to save another, no matter what the danger. To this prohibition, however, he attached the noteworthy qualification, which he attributed to Augustine, "It is licit nevertheless to conceal the truth prudently under some dissimulation" *(Licet tamen veritatem occultare prudenter sub aliqua dissimulatione, ut*

[40] Ibid., q. 89, art. 7 (39:224–225).

[41] Ibid., q. 110, arts. 1, 2 (41:148–153).

[42] The book of Judith, excluded as apocryphal from the Authorized Version, is included in the Vulgate among the canonical scriptures.

[43] *Summa Theologiae,* 2a2ae, q. 110, art. 3 (41:155–159).

Augustinus dicit).[44] In this dictum, Aquinas went beyond the opinion in Augustine's *Against Lying* (quoted above) to which he referred. Although Augustine did there distinguish concealment of the truth from lying, he said nothing about the licitness of dissimulation.

Although he judged all lying to be sinful, Aquinas held that not every lie was a mortal sin; its character depended on the will and the intention. Lies that injured God or one's neighbor and were against charity were mortal sins. On the other hand, humorous and helpful lies, which intend either harmless pleasure or service to another, were not in this category. He accordingly judged that the Egyptian midwives sinned by their lie in outward act but that their goodness to the Jews and reverential fear of God gained an eternal reward.[45]

In examining the question of deception *(simulatio)* and hypocrisy *(hupocrisis)*, Aquinas recurred to scriptural cases we have already encountered, such as Christ's pretense to his disciples that he would go further, Jehu's feigning to worship Baal, and David's feigning of madness. In this context he cited, as did the *Decretum,* Jerome's pointed statement on such precedents in his Galatians commentary that dissimulation was sometimes acceptable.[46]

Aquinas declared that deception, which meant a false signification by outward acts, was identical with lying. But he also observed that to pretend *(fingere)* is not always to lie, for a pretense sometimes has reference to a further meaning and conveys a truth figuratively. Hence Jesus in feigning to his disciples that he would go further was communicating figuratively that the truth about himself was far removed from their way of thinking. David's feigning was likewise figurative. As for Jehu, his dissimulation was wicked in not departing from idolatry, but he received praise and an earthly reward for destroying Baal's worship.

Here as elsewhere Aquinas stressed the difference between concealing the truth and lying either verbally or in actions: to say or signify by actions what is false is to lie, but to keep silent or refrain from conveying the truth by other signs is not.[47] He also equated hypocrisy with lying as a species of dissembling, although he conceded that it was not always a mortal sin if its end was not against charity.[48]

[44] Ibid. (pp. 160–161).
[45] Ibid., art. 4 (pp. 164–167).
[46] Ibid., q. 111, art. 1 (pp. 168–169).
[47] Ibid. (pp. 170–173).
[48] Ibid., arts. 2–4 (pp. 173–180).

The Franciscan Nicholas of Lyra discussed another crucial Old Testament text relating to the question of dissimulation. A learned Hebraist and master in the theological faculty of the University of Paris, Nicholas was one of the greatest biblical scholars of the Middle Ages. Composed during the first half of the fourteenth century, his *postilla* or exegeses on the scriptures were known to all students of the Bible. Many early printed editions of the Bible included them as glosses in the margin of the text.[49]

Nicholas used the story of Naaman (4 Kings 5:17–19 in the Vulgate; 2 Kings 5:17–19 in the Authorized Version) in commenting on dissimulation. Naaman, a great captain and servant of the king of Syria, was healed of leprosy by the prophet Elisha, and in gratitude he announced his conversion to the God of Israel, vowing never to make sacrifices or burnt offerings to other gods. Nevertheless, he begged Elisha for the Lord's pardon when he accompanied the king his master, who would lean upon his arm, into the temple of the idol Rimmon and bowed down with him there. To this request Elisha replied by bidding Naaman to go in peace.

Nicholas' first observation on this episode was that "not only the worship of idols but even to simulate this worship is sin." He then noted the opinion held by some that because Naaman was a neophyte newly converted to the Jewish law, Elisha dispensed him. He rejected this view, however, on the ground that Naaman was not, properly speaking, a new convert obliged to follow the law of Moses, but rather one who had come to believe in the true God as did many Gentiles who were saved without observing the Mosaic law. He also pointed out that things "evil in themselves" were not dispensable and that one such evil was the "simulation of idolatry."

He then went on to explain Elisha's answer. According to Nicholas, the prophet told Naaman that the action he feared as unlawful was lawful. Naaman had a duty to assist his king, and this was not illicit in its own nature. Moreover, he could perform this duty whether outside or within the idol's temple, just as a Christian girl captured by the Saracens may carry her mistress's train into a Muslim temple without worshiping Muhammad. What Naaman asked of Elisha, therefore, was only that he might perform the same duty to his master in the idol's temple as he lawfully did elsewhere. He sought this permission

---

[49] For an account of Nicholas of Lyra, see *Dictionnaire de theologie catholique*, s.v.

not from reverence to the idol but lest he incur the king's displeasure. This was what Elisha granted him, Nicholas concludes, and it was not unlawful.[50]

As his reference to other opinions suggests, Nicholas of Lyra was probably not the first commentator to deal with the issue of dissimulation in the case of Naaman the Syrian. His work, however, was so widely known that it would have served to emphasize the pertinence of the example of Naaman in determining whether a dissimulated submission to idolatry was ever lawful. This example was to be extensively debated in the sixteenth century and repeatedly cited as a leading precedent by those who attempted to justify the concealment of belief through pretended conformity.

In the confessional conflicts, persecution, and enforced conformity of the Reformation, the problem of dissimulation assumed a greater relevance than ever before. Several celebrated Christian theologians of the early sixteenth century treated Peter's dissimulation in Paul's letter to the Galatians. As we have seen, this text posed the issue of dissimulation in the sharpest terms. It did so, moreover, with regard to the licitness of pretending conformity to rites and practices that the believer's conscience repudiated as sinful or unnecessary.

The letter to the Galatians was one of Martin Luther's favorite scriptural books because it provided such ample scope for the dialectic of difference between the law and the gospel which lay at the heart of his religious thought. His commentary on it, first published in 1535, was among his most influential and widely read works.[51] Its fundamental theme was the principle of justification by faith in Christ alone and the rejection of every other conception of righteousness, legal, moral, and civil, as incapable of taking away sin. For Luther the Christian's liberty from the tyranny of works prescribed by the Catholic church was identical with the emancipation from bondage to the law

[50] "Ad IIII Regum Cap. V," in *Textus Bibliae cum Glossa Ordinaria, Nicolai de Lyra Postilla . . .* (Basel, 1506–1508).

[51] *In Epistolam S. Pauli ad Galatas Commentarius,* in *Werke,* 60 vols. (Weimar: H. Böhlau, 1883–1979), vol. 40. I quote from the Elizabethan translation, *A Commentarie of M. Doctor Martin Luther upon the Epistle of S. Paul to the Galatians* (London, 1575), which is printed in a revised version in Martin Luther, *A Commentary on St. Paul's Epistle to the Galatians,* ed. Philip S. Watson (Westwood, N.J.: Revell, 1953).

which Paul preached in Galatians. Like Augustine, Luther held that in observing Jewish practices, Paul never pretended that they were necessary to salvation; when he behaved as a Jew with the Jews and as a Gentile with the Gentiles, eating and drinking with the latter what the law forbade, abstaining with the former from everything prohibited by the law, Paul only "laboured to serve & please all men that he might gaine all."[52] Peter's offense, therefore, was not that he ate with the Jews but that he dissimulated, thus conveying the belief that without observance of the law a man cannot be saved. This action, according to Luther, fully justified Paul's rebuke.

Luther rejected Jerome's interpretation of Galatians with the flat statement, "Jerome neither understood this place nor the whole epistle besides." He denied that Paul's reproof was feigned, pointing out that Peter dissembled through fear and that if Paul had not corrected him, both Jews and Gentiles would have been deprived of the liberty that is in Christ and the gospel thereby endangered. Luther used the incident to condemn dissembling and to underscore the difference between the law and the gospel as "the summe of all Christian doctrine." "In this matter," he declared, "we should doe nothing by dissimulation, or give place to any man, if we will retaine the truth of the gospell and faith sound and incorrupt."[53]

As might be expected, Erasmus' treatment of the Galatians text was very different from Luther's. The great humanist, whose efforts to mediate and preserve his independence were to bring mistrust, reproach, and attacks on him from both sides of the great religious divide that started to open in the 1520s, owed part of his European fame to his work as an editor and translator of the New Testament and of the works of Jerome. Something of his attitude to Peter's dissimulation comes through in his *Paraphrase* of the letter to the Galatians (1519), one of several paraphrases of Paul's letters and other New Testament books. In it Erasmus used his own words but preserved Paul's first-person form of address. Thus he made Paul say that Peter's dissimulation proceeded from "a pious mind" but was nevertheless "inadvised" and threatened to bring about the destruction of many. Erasmus' palliating reference in this context to Peter's pious mind had no basis in the original of Paul's words in Galatians.[54]

[52] *A Commentarie of M. Doctor Martin Luther*, fol. 52r.

[53] Ibid., fols. 53r–56r.

[54] *Paraphrasis in Novum Testamentum*, in *Opera*, ed. Jean Leclerc, 10 vols. (1703–1706; repr., London: Gregg, 1961–1962), 7:949.

In the *Annotationes* to his 1516 edition of the New Testament, Erasmus commented at length on the controverted episode in Galatians. Besides remarking on Peter's seniority as an apostle and summarizing Aquinas' exposition of the text, it discussed the *magnifica disputatio* between Jerome and Augustine. Erasmus' interpretation resembled Jerome's. He did not exactly acquit Peter of wrongdoing but tried to excuse his conduct as vacillation and no more than a light offense. Observing that what Jerome called dissimulation Augustine called a lie, he commented, "I do not see why in our hatred of the lie we should treat Peter as harshly as Augustine did." In agreement with Jerome he also defended the use of dissimulation: "No one denies that it is sometimes right for a pious man to dissimulate" *(neque quisquam negat, pium hominem alicubi recte simulare et dissimulare)*.[55]

Erasmus' view reflected his well-known disposition to evasion and compromise. Elsewhere he praised Paul for his flexibility, accommodation, and pious cunning as an exemplary preacher of the gospel who adapted himself to all kinds of men and circumstances. Erasmus favored reserve and economy or opportuneness in communicating the truth, believing that it might be withheld from those not yet fully ready for it. "A prudent steward," he wrote to a friend in 1521, "will husband the truth," revealing only as much as necessary for the business and persons concerned.[56] He compared both Paul and himself to a chameleon, to Proteus, and to Vertumnus as beings without fixity who turn all ways. Such qualities were easily perceived as dissimulation by his critics. It is not surprising that former admirers such as the humanist knight Ulrich von Hutten, who became a passionate supporter of Luther, accused him of deception and dishonesty when he refused to enlist himself as a partisan in the reformer's cause.[57]

Calvin's commentary on Galatians, published in 1548, was written during the period in which he was also waging his polemic against

---

[55] Erasmus' *Annotationes* to Galatians 2:11–14 are printed with his *Novum Testamentum*, in *Opera*, 6:807–810.

[56] *The Correspondence of Erasmus*, 8 vols. (Toronto: University of Toronto Press, 1974–1988), 8:203.

[57] See the discussion and passages cited in Biondi, "La giustificazione della simulazione"; P. G. Bietenholz, " 'Haushalten mit der Wahrheit': Erasmus im Dilemma der Kompromissbereitschaft," *Basler Zeitschrift für Geschichte und Altertumskunde*, 86, no. 2 (1986); idem, preface to *The Correspondence of Erasmus*, 8:xiii–xiv. On Hutten's quarrel with Erasmus see Hajo Holborn, *Ulrich von Hutten and the German Reformation* (New York: Harper & Row, 1966), chap. 12.

Nicodemism and religious dissimulation. To him, as to Luther, Paul's letter was a declaration of the doctrine of justification by faith against the delusion of salvation by the works of the law. His explanation of the contested text was akin to Augustine's. Not surprisingly, he termed Jerome's exposition "unapt," "frivolous," and "vayne," dismissing as groundless the argument that the disagreement of Peter and Paul was feigned as a sort of prearranged match or prank to be played before the people. According to Calvin, Paul's public reproof of Peter was salutary and necessary to preserve Christian liberty. Whereas Paul accommodated himself to the Jews only insofar as was consistent with Christian liberty, Peter's action would have forced the Gentiles into slavery to the law and was done from the desire to please, not to edify. Thus Paul was right to oppose Peter's dissimulation, because he saw that it would injure the church. One of the conclusions Calvin drew was "how warily we must attemper our selves to please men: lest we swerve aside from the right course, with too much desire to please, or else with preposterous feare to offend." If this might happen to Peter, he declared, "how much more easilye shall it happen to us, except we take very good heede."[58]

Finally, in marked contrast to Calvin's was the earlier treatment of the Galatians text by the distinguished French humanist, philosopher, biblical scholar, and reformer *avant la réforme* Jacques Lefèvre d'Etaples. Though agreeing with Augustine that Peter wrongfully dissimulated, Lefèvre held that dissimulation as such was neither good nor bad but indifferent, and depended upon its end. As an example he cited the by now familiar instance of Christ's simulating to his disciples on the way to Emmaus that he would go further. If dissimulation edified, Lefèvre maintained, it was good, whereas if it took away charity and worked against edification it was bad. Paul himself dissimulated in observing Jewish rites, he said, but all of Paul's actions, even his dissimulation, were spiritual.[59]

Lefèvre published his edition of Paul's epistles in 1512. His later failure to align himself with the Protestant reform and risk martyrdom, as some of his own friends and disciples did, gave rise to a

[58] *Commentarius in Epistolam Pauli ad Galatas,* in *Opera,* ed. Johann Baum, Eduard Cunitz, and Eduard Reuss, 59 vols. (Brunswick, 1863–1896), vol. 50. I quote from the Elizabethan translation, *A Commentarie of M. J. Calvine upon the Epistle to the Galatians* (London, 1581), pp. 36–38.

[59] *Sancti Pauli Epistolae XIV . . . cum Commentariis,* cited and discussed by Biondi, "La giustificazione della simulazione," pp. 18–19.

belief among the latter that he was guilty of dissimulating his true convictions. Before his death in 1536, he was reported to have been torn by remorse and fear of damnation for not having testified openly to his faith. There is no knowing whether there is any truth to this story, which is attributed to Calvin's colleague and fellow Protestant Guillaume Farel.[60] Nevertheless, it underscores the importance of the problem of dissimulation during these early decades of the Reformation, when Calvin and other reformers were outspokenly demanding an open commitment to Protestantism.

[60] See A-L. Herminjard, *Correspondance des réformateurs dans les pays de langue francaise,* 9 vols. (1866–1897; repr. Nieuwkoop: B. de Graff, 1965–66), 3:400n. Lefèvre's religious position in relation to Protestantism is delineated in Eugene F. Rice, Jr., "Introduction," in *The Prefatory Epistles of Jacques Lefèvre d'Etaples and Related Texts* (New York: Columbia University Press, 1972), esp. pp. xxii–xxiii. He is depicted as being in agreement with the Protestant reformers in some things, but also as holding that both faith and works were necessary to salvation and as retaining his belief in the freedom of the will, contrary to Luther.

CHAPTER 3

The Marranos and Crypto-Judaism

The Inquisition was established in Castile by the bull of 1 November 1478, which Pope Sixtus IV addressed to the Spanish monarchs Ferdinand and Isabella. The papal statement referred to the number of those who despite regeneration in Christ through the holy water of baptism "have by their own will returned secretly" to the practice of Jewish superstition. Such people, it declared, incurred the penalty of heresy, and by reason of their crimes and the tolerance extended them afflicted the land with innumerable evils. It authorized the sovereigns to appoint three bishops or other suitable men with full powers as inquisitors of heresy in every diocese and city. Five years later the jurisdiction of the Inquisition was extended to Aragon.[1]

From this small beginning arose the Spanish Inquisition or Holy Office, the main motive of whose foundation was the eradication of crypto-Judaism among the *conversos,* the New Christians or *nuevos Cristianos* of Jewish descent. Although there had been earlier types of inquisition in medieval Europe, including several regions of Spain, this one developed into a unique bureaucratic organization that achieved an extraordinary amplitude and penetration in the Spanish kingdoms. Eventually it evolved into twenty-one permanent tribunals, fourteen of which were located in peninsular Spain and the rest in the Mediterranean, Atlantic, and American possessions of the Spanish monarchy. In addition to its salaried officials, who were largely clergy, it had a considerable number of unsalaried agents, the familiars and

[1] Guy Testas and Jean Testas, *L'Inquisition,* 4th ed. (Paris: Presses Universitaires de France, 1983), pp. 69–70, prints extracts from Sixtus IV's bull; see also H. C. Lea, *A History of the Inquisition of Spain,* 4 vols. (New York: Macmillan, 1922), 1:157–159.

commissioners, who served as informers and assistants in each tribunal district and enjoyed various privileges in return for their services. The entire body was under the direction of the *Suprema* or Supreme Council, presided over by the inquisitor general, all of whose members were appointed by the crown. Quite soon the Inquisition, which was not abolished until 1834, became one of the most feared and powerful of royal institutions. In a land sharply divided by the regionalism and autonomism of its separate states, it was also the only centrally administered institution other than the monarchy itself whose authority transcended all frontiers and jurisdictional boundaries and was common to the whole of Spain.[2]

Crypto-Judaism, the earliest target of the Inquisition, stands somewhat apart from the other manifestations of religious dissimulation in early modern Europe, which were related to the confessional divisions within Christian society and the enforcement of orthodoxy and conformity by one Christian denomination upon the members of another. Crypto-Judaism, in contrast, reflected the dominant Christian society's religious and cultural oppression of a non-Christian minority in its midst. True, canon law and the Inquisition treated Christians who reverted to Judaism as heretics, not as Jews; they were regarded as apostates and rebels against the faith of Christ. In their own minds, however, the *conversos* who clandestinely practiced some semblance,

---

[2] Lea's great work remains the fullest, most detailed institutional history of the Spanish Inquisition. A recent short survey is Henry A. Kamen's *Inquisition and Society in Spain in the Sixteenth and Seventeenth Centuries* (Bloomington: Indiana University Press, 1985). Edward Peters, *Inquisition* (New York: Free Press, 1988), contains an account of the Spanish and other inquisitions and is concerned to separate the reality from the myths about them. Since the 1970s, an explosion of research on the Spanish Inquisition has shed new light on its functioning and begun to exploit the wealth of information in its archives to illuminate important aspects of social history. For some descriptions of this work with many bibliographical references, see the essays in Bartolome Bennassar, ed., *L'Inquisition espagnole* (Paris: Hachette, 1979); J. Pérez Villanueva, ed., *La Inquisición española: Nueva vision, nuevos horizontes* (Madrid: Siglo Veintiuno de España, 1980); Angel Alcalá, ed., *Inquisición española y mentalidad inquisitorial* (Barcelona: Editorial Ariel, 1984); Gustav Hennigsen and John Tedeschi, eds., *The Inquisition in Early Modern Europe* (De Kalb: Northern Illinois University Press, 1986); Geoffrey Parker, "Some Recent Work on the Inquisition in Spain and Italy," *Journal of Modern History*, 54, no. 3 (1982). On the Inquisition's effects on Spanish life, see David Peyre, "L'Inquisition, ou la politique de la présence," and Bartolome Bennassar, "Le pouvoir inquisitorial" and "L'Inquisition, ou la pédagogie de la peur," all in Bennassar, *L'Inquisition espagnole.*

however impoverished, of Judaism, felt themselves to be Jews, even if compelled to act as Catholics.

What unites them with other persecuted religious groups of the early modern era is the place dissimulation occupied in their lives. As Julio Caro Baroja, author of the most comprehensive historical and sociological study of modern Spanish Jewry, has observed, this "dissimulation went to such extremes that for years it deceived the shrewdest agents of the inquisitorial power."[3] The lives of *converso* Judaizers were based on secrecy and steeped in dissimulation, both its rationale and its practice. This was probably the case to an even greater degree than that of the Christians who were also forced to dissimulate to escape persecution by church or state during the Reformation and Counter-Reformation. Between these Christians and crypto-Jews, moreover, there were definite affinities and resemblances, despite the profound differences in beliefs, history, and tradition that separated them.

In medieval Spain Jews had long coexisted with Christians in relative tolerance and peace. Favored by Christian rulers who benefited from their presence, many Jews attained prominent positions in government, finance, and commerce. During the fourteenth century, however, jealousy and resentment of Jewish influence and wealth strongly increased. In 1391 the massacres of thousands in the Jewish quarters of many cities throughout Spain resulted in the conversion of considerable numbers of Jews. The process of conversion continued steadily during the fifteenth century in consequence of recurrent anti-Semitic outbreaks together with the introduction of various discriminatory measures and other pressures. This was the origin of the *converso* problem, which sprang from the existence in Spain by the mid-fifteenth century of a conspicuous minority of New Christians of Jewish origin.

The continuing proximity and associations in various relationships of Jews and *conversos* fostered suspicion among Old Christians that the *conversos* had merely assumed the guise of Christianity while remaining Jews at heart. The word *marrano,* meaning "pig" or "unclean," came to be applied throughout western Europe to Jews who pretended to be Christians while adhering secretly to Judaism.[4]

[3] Julio Caro Baroja, *Los judíos en la españa moderna y contemporánea,* 3 vols. (Madrid: Ediciones ISTMO, 1978), 1:415–416.

[4] On the origin and meaning of the term *Marrano* see ibid., pp. 405–406; Albert A. Sicroff, *Les controverses des statuts de "Pureté de sang" en Espagne du XVe au XVIIe*

Conversos were obliged to take Christian names at baptism, and laws were also instituted requiring them to segregate themselves from Jews. Nevertheless, persisting suspicion of crypto-Judaism, plus the fact that the *conversos* included many outstanding men who played a significant role in royal and municipal government, commerce, the professions, and even the church, drew widespread animosity upon them. Hence Christian anti-Semitism extended itself equally to the *conversos*, who were accused of Judaism and resented as well for their influential position in society.[5]

Writers and popular preachers belonging to the religious orders carried on a steady propaganda against Jews and *conversos* alike, promoting an image of the *converso* as a nefarious dissembler and secret enemy of Christianity. This odium was compounded by the adoption of statutes of *limpieza de sangre* or blood purity, which barred persons of non-Christian descent from holding office or membership in particular institutions. The earliest of these, enacted in 1449 by the city of Toledo following an outbreak of violence against *conversos*, prohibited the latter from holding any office in the city or the territory under its jurisdiction. In justification of this action, the Toledo ordinance

---

siècle (Paris: Études de Littéraire Étrangère et Comparée, 1960), p. 250 and n. I have not seen the work by Arturo Farinelli, *Marrano (storia di uno vituperio)* (Geneva: Biblioteca dell'Archivum Romanicum, 1925).

[5] Besides the *conversos* of Jewish origin, the Moriscos, the offspring of the Muslim inhabitants of medieval Spain, were likewise victims of oppression by the dominant Christian society. After the Christian reconquest of Spain, completed in 1492 with the fall of Granada, the Moors there and in Valencia and Aragon were increasingly subjected to forced Christianization, notwithstanding the original promises of the Catholic sovereigns for the preservation of their religion and culture. They thus became a despised and persecuted minority destined eventually to expulsion from Spain in 1609. The survival of Islam among them made them no less a concern of the Inquisition than were *converso* Judaizers. In certain tribunals, trials of Moriscos at times outnumbered other cases; see e.g., Ricard García Cárcel, *Herejía y sociedad en el siglo XVI. La Inquisición en Valencia 1530–1609* (Barcelona: Ediciones Peninsula, 1980), pp. 221–243. Most Moriscos, however, were agricultural workers and artisans and never occupied the important position in Spanish society that many *conversos* did. They often lived apart in their own villages or in separate quarters of towns, and their attachment to Islam and its rites was frequently unconcealed. On their history and relation to the Inquisition, see Lea, *History of the Inquisition,* vol. 3, bk. 7, chap. 2; Julio Caro Baroja, *Los Moriscos del reino de Granada,* 2d ed. (Madrid: Instituto de Estudios Políticos, 1957); Kamen, *Inquisition and Society,* chap 6; Antonio Domínguez Ortiz, *Historia de los Moriscos. Vida y tragedia de una Minoría* (Madrid: Revista de Occidente, 1978).

recited a harsh indictment of the New Christians, affirming that they were not truly converted but held Jewish beliefs, and that they slandered Christians with the accusation of adoring as a god and savior a man of the Jews who had been hung.[6] Statutes of blood purity were always opposed by some churchmen as introducing an unjust discrimination among Christians and hindering the assimilation of *conversos*. At first they were also condemned by the pope and crown. Nevertheless, over time *limpieza* became a requirement for admission to the great military orders of the kingdom, to cathedral chapters, religious orders and confraternities, the *colegios mayores* of the universities, and many other institutions and offices. In this way, blood purity became an obsession among Spaniards, giving rise to its own brand of dissimulation as aspirants to honors and positions sought to prove their eligibility by fictitious genealogies concealing any stain of Jewish ancestry.

The situation of *conversos* was full of paradoxes. At the will of Christian society they or their immediate forebears had been compelled by various means to receive baptism, yet they were not accepted among Christians as equals. They were scorned as secret Jews and subjected to racial anti-Semitism, yet possessed opportunities and rights as baptized Christians that were unavailable to Jews. They intermarried with Old Christians, including many eminent noble families. They became clergy and even inquisitors.[7] Many of them enjoyed rank and affluence and were indispensable both to the economic life of Spain and to the Spanish sovereigns in the administration of their kingdoms. Still another paradox was that some *conversos* were themselves anti-Semites; because they felt compromised by the presence of the Jews, they joined in the attack upon them and their religion.

A widespread opinion maintained that the *conversos* were contaminated by Jewish proximity and association and that only the removal of the Jews from Spain could eliminate the problem. This was the policy eventually resolved upon by Ferdinand and Isabella. The royal edict of March 1492, which was issued also in the name of the Inquisitor General Torquemada, ordered the expulsion of the Jewish inhabi-

---

[6] Sicroff, *Les controverses des statuts,* pp. 32–35. For the operation of *limpieza* in the case of a famous writer, see Stephen Gilman, *The Spain of Fernando de Rojas* (Princeton: Princeton University Press, 1972).

[7] The first inquisitor general of the Holy Office, the Dominican prior Tómas de Torquemada, and his immediate successor, Diego Deza, bishop of Jaen, were both of Jewish descent; Lea, *History of the Inquisition,* 1:120.

tants from all territories of the crowns of Castile and Aragon by the following August under pain of death unless they accepted baptism. The edict stated that this step had been made necessary by the failure of all previous measures to prevent the Jews from influencing the *conversos* and injuring the Christian faith.[8]

The expulsion of 1492, the culmination of a century of religious and racial anti-Semitism, marked the final blow in the destruction of Spanish Jewry. Between 150,000 and 170,000 Jews may have been driven into exile, while possibly another 50,000 accepted baptism. This event occurred at a time when Spain's population amounted to perhaps five or five and one-half million.[9] Some of the Jews who were expelled went to Italy, France, North Africa, and Turkey, but the large majority sought refuge in Portugal. There they were to find no rest either, for in 1497 King Manuel of Portugal ordered the expulsion of all Jews over the age of fourteen, an act resulting in the sudden conversion of virtually the entire Jewish population. Owing to the presence of a sizable minority of *conversos* and the problem of crypto-Judaism in Portugal, the Inquisition was established there in 1537.[10]

Conversion on the scale that occurred among the Spanish Jews from the end of the fourteenth century to the expulsion of 1492 cannot be explained solely as the effect of physical coercion or terror. Jews had always known violence and suffering in their resistance to alien religions and had drawn from this experience some of their profoundest inspiration. Sacrificial martyrdom at the hands of pagan, Christian, and Muslim persecutors was a keynote of all Jewish history.

[8] Yitzhak Baer, *A History of the Jews in Christian Spain*, 2 vols. (Philadelphia: Jewish Publication Society, 1961), 2:433–434.

[9] For estimates of the number expelled, see ibid., pp. 438, 510–511n; Jaime Vicens Vives, *Historia social y economica de España y America*, 4 vols. (Barcelona: Editorial Teide, 1957–1959), 2:410. I have taken the estimate of Spanish population from J. M. Batista i Roca in *The New Cambridge Modern History*, vol. 1: *The Renaissance*, ed. G. M. Potter (Cambridge: Cambridge University Press, 1957), p. 316. See also Caro Baroja, *Los judios*, 1:198–205.

[10] Baer, *A History of the Jews*, 2:438; Lea, *History of the Inquisition*, 3:237. On the difference between the character of the conversion of the Jews of Spain and Portugal, see Y. H. Yerushalmi, *From Spanish Court to Italian Ghetto: A Study in Seventeenth-Century Marranism and Jewish Apologetics* (New York: Columbia University Press, 1971), pp. 3–8. I. S. Révah, "Les Marranes portugais et l'Inquisition au XVIe siècle," in *The Sephardic Heritage*, ed. R. D. Barnett (London: Ballantine, Mitchell, 1971), discusses the relation of the Portuguese *conversos* to the Inquisition.

Even in the recent past the Jews of northern Europe had died sanctifying the name of God during the crusaders' massacres.

In Spain, however, there was never one unique or supreme moment when the Jews confronted the choice of martyrdom. Physical violence, moral intimidation, and peaceful evangelization all combined to support a sustained policy of systematic conversion by church and state. Moreover, the process of conversion was facilitated by contacts with secular culture and powerful currents of rationalism, worldliness, and unbelief stemming from Averroistic Aristotelian philosophy, which had made considerable inroads on Jewish faith and weakened its ties with tradition.[11] This was especially true of the educated elite of Jews who were heavily represented among the *conversos*. Under the influence of rationalistic and naturalistic ideas, such Jews became skeptical of the authority of biblical law and developed a philosophical religion of the intellect. While the majority of small tradespeople and artisans apparently remained steadfast in their Judaism, the *conversos* included many members of the aristocracy of the Jewish communities. Thus most of the apostates whose names have been identified apparently came from the wealthy and cultured sectors of the Jewish population.[12] One of the best-known *conversos*, Solomon Halevi, was the chief rabbi of Burgos and a royal fiscal official and philosopher who at the age of forty during the massacres of 1391 was baptized under the name Pablo de Santa Maria together with two of his brothers and five sons. He was later to become bishop of Burgos, a papal legate, and a prominent polemicist against Judaism.[13] Another celebrated convert, Joshua Halorki, was a rabbi and papal physician whose intellectual doubts regarding Judaism led him to accept Christianity in 1410. Taking the baptismal name Gerónimo de Santa Fe, he turned into a leading anti-Jewish propagandist.[14] In 1492 at the time of the expulsion, Abraham Seneor, the last chief rabbi of Castile, a great royal tax

[11] Baer, *A History of the Jews,* 2:137, 148, 163, and chap. 10; see also John Edwards, "Religious Belief and Social Conformity: The 'Converso' Problem in Late-Medieval Córdoba," *Transactions of the Royal Historical Society,* 5th ser., 31 (1984).

[12] Baer, *A History of the Jews,* 2:130.

[13] Ibid., pp. 139–141; Lea, *History of the Inquisition,* 1:114.

[14] Baer, *A History of the Jews,* 2:139–141, 171; Lea, *History of the Inquisition,* 1:114–115. In 1413–14, Gerónimo de Santa Fe took a leading part in the Disputation of Tortosa, a debate held between Christian and Jewish theologians intended to demonstrate the errors of the Jewish religion and conducted in the presence of the anti-pope Benedict XIII. This event was widely known to the Jews, and a

farmer and the most important figure among the Spanish Jews, was converted with his son-in-law and others of his family and underwent baptism with great ceremony. It was with reason that another rabbi lamented during the dark days of the expulsion that "most of the Jews and their great men and their nobility and their magistrates remained in their houses and converted."[15]

How widespread was Marranism among the *conversos?* Owing to the obscurities and complexities of *converso* history, this is a question that can never be adequately answered. The main evidence for crypto-Judaism derives from the trial records of the Inquisition, which in the first decades of its existence was far more preoccupied with Jewish heresy than with any other type of crime. Even so, clusters of Judaizers were able to escape its notice for a time. In the 1560s and 1580s, for example, the Inquisition discovered and eliminated a number of surviving communities of Judaizers in Alburquerque and other towns in the province of Extremadura, near the Portuguese frontier.[16] It is also well known that many *conversos* who emigrated from Spain and Portugal in the sixteenth and seventeenth centuries affiliated themselves with or established Jewish communities in the places where they settled. Rabbinical *responsa* issued outside Spain during the fifteenth century and later also attest that many emigrant *conversos* sought to return to Judaism; it had to be determined whether, having submitted to idolatry, they still remained part of Israel. Likewise, *con-*

---

spate of conversions was reported to have ensued as a result of Gerónimo's arguments.

[15] Baer, *A History of the Jews,* 2:436, 510n. The story was told that Abraham Seneor accepted baptism because Isabella had sworn that she would destroy all the Jewish communities if he refused. Concerning the mass conversion of Jews and its reasons, see, besides Bear, I. S. Révah, "Les Marranes," *Révue des études juives,* 3d ser., 118 (1959–60); Antonio Domínguez Ortiz, "Historical Research on Spanish *Conversos* in the Last Fifteen Years," and Francisco Márquez Villanueva, "The *Converso* Problem: An Assessment," both in *Collected Studies in Honour of Américo Castro's Eightieth Year,* ed. Marcel Hornik (Oxford: Lincombe Lodge Research Library, 1965).

[16] Catherine Brault-Noble and Marie-Jose Marc, "L'unification religieuse et sociale: La repression des minorités," in Bennassar, *L'Inquisition espagnole,* pp. 149–151; J. Contreras and Gustav Hennigsen, "Forty-four Thousand Cases of the Spanish Inquisition (1540–1700): Analysis of a Historical Data Bank," in Hennigsen and Tedeschi, *Inquisition in Early Modern Europe,* p. 124; see also Antonio Rodriguez-Moñino, "Les judaisantes á Badajoz de 1493 à 1599," *Revue des études juives,* 136 (1956).

versos who had apparently been cut off for generations from almost all connection with Judaism nevertheless left Spain in order to live as Jews. Thus Fernando Cardoso, educated at the university of Valladolid, an eminent Spanish court physician, philosopher, and man of science, in 1648 at the age of forty-four left Spain for Italy, returning to the Jewish fold in Verona, where he later wrote under his Hebrew name of Isaac Cardoso a famous defense of the Jews titled *Las excellencias de los hebreos.*[17]

Given the massive scale of Jewish conversion, however, it appears unlikely that Marranism was ever more than a relatively small phenomenon among the *conversos*. The claim of one of the principal historians of Spanish Jewry that "*conversos* and Jews were one people, united by bonds of religion, destiny, and messianic hope," may perhaps have been partially true of the fifteenth century.[18] During the century following the creation of the Inquisition, though, the odds against clandestine Jewish survival in Spain became overwhelming. Not only was the Holy Office relentless in its pursuit of crypto-Judaism, but also there occurred an inevitable decline of Jewish memory, a fading of religious knowledge with the disappearance of the conditions in which the Mosaic laws or *mitzwot* could be observed, and a loss of contact with the sources of tradition in books and rabbinical teaching. At the same time, the *conversos,* notwithstanding their ambiguous position, were being steadily assimilated into the life of Christian Spain. There can be no doubt that many were genuine Catholics. More than that, out of their number came saints, mystics, churchmen, jurists, philosophers, and other figures who contributed significantly to the golden age of Spanish civilization in the sixteenth and seventeenth centuries.[19]

---

[17] See the analysis of Marranism and the survival of Judaism in Révah, "Les Marranes"; the rabbinical *responsa* are touched on by Baer, *A History of the Jews* (2:506), and discussed in detail in Benzion Netanyahu, *The Marranos of Spain: From the Late XIVth to the Early XVIth Centuries according to the Contemporary Hebrew Sources* (New York: American Academy for Jewish Research, 1966). For an account of the life and career of Fernando Cardoso in the context of Marranism, see Yerushalmi, *From Spanish Court to Italian Ghetto.* In looking for an explanation of Cardoso's return to Judaism, Yerushalmi notes (pp. 90–92) a statement by Fernando's brother Miguel that their parents told the latter when he was six years old that he was a Jew.

[18] Baer, *A History of the Jews,* 2:424.

[19] See Révah, "Les Marranes"; and Márquez Villanueva, "The *Converso* Problem"; the latter argues convincingly that the Judaizers were only a small and

The Inquisition dealt both with the major heresies of Judaism, Islam,[20] Protestantism, and illuminism (the *alumbrados*) and with a range of lesser offenses, including witchcraft, sorcery, and superstition, blasphemy and scandalous acts against religion, bigamy and sexual transgressions, solicitation by clergy in the confessional, and contempts against the Holy Office itself. Quantitative investigation of the Inquisition's archives has shown that from its creation until about 1530, trials for Jewish heresy overwhelmingly outnumbered all other categories of cases. Between 1484 and 1530 in Valencia, for example, the Inquisition tried 2,354 people, more than 90 percent of them as Judaizers. More than 99 percent of the Toledo tribunal's cases from its foundation in 1483 until 1500 were likewise for crypto-Judaism. For the rest of the century the number of cases of Jewish heresy declined sharply, doubtless as a result of the Holy Office's terrible efficiency in the preceding years.

In 1580, however, Philip II of Spain annexed the crown of Portugal in a conquest that lasted until 1640, and a stream of Portuguese *converso* emigration into Spain began. Unlike the Spanish Jews, the Portuguese Jews had converted as a community en masse at the end of the fifteenth century. Having undergone no gradual conversion, they apparently retained a considerable attachment to Judaism. As a consequence, the seventeenth century brought a resurgence of trials for Jewish heresy, though not in the same proportions as in the first decades of the Inquisition.[21] From the evidence of inquisitional trials

---

undistinguished minority among the *conversos*. The well-known significance of the *conversos'* role in Spanish civilization is stressed by Américo Castro, *The Spaniards: An Introduction to Their History* (Berkeley: University of California Press, 1971).

[20] Above, note 5.

[21] Jaime Contreras and Gustav Hennigsen have made the most comprehensive quantitative analysis to date of the Inquisition's activity based on an examination of summaries in its records of more than 40,000 cases from 1540 to 1700, about half the total number in this period. Among their findings is that 60 percent of these cases dealt with lesser offenses ("delitos menores") and 40 percent with the greater heresies, which involved persecution of religious minorities. Their data are summarized in Gustav Hennigsen, "La elocuencia de los numeros: Promesas de las 'Relaciones de causas' para la nueva historia social," in Alcalá, *Inquisición española;* and more fully in Contreras and Hennigsen, "Forty-four Thousand Cases." For a comparison of the data on cases of the Inquisition of Valencia with other tribunals, see Ricard García Cárcel, *Origines de la Inquisición española. El tribunal de Valencia 1478–1530* (Barcelona: Ediciones Peninsula, 1976), pp. 167–170; idem, *Herejía y sociedad,* pp. 220–221. Jean-Pierre Dedieu provides data on the Toledo Inquisition in "Les quatre temps de l'Inquisition," in Bennassar,

and literary sources, it is possible to form a vivid conception of crypto-Judaism and its methods of dissimulation.[22]

In 1460 a Franciscan friar, Alonso de Espina, published *The Fortress of Faith (Fortalitium Fidei)*, a defense of Catholicism against the Jews and other enemies. Along with its anti-Semitic libels it contained a description of the practices of Judaizers, including circumcision, the gift of oil for synagogue lamps, observance of the sabbath and Jewish funeral rites, and Jewish education of sons in the synagogue. It also mentioned various transgressions against Christianity, such as avoiding the sacraments, working on Sunday, unwillingness to mention the names Jesus and Mary, attending mass solely so as not to appear conspicuous, pretending that it would be dangerous for newborn infants to be baptized in church in order to have them baptized at home without ecclesiastical ceremony, contempt of the Host, and

---

L'Inquisition espagnole; and "The Archives of the Holy Office of Toledo as a Source for Historical Anthropology," in Hennigsen and Tedeschi, *Inquisition in Early Modern Europe,* app. 4.

[22] A few scholars have denied the reliability of the Inquisition's records, contending that crypto-Judaism was largely a hoax and fiction invented by the Inquisition for propaganda purposes and as an excuse to confiscate Jewish wealth; see Netanyahu, *The Marranos of Spain;* Ellis Rivkin, "The Utilization of Non-Jewish Sources for the Reconstruction of Jewish History," *Jewish Quarterly Review,* 48, no. 2 (1957–58); Antonio José Saraiva, *Historia de cultura em Portugal,* 3 vols. (Lisbon: Jornal de Foro, 1950–1962), vol. 3. Most historians of the Inquisition and Iberian Jewry rightly reject this thesis as unfounded, for it would entail the highly improbable conclusion that the examinations and trials in the Inquisition's various tribunals, which were not only carefully recorded but kept in the strictest secrecy solely for the use of the inquisitors, were deliberate transcriptions of lies describing nonexistent practices; see Révah, "Les Marranes," pp. 45–51 and passim; Gerard Nahon, "Les Marranes espagnoles et portugais et les communautés juives dans la historiographie récente, (1960–1975)," *Révue des études juives,* 136 (1977), 308–309, 313; Yerushalmi, *From Spanish Court to Italian Ghetto,* pp. 21–24; B. Lorence, "The Inquisition and the New Christians in the Iberian Peninsula— Main Historiographic Issues and Controversies," in *The Sepharadi and Oriental Heritage,* ed. Issachar Ben-Ami (Jerusalem: Magnes Press, 1982), pp. 18–20. The majority of historians of today, even when most critical of the Inquisition's activity and methods, are in accord that, given its assumptions, its procedures, which were clearly prescribed in its regulations, were by no means arbitrary and compared favorably in certain respects with those of secular and other ecclesiastical courts in Europe in their concern for evidence and justice. Hennigsen has noted, for example, that death sentences became exceptional from the sixteenth century on; "La elocuencia de los numeros," p. 221. In its use of torture too, it was far more sparing than has been generally supposed.

false confessions to priests naming only good actions. A third category of offenses included the marriage of relations within the prohibited degrees, underscoring the *conversos'* alleged proclivity for intermarrying among themselves rather than with Old Christians.[23]

Written several decades before the founding of the Inquisition and the expulsion of 1492, and at a period when *conversos* and Jews still lived together, Espina's treatise catalogued practices that would have become far more difficult and dangerous to follow later. His list, however, paralleled descriptions that the Inquisition subsequently drew up for the guidance of its officials in identifying Judaizers, and can be confirmed from its records. One striking case of the persistence of an illicit Jewish existence in the aftermath of formal conversion involved the *conversos* of Ciudad Real.

In the Castilian city of Ciudad Real, on the road between Toledo and Cordova, the Jewish community had been completely eliminated in the twenty years following the massacre of 1391. By 1412, as a result of conversion and probably also some emigration, not a single Jew remained. What survived instead was a community of *conversos* who preserved their Judaism clandestinely. This community underwent anti-Semitic violence several times before the Inquisition's arrival in 1483. The tribunal operated in Ciudad Real from 1483 to 1485, when it was transferred to Toledo. From 1483 to 1527 it heard 124 cases of heresy against the *conversos* of Ciudad Real, many of which involved multiple accused such as husbands and wives or other persons. In these proceedings, defendants who had fled were tried *in absentia;* those who were already dead were tried posthumously. Not only did many of the accused confess, but children testified against their parents, servants against their masters, and husbands and wives and relatives and friends against one another. Informers also played a part. The most important was Fernán Falcón, a second- or third-generation *converso* on whom the tribunal relied heavily. He was called to testify in a large number of cases, including that of his own father. Among those tried, some abjured and were then penanced and reconciled, while others were sentenced to death and handed over to the secular arm for execution. In its two years at Ciudad Real, the tribunal, according to one estimate, burned 52 heretics, condemned 220 fugitives, and reconciled 182

---

[23] See the summary and discussion of Espina's book in Baer, *A History of the Jews,* 2:283–289; Haim Beinart, *Los conversos ante el tribunal de la Inquisición* (Barcelona: Riopiedras Ediciones, 1984), pp. 19–23. Lea, *History of the Inquisition,* 1:149n, rejects suggestions that Espina was himself a *converso.*

people as penitents. Its repression put an end to the city's *converso* community, and the evidence it gathered from confessions and witnesses provides an illuminating insight into underground Judaism and its subterfuges.[24]

Many of the accused in Ciudad Real were age sixty or older, and the beginning of their attempt to observe the Jewish commandments apparently went back a long way.[25] After the disappearance of Jews from the town, the local *conversos* formed the three confraternities of St. John, St. Michael, and All Saints, which were probably intended as funerary societies. Through these associations they were able to purchase the land that had formerly been the Jewish cemetery. Later investigation revealed that *conversos* had been interred there in accordance with Jewish rites. The same investigation disclosed that the *conversos* continued to possess many Hebrew books, which they kept hidden in wells and pits.[26]

The *conversos* of Ciudad Real included several public figures who made a significant contribution to Jewish survival. The most prominent and most faithful of these was Sancho de Ciudad, a wealthy fiscal official of the crown and member of the municipal council. At times he apparently made scarcely any effort to conceal his Judaism. He had arranged to be circumcised in 1463, and his house was one of the principal places at which *conversos* gathered secretly for worship. In anticipation of the Inquisition's arrival he attempted to flee Spain with his family but was captured and returned. He and the other fugitives who accompanied him went to the stake in Toledo in 1486.[27]

Another prominent *converso* was Juan González Pintado, secretary

---

[24] Haim Beinart has published the documents of these proceedings in *Records of the Trials of the Spanish Inquisition in Ciudad Real*, 4 vols. (Jerusalem: Israel Academy of Sciences and Humanities, 1974–1977). The preface and introduction to vol. 1 contain an account of the history and procedure of the tribunal; a chronological summary of its activity in Ciudad Real is in 1:615–638. Volume 4 includes "Biographical Notes" on many of the defendants and other participants in the trials. Beinart provides no estimate of the total number of people tried in these cases, nor does he indicate how many of the accused were reconciled or condemned to the stake. I have used the figures in Lea, *History of the Inquisition*, 1:168. My discussion relies on Beinart's *Los conversos*, a detailed story of the working of the tribunal and the crypto-Judaism of the *conversos* in Cuidad Real based on the trial records; for Falcón and other informers, see ibid., pp. 151–152.

[25] Beinart, *Los conversos*, p. 67n.

[26] Ibid., pp. 92–93.

[27] Ibid., pp. 226–231.

to two former kings of Castile. The date of his return to Judaism is uncertain. In the 1440s, probably to maintain his Christian credentials, he had built a chapel in the church of St. Dominic and had also given the church an image of the Virgin. In 1483 he was condemned to the flames for having observed the sabbath and Jewish dietary laws, and for other offenses against the Christian faith.[28]

Yet another leading Judaizer was Juan González Daza, a notary described as scrupulously observant of the *mitzwot*. According to the testimony against him, he attended church, prayed, and heard mass to conceal his Judaism by posing as a Christian. He too was condemned to be burned.[29]

In addition to such notables, we learn of men such as Juan Falcón, father of the informer Fernán Falcón, who was condemned and his bones exhumed and burned in 1485. He had been a devout Jew since the 1440s, serving as ritual slaughterer for some of the *conversos*. Juan de Fez, a tax farmer tried with his wife, attributed their Jewish observances to the influence of others. One of his offenses was washing the consecrated baptismal water from his twin sons. Both de Fez and his wife were burned in 1484; later some of their six children were also tried, including a daughter who was sentenced to death.[30]

Among the defendants were *converso* women with a profound attachment to Judaism. Foremost of these was María Díaz de la Cerera, who exerted a strong influence in the community. Reputed to possess a considerable knowledge of the Mosaic laws, she celebrated all the holy days and instructed young women in the Jewish precepts before marriage. Both she and her equally faithful sister, Leonor González, fled with other *conversos* to Portugal just before the Inquisition arrived in Ciudad Real. Leonor was sentenced to be burned in effigy; subsequently her son induced her to return and stand trial, and she was sent to the stake in Toledo in 1492.[31]

It was revealed that eighteen houses had served at various times as secret meeting places for communal worship and prayer. Jews from other towns had aided observance of the *mitzwot;* thus, in 1462 a visiting cloth dealer had circumcised ten men.[32] Numerous precautions and deceptions were used to escape discovery of Jewish practices in a

[28] Ibid., pp. 232–234.
[29] Ibid., pp. 237–238.
[30] Ibid., pp. 234, 240–241; Beinart, *Records,* 4:447–448.
[31] Beinart, *Los conversos,* pp. 248–250.
[32] Ibid., pp. 273, 274–275, 270.

small civic society in which people were apt to be acquainted or to know about one another's activities. If families went to relatives to celebrate the sabbath, the women carried their spindles and distaffs with them to give neighbors the impression that they intended to work on Saturday. Another subterfuge was to pretend illness on the sabbath eve as an excuse not to work on the following day. Witnesses testified that the Judaizers kept their doings secret so that Christians would not see or understand them.[33] One *conversa* confessed that she had not dared celebrate the sabbath openly for fear of her husband and daughters, but had kept it in her heart, her thoughts, and her intentions. Another admitted that she had had her child baptized as a Christian on the sabbath in order to observe it as a festive day.[34] *Conversos* were accused of hatred and contempt for the Christian religion. At church they tried to avoid participation in prayers and ceremonies, and they customarily washed off the water used in the sacrament of baptism.[35]

Such was the plight of Marranos forced to dissimulate in their double existence but nevertheless not justly guilty of betraying the Christian faith, since it was a religion in which they had no belief. The situation in Ciudad Real repeated itself throughout the Iberian peninsula. In 1500 in Valencia the Inquisition discovered a secret synagogue in the house of Salvador Vives Valeriola and his son Miguel, who were leading citizens. A room furnished with lamps, candles, and a table with a rich cloth had been set aside for the sabbath and other Jewish observances. Salvador Vives died before his condemnation, but his son and wife were burned in 1501.[36]

These Viveses were the uncle, aunt, and cousin of Juan Luis Vives, one of Spain's greatest Christian humanists in the sixteenth century, a friend of Erasmus, classical scholar, educational and social reformer, and tutor in England to Henry VIII's daughter Mary. Completely of Jewish extraction, Vives was nonetheless a sincere Catholic. His entire family, however, were *converso* Judaizers, and all of them besides the three mentioned above—his father, mother, brother, sister, and sister-in-law—became victims of the Inquisition. His mother, Blanquina March, was not condemned until 1529, more than twenty years after her death. Though a baptized Christian, she was charged with having

[33] Ibid., pp. 265–266, 267.
[34] Ibid., p. 297.
[35] Ibid., pp. 311–313.
[36] García Cárcel, *Orígines,* pp. 75–76.

believed all her life in the law of Moses and the coming of the messiah. A declaration of her Christian faith which she had given before the tribunal as a young woman was pronounced *ficta y simulada* and made with malice. Despite her solemn and repeated later renunciations of Judaism, she was stated to have lived exclusively with Judaizers. Her fortune was confiscated and her remains exhumed and burned, in accord with the Inquisition's rule in cases of those posthumously condemned for heresy.[37] It has been suggested that Juan Luis Vives' continued refusal to live in Spain was a result of the extermination of his family at the hands of the Inquisition.[38] By 1530 the Holy Office's pursuit of crypto-Judaism had destroyed all vestiges of the Jewish community in Valencia.[39]

Marranism also existed in some of the religious orders. The Hieronymites, the order of San Jerónimo, contained numerous *conversos*. Owing to concern about apostasy among its members, in 1486 the general council of the order launched an internal investigation and purge of crypto-Judaism. The ensuing proceedings revealed a variety of Jewish beliefs and practices among the monks such as sabbath observance, fasting on the Day of Atonement by feigning illness, the reading of Hebrew books, praising the law of Moses, and avoidance of making the sign of the cross. Fray García de Zapata, prior of the Hieronymite monastery of La Sisla, near Toledo, used to celebrate Sukkoth, the Feast of Tabernacles, annually with two other monks. To do this, he would feign illness every September, and two Jewish physicians would visit him and erect the traditional tabernacle, which they said was necessary to treat his ailment. Several of the accused monks were acquitted or punished by the order itself; others were handed over to the secular authorities. At least three were burned.[40] In the latter part of the sixteenth century the Hieronymite order was to harbor another kind of dissimulators, Christian Nicodemites, in the royal monastery of the Escorial itself.

By the middle decades of the seventeenth century, several thousand

---

[37] See Hornik, *Collected Studies*, pp. 12–28.

[38] Domínguez Ortiz, "Historical Research on Spanish *Conversos*," p. 76; for Vives' career and work as a humanist, see Marcel Bataillon, *Erasmo y España*, 2d ed. (Madrid: Fondo de Cultura Económica, 1966).

[39] García Cárcel, *Herejía*, p. 220.

[40] See Sicroff, *Les controverses des statuts*, pp. 77–78; Haim Beinart, "The Judaizing Movement in the Order of San Jerónimo in Castile," in *Scripta Hierosolymitana* (Jerusalem: Hebrew University, 1961), vol. 7.

conversos of Portugal, among whom crypto-Judaism was widespread, had purchased from the crown the right to trade and settle in Spain, and the government had come to depend on some of these emigrant financiers and merchants for loans. The wealthiest of them, Manuel Cortizos, enjoyed the favor of Philip IV and the count-duke of Olivares, the all-powerful favorite and minister who until his fall in 1643 controlled the affairs of Spain. To all appearances a Christian, Cortizos had been rewarded with honors and offices for his services to the monarchy. Nonetheless, after his death in 1649 the Inquisition instituted proceedings against him, his widow, and other family members. He was shown to have engaged in Jewish practices and to have associated himself with the synagogue in Amsterdam. Despite abundant proofs of his and his relations' devotion to the Mosaic law, influence from on high exerted on their behalf spared them from punishment. Another financier and a confidant of Olivares, Juan Nuñez Saravia, who was also in the good graces of the Jesuits, had been denounced for Jewish heresy as early as 1613 but was able to get off with payment of a heavy fine. He tried to cover up his real beliefs through gifts to the church, the display of pious images, and similar expressions of Catholicism. In 1637 following renewed accusations he was tried by the Inquisition. Though tortured briefly, he would say nothing, but later admitted to a number of offenses, including observance of some of the Mosaic laws; protection of persons punished by the Holy Office; sheltering Jews who came to Madrid from Amsterdam, Hamburg, Turkey, and other places; arranging for his elderly father to be circumcised by a foreign rabbi before he died; and paying for lamps in synagogues in Holland. Nuñez abjured and escaped with no worse than a large fine.[41]

Conversos who went abroad and continued to dissimulate sometimes got into trouble for Judaizing. The sixteenth-century records of the Venetian Inquisition, founded in 1547, include about seventy cases of crypto-Judaism. As the Venetian republic was eager to attract Spanish and Portuguese Marranos, it was willing to protect them without inquiring into their past behavior provided they lived openly as Jews, wearing the obligatory yellow hat and residing in the city's ghetto. In a case of 1555, the defendant, Tristao da Costa, otherwise known as

[41] Caro Baroja, *Los judios,* 2:66–75, 115–134, describes the case of Nuñez Saravia and the complicated story of Cortizos and his family; for an account of crypto-Judaism in the reign of Philip IV see ibid., chaps. 1–8; idem, *La sociedad criptojudia en la corte de Felipe IV* (Madrid: Editorial Maestre, 1963).

Abraham Habibi, a Portuguese baptized as an infant and educated at the university of Salamanca, admitted that he had always lived privately as a Jew and conformed to Christianity solely from fear and expediency. In Portugal and Spain he had avoided all contact with the Christian sacraments but had married a *conversa* by Christian rites and had had all his children baptized. If he had not done so with his eldest son, he stated, he would have been burned. The difficulty of getting his large fortune out of Portugal had hindered his departure from the country. In 1543, however, the da Costa family migrated to the Low Countries and thence to Ferrara, Italy. From there Tristao and some of his family moved on to Venice, but his wife and three sons went to Salonika, where she had them circumcised and given Jewish names. For eight years Tristao lived in Venice, dissembling as a Christian in order to conduct his business. He had come there, he explained, because he believed that Venice was "a free city with no Inquisition." Some of his relatives finally denounced him to the authorities on account of a family quarrel. His crypto-Judaism consisted of only a few practices, mainly adherence to the dietary laws, without any formal acts of worship. During his interrogation the tribunal asked him whether he valued his faith or his goods more highly. "The faith, of course," was his reply, "but after the faith I want my goods, in order to have the means to live." Because he had arrived in Venice under a safe conduct from the Council of Ten, he was not punished but deported.[42]

Crypto-Judaism seems to have involved fundamentally a repetition of the same situations and the same dilemmas. Depending on the endurance of memory and the depth of commitment, Marranos accepted the risk of Jewish observance despite constant pressure from the dominant Christian society. They did so, of course, with many kinds of compromises and limitations. Conditions of clandestinity made certain observances highly difficult or impossible. Moreover, as knowledge of the Hebrew language and Jewish teaching decayed, and as separation from normative Judaism increased, Marrano religion could only con-

---

[42] This case forms part of the illuminating discussion of the dilemmas and complexities of Marranism by B. Pullan, *The Jews of Europe and the Inquisition of Venice, 1550–1670* (Totowa, N.J.: Barnes & Noble, 1983), pp. 213–214. The records of about 1,550 trials of the Venetian Inquisition surviving from the sixteenth century indicate that about 5 percent involved crypto-Judaism; for the seventeenth century, 1,480 trials survive, of which about 34 concern Jews and Judaizers.

serve the ancestral faith in a modified and impoverished form, with
losses, suppressions, and additions that even included Christian elements. Sometimes customs were retained long after knowledge of their
reason had disappeared. A Judaizing practice that the Inquisition noted
and ridiculed in the seventeenth century was that of sweeping the dirt
away from the entrance and into the room. Its origin lay in reverence
for the *mezuzah,* the little receptacle containing a script of the Mosaic
law which Jews placed on their doorposts. Although *mezuzot* no longer
existed, the custom apparently persisted.[43] And always hanging over the
Judaizer was the danger of exposure of his religious secret. Some
writers have suggested that endogamy was prevalent among the *conversos* because of the need to preserve religious secrecy.[44] Yet not even
the closest family ties could guarantee security. As the Inquisition's
records show, family members repeatedly informed and testified against
one another. Hard and dangerous also would have been the decision
when to initiate children into the Jewish faith. A Marrano writer of the
seventeenth century, Isaac Orobio de Castro, who was persecuted by
the Inquisition in Spain before migrating to Amsterdam, stated that
parents did not consider it safe to divulge the truth to their children
until they were twenty years old.[45]

Orobio de Castro also declared that it was impossible to live in
Spain without dissimulation. But how then did Marranos defend their
dissembling and double life? Against them was Judaism's fierce horror
and condemnation of idolatry, of which they were guilty by submitting to conversion and pretending to be Christians. Against them
too was the hallowed history of Jewish martyrdom, in which they
could claim no share because of their subterfuges. Most Marranos
detected in their Judaizing sought to be reconciled by the Holy Office
as repentant heretics; only a few were willing to die for the sake of
their beliefs. Marranism, however, found a rationale for its refusal of
martyrdom and its choice of external conformity to an idolatrous religion in the resources of Jewish tradition.

One of the doctrines invoked by Marranos was that God had given
the Jews the law in order to live and not to die. Its source was Deuter-

---

[43] See the discussion of Marrano religion in Cecil Roth, *A History of the Marranos,* 4th ed. (New York: Schocken, 1974), chap. 8; Yerushalmi, *From Spanish
Court to Italian Ghetto,* pp. 35–40. Révah, "Les Marranes," pp. 53–55, characterizes
it as a "potential Judaism."

[44] Caro Baroja, *Los judios,* 1:416–423.

[45] Yerushalmi, *From Spanish Court to Italian Ghetto,* p. 64.

onomy 5:33: "Ye shall walk in all the ways in which the Lord your God hath commanded you, that you may live," and the similar promise contained in Leviticus 18:5. This was an argument Marranos apparently used before the Inquisition. A Spanish author of the later sixteenth century who accused them of cowardice and prevarication observed that they denied to the Inquisition that they were Jews and committed many perjuries. When they finally confessed, he said, they acknowledged their errors and asked to be reconciled; then, according to the writer, on being asked "why they would not die for the Jewish law if they believe it brings them salvation, they reply that it is not for fear of death but because the law was not given them that they should die for it but that they may live."[46]

This justification rested on an interpretation belonging to the domain of religious casuistry. It was similar, as we shall see, to some of the casuistical doctrines that Christian moral theologians developed to direct consciences in questions of life and death under persecution. Behind it lay the authority of one of the greatest of Jewish thinkers, legists, and spiritual guides, the twelfth-century philosopher Maimonides, who had affirmed the identical doctrine in his *Epistle on Martyrdom*. Maimonides composed this tract in response to the plight of the Moroccan Jews under the fanatical persecution of the Almohad sect of Muslims, which threatened them with death unless they made a public profession of Islam. The same persecution had already driven him and his family from Spain and eventually to Cairo, where he wrote his epistle in about 1165. What especially provoked it was his opposition to the opinion of a Moroccan rabbi who not only condemned any compliance by Jews with the Almohad decree but also had ruled that a forced convert would sin additionally with every commandment of Judaism that he performed. The harshness of this judgment aroused Maimonides' profound indignation.

In dealing with the question of forced conversion, Maimonides reserved his highest praise for those who accept martyrdom to sanctify God's name. The burden of his letter, however, was a compassionate concern for the many who were incapable of such heroism. He accordingly cited Old Testament examples to show that God had

[46] Diego de Simancas, *Defensio Statuti Toletani* (Antwerp, 1575), cited in Caro Baroja, *Los judios,* 1:450–451 and n. This work was a defense of the *limpieza* statute promulgated in 1547 by the cathedral chapter of Toledo at the instigation of the archbishop of Toledo, Juan Martínez Silíceo; see Sicroff, *Les controverses des statuts,* chap. 3.

always been merciful to sinners who sinned under duress and had rebuked those who wanted to punish them. These unfortunate rebels against God did not sin for the sake of worldly pleasures or status, Maimonides said, but "fled before swords . . . the whetted sword, before the bow that was drawn" (Isaiah 21:15). They were not rebels by choice; therefore, God did not abandon them, "for He did not scorn, He did not spurn the plea of the lowly" (Psalms 22:25).[47]

Maimonides thus laid great stress on duress and fear as extenuating circumstances. He went on to mention with approval the example of sages who dissimulated under persecution. Thus Rabbi Meir denied his identity and pretended to eat pork to prove that he was not a Jew; Rabbi Eliezer used equivocation when seized and questioned by heretics, feigning by his double language "that he was a heretic, although . . . sincerely devoted to God." Under the wicked king Nebuchadnezzar the Jews of Babylon who were forced to bow to idols did not separate themselves from Israel because they only pretended. It was therefore inconceivable, he concluded, that God would not reward Jews who despite the exigencies of forced conversion performed the commandments secretly.[48]

In Maimonides' judgment, force removed culpability, and one who profaned God's name under compulsion, even though he had acted improperly, is not punishable. According to the Talmud, he noted, the law excused the forced individual because he was not a deliberate profaner of God's name. Likewise, although a false oath was a profanation, the Mishnah nevertheless permitted false oaths to be sworn to murderers and robbers. The law was therefore not the same for the person who acted under duress and one who acted voluntarily. It is at this point that Maimonides invoked the fundamental principle that the law was made so that man should live and not die.[49]

With regard to the Almohad persecution, Maimonides believed that although Jews were compelled to acknowledge Muhammad as God's prophet in speech, they were not required to perform any actions. Consequently, though holding that the person who refuses and suffers

[47] Moses Maimonides, *The Epistle on Martyrdom*, in *Crisis and Leadership: Epistles of Maimonides* (Philadelphia: Jewish Publication Society, 1985), p. 19. This work is translated with a historical introduction by Abraham Halkin and comments by David Hartman.

[48] Ibid., pp. 20, 23.

[49] Ibid., pp. 29–30. Maimonides apparently cites this principle not from Deuteronomy, but from the similar verse in Leviticus 18:5.

martyrdom is most praiseworthy, he concluded that "if anyone comes to ask me whether to surrender his life or acknowledge, I tell him to confess and not choose death." Along with this conclusion, however, he declared that Jews were obliged to flee the land of persecution, leaving family, home, and possessions to go where they could observe the law freely, for the law was more precious than all other things. And if flight was impossible, then one who complied with his persecutors should look on himself with blame and strive to observe as much of the law as he could in private. For every precept a man fulfilled under such persecution, "God will reward him doubly, because he acted so for God only, and not to show off or be accepted as an observant individual. The reward is much greater for a person who fulfills the Law and knows that if he is caught, he and all he has will perish."[50]

Maimonides therefore advocated what a modern commentator has called a "Marrano" type of compromise to the dilemma of forced conversion.[51] From the Jewish standpoint, however, *conversos* could be regarded either as forced converts *(anusim)* or as apostates *(meshumadim)*. Later rabbinical *responsa* reflected a diversity of attitudes toward the religious status of *conversos*. These ran the gamut from treating them as Jews to considering them as apostates and worse than non-Jews. The former chief rabbi of Valencia, Isaac bar Sheshet Perfet, who escaped from the massacre of 1391 to North Africa, where he became chief rabbi of Algiers, held that most *conversos* were apostates, having ceased to be Jews because of their failure to flee conversion. The only valid excuse he would allow for not emigrating was lack of means and refusal to leave family behind lest it be lost to Judaism. On the other hand, his successor in Algiers, another rabbi who had also fled Spain, contended that even those who remained behind and submitted to conversion might still be Jews if they did not practice Christianity willingly. As only God could know the individual's inner self, such people should be presumed Jews unless there was proof to the contrary.[52]

Like Maimonides, with his emphasis on the importance of duress, fifteenth-century Jewish writers discussed whether fear of death and suffering took away free will and made submission to conversion an

---

[50] Ibid., pp. 30–31, 33.

[51] Hartman, ibid., p. 62.

[52] Révah, "Les Marranes," pp. 520–521; Netanyahu, *The Marranos of Spain,* pp. 31, 33–34.

involuntary act. Isaac Caro, a Castilian rabbi who left Spain in 1492, rejected Maimonides' argument exonerating the convert who yielded to compulsion. In his view, conversion even when caused by fear of death remained an act of free will and was therefore to be condemned. According to a modern scholar, most Jewish authorities who emigrated from Spain at the time of the expulsion denounced forced conversion as nonetheless voluntary and maintained that sanctification of God's name even at the cost of death was the only course for the faithful to follow if they wished to abide by the divine law.[53]

Marranos possessed a further rationale for dissimulation in the distinction between intention and appearance, inner and outer, heart and mouth, a theme also common in sixteenth-century Christian justifications of religious dissimulation. For this they cited the epistle of Jeremiah in the apocryphal book of Baruch. The latter was included in the Vulgate as part of the Old Testament canon and thus would have been easily accessible to Marranos despite their lack of knowledge of Hebrew and the disappearance of the Hebrew scriptures. In this text, the prophet exhorted his oppressed brethren in Babylonian exile: "When you see a multitude before you and behind you bowing down, say in your hearts, thou only are to be adored, O Lord" (Baruch 6:5). Marranos could also apply this passage to themselves as a permission to worship alien gods if compelled by necessity, provided they remained faithful in their heart to the God of Israel.[54]

A Portuguese *converso*, Antonio Homem, executed by the Portuguese Inquisition in 1618 for Jewish heresy, used this doctrine as an argument. Holder of the prime chair of canon law at the university of Coimbra, a noted preacher, canonist, and confessor, Homem was nevertheless the leader of a group of *conversos* including canons and students at Coimbra, which met in secret to observe Jewish holy days, fasts, and other commandments of the Mosaic law. In a sermon preached at one of these clandestine services (which had also assimilated some Christian elements), he declared that it was sufficient in conditions of persecution to have the intention of performing those precepts of the law which could not be safely practiced.[55] Earlier, the Spanish rabbi Isaac Caro had taken note of the same plea only to reject

---

53 Netanyahu, *The Marranos of Spain*, pp. 157–158.

54 Roth, *A History of the Marranos*, p. 170; Yerushalmi, *From Spanish Court to Italian Ghetto*, p. 38n.

55 Roth, *A History of the Marranos*, p. 170; Caro Baroja, *Los judios*, 1:327–341, describes the extraordinary case of Antonio Homem.

it as a self-serving delusion. He referred to the excuse of Marranos who said that they had converted because unable to withstand so much suffering but still continued to serve God in their hearts while worshiping a foreign deity. Such people, he held, who declared that they followed two laws, would suffer divine punishment for honoring the law of the Gentiles.[56]

Crypto-Jews found still another justification for their double life in the example of the biblical heroine Esther. The book of Esther relates how Ahasuerus, king of Persia, chose Esther, niece of the Jew Mordecai, from among many women to be his queen and how she preserved the Jews from the destruction planned by the wicked vizier Haman. When first brought to the king, Esther, like the Marranos, concealed her Jewish identity: she "had not shewed her people nor her kindred: for Mordecai had charged her that she should not shew it" (Esther 2:10). According to the Inquisition's records, the fast of Esther, which initiated the festival of Purim, had an importance second to none for Marranos and was often observed by them with exceptional austerity. By dissimulating her true faith to save her people, the Jewish Esther could be seen in the Marrano rationale as the archetypal Marrano.[57]

Because Judaism at the end of the fifteenth century was completely proscribed in Spain and Portugal and Jewish heresy carried the threat of death at the hands of the Inquisition, the situation of crypto-Jews was more extreme than that of some dissenting and heretical Christian groups that faced persecution in this period. There was nevertheless a clear resemblance between the plight of Marranos and of persecuted Christians, both Protestant and Catholic, alien and indifferent though each was to the other. Like Marranos, both Protestants under the rule of Catholic princes and Catholics in England, where their religion was illegal from the beginning of Elizabeth I's reign, were threatened with penalties and dangers unless they conformed to state churches. Among both, as we shall see, doctrines licensing a pretended and deceitful conformity emerged. These doctrines contained features that closely paralleled the Marrano rationale. The theory and practice of dissimulation as we have seen it in the case of crypto-Judaism were never a peculiarity of any single religious body. They were the inevitable consequence of Christian religious oppression against Jews and

[56] Netanyahu, *The Marranos of Spain*, p. 159.

[57] Roth, *A History of the Marranos*, p. 168; Yerushalmi, *From Spanish Court to Italian Ghetto*, p. 38n.

Christians alike, as well as the common product of a religious tradition based on the scriptures.

In certain instances, the relationship between persecuted Marranos and Christian groups may have been even closer than mere resemblance. It has been suggested, for example, that there may have been a link between Marrano clandestinity and the Spanish heretics known as the *alumbrados* or illuminists, who were condemned by the Inquisition during the 1520s. Like the Marranos, the *alumbrados* combined an intimate inward religion of indifference to external forms with an outward profession of conventional Catholicism. Believing in personal illumination and a direct relation to the divine will, they eliminated all intermediaries between God and man and rejected works, intercession of saints, and practices such as confession and vocal prayer. It is perhaps significant, therefore, that the inspirers of the *alumbrado* movement, Isabel de la Cruz, Pedro Ruiz de Alcaraz, and the priest Gaspar de Bedoya, were all New Christians. Is it possible that their interiorization of religion and its accompanying dissimulation owed something to Marrano example?

One of the notable personalities who came under *alumbrado* influence was the Spanish reformer Juan de Valdés, who subsequently went to Italy. There he was to play a crucial part as leader of a circle of distinguished men and women in Naples whom he imbued with evangelical and Protestant beliefs. Valdés and his followers were obliged to resort to dissimulation to avoid persecution as heretics.[58] Likewise, in the 1560s there were a number of Marranos living in Antwerp who became Calvinists or carried their crypto-Judaism into the Reformed church and took part in the revolt against Spanish rule.[59]

These possible connections between Marranism and certain forms of Christian dissent are tantalizing to consider, although they must of course be largely speculative. They are not beyond the bounds of probability, however, and only serve to emphasize the complexity of the Marrano phenomenon in its clandestine and duplicitous existence.

[58] Marcel Bataillon, "Juan de Valdés Nicodemite?" and Augustin Redondo, "Les premiers illuminés Castillans et Luther," in *Aspects du libertinisme au XVIe siècle* (Paris: Vrin, 1974); see below, Chapter 5.

[59] Paul Hauben, "Marcos Pérez and Marrano Calvinism in the Dutch Revolt," *Bibliothèque d'humanisme et Renaissance,* 29, no. 1 (1967); Geoffrey Parker, *The Dutch Revolt* (London: Allen Lane, 1977), p. 60.

CHAPTER 4

Calvin and Nicodemism

The problem of believers who dissimulated under persecution confronted the Christian church from an early period. Its importance may be gauged from a work by the church father Cyprian, bishop of Carthage, written in the wake of the severe persecution of Christians by the emperor Decius in 249–251. During this fearful time Cyprian went into hiding, not because of cowardice but so that he might be able from concealment to encourage his flock by letters. On his return he composed his tract, *The Lapsed (De Lapsis)*, which extolled the heroism of the confessors and martyrs of Christ and branded the apostates who had publicly renounced their faith.

The apostasy in the Decian persecution was apparently on a massive scale.[1] Cyprian blamed some in the Christian community for not fleeing as they could easily have done had it not been for their greed to preserve their property. Many believers did not even await arrest but sped voluntarily to perform the compulsory sacrifice to the pagan gods which the emperor demanded. All who obeyed the imperial decree received a certificate attesting their compliance. Some Christians, however, managed to buy or obtain these certificates without actually sacrificing. Cyprian nevertheless considered them also guilty of apostasy, even if in a lesser degree, and pronounced them condemned by the scriptural saying "Ye cannot serve two masters" (Matthew 6:24). To all these renegades he prescribed heavy penances for their pollution by idolatry. He demonstrated his own fidelity when only a few years

[1] See W. H. C. Frend, *The Rise of Christianity* (Philadelphia: Fortress Press, 1984), pp. 320–321, 410.

later he perished as a martyr during the persecution under the emperor Valerian in 258.[2]

The question of flight as an alternative to martyrdom was also discussed in the early church, just as later it engaged the religious authorities of Spanish Jewry and Protestant theologians of the Reformation. The third-century church father Tertullian strongly opposed flight and exalted martyrdom, and in the following century Athanasius, bishop of Alexandria, defended his flight from Arian persecution in *Apology for His Flight* (*De Sua Fuga,* ca. 357). Athanasius did not abandon his previous commendation of martyrdom; instead, he advanced a theological justification of flight as lawful in certain circumstances. In support he cited Jesus' words in Matthew 10:23: "But when they persecute you in this city, flee ye into another," and pointed out that Christ as divine Logos had hidden himself too. Flight, he argued, can sometimes be an act of witness against evil. Thus men may flee persecution, even though they must also be prepared, as Christ was, to accept death for the truth when the time comes.[3]

Casuistry of the religious conscience in the avoidance of martyrdom was therefore an old story in Christian tradition. In the Middle Ages the heretical Vaudois or Waldensians were well known for resorting to dissimulation in the hope of escaping detection. The guide that the inquisitor Bernard Gui drew up about 1322 for use by officials of the papal inquisition in France described their methods of "duplicity and deceit of words" in detail. We have no reason to question the essential accuracy of his account.

According to Gui, the Vaudois used equivocation to answer different questions from the ones their interrogators put to them, they responded to one question by asking another, and they pretended to believe anything the inquisitor wanted them to believe. Thus if asked their creed, they said they believed whatever a good Christian ought to believe. Asked to state what that was, they replied that it was what the holy church believed. Asked then what they called the holy church, they answered that it was what the inquisitor believed the holy church was. When the inquisitor declared that this was the

[2] *The Lapsed (De Lapsis),* ed. Maurice Bévenot (Westminster: Newman Press, 1957).

[3] *Apology for His Flight, Historical Tracts of S. Athanasius* (Oxford, 1843). My discussion is based on Alvyn Pettersen, "To Flee or Not to Flee: An Assessment of Athanasius's *De Sua Fuga,*" in *Persecution and Toleration,* ed. W. J. Sheils (Oxford: Blackwell, 1984).

Roman church ruled by the pope and the prelates under his authority, they said, "Yes, I also believe that," meaning only that they believed this was the inquisitor's belief.[4]

Gui also mentioned the practice of another heretical sect, the pseudo-Apostles, who would swear oaths which they inwardly retracted on the ground that they were not bound to speak the truth to unbelievers. To escape the inquisitors, they held it lawful to deny the truth as long as they kept it in their hearts.[5]

Another inquisitorial manual, the *Directorium Inquisitorum,* composed around 1376 by the Dominican Nicholas Eymerich, inquisitor general of Catalonia, Aragon, Valencia, and Mallorca, throws additional light on heretics' methods of dissimulation. First printed in 1503, it was reprinted five times between 1578 and 1607. To provide uniformity in inquisitorial practice, an enlarged edition was produced in 1578 at the order of the Roman Inquisition, with a commentary by Francisco Peña, a canonist of the papal curia. Peña's revision became the standard handbook for papal inquisitors in the late sixteenth and seventeenth centuries.[6]

In discussing what he called "the modern heresies," Eymerich described the ruses used by both the Vaudois and the Beghards, "who have become masters in the art of hiding the truth" and whose dissimulation made their examination very difficult. He listed ten tricks they employed to reply without confessing. One was an equivocation that consisted in adding a mental condition to an answer—what would later be termed mental reservation or restriction. Thus, if asked whether they believed that marriage was a sacrament, they replied that they did if God willed it, mentally understanding that God did not will them to believe it. Or if shown the Host and asked if it was the true body of Christ, they said that it was, mentally referring to a stone or to their own body in the sense that either of these is of God

[4] Bernardus Gui, *Practica Officii Inquisitionis,* translated as *Manuel de l'Inquisiteur,* ed. Guillaume Mollat, 2 vols. (Paris: Champion, 1926–27), 2:63, 65–67, 73, 75.

[5] Ibid., pp. 93, 97.

[6] Nicholas Eymerich, *Directorium Inquisitorum,* abridged text based on the Roman edition of 1578 and translated as *Le manuel des Inquisiteurs,* ed. Luis Sala-Molins (Paris: Mouton, 1973), pp. 11–18. On Eymerich's and Peña's contributions see Edward Peters, "Editing Inquisitors' Manuals in the Sixteenth Century: Francisco Peña and the *Directorium Inquisitorum* of Nicholas Eymeric," *Library Chronicle,* 40, no. 1 (1974); A. Borromeo, "A proposito del *Directorium Inquisitorum* de Nicolas Eymericke e delle sue edizione cinquecentesche," *Critica storica,* 20, no. 4 (1983). I owe the last two references to Professor Edward Peters.

and Christ. Sometimes, according to Eymerich, they used equivocation to answer a different question from the one the inquisitor intended. For example, in the case of oaths, which the Vaudois opposed, the question "Do you think it is a sin to swear an oath in judgment?" elicited the response that someone who told the truth did not sin or that it was a great sin to swear vainly. To evade answering, they also feigned surprise when queried about a belief, replying, "Could I believe anything else? My God, why ask me such a question, do you think I am a Jew, I am a Christian, yes." Another of their tricks was to simulate stupidity or madness. "I have seen this a thousand times to escape torture or death," Eymerich noted.[7]

In determining whether a heretic was really mad, Peña observed that torture would prove whether or not he was pretending; "he will have difficulty continuing his comedy in his pain." Eymerich also outlined ten ways for an inquisitor to expose the ruses of heretics. These included the use of spies and of promises that need not be kept, both designed to enable the inquisitor to obtain the truth without resorting to torture. Peña discussed at some length whether false promises were prohibited. He concluded that "it is necessary to distinguish between lie and lie and deception and deception." A deception that aimed only to deceive was forbidden and could not be used to enforce the law. In contrast, a lie that was judicially employed for the benefit of the law, common good, and reason was always praiseworthy, especially if its purpose was to detect heresy and convert sinners. Peña questioned Eymerich's claim that it was permissible for the inquisitor to trick an accused heretic with a promise of mercy, since the inquisitor could not keep his word. Pointing out that authorities on the question differed, he concluded that the inquisitor should make no promise that he could not keep without sin; if, however, the inquisitor reduced the deserved punishment of a heretic even by only a little, he would have kept his promise of mercy. In these instances the Inquisition's dissimulation matched that of its victims.[8]

It would be surprising if the pious Vaudois did not have some theological rationale to justify the subterfuges by which they tried to outwit their persecutors. If they did, however, there seems to be no evidence of what that rationale was. Moreover, according to the description in the inquisitors' manuals their dissimulation had such a deliberate char-

[7] *Directorium Inquisitorium*, pp. 126–129.
[8] Ibid., pp. 129–134.

acter that it seems likely the members of the sect received instruction in its methods in the event of being interrogated about their beliefs.

There is further evidence concerning the use of dissimulation by the Vaudois. To remain faithful to their heterodox creed, many of them had emigrated to some of the high and inaccessible Alpine valleys of Dauphiné and Piedmont. Even so, they were persecuted on both the French and Italian sides of the Alps. In self-protection, they not only engaged in clandestine worship but also attended Catholic services and mass. They even went to Catholic priests for confession, while confessing as well to their own *barbes* or pastors. These traveled among the Vaudois communities as preachers and teachers, acting as traders or pretending to be *colporteurs* and carrying needles and pins as a secret sign.

Beginning in the 1530s the Vaudois of the Alps gradually merged into the Swiss Reformation following discussions between their representatives and the Protestant ministers Johannes Oecolampadius, Martin Bucer, and Guillaume Farel. These reformers dealt with the Vaudois sympathetically but reprehended their dissimulation. Admonishing them to serve God in truth without deception, they bade them to cease participating in popish masses, for there could be no compromise with the AntiChrist.[9]

The Lollards, the proto-Protestant English heretics who sprang from the teachings of John Wyclif, also probably harbored a doctrine of dissimulation. Opposed to Catholic beliefs and accustomed to gather in secret conventicles, they attempted at the same time to avoid suspicion by attending their parish churches. Some thought they might derive spiritual benefit from receiving communion from the priest if they inwardly rejected the official teaching concerning this rite. Lollardy's survival into the sixteenth century may have been partly the result of such practices as well as of members' frequent pretended recantations when caught by the ecclesiastical authorities.[10]

[9] Giovanni Gonnet, "Les relations des Vaudois des Alpes avec les Réformateurs en 1532," *Bibliothèque d'humanisme et Renaissance,"* 23, no. 1 (1961), 38, 50; Gabriel Audisio, "Une organisation clandestine: Les barbes vaudois. Approche à partir du procès inquisitorial de P. Griot (Apt, 1532)," in *Histoire et clandestinité du Moyen Age à la Première Guerre Mondiale,* ed. Michel Tilloy et al. (Albi: Ateliers Professionels, 1979); Evan Cameron, *The Reformation of the Heretics. The Waldenses of the Alps 1480–1580* (Oxford: Clarendon Press, 1984), pp. 68, 75, 87, 103, 118, 205.

[10] John Thomson, *The Later Lollards 1414–1520* (Oxford: Oxford University Press, 1965), pp. 6, 247.

With the Reformation, the problem of dissimulation acquired new urgency and importance. The dissemination of Protestant heresy amid confessional intolerance and persecution resulted in outward conformity to the Catholic church by a spectrum of groups and individuals who had inwardly broken with fundamental Catholic beliefs. These crypto-Protestants and other kinds of dissemblers based their participation in Catholic services on a variety of arguments. Protestant reformers generally condemned such conduct, however, insisting that there could be no concessions to Catholic idolatry and that the true Christian must give a sincere, undisguised testimony of his faith. As a result, the licitness of religious dissimulation became a widely debated topic.

No Protestant leader subjected the phenomenon of dissimulation and its rationales to closer scrutiny than the Genevan reformer John Calvin. Calvin rejected it in a succession of works that contain the most significant and influential Protestant discussions of the subject during the Reformation.

Among Calvin's targets were people whom he called Nicodemites. These justified themselves by the precedent of the Pharisee Nicodemus, a believer in Christ who kept his faith hidden because of fear (John 3:1-2). The Nicodemites were not the only dissimulators Calvin denounced, however, and his neologism was not widely used in the sixteenth century. From it, nevertheless, derives the name "Nicodemism," which modern parlance has adopted as a general term for the theory and practice of religious dissimulation.

In his study of the development of Nicodemism, Carlo Ginzburg has claimed that the doctrine of dissimulation was first formulated by a sixteenth-century German Protestant, Otto Brunfels (1488–1534). Best known in his lifetime as a physician and botanist, Brunfels was a Christian humanist belonging to the radical wing of the Reformation who diverged from Luther by his opposition to earthly powers and his attraction to religious spiritualism and esotericism. The suppression of the peasant revolt of 1525 confirmed his vision of the world as a place in which the wicked triumph and the lovers of truth are few and always persecuted. In 1527 he published a collection of biblical texts accompanied by short commentaries, *Twelve Books of Pandects of the Old and New Testament,* which covered a wide variety of subjects and included some scattered remarks in defense of dissimulation. The work was dedicated to the reformer Jacques Lefèvre d'Etaples, whom

Brunfels had known during the former's brief stay in Strasbourg in 1525–26.[11]

Brunfels maintained in the *Pandects* that "we may feign and dissimulate among unbelievers and the obstinate." Distinguishing between inner belief and outward conformity, he declared that only the former mattered because "God weighs the heart." Led by his spiritualist conception of liberty to regard external forms as irrelevant, he asserted that "it is licit to feign and dissimulate in the presence of the impious to avoid or prevent danger. Moreover, we may humble ourselves to them for the glory of God and nevertheless pray in our heart for God to destroy them." Elsewhere he pointed out that "even the saints used worldly prudence," and in an admonition to shun lying he nevertheless observed that "certain fathers of the Old Law lied without sinning."[12]

As scriptural precedents Brunfels adduced the example of Naaman the Syrian, who was permitted by the prophet Elisha to bow before the idol Rimmon because he had God in his heart; and of Abraham and Sarah, the Egyptian midwives, David, Esther, Judith, and the apostle Paul. From Paul's first letter to the Corinthians he quoted the saying "I am made all things to all men" as support for the principle of accommodation to times and circumstances. Brunfels' use of this passage led Ginzburg to comment, "Thanks to the *Pandects,* these words . . . were destined to become the slogan of the theorists of dissimulation."[13]

As has already been shown in our survey of the sources, Brunfels' ideas on dissimulation were not original. The merits of dissimulation and lying had already been discussed by theologians and canonists for many centuries, and virtually all the biblical precedents Brunfels cited were already commonplaces. Moreover, his brief remarks in favor of dissimulation, mingled among a large miscellany of topics, were contradicted by other comments that condemned lying and exhorted the pious to resist the wicked and impious even at the risk of imminent physical danger. Ginzburg has further suggested that Jacques Lefèvre d'Etaples was indebted to Brunfels for his Nicodemism. It is far more

[11] Carlo Ginzburg, *Il Nicodemismo. Simulazione e dissimulazione nell'Europa del '500* (Turin: Einaudi, 1970), chaps. 1–2; Otto Brunfels, *Pandectarum Veteris & Novi Testamenti, Libri Duodecim* (Strasbourg, 1528).

[12] Brunfels, *Pandectarum,* pp. 85, 322, 332–334; Ginzburg, *Il Nicodemismo,* chap. 3.

[13] Brunfels, *Pandectarum,* pp. 208–209; Ginzburg, *Il Nicodemismo,* p. 76.

likely, however, that Lefèvre, a much older man and an eminent biblical scholar, was Brunfels' instructor in this doctrine.[14] It is also significant that Calvin never mentioned Brunfels' opinions in any of his
writings against dissimulation, as he probably would have done if they
had exercised influence in the promotion of Nicodemism.

Nicodemism existed in many countries and among diverse groups.
Its practitioners ranged from Catholic evangelical reformers and
philo-Protestants who covertly accepted the Protestant doctrine of justification by faith alone, to crypto-converts and members of Protestant
congregations forced to live under persecuting regimes, to an array of
spiritualists and sectaries whose beliefs lay well outside the bounds
of Protestant orthodoxy. The use of dissimulation among such different kinds of believers reflected a blend of motives and reasons.
Pragmatic concerns arising from the fear of martyrdom or loss of
property and livelihood were nearly always prominent among them.
In addition, there was the idea that superstitious ceremonies and outer
forms belonged to the realm of adiaphora, of things indifferent to the
true Christian, who might therefore participate in Catholic rites if
necessary. There was also the belief that charity for weak and erring
brethren still in thrall to popish idolatry demanded condescension to
their infirmity rather than offending them by condemnation or separation. Arguments based on these considerations buttressed by scriptural
precedents constituted the substance of Nicodemism as a theory of
dissimulation.

For Calvin, however, Nicodemism was a betrayal of Christ. In
polemics of lucid, forceful prose he probed all aspects of dissimulation
and denounced both it and its exponents. In these compositions he
spoke both as an evangelist and as the leader of a religious revolution.
He was inflexible toward the backsliders and renegades on whom he
poured his withering scorn.[15]

[14] Ginzburg, *Il Nicodemismo*, pp. 87–88; for other criticisms of Ginzburg's study,
see Albano Biondi, "La giustificazione della simulazione nel cinquecento," in
Eresia e riforma nell'Italia del cinquecento (De Kalb: Northern Illinois University
Press, 1974); Carlos Eire, *War against the Idols. The Reformation of Worship from
Erasmus to Calvin* (Cambridge: Cambridge University Press, 1986), chap. 7. The
latter also contains an account of Calvin's view of Catholic worship as idolatry
and his attitude toward Nicodemism (chaps. 6–7) but goes astray in denying that
Nicodemism entailed a theory of dissimulation.

[15] Eugénie Droz criticizes Calvin's views as brutal and violent, believes they
alienated many from the Reform, and holds that there was no theological justification for Calvin to have limited French evangelicals' alternatives to martyrdom

Calvin's first published works on the subject of dissimulation appeared in 1537 in the form of two letters to onetime friends. His disciple and colleague, Theodore Beza, described the occasion of their composition as follows:

> . . . Calvin seeing many persons in France though they had a thorough knowledge of the truth, yet consulting their ease, and holding it enough to worship Christ in mind while they gave outward attendance on popish rites, published two most elegant letters, one on shunning idolatry, addressed to Nicholas [Du] Chemin, the other on the popish priesthood . . . to Gerard Roussel . . . [16]

The letter to Roussel, a reformer and associate of Lefèvre d'Etaples who despite his sympathies never became a Protestant and had just accepted a bishopric, condemned the assumption of any office in the corrupt Roman church.[17] The letter to Du Chemin criticized the subterfuges and defenses of those who indulged in "crafty dissimulation" by participating without belief in popish services.[18] All arguments used in these defenses depended heavily on the distinction between outward conformity and what is in the mind or heart, for which several scriptural examples were alleged. This was a standard ingredient in the casuistry of Nicodemism which Calvin addressed repeatedly.

Calvin discussed the question of dissimulation again in 1543 in *A Little Treatise Showing What a Faithful Man Instructed in the Truth of the Gospel Ought to Do When Living among Papists*,[19] and the next year in

---

or exile; "Calvin et les Nicodémites," in *Chemins de l'heresie*, 4 vols. (Geneva: Slatkine, 1970–1974), 1:145, 154–157. This essay contains a list of Calvin's polemics against Nicodemism, including editions and translations.

[16] Theodore de Beza, *The Life of John Calvin*, in *Tracts Relating to the Reformation by John Calvin* (Edinburgh, 1860), p. xxviii.

[17] *De Christiani Hominis Officio in Sacerdotiis Papalis Ecclesiae vel Administrandis vel Abiiciendis*, in *Opera*, 59 vols., ed. Johann Baum, Eduard Cunitz, and Eduard Reuss (Brunswick, 1863–1896), vol. 5. Beza, *The Life of John Calvin*, p. xxviii, mentions Roussel's failure to keep a straight course, which elicited Calvin's work.

[18] *De Fugiendis Impiorum Illicitis Sacris et Puritate Christianae Religionis Observanda*, ibid., col. 244.

[19] *Petit traicté monstrant que c'est que doit faire un homme fidele cognoissant la verité de l'evangile quand il est entre les papistes*, *Opera*, vol. 6. I quote from the English translation, *The Mynde of the Godly and Excellent Learned Man . . . Calvin, What a Faithfull Man Which Is Instruct in the Word of God, Ought to Do, Dwelling amongst the Papists* (Ipswich, 1548). The English version lacks the brief epistle to a friend dissuading him from participation in Catholic ceremonies, dated September 1540 at Strasbourg, which comes at the conclusion of the 1543 French edition.

The Excuse of John Calvin against the Complaint of Messieurs the Nicodemites of His Too Great Severity.[20] That Calvin considered these two works important is shown by the fact that he reprinted them several times and also published them together in 1549 and 1550 in an edition titled The Avoidance of Superstition, which included statements by the reformers Martin Bucer, Philipp Melanchthon, and Peter Martyr Vermigli, whose support he had sought.[21] Between them, they contain Calvin's fullest, most detailed discussion of dissimulation, though not his last by any means.

In the Little Treatise, Calvin attributed Protestants' conformity to Catholic worship to nothing but self-love and desire for an easy life. Bitingly he referred to men who "hyde their cristianitie," never speaking the word of God "except it be to their chief frendes and familyars and that shut up in a chamber suerly." Such people had never learned the first lesson in the school of Christ, which was to forsake themselves. Condemning their "carnal pretence" and "perverse subtilitie," he declared that God demanded to be worshiped openly, not secretly, and that those ashamed of Christ before men would find Christ ashamed of them at the last day.[22]

He presented a revealing picture of the ways of the feigners and dissemblers who want to "kepe themselves in the favour of the world." On Sundays and holy days they went to mass. They polluted themselves by Catholic marriage rites, and their children were not rightly baptized but were defiled by profane ceremonies. They failed to instruct their servants in God's word from fear of the danger of speaking to them. Although they said they professed the gospel, they went to confession at Easter. He had set forth this description, said Calvin, as a "myrour before men" whereby every faithful man who lived among papists could behold his faults and "the cursed estate wherein he is."[23]

Calvin next turned directly to the arguments to determine whether "a man may feine and counterfaict . . . against the truth" by participating in Catholic ceremonies. He rejected the distinction between inner intention and outer conformity, insisting that God must be wor-

[20] Excuse à messieurs les Nicodémites sur la complaincte qu'ilz font de sa trop grand rigueur, in Opera, vol. 6.
[21] De Vitandis Superstitionibus, ibid. See also Droz, "Calvin et les Nicodémites," pp. 152–153.
[22] The Mynde of the Godly, sigs. B–Biiii.
[23] Ibid., sigs. E–Eiiii.

shiped purely in body as well as in spirit because both were God's and the body must not be polluted by worshiping idols. The only cause of such feigning, he contended, was "to avoyde daunger," but the body should rather be cast into a burning furnace than be guilty of dissembling.[24]

He then examined some of the scriptural precedents pleaded by the defenders of dissimulation. The first was the case of Naaman the Syrian, which he noted was commonly alleged to prove that dissimulation was permissible in similar circumstances. This example he dismissed on the ground that Naaman was uncircumcised and possessed only a little spark of the truth, unlike the Christian who has full knowledge and is obliged to glorify God. Moreover, Naaman did actually forsake idolatry, accompanying his king into the idol's temple only as a service and courtesy.

A second example was Jeremiah's letter in the book of Baruch where the captive Israelites were bidden to give glory to God in their hearts when they saw the Babylonians worshiping idols. Here Calvin commented that he did not require the faithful to openly insult or tear down the ornaments of Catholic idolatry, but merely to abstain from participating in it.

He also considered the conduct of Paul, who, according to the dissemblers, sinned no more in conforming to Jewish ceremonies than they did in attending mass. To this precedent he replied that there could be no comparison between the Jewish laws instituted by God and popish abominations. Besides, Paul was a Jew with the Jews to win them to the gospel, not a dissimulator seeking to keep in favor with the world.[25]

Calvin passed a scathing judgment on all these reasonings. "Let us not mocke with God," he exclaimed. "If there were no feare of losynge . . . lyfe or . . . goodes or auctoryte . . . wold a man fynd among a hundred yea . . . amonge a thousande [one] which wolde dissemble so as all men do nowe?"[26]

Referring to yet other arguments in the rationale of Nicodemism, Calvin noted that some claimed they dissembled so as not to offend weaker Christians, just as Paul sought by his accommodation to avoid offending those still weak in faith. These people also said that their conformity to Catholic rites was only a light fault that God would

[24] Ibid., sigs. C, Cii–iiii.
[25] Ibid., sigs. Fi–iiii.
[26] Ibid., sig. Fiiii.

easily pardon because it did not proceed from the heart. They maintained too that no good could come if all the faithful were to declare themselves, as this would result only in persecution, while if they should remove themselves from idolatry, the lands where AntiChrist reigns would be destitute of true Christians. How, they asked, could the gospel be multiplied without the seed, should those of better zeal and knowledge depart?

Calvin dismissed such justifications as no more than self-serving counsels of "my Ladye worldely wysdom." Paul avoided offending the weak in order to edify and unburden conscience, not to harden unbelievers by his example or to escape the displeasure of worldly people. Furthermore, all God's ordinances were to be kept, and idolatry was no small fault. If the faithful were endangered by persecution, they should look to God as their refuge. If those with knowledge of the truth did only half their duty, the whole earth would be filled with the gospel, for the seed of God could not be extinct, and for every person who departed, God would raise up four more.[27]

Calvin also confronted the touchy issue of his own good faith in his attack on Nicodemism. To the charge that it was easy for him to talk because he was safe and far from danger, he countered that he spoke nothing but what his conscience compelled and would blaspheme the truth to speak otherwise. If he himself had been in a place where he could not shun idolatry without peril, he would pray for strength to prefer God's glory to his own life. If he failed to follow his own preaching, then "wo be unto me," for he would convict himself out of his own mouth. He required nothing of the faithful but to follow the example "of that which so manye thousand Martyres have done before us, men and Women, Ryche and Poore, great and small." If these martyrs "had . . . thought it lawful to escape by symulation or dissemblynge, when men wold constrain them . . . unto Idolatry," they need not have undergone such torment. But they knew that it was mocking God to pretend that one honored him in the heart when one betrayed the truth before men.[28]

Calvin also denied that he condemned or reproved the faithful dispersed in France, Flanders, England, and other realms because they were forced to use superstitious ceremonies. Rather he pitied them, mourned for them, and did not reject them as brethren. Yet he had to

[27] Ibid., sigs. G–Giiii, H, Hiii–iiii, I–Iii.
[28] Ibid., sigs. Iiii–iiii.

speak as conscience dictated and could not cease to condemn their vices. As his final counsel, he exhorted the faithful to flee persecution as the best recourse. Let them leave the Egypt or Babylon in which they dwelt for a place where they could openly profess the truth in an assembly of Christians. If this was impossible, then let them shun idolatry and worship God privately despite the danger of death, because God's glory was more precious than "this vayne and transitory lyfe whiche . . . is nothing but a shadow." He knew that most would say that they had father, mother, and households and would ask "how can we well get awaye?" These people should at least cease to justify themselves and should bewail and accuse their weakness, confess their sin to God, and pray for deliverance from bondage into a right form of the church.[29]

Calvin's *Little Treatise* showed clearly not only his unyielding attitude toward Nicodemism but also his thorough knowledge of its concepts and rationales. It is impossible to be sure of the work's effect on the faithful Protestants it sought to convince. We know that in 1543 the Calvinist minister Valerand Poullain distributed 200 copies of the *Little Treatise* in Tournai, Lille, Douai, and Arras, where it provoked a very hostile reaction in some readers. Poullain nevertheless distributed other copies in both France and the Netherlands, and the work was also soon issued several times in English, French, and Latin.[30]

Neither in the *Little Treatise* nor in any of his earlier writings did Calvin use the term *Nicodemites*. This label appeared for the first time in 1544, in his renewed critique of dissimulation, the polemical *Excuse against the Nicodemites*. A French scholar has recently proposed a plausible explanation of how he came to invent the neologism.

One of the former associates whom Calvin considered a dissembler was Gérard Roussel (1480–1550), bishop of Oléron, to whom he had addressed his tract of 1537 against the Catholic priesthood. Like Lefèvre d'Etaples a prominent figure in the first phase of the French Reformation, Roussel combined mystical tendencies with Protestant leanings while sanctioning conformity to ceremonies as things indifferent. Once, when reproached by Calvin's friend and fellow reformer Guillaume Farel for accepting office in the Catholic church, he had replied

---

[29] Ibid., sigs. Iiiii, K–Kii.
[30] Droz, "Calvin et les Nicodémites," p. 145 and n; Phyllis Mack, *Calvinist Preaching and Iconoclasm in the Netherlands 1544–69* (Cambridge: Cambridge University Press, 1978), pp. 51–53; Calvin, *Opera*, 6:xxxii–xxxiii.

that it required more courage than he possessed to live according to the
new doctrines.[31] During the 1540s Roussel inspired an evangelical
reform movement among Catholics in the southwest region of France,
where his efforts were supported by his patroness Margaret, queen of
Navarre, Francis I's sister. For this movement he composed an exposition of the faith which ascribed vital importance to Jesus' answer to the
Pharisee Nicodemus' question how a man can be born again: "Except a
man be born of water and of the Spirit, he cannot enter into the
kingdom of God" (John 3:4–5). Calvin accordingly associated Roussel
and his followers with Nicodemus, by whose example they also justified their participation in Catholic rites.[32]

In form the *Excuse* was Calvin's answer to those who blamed his
severity toward their pretended conformity to Catholicism. Although
it focused on the precedent of Nicodemus, it repeated most of the
arguments in the *Little Treatise* and was perhaps even more hard-
hitting. Calvin took care to explain that he was not speaking to those
who remained through weakness in the Babylonian captivity of Catholic superstition but confessed their wrongdoing and begged God for
mercy; he addressed only those who sought to justify themselves with
every possible subterfuge and even borrowed the name of Nicodemus
as their buckler. As in the *Little Treatise,* he heaped contempt on the
dissociation between interior affection and outer appearance as merely
a pretext for compliance with idolatry. Not mincing words, he compared those who used such "wicked and perverse excuses" to people
who carried ordure from the sewers and were so inured to the bad
odor that they scoffed at others offended by it.[33]

[31] See the introduction by Albert Autin, ed., *Jean Calvin. Traité des reliques suivi de
l'Excuse à messieurs les Nicodémites* (Paris: Editions Bossard, 1921), pp. 49–56; for
Calvin's and others' disapproval of Roussel's conformity to Catholic rites, see
A.-L. Herminjard, *Correspondance des Reformateurs dans les pays de langue française,*
9 vols. (1866–1897; repr., Nieuwkoop: B. de Graaf, 1965–66), 6:39n, 121n, 439n.
Charles Schmidt, *Gérard Roussel* (1845; repr., Geneva: Slatkine, 1970), brings out
Roussel's "demi-protestantisme" and inability to break with the Catholic church,
all rationalized by his belief in the indifference of external forms; see esp. pp. 5–6,
118–119. Eire, *War against the Idols,* chap. 5, discusses Roussel and Lefèvre d'Etaples
in relation to the Reformation.

[32] See Maurice Causse, "La 'Familière exposition' de Gérard Roussel et
l'aventure 'Nicodémite' en Guyenne," *Bulletin de la Societé de l'histoire du Protestant-
isme française,* 131, no. 1 (1985); idem, "La dissimulation de Marguerite de
Navarre," ibid., 132, no. 3 (1986).

[33] *Excuse,* pp. 203–207.

The most interesting part of the *Excuse* is its discussion of the various sorts of Nicodemites, who, according to Calvin, were not all of the same kind. Representatives of nearly all social groups attracted to the Reformation appeared in Calvin's gallery of dissimulators. First were the preachers who professed the gospel but made it sweet and easy for their auditors in order to gain benefices and money. They said mass knowing it to be an abomination and induced others to follow their example, covering their idolatry under the pretext of edifying. Next were the ecclesiastical dignitaries who were content to have the gospel as long as it did not hinder their pleasure. Included with them in the practice of idolatry were the court favorites and ladies, all of whom called Calvin inhuman because he would lead them to beggary and the stake. Third were those who turned Christianity into a philosophy, showing no care for reformation or courage for anything dangerous. To these persons religion was a Platonic idea that tolerated the existence of papal superstition. Most men of letters belonged to this category, as well as judges, lawyers, physicians, and philosophers or dialecticians, all of whom colored the truth of the gospel and maintained that evil was good. Fourth were the merchants and common people who regarded only their profit and therefore did not want Calvin as their doctor. Finally, Calvin mentioned the "Lucianists" and "Epicureans," contemners of God who feigned adherence to the Word while in their hearts they mocked and considered it no more than a fable. These last, however, he distinguished from the preceding four groups, who retained a spark of the fear of God and reverence for the Word even though they had not learned to renounce themselves and the world in order to serve God.[34]

Calvin countered every objection of the Nicodemites with the same unbending logic. Of the complaint that he was too extreme, he asked if it was a light vice to dissimulate by pretending consent to abominations against the gospel. Christ had said that those who hold their souls precious in this world will lose them: did people who dissimulated on the plea that they risked death if they openly declared their religion imagine they could constrain Christ to retract his sentence? Some said they could not endure the burden; but what would have become of Christianity if the faithful of the primitive church had thought like this? He swept aside as blasphemy the contention based on "human prudence" that the best means to advance the gospel was to participate

---

[34] Ibid., pp. 210–214.

in popish idolatry and advance little by little. If the apostles had held this "fantasy," it would have spelled the end of Christianity. He rejected as hypocrites those who alleged that "we dissimulate . . . and do many things contrary to our heart to win over our neighbors and sow the seed daily so that by these means the church will be preserved and increased." The ones who said this, he commented, could not even form a church of ten members in a village with their "so great discretion and circumspect wisdom"; moreover, it was not the gospel that motivated them, but "fear for their skin."[35]

Calvin's crowning blow against the Nicodemites was to deny them any claim to the name. Hence he proceeded to show that they had no right to hide under the robe of Nicodemus, because they did not resemble him. This point was further emphasized in the *Excuse*'s 1549 Latin version, whose title termed the Nicodemites "pseudo-nicedemos."[36] Calvin explained that although Nicodemus first came to Jesus secretly by night, he then saw the light and openly declared himself. After the crucifixion, moreover, he went with Joseph of Arimathea to ask Pilate for Jesus' body, fearing neither contempt, hatred, scandal, nor persecution. "This is what it means to Nicodemize," Calvin affirmed, if the example of Nicodemus was to be followed when he became a true Christian and not in the time of his ignorance. Thus "the true way of Nicodemizing" was to adapt to the time so as to advance daily in giving glory to God. Those who tried to defend the licitness of dissimulation with the buckler of Nicodemus not only polluted themselves with idolatry but showed a hundred times less constancy after Christ's resurrection than did Nicodemus at the time of Christ's death.[37]

Not only Nicodemites came under Calvin's fire for dissimulation. In 1545 he published a treatise attacking the libertines.[38] Believers in an antidogmatic Christian spiritualism with mystical features that expressed indifference to external forms, the libertines stood for a type of sectarianism whose followers often resorted to concealment and

---

[35] Ibid., pp. 229–233.

[36] *Excusatio ad Pseudonicedemos, Opera*, 6:xxxiii.

[37] *Excuse*, pp. 240–244; Calvin here follows the story of Nicodemus as told in John 19:39.

[38] *Contre la secte phantastique et furieuse des libertins que se nomment spirituelz*, in *Opera*, vol. 7. Benjamin Farley provides a helpful introduction to this work in his edition *John Calvin: Treatises against the Anabaptists and the Libertines* (Grand Rapids, Mich.: Baker Book House, 1981), pp. 161–186.

deception. Although Calvin's target in this particular case was several men who had found refuge at the court of Margaret of Navarre and shared a common indifferentism with Roussel, their propensity to dissimulate resembled that of other kinds of spiritualists in Reformation Europe.[39] Calvin described the libertines as those who "under cover of liberty simulate consent to all impiety and idolatry" by pretending an acceptance of popish abominations that they derided in their hearts. They possessed the same "duplicity of heart and language" as the Priscillianist heretics whom Augustine had denounced for approving lying. Calvin strove to refute the biblical examples they invoked for their practices, such as that of Christ speaking in parables and bidding his disciples to be "wise as serpents" (Matthew 10:16). In their method of allegorizing scripture and use of strange and incomprehensible language, he saw further proof of their equivocation and malicious cunning.[40]

The libertines continued to be a source of concern to Calvin. In 1562 he replied to a criticism of his writings against Nicodemism by the Hollander Dirck Coornhert, an Erasmian humanist and tolerant spiritualist who in the name of Christian liberty viewed ceremonies as indifferent and declared that it was wicked to instruct Christians to abstain from Catholic worship at the price of martyrdom.[41] Calvin's answer, dedicated "to the faithful of the Low Countries," treated Coornhert as merely another of the dissemblers who separated comportment from belief so as to justify conformity to idolatry. Besides reiterating some of his previous arguments, he recalled the example of Paul, in Galatians 2:11–14, who always refused to play the "beau semblant" and demonstrated his dislike of hypocrisy by reprimanding

---

[39] Below, Chapter 6. For a discussion of the spiritual libertines and their beliefs see Henri Busson, *Le rationalisme dans la littérature française de la Renaissance (1533–1601)*, rev. ed. (Paris: Vrin, 1957), chap. 10; Jean Wirth, "Libertins et Epicuriens; Aspects de l'irreligion au XVIe siècle,"*Bibliothèque d'humanisme et Renaissance*, 39, no. 3 (1977); J. Margolin, "Reflexions sur l'emploi du terme libertin au XVIe siècle," in *Aspects du libertinisme au XVIe siècle* (Paris: Vrin, 1974). G. H. Williams, *The Radical Reformation* (Philadelphia: Westminster Press, 1962), provides a survey of spiritualism and its exponents during the Reformation.

[40] *Contre la secte des libertins*, cols. 209, 171, 158, 173.

[41] *Response à un certain holandois lequel sous ombre de faire les Chrestiens tout spirituels permet de polluer leur corps en toutes idolatries*, in *Opera*, vol. 9. Coornhert's tract, *Justification of Roman Ceremonies*, was published anonymously in 1562; see Olga Rinck-Wagner, *Dirck Volckertszoon Coornhert 1522–1572* (1919; repr., Vaduz: Kraus, 1965), chap. 3.

Peter for dissimulating. Coornhert had also spoken of the need for prudence and discretion on the part of believers. Ironically assenting, Calvin commented that this sort of discretion was the kind that defrauded God of his rights; as for prudence, in the faithful it could not be a "cunning to deceive" but must be joined according to Christ's command with the simplicity of the dove.[42]

In his long battle with the hydra of Nicodemism, Calvin identified still another type of thinking besides that of the spiritualists and libertines which gave rise to dissimulation. This was exemplified by the people who in the interests of religious peace sought a doctrinal compromise between Protestantism and Catholicism. Calvin and their other opponents characterized them as moderates, mediators, temporizers, or "moyenneurs." In 1548 the Holy Roman emperor Charles V and the German imperial diet decreed the Interim, a formula of religious settlement of a largely Catholic character but offered as a compromise and imposed on the Protestants of Germany despite the opposition of most of their leaders.[43] In 1549 Calvin published a treatise against the Interim as a false settlement, ascribing it to the "mediatores" and "moderatores" of whom he harbored the strongest suspicions.[44] In his view, these conciliators mixed God's truth with human vagaries and were guilty of deceit in their desire for a specious unity. In the French edition of the same year he called them "moyenneurs" and "moderateurs," perhaps the first appearance of the terms in this context.[45]

The position of the *moyenneurs* comprised elements of both adiaphorism and Erasmian irenicism. They held that some aspects of doctrine, ritual, and church organization should be treated as indifferent for the sake of peace. Among their leading spokesmen at this period were the Lutheran Philipp Melanchthon and the Romanist theologian George Cassander. In France a celebrated legal scholar, François Baudouin, became a prominent advocate of the same *via media*. A convert to Protestantism and onetime disciple of Calvin, Baudouin had nevertheless not scrupled to participate in Catholic services for his own

---

[42] *Response,* cols. 581, 610–611, 614, 625.

[43] See the account of the Interim in Franz Lau and Ernst Bizer, *A History of the Reformation in Germany to 1555* (London: Black, 1969), pp. 208–219.

[44] *Interim Adultero-Germanum,* in *Opera,* 7: cols. 610, 613, 618.

[45] *Le vraye façon de réformer l'eglise chrestienne,* quoted in Mario Turchetti, *Concordia e toleranza. François Bauduin (1520–1573) e i "moyenneurs"* (Geneva: Droz, 1984), p. 333.

safety. He had conformed while living in Bourges, the great university center of legal studies, as had other lawyers who accepted the reformed faith. He broke with Calvin and eventually returned to Catholicism, though still pinning his hopes on a religious compromise.[46] Protestants denounced him as a chameleon and apostate who had changed his faith seven times. Pierre Viret, a luminary among the ministers of the French reformed church, included him with the *moyenneurs* and *temporiseurs* who by mingling all religions together corrupted the true religion under pretext of the public peace.[47] Calvin too pursued Baudouin relentlessly, referring to him in a 1561 pamphlet as a cunning and tricky *moyenneur,* a neuter, enemy of the gospel, and dissimulator.[48]

It can hardly be maintained that Calvin was just to all of those against whom he pronounced his uniform judgment for the sin of dissimulation. His verdict was even more unsparing than Augustine's condemnation of the lie. Though blaming all lying as sinful, Augustine had recognized different degrees of sinfulness and culpability depending on the motive of the liar. Calvin did not bother about such distinctions. He was convinced that Nicodemism in all its varieties was purely opportunistic and proceeded solely from cowardice. He refused to acknowledge that it could sometimes be based on conscientious motives or that the spiritualists' belief in the indifference of ceremonies might itself be a religious principle. For the irenicism that sought accommodation and concord between Catholics and Protestants he had only contempt. He could not comprehend the ideas or credit the sincerity of those who on both religious and political grounds hoped for an end to religious strife through compromise. Though not lacking compassion for Christians under Catholic rule who were forced to attend Catholic worship, he was merciless toward their conformity. No casuistical reasoning could persuade him to temper his attitude. The faithful must shun popish rites at whatever cost; the only

---

[46] Turchetti, *Concordia e toleranza,* contains a discussion of the *moyenneurs* and the views and activity of Baudouin. Donald Kelley, *François Hotman: A Revolutionary's Ordeal* (Princeton: Princeton University Press, 1973), describes Baudouin's relation to Calvin and to Nicodemism.

[47] *L'interim fait par dialogues* (Lyons, 1565), pp. 2–3, and see the entire dialogue, "Les moyenneurs," from which the citation is taken. Viret's writings against Nicodemism are discussed below, Chapter 6.

[48] *Response à un cauteleux et ruse moyenneur,* quoted in Turchetti, *Concordia e toleranza,* p. 282n.

alternatives were flight or martyrdom. Few can doubt that Calvin himself would have undergone martyrdom if necessary to demonstrate his faith. Having abandoned his own country and come to Geneva as an exile, he nevertheless gave little consideration to the obstacles that could make religious emigration impracticable or impossible. It is also likely that by urging flight he hoped to attract religious refugees to Geneva who would support him in his conflicts with his opponents in the city. All denials or disagreements with his views he rejected as worthless rationalizations. Calvin's dealings with Nicodemism demonstrate both his heroic religious commitment and his moral and intellectual intolerance. His writings against dissimulation offer an unparalleled insight into the realities of religious choice during the Reformation, as well as Calvin's own strengths and limitations as a religious thinker and leader.

CHAPTER 5

Nicodemism in Italy

Although Calvin's discussion of religious dissimulation was aimed mainly at France and the francophone regions where the Reformation had taken root, some Italian exponents of Nicodemism also attracted his notice and provoked his criticism. Moreover, as a result of Protestant leaders' concern over the compromises adopted by reformed believers in Italy, in 1553 his *Little Treatise* and *Excuse* were published with several related writings in an Italian translation by Celso Martinengo, the pastor of the Italian refugee congregation in Geneva.[1] Well before this date, however, from at least the 1530s, the evangelical reformer Juan de Valdés and his disciples had been among the first Christians in Italy to conceal an inner detachment from the Catholic church and a receptiveness to the Protestant doctrine of justification by faith under a mask of equivocation and opportunistic conformity in order to avert persecution.

Born in 1500 to a noble family of Castile, Valdés was educated in Spain, where he absorbed the influence both of Erasmus' Christian humanism and of the heterodox *alumbrados* or illuminists. Erasmus advocated an inner piety based on scripture and a critical attitude to ritualistic good works and formalism. The *alumbrados* stressed abandonment of self, mysticism, and inward illumination through an immediate relationship with Christ. Together, they fostered a distinctive form of spirituality which devalued dogma and ceremonial. It was probably no accident that most of the *alumbrados*, including Valdés' own mentors, were *conversos*. Owing perhaps to their ambiguous posi-

---

[1] *Del fuggir le superstitioni* (Geneva, 1553); Eugenie Droz, "Calvin et les Nicodémites," in *Chemins de l'heresie*, 4 vols. (Geneva: Slatkine, 1970–1974), 1:159–165.

tion as New Christians, some *conversos* were especially susceptible to a version of Christianity which placed cultivation of an interior personal faith above external observances. Through the *converso* experience there may also have been a connection between Marranism and the tendency of the *alumbrados* to dissimulate their deviation from orthodox beliefs. Somewhat like the Marranos, the illuminists founded their religion on an inward faith of subjective immediacy which made ritualistic and intercessory practices essentially superfluous but nevertheless outwardly conformed to a conventional Catholicism on grounds of expediency.[2]

In Spain Erasmus' writings and the doctrines of the *alumbrados* incurred the accusation of heresy. Falling under the Inquisition's suspicion himself because of a book he had written on Christian doctrine, Valdés went in 1534 to Italy, where he had powerful connections. Three years later he settled in Naples as an official of Spanish imperial administration. He remained there till his death in 1541, surrounded by a group of friends who took him as their spiritual guide.

Valdés and his followers belonged to the widespread current of Catholic evangelism in Italy which strove for a renewal of religion and the church in the years just preceding and following the beginning of the Reformation, before the confessional divide in Europe had hardened forever. Evangelicals made the word of God in the New Testament, especially Paul's letters, the anchorage of their faith. While pursuing both a personal sanctity and a more public activity to revitalize religion many looked expectantly to the convocation of a church council that they hoped would ordain necessary reforms and achieve a *modus vivendi* with the basic Protestant doctrine of justification by faith. During the 1530s, before the upsurge of the Counter-Reformation, the religious situation still seemed fluid enough for evangelicals to imagine that Christendom might yet be reunited.[3]

[2] Marcel Bataillon, *Erasmo y España,* 2d ed. (Madrid: Fondo de Cultura Económica, 1966), chap. 4, discusses Erasmianism, illuminism, and the work of Valdés in Spain. For speculation about a connection between Marranism, illuminism, and Valdés, see idem, "Juan de Valdés Nicodemite?" in *Aspects du libertinisme au XVIe siècle* (Paris: Vrin, 1974). See also José Nieto, *Juan de Valdes and the Origins of the Spanish and Italian Reformation* (Geneva: Droz, 1970), chaps. 1–2.

[3] See Delio Cantimori, "Nicodemismo e speranze conciliari nel cinquecento italiano," in *Studi di storia* (Turin: Einaudi, 1959). Dermont Fenlon, *Heresy and Obedience in Tridentine Italy. Cardinal Pole and the Counter-Reformation* (Cambridge: Cambridge University Press, 1972), examines both the evangelicals' hopes and the shock of their ultimate disappointment and throws extensive light on the psychology and rationale of Italian Nicodemism. See also Eva-Marie Jung, "On the Nature of Evan-

The *spirituali,* as Valdés' disciples called themselves, were an elite that included famous churchmen, distinguished women, and eminent intellectuals. Among them were Bernardino Ochino, vicar general of the Capuchin order; the Augustinian abbot Peter Martyr Vermigli; Pietro Carnesecchi, a prelate of the papal curia; Pier Paolo Vergerio, bishop of Capo d'Istria; Vittoria Colonna and Giulia Gonzaga, both from Italian princely families and the former an intimate friend of Michelangelo; and Marcantonio Flaminio, humanist, poet, and religious writer. After Valdés' death some of his friends went to Viterbo, where the highborn Englishman Cardinal Reginald Pole, who shared the evangelicals' outlook, was papal governor. In Pole's household the devout atmosphere and edifying discussions of the earlier Valdesian circle were recreated for a time.[4]

The fundamental concern of Valdés and his followers was justification by faith. Whether or not he was a fully self-conscious heretic, his theological orientation, which may have been directly influenced by Luther's teaching, was basically Protestant. Certainly its implicit tendency was to undermine the mediatorial role of the church.[5] Despite these beliefs, however, he maintained the external posture of a conforming Catholic and died in the bosom of the church. "Were it permitted to true Christians to live Christianly," he wrote in one of his tracts, "they would not have to hide as they do."[6] The rationale for his Nicodemism is unclear. He could have defended it on the basis of a well-grounded fear of persecution or justified himself on the principle that Catholic dogma and sacraments were meaningless or superfluous to a spiritual Christian.[7]

Delio Cantimori has observed that the popularity of Nicodemism in

---

gelism in Sixteenth-Century Italy," *Journal of the History of Ideas,* 14, no. 4 (1953); criticized by Elisabeth Gleason, "On the Nature of Sixteenth-Century Italian Evangelism: Scholarship, 1953–1978," *Sixteenth Century Journal,* 9, no. 3 (1978).

[4] See the list of Valdés' disciples in Angel Mergal's introduction to several of his works, in George H. Williams, ed., *Spiritual and Anabaptist Writers* (Philadelphia: Westminster Press, 1957), pp. 304–305; Delio Cantimori, "Italy and the Papacy," in *The New Cambridge Modern History,* vol. 2 (Cambridge: Cambridge University Press, 1958), pp. 265–267, gives an account of Valdés and Valdesianism; Fenlon, *Heresy and Obedience,* chap. 5, describes the Viterbo circle.

[5] Nieto, *Juan de Valdes,* pp. 166–167, holds that Valdés made a conscious and radical break with Catholicism; Fenlon, *Heresy and Obedience,* pp. 69–70, characterizes him as implicitly Protestant and suggests that he must surely have been influenced by Luther.

[6] Valdés, *Trattateli,* quoted in Nieto, *Juan de Valdes,* p. 165.

[7] Nieto, *Juan de Valdes,* p. 166; Cantimori, "Italy and the Papacy," p. 268.

Italy was largely a result of Valdés' teachings.[8] Religious dissimulation was indeed a note not only of Valdés' circle but of Italian evangelism generally.[9] Most Valdesians were compelled to resort to some degree of duplicity because of their dubious relation to Catholic orthodoxy. According to the confession of Carnesecchi, who was later executed as a heretic, it was in Cardinal Pole's household at Viterbo that he first read the writings of Luther, Bucer, and Calvin. Another member of the group, Marcantonio Flaminio, was the coauthor of the most significant and popular devotional work of the Italian Reformation, *The Benefit of Christ Crucified (Il beneficio di Cristo),* published anonymously in 1543, which expounded the doctrine of justification by faith and also incorporated whole passages from Calvin's *Institutes of the Christian Religion.* Pole himself, always cautious and prudent, was genuinely loyal to the church; yet his desire for reconciliation with the Protestant conception of justification inevitably forced him into a posture of evasiveness and equivocation.[10]

In 1541 a conference of Catholic and Protestant theologians was held in Regensburg to discuss reunion, in which Pole's friend and distinguished fellow evangelical, Cardinal Contarini, took a leading part. The meeting ended in failure. The next year Pope Paul III, alarmed by the extent of heresy in Italy, established the Roman Inquisition. These developments were deeply discouraging to the evangelicals. Their orthodoxy doubted, they were looked on with intense suspicion, and the next few years witnessed the gradual disintegration of their hopes as the proceedings of the Council of Trent made it evident that the church would draw a clear and definitive line against any accommodation with Protestantism.

[8] "Italy and the Papacy," p. 268.

[9] Fenlon shows this clearly; Jung also emphasizes the point in her negative judgment on Italian evangelism and its "hypocritical submissiveness." For a penetrating and nuanced account of the Nicodemism of the evangelicals and adherents of the Reformation in Italy, see Antonio Rotondó, "Atteggiamenti della vita morale italiana del cinquecento. La pratica nicodemitica," *Rivista storica italiana,* 79, no. 4 (1967).

[10] Nieto, *Juan de Valdés,* p. 148; Fenlon, *Heresy and Obedience,* chaps. 5–6, discusses Pole's position, the doctrinal features of *Il beneficio di Cristo,* and Flaminio's contribution. The other and principal author was Benedetto da Mantova, a Benedictine monk. The nature of this work has been debated; see Ruth Prelowski's introduction to her translation of the *Beneficio* in *Italian Reformation Studies in Honor of Laelius Socinus,* ed. John Tedeschi (Florence: Le Monnier, 1965); and Barry Collett, *Italian Benedictine Scholars and the Reformation* (Oxford: Clarendon Press, 1985), chap. 8.

At this juncture Valdés' disciples took diverse paths. Immediately after the creation of the Roman Inquisition, Ochino and Vermigli fled to Protestant territory. The defection of these two noted ecclesiastics created a scandal in the church and threatened the safety of their friends who remained in Italy. Explaining his flight to Vittoria Colonna, Ochino wrote that he could no longer remain in Italy and "preach Christ masked." In 1549 Bishop Vergerio also fled his native soil for the Grisons to launch a new life as a Protestant.[11] Flaminio underwent a reconversion to the church and submitted to its teachings. Carnesecchi continued to dissemble his beliefs until he was executed in 1567. Vittoria Colonna (d. 1547) and Giulia Gonzaga (d. 1566) persisted in their Nicodemism with all its ambiguities until their deaths. As her spiritual director Pole had advised Colonna "to believe as if her salvation depended upon faith alone, [but] to act . . . as if it depended upon good works," a typical Nicodemite position. After the death of Gonzaga, Pope Pius V, who as an inquisitor had seen her confiscated papers, said that he would have had her burned alive had she lived.[12]

Cardinal Pole, the friend and patron of these *spirituali,* was appointed a papal legate to the Council of Trent at its opening in 1545 but soon withdrew from it. Though ultimately disappointed by its uncompromising decree on justification, he was unwilling to abandon the church in whose unity he deeply believed. Nevertheless, his equivocal conduct and doctrinal reservations rendered him suspect to the orthodox, while his circumspection and failure to speak out evoked charges of dishonesty from the evangelicals who had openly joined the Reformation. In 1555 Vergerio in one of a series of attacks denounced Pole for his "most subtle cunning in concealing the truth" concerning justification by faith and for influencing others to do likewise. After more than two decades of dissimulation, Pole returned to England in 1554 as papal legate during the rule of Mary Tudor. There he became archbishop of Canterbury and by a horrible irony finished

[11] Ochino's statement is quoted in Rotondó, "Atteggiamenti della vita morale italiana," p. 1018; for his and Vermigli's flight, see Philip McNair, *Peter Martyr in Italy. An Anatomy of Apostasy* (Oxford: Clarendon Press, 1967), chaps. 9–10; for Vergerio, Anne Jacobson Schutte, *Pier Paolo Vergerio: The Making of an Italian Reformer* (Geneva: Droz, 1977), chaps. 7–9.

[12] Fenlon, *Heresy and Obedience,* pp. 93–94 (Flaminio), 278–279 (Carnesecchi), 96, 280n (Colonna, Gonzaga). In his testimony to the Inquisition Carnesecchi revealed many details about the Nicodemism of the Valdesians.

his career as a prime instrument in the queen's bloody persecution of Protestants.[13]

In Italy Protestants and philo-Protestants were scattered, weak, and constantly exposed to the risk of persecution by the repressive organs of the Counter-Reformation, aided by the power of the secular authorities. The rigorous enforcement of orthodoxy made it nearly impossible to maintain underground congregations for Protestant worship. Believers who had withdrawn spiritually from the Catholic church had to resort to many subterfuges and compromises. Forced to walk a razor's edge between their genuine convictions and the dominant Catholic order's exaction of conformity, it was easy for converts to the Reformation to fall into all kinds of doctrinal, intellectual, and psychological equivocations.[14] The case of Francesco Spiera, a lawyer in the town of Cittadella, furnished a notorious example of the stresses and contortions imposed by the balancing act of Nicodemism.

Spiera had been converted to the doctrines of justification by faith and predestination. His opinions became known, and in 1548 he was summoned before the Inquisition of Venice, a branch of the Roman Inquisition. There he abjured and consented to acknowledge his errors before his fellow citizens. Following this decision he was stricken with guilt and shame that he had denied Christ. The friends whom he consulted nevertheless advised him to preserve himself and his family, urging that the confession of his errors was only a trivial matter. With a heavy heart Spiera went through with his public recantation in the presence of nearly two thousand witnesses and was fined thirty pieces of gold. Immediately thereafter he broke down in what was probably a hysterical illness, convinced that he had betrayed Christ and was eternally damned. He lay ill in Padua suffering paroxysms, seeing devils, weeping and discoursing of his sin, all the while visited by crowds of people. None of the efforts of his physicians, churchmen, and friends to relieve his despair had any effect. He would only repeat that he was devoid of faith or hope. After eight weeks in this condition he died, the victim of his terrified, remorseful conscience.[15]

---

[13] Ibid., chaps. 8–12 and pp. 267 n, 282.

[14] Cantimori, "Nicodemismo e speranze conciliari," p. 532.

[15] I have used the account of Spiera's case in Schutte, *Pier Paolo Vergerio,* pp. 239–242, and in *A Relation of the Fearefull Estate of Francis Spiera in the Year 1548* (London, 1638), which is largely based on contemporary eyewitness accounts and is attributed to Nicholas Bacon in Alfred W. Pollard and G. R. Redgrave, *Short-*

Spiera's case attracted considerable attention, and several accounts of it were published soon afterward. One of these was written by Vergerio, who had witnessed the unhappy man's sufferings. He drew the lesson that Spiera had been made an example of God's punishment on those who deny him and merely play the Christian rather than being one in deed. At the time Vergerio himself was under a charge of heresy by the Inquisition from which he was seeking exoneration. It was probably the spectacle of Spiera's end that caused him to give up further attempts at compromise with Catholicism and precipitated his decision a few months later to abandon his bishopric and Venetian territory and identify openly with Protestantism.[16] In 1550 Calvin described Spiera as a perfidious dissimulator and an example of divine judgment for present and future ages.[17] In 1562 he referred to Spiera as a coward who had renounced his faith in order to save his life.[18] As late as 1638 an English narrative of Spiera's case was published in London. The author interpreted the story as a warning both not to act against conscience and not to pry into God's secret judgment on reprobation and damnation.[19]

Giorgio Siculo, a Benedictine monk, expressed a very different attitude toward Spiera's fate in 1550 in a published letter addressed to the citizens of Riva di Trento, where he had previously preached. Siculo linked his discussion of Spiera with an explicit defense of religious dissimulation, apparently the first such justification to be published in Italy.[20]

Siculo's mystical and spiritualistic message, which he communicated to conventicles of his followers in Bologna and Ferrara, was similar in some respects to that of Valdés. Having repudiated the cen-

---

Title Catalogue . . . 1475–1640, 2d ed., 2 vols. (London: Bibliographical Society, 1986), no. 1177.5. I owe my knowledge of the existence of this tract to Professor Paul Seaver.

[16] Pier Paolo Vergerio, *La historia di M. Francesco Spiera* (wr. 1548, pub. 1551), is discussed in Schutte, *Pier Paolo Vergerio*, pp. 242–246.

[17] Preface to *Francisci Spierae . . . Historia*, in John Calvin, *Opera*, 59 vols., ed. Johann Baum, Eduard Cunitz, and Eduard Reuss (Brunswick, 1863–1896), 10:lxx–lxxi, cols. 855–858.

[18] *Response à un certain holandois lequel sous ombre de faire les Chrestiens tout spirituels permet de polluer leur corps en toutes idolatries;* ibid., 9: col. 622.

[19] *A Relation of the Fearefull Estate of Francis Spiera.*

[20] *Epistola di Giorgio Siculo servo fidele di Jesu Cristo alle cittadini di riva di Trento* (Bologna, 1550); Delio Cantimori, *Eretici italiani del cinquecento* (1939; repr., Florence: Sansoni, 1967), chap. 8; Carlo Ginzburg, *Il Nicodemismo, Simulazione e dissimulazion nell'Europa del '500* (Turin: Einaudi, 1970), pp. 163, 170–173.

tral dogmas of the Catholic church as diabolical inventions, he was executed in Ferrara in 1551 for heresy. But he was likewise opposed to Protestantism and condemned the doctrine of predestination as false and pernicious. Convinced of the existence of free will and of the infinite efficacy of the *beneficio di Cristo* in behalf of sinners, he held that no one was excluded from God's mercy. In Siculo's opinion, Spiera's despair and dreadful end were the result of his erroneous belief in predestination. Desiring to console Protestants in Italy, France, and elsewhere who were compelled to live under the yoke of the Roman church, he affirmed that it was no sin to adhere outwardly to Catholic worship if the situation required it. He maintained further that Christians despite lack of belief might conform to the doctrine and discipline imposed by lawful superiors, and that in doing so they neither denied Christ nor were among the reprobate. In part his attitude was based on a consignment of ceremonies to the realm of indifferent things. As proof of his view Siculo stressed the example of Paul, who sometimes conformed to the Jewish law in order not to scandalize or offend weaker brethren.[21]

There can be little question that fear and physical danger caused most of the Italians attracted to the Reformation to disguise their convictions behind a facade of participation in Catholic worship. As part of their opposition to this deceit, Protestant ministers urged recourse to flight. The three ex-ecclesiastics Ochino, Vermigli, and Vergerio had all fled rather than go on pretending to accept Catholic idolatry. Ochino admitted that he had engaged in dissimulation in the belief that he could utilize the "disguise of my habit and of the extrinsic . . . sanctity of my life" to preach the true gospel. Finally, though, flight in accord with Christ's advice to leave the place of persecution (Matthew 10:23) had extricated him from this false position.[22] Peter Martyr Vermigli, who had converted many people in Lucca to Protestantism before leaving Italy, later wrote to his brethren there to explain his departure and deplore their failure to take flight. He blamed them for their weakness and cowardice in abjuring under persecution, a betrayal he attributed to their love of riches and the flesh. If they were unable to endure martyrdom, he said, they should

[21] Barry Collett, *Italian Benedictine Scholars* (Oxford: Clarendon Press, 1986), chap. 10, discusses Siculo's theological ideas.

[22] Quoted in Schutte, *Pier Paolo Vergerio,* pp. 254, 256. Roland Bainton, *Bernardino Ochino esule e riformatore senese del cinquecento* (Florence: Sansoni, 1940), does not mention dissimulation or Nicodemism.

have fled rather than forsaken their faith. To those who were "fallen" he prescribed repentance and prayers for God's forgiveness.[23]

In other works concerned with the guidance of conscience, Vermigli dealt with the casuistry of flight in considerable detail. While holding it lawful for the godly to flee persecution, he insisted that flight must always respect the glory of God and not proceed solely from fear or infirmity, because Christians must also be ready to die for the Lord. Furthermore, flight must not injure one's neighbor. Pastors could not flee if their absence would endanger their flock and if no others remained to take their place. In general he laid it down that "there can be nothing absolutelie commanded [about flight]. For everie man . . . must examine and make trial of himselfe, when he taketh in hand to flie awaie."[24]

Vergerio also defended the legitimacy of flight. In some tracts recording his spiritual evolution which appeared in 1550 after his departure from Italy, he exhorted his Christian readers to shun deception. "Stand fast in the truth," he urged, "and do not dissimulate, do not disguise yourselves." His counsel to believers was to flee persecution as Christ and the apostles had done. Christ had never permitted dissimulation, but when persecuted in one place had sought refuge in another. God teaches the elect, as he himself had been taught, Vergerio wrote, "that they should escape from dangers until, by a special revelation, they recognize that their hour has come."[25]

Vergerio's argument formed part of a larger debate about flight which took place among Italian Protestants at this difficult time. In a work with the self-explanatory title *Exhortation to Martyrdom* (1556), another Italian Protestant exile, Giulio Della Rovere, a pastor in Zurich, castigated Italians for denying their faith as soon as they found themselves in danger and then becoming confessors again once they had arrived in the Swiss cantons.[26] He admonished that the time had passed for disputes about religion and that deeds were necessary; hence

[23] "To the Brethren of the Citie of Lucca," in *The Common Places of Peter Martyr* (London, 1583), separately paginated, pp. 140–144.

[24] *The Common Places*, pp. 287–290; see also idem, "An Epistle . . . to a Friende . . . Touching the Flying Awaie in Time of Persecution," in ibid.

[25] Vergerio dealt with flight in two of his *Dodici Trattateli* (Basel, 1550); my discussion is based on Schutte, *Pier Paolo Vergerio,* pp. 251, 255–260.

[26] Giulio Della Rovere (also known as Giulio da Milano), *Esortazione al martirio* (Zurich, 1552); my discussion is based on Cantimori, "Nicodemismo e speranze conciliari," pp. 527–528. Cantimori surveys the debate on flight in *Prospettive di storia ereticale del cinquecento* (Bari: Laterza, 1960), chap. 4.

all must follow Christ by taking the cross on their shoulders and preparing for martyrdom. Although the believers in Italy were like dead and scattered members, lacking spiritual guides and churches governed by the word of God, if they would unite themselves into properly organized churches they would become more strongly attached to the faith. Accordingly, Rovere largely condemned flight as an act of weakness. While conceding that it was excusable for itinerant preachers to flee persecution, he held that resident pastors and their flocks must remain where they were. Martyrdom if necessary was the true Christian's choice.

Calvin, on the other hand, had strongly advocated flight in his writings against dissimulation. When these appeared in an Italian version in 1553, the anonymous translator took up the subject of flight in his preface. He painted a bleak picture of the Reformation's prospects in Italy: there were no Italian princes who supported the gospel, nor any form of true church, and no true piety to sustain Christians amid the dangers of so much corruption. Fear caused many to deny their faith, some by their own will, others on account of force. The writer saw no hope that the situation would improve, and recommended flight to Protestant territory as the only way to avoid dissimulation and other perils. He argued forcibly against the notion that flight was wrong; deprived of this alternative, believers might lose hope and resign themselves to renouncing their faith if God did not give them the power to endure. Distinguishing between voluntary departure and flight under compulsion, he justified the former as itself equivalent to a confession of faith, though in a lesser degree than martyrdom. Against the assumption that many would flee if exhorted, he offered a barbed reassurance. Few would do so, he maintained, most being attached to their property, their comforts, and "the sweet . . . delights of the beautiful land of Italy." For every person who chose to depart, a thousand would prefer to remain.[27]

The discussion of flight by Italian Protestants faced with increasing persecution at the midpoint of the sixteenth century casts into sharp relief the moral problems besetting the men and women who had renounced their spiritual allegiance to the Catholic church. It also explains why Nicodemism became so common in Italy. Rather than

[27] John Calvin, *Del fuggir le superstitioni* (Geneva, 1553); Droz, "Calvin et les Nicodémites," pp. 159–165, has identified the translator as Celso Martinengo. I have relied on the summary of the preface in Delio Cantimori, "Spigolature per la storia del Nicodemismo italiano," in *Ginevra e l'Italia* (Florence: Sansoni, 1959).

suffer a martyr's death or the costly social and economic uprooting incident to exile, most of the Reformation's Italian adherents chose to take refuge in dissimulation.

Of the Italians affected by evangelism and the Reformation who ceased to be Catholic, most presumably became Protestants in due course. However, there was also a minority whose beliefs diverged as widely from the mainstream Protestantism of Luther, Calvin, and the Swiss Reformation as they did from Catholicism. Calvin noted as a distinctive characteristic of the Italians their restless minds and "inanis curiositas," which carried them into all sorts of useless speculations and dangerous heresies. The proof of this was that they were well represented in fringe movements such as anabaptism and antitrinitarianism with its mingling of spiritualistic and rationalistic elements.[28] Such people often persisted in prudential dissimulation even if they eventually left Italy for Protestant territory, because their religious convictions made them as liable to persecution by Protestant authorities as they had been in their native land. In such cases Nicodemism could be associated with highly unorthodox ideas.

A striking example appears in a defense of dissimulation composed about 1538 by a Sienese aristocrat, Bartolomeo Carli Piccolimini, as part of a treatise on prudence which, though never printed, was known to some of his contemporaries.[29] Carli's faith had been largely shaped by Valdesian teaching. For him Catholicism was a religion of the ignorant and foolish, and its external ceremonials devoid of meaning. His own religion aimed at a personal illumination in the belief that he formed one of a small minority directly inspired by God. In dealing with the relation of prudence to the religious life, Carli stressed the necessity of dissimulation for survival: because a reputation for heresy must bring ruin, a wise man would render an external

[28] Calvin's statement is quoted in Albano Biondi, "La giustificazione della simulazione nel cinquecento," in *Eresia e riforma nell'Italia del cinquecento* (De Kalb: Northern Illinois University Press, 1974), p. 54; George H. Williams, *The Radical Reformation* (Philadelphia: Westminster Press, 1962), chaps. 22, 24, surveys Italian reformers' involvement with anabaptism and antitrinitarianism.

[29] My discussion of Carli's treatise is based on Rita Belladonna, "Pontanus, Machiavelli, and a Case of Religious Dissimulation in Early Sixteenth-Century Siena," *Bibliothèque d'humanisme et Renaissance*, 37, no. 3 (1975); and idem, "Aristotle, Machiavelli, and Religious Dissimulation: Bartolomeo Carli Piccolimini's *Trattati Nove della Prudenza*," in *Peter Martyr Vermigli and Italian Reform*, ed. Joseph C. McLellan (Waterloo, Ont.: Wilfred Laurier University Press, 1980).

conformity. As a further reason for outwardly respecting religion he pointed to its crucial role in maintaining the authority of states and rulers. Like Machiavelli, whose writings he held in high esteem, in justifying dissimulation he emphasized the vital political function of religion. A reminiscence of *The Prince* also appeared in his remark that the *prudente* must sometimes act the "fox" and sometimes the "dove."

Another influence on Carli was the fifteenth-century humanist Giovanni Pontano, who had similarly endorsed dissimulation in a treatise of the 1490s on the theme of prudence.[30] Though acknowledging that good men looked down on falsity and dissembling, Pontano contended that both were unavoidable. Owing to the inconstancy of fortune and the variability of human affairs, even men most renowned for virtue sometimes found it necessary to dissimulate. It is noteworthy that Carli's advocacy of dissimulation in religion did not rely on any biblical precedents. Instead he gave the secular reasonings of Machiavelli and Pontano a religious application and based the rationale of his Nicodemism mainly on prudential considerations.

Two other highly heterodox thinkers who made a principle of dissimulation were Lelio Sozzini (1525–1562) and his more famous nephew Fausto Sozzini (1539–1604). Both Sienese patricians like Carli, the Sozzinis contributed significantly to the formation of antitrinitarianism or Socinianism, a heresy regarded with horror and hatred by most Protestants. Lelio, educated in jurisprudence and philosophy, was a religious rationalist who developed a marked partiality toward anabaptism and other radical beliefs during the 1540s. Having fallen under suspicion of heresy in Venice, in 1547 he joined the diaspora of Italian religious emigrants, first in the Grisons and then in Switzerland. Although he traveled widely in Europe thereafter, he lived mainly in Switzerland, where his intellectual qualities and personal distinction brought him into friendly relations with Calvin and other leading figures of the Reformation. His associations with anabaptists and spiritualists among the Italian exiles led him to be skeptical of the importance of ceremonies. Like the anabaptists, he embraced psychopannychism, a heresy that held that the soul is not immortal but dies or sleeps until the resurrection.[31] He showed great prudence and reserve, however, in disclosing his beliefs. Rather than

---

[30] Johannes Jovianus Pontanus, "De Simulatione et Dissimulatione," in *De Prudentia Libri V Ioannis Ioanni Pontani, Opera* (ed. Venice, 1518).

[31] Calvin's treatise *Psychopannychia* (1542) (*Opera*, vol. 7), directed against this doctrine, is discussed in Williams, *Radical Reformation*, pp. 581–586.

expressing his own views, he professed to be always in search of knowledge from others. As a result he came to be regarded as a subtle and cunning hypocrite who dissimulated to conceal his heresies.

In 1549 Sozzini addressed a number of casuistical queries to Calvin. After praising the latter's writings against participation in Catholic worship, he said he wished to know whether it was permissible to marry a woman who had the true faith but conformed to impious ceremonies, or to baptize an infant in the Catholic church, or to attend mass. He also asked whether it was necessary to believe in the resurrection of the body. These questions, framed with many particulars, were in themselves a subtle exercise in Nicodemism. Under cover of seeking information, they insinuated reservations that undermined Calvin's fundamental position on the subjects addressed. The reformer nevertheless sent a courteous reply repeating his condemnation of outward conformity to idolatry and stating his firm belief in a bodily resurrection. Sozzini continued to press questions in further correspondence until Calvin, growing impatient, terminated the discussion. Wary of Sozzini's attitude, he cautioned the Italian against his "monstrous questions," speculations, and "vice of curiosity," warning that he would get into trouble if he did not cure his "itch for inquiry."[32]

In 1553 Calvin acted as the prime mover in the case of the archheretic Michael Servetus, who was tried and burned alive in Geneva for his antitrinitarian and other unorthodox beliefs. This notorious example of Protestant persecution provoked a storm of controversy and gave rise to the well-known work by Sebastian Castellio, *On Heretics and Whether They Should Be Persecuted,* a protest against Servetus' death and plea for religious tolerance. Lelio Sozzini was an intimate of Castellio, and Calvin and Theodore Beza rightly suspected that he had a hand in the preparation of Castellio's book.[33] By this time he was widely rumored to hold many heretical opinions. There can be little doubt that his skeptical turn of mind led him to favor tolerance and to reject basic dogmas.

In 1555, at the behest of the Zurich reformer Henry Bullinger, Soz-

---

[32] See Cantimori, *Eretici italiani,* chap. 14; Earl Wilbur, *A History of Unitarianism* (Cambridge, Mass.: Harvard University Press, 1947), pp. 239–247; Ralph Lazzaro translates Sozzini's questions and Calvin's replies in "Four Letters from the Socinus-Calvin Correspondence (1549)," in Tedeschi, *Italian Reformation Studies in Honor of Laelius Socinus.*

[33] Beza, in his *Life of Calvin,* printed in *Tracts Relating to the Reformation by John Calvin* (Edinburgh, 1860), also speaks of Sozzini as a skeptic; pp. liv, xlvi.

zini drew up a confession of faith in order to prove his orthodoxy.[34] This artfully contrived statement abounded in equivocation, using orthodox phraseology to convey the impression of freedom from heresy while leaving the door open to various heretical views. Thus Sozzini stated that he abhorred the errors of the anabaptists and Servetus but never indicated what they were. He did not endorse the Apostle's and other ancient creeds, but declared only that he honored them as far as he ought. Neither did he avow his faith in the trinity, though allowing that it had been a doctrine current for many centuries. He affirmed that he accepted all things necessary for salvation without naming any of them.

This confession of faith, which reassured Bullinger, must be regarded as a masterpiece of Nicodemism. Especially in the aftermath of Servetus' death, Sozzini could not have expressed his true convictions in Protestant Switzerland without great danger; hence he resorted to ambiguities and generalities. Throughout the document he refrained from committing himself to any particular propositions on disputed points. Despite his seeming orthodoxy, the author of such an evasive statement could have held many heretical beliefs.

Lelio Sozzini left few writings at his death, but his antitrinitarian principles were developed fully in the works of Fausto, his nephew and heir. This bold and original thinker carried the rationalist strain of the radical Reformation to its furthest point by his methods of scriptural interpretation, his rejection of the divinity of Christ's nature, and his denial of the immortality of the soul. His heterodoxy during a career that took him from Italy, France, and Switzerland to central Europe and Poland, where he spent the last twenty-five years of his life, impelled him to conceal his beliefs under a prudential Nicodemism. Thus while staying in Lyons he was accustomed to take the Catholic sacrament. Later, in Switzerland, despite being on close terms with many heterodox Italians, he gave assurances of his trinitarian orthodoxy in order to be admitted to the Italian Protestant church in Geneva. From 1563 to 1574, when he lived in Florence as a courtier of the grand duke of Tuscany, he conformed to the Catholic

[34] Translated and discussed in E. M. Hulme, "Lelio Sozzini's Confession of Faith," in *Persecution and Liberty: Essays in Honor of G. L. Burr* (New York: Century, 1931), pp. 214–216; see also Wilbur, *History of Unitarianism*, p. 245; Cantimori, *Eretici italiani*, pp. 181–183.

church. For many years he also never published any of his works under his own name.

Fausto Sozzini exhibited a flexibility in adapting to different religions which was barely separable from duplicity and hypocrisy. Among the reasons he gave for external conformity was the need to avoid disturbances and scandals that might offend weak brethren and drive them from the true worship of God. As he attributed no significance to ceremonies, he could take this position without difficulty. He was prepared to sanction dissimulation provided one kept the truth within. In explaining his attitude at a conference of Unitarian theologians at Rakow in 1601, he stressed the necessity of accommodation to times and conditions as long as true believers were so few. He also urged the need for caution and prudence in speaking of doctrines such as the mortality of the soul. In defending dissimulation as not necessarily sinful, he cited the precedent discussed earlier by Augustine, Aquinas, and Lefèvre d'Etaples, that Christ himself dissimulated *(simulavit)* to his disciples on the road to Emmaus (Luke 24:28). Sozzini's remarks indicate that he had developed a justification compounded of prudential and religious reasons to permit the dissembling of belief to escape persecutors and enemies.[35]

A final example of the linkage between extreme heterodoxy and dissimulation among the Italians is provided by the Florentine heretic Francesco Pucci (1543–1597). Educated for the priesthood, Pucci embarked in 1571 on a life of wandering across Europe during which he met other visionaries like himself. In Switzerland he knew Fausto Sozzini, with whom he debated the immortality of the soul. Later, in Prague, he consorted with the famous English scientist-magus John Dee and took part in his séances. In Pucci's case heresy fused with occult, hermetic, and magical beliefs, a combination considerably more typical of the later than of the earlier sixteenth century. He was repelled by all existing religions and their divisions. A mystic, chiliast, and prophet who believed himself to possess a new revelation, he looked for the restoration of the world to concord and unity through

[35] My discussion is based on Rotondó, "Atteggiamenti della vita morale italiana," pp. 991–993, 999–1011; and Wilbur, *History of Unitarianism*, pp. 387–391. Cantimori, *Eretici italiani*, though acknowledging in Sozzini a subtlety and ambiguity bordering on "hypocritical dissimulation," observes that one cannot speak in his case of Nicodemism, a judgment I find difficult to understand.

the rule of a spiritual elite. In the hope of propagating his revelation more widely he sought reconciliation with the Catholic church. Eventually arrested and tried by the Inquisition for heresy, he was executed in 1597 in Rome.

Pucci developed dissimulation into a system by making it the *modus operandi* in a plan for an underground society dedicated to the creation of a utopian new order. This order was to be based on a universal religion of Christian character but reflecting the light of natural reason. In an anonymous work of 1581, *The Form of a Catholic Republic,* he described his proposed secret organization, whose members were to be distributed throughout Europe.[36] Subject to strict moral discipline, they would constitute a sort of state within existing states and conduct clandestine activity and propaganda to realize their goal. Where the Inquisition maintained guard, they were to elude its vigilance by various devices. They would know, for example, how to talk and write secretly in the presence of third parties by means of disguised speech. To refer to the iniquity of their adversaries they would use irony, antiphrasis, allegory, and other equivocal language. By conversing in this manner in shops, churches, squares, and even in homes, they would be able to name things in other terms and thus draw out people's opinions. Pucci declared that God saw the heart and succored those united in soul who acted covertly for the true religion and public good. God would therefore reward all who helped to further the secret society's aims either openly or in secret.

Cantimori has characterized this fantastic scheme as "a codification of Nicodemism" in the sense not of a defense against persecution but of a consciously organized attempt to transform states and religion.[37] It did certainly signify the extension of dissimulation to the point where it became an entire way of life. The members of Pucci's secret republic were not only to conceal their identity but also to engage in surveillance and espionage against both outsiders and one another. He did not put forward any theological rationale for such duplicity, appar-

---

[36] *Forma d'una republica catholica,* printed in Delio Cantimori and E. Feist, *Per la storia degli eretici italiani del secolo XVI in Europa* (Rome: Reale Accademia d'Italia, 1937), pp. 200–202; Cantimori, *Eretici italiani,* pp. 381–404, attributes this anonymous work to Pucci and analyzes it in relation to his other writings; see also Robert Evans, *Rudolf II and His World* (Oxford: Clarendon Press, 1974), pp. 102–104; Miriam Eliav-Feldon, "Secret Societies, Utopias, and Peace Pleas: The Case of Francesco Pucci," *Journal of Medieval and Renaissance Studies,* 14, no. 2 (1984).

[37] *Eretici italiani,* p. 392.

ently simply taking for granted that it was necessary to the attainment of the new order and therefore approved by God. With Pucci dissimulation went beyond the Nicodemism against which Calvin inveighed and became linked to the vision of a perfected society. He saw it as a permanent refuge of inwardness for those who had no spiritual home in any of the existing churches and were driven by a longing to escape from religious wars and hatreds into a world of harmony and peace.

CHAPTER 6

Nicodemism: Controversialists, Sectarians, Familists

W e are accustomed to think of the Reformation as a time when religious men and women were forced to make a fundamental decision between Catholicism and Protestantism. Conversion and the commitment and constancy that spring from faith, martyrdom, or exile for the sake of belief were all vital aspects of Protestantism in the first two or three generations of its existence. Those who suffered for the sake of their religion were commemorated in the martyrologies compiled by contemporary Protestant writers as a tribute to the victims of persecution and an inspiration to believers. Yet this conception of the Reformation represents no more than a partial view. As we have seen, alongside the martyrs and exiles were a considerable number of Protestants in the sixteenth century who chose instead to disguise their faith under a pretended conformity to the Catholic church. In all countries in which Protestantism won converts, Nicodemism became a common response to confessional persecution and division, and its pervasiveness made it a serious concern to Protestant pastors and leaders. Issued in 1549 and 1550 under the title *The Avoidance of Superstition (De Vitandis Superstitionibus)*, Calvin's principal works against Nicodemism were disseminated throughout Europe. Other Protestant authorities also grappled with the problem of religious dissimulation, striving to undermine its arguments and to persuade believers not to imperil their salvation by participating in popish idolatry. At the same time there were sectarians who remained immune to such exhortations and approved and practiced dissimulation on various grounds.

After Charles V's promulgation in Germany of the Interim in 1548, one of the Protestant ministers who went into exile rather than conform to its provisions was the Augsburg preacher Wolfgang Musculus

(1497–1563).[1] In Switzerland, where he spent the remainder of his life, Musculus published in 1549 a group of Latin dialogues, *Proscaerus,* meaning timeserver or temporizer, stigmatizing the dissemblers who participated in impious ceremonies and written in the knowledge that some in his own congregation who had seemed strongest in the faith were attending the Catholic mass. The work was shortly published in French as *Le temporiseur* and then appeared in English in 1555 with the title *The Temporysour: The Observer of Tyme, or He That Chaungeth with the Tyme.*[2] Printed by a clandestine press in the duchy of Cleves, this version was addressed to the Protestants who, under the rule of Mary Tudor, were legally required to participate in Catholic services. In his preface the translator, an English Protestant exile, reproached his countrymen for submitting to idolatry. More than once he spoke of the "dissimulate hypocrisie" of those who "cloke and dissemble their faith." He explained that he had translated this profitable work to counter the arguments and excuses used to defend conformity to popish worship.[3]

The Temporysour consists of four brief dialogues in which the main participants are Temporiser, a defender of Nicodemism sorely perplexed in conscience; and Eusebius, a faithful Christian who abstains from Catholic ceremonies. The essential issue between them is the legitimacy of dissimulation. At the outset Temporiser protests that he conforms from fear and to avoid danger to himself, his wife, and his family. Eusebius responds that he nevertheless has a choice and should obey God rather than man. Temporiser advances as an excuse the much-invoked distinction between belief and conformity. "When I go to the papisticall services," he avers, "I judge it no great matter to dissemble outwardly, seyinge I do reserve faith perfectly in my hart." Eusebius answers that real faith cannot be hidden and must be manifested. When Temporiser cites Christ's command to his disciples to be as wise as serpents, to beware of men who will deliver them up, and

---

[1] For the Interim, see Chapter 4.

[2] For details of the publication, editions, and translations of Musculus' *Proscaerus* see Eugenie Droz, "Musculus, Poullain, et les temporiseurs," in *Chemins de l'heresie,* 4 vols. (Geneva: Slatkine, 1970–1974), vol. 1, which also contains the Calvinist pastor Valerand Poullain's French translation. The English translator, Robert Pownall, who signed only his initials, was a Protestant minister in Germany; see *DNB,* s.v. His version is derived from the French text. *Proscaerus* is discussed by Carlo Ginzburg, *Il Nicodemismo. Simulazione e dissimulazione nell' Europa del '500* (Turin: Einaudi, 1970).

[3] *The Temporysour* (Wesel? 1555), sigs. Aiiii–v.

not to cast pearls before swine and dogs, Eusebius retorts that he is foolish to deny his faith, as all Temporiser's neighbors must know he is dissimulating because he has publicly professed the gospel for twenty years.[4]

Still unconvinced, Temporiser argues that he cannot understand why his dissembling should be blamed, seeing that he conforms only in obedience to the magistrate and to escape danger. He also points out that some conformists justify themselves by the examples of Naaman the Syrian, Nicodemus, and Joseph of Arimathea, all of whom kept the faith secretly in their hearts while communicating with the adversaries of the truth. "Yf [their] dissimulation . . . did not hinder their salvation," he demands, "wherefore then is it damnable to us?" Eusebius, however, refutes these precedents. Neither Naaman, Nicodemus, nor Joseph had adhered openly to the gospel and therefore did not openly renounce it by their conformity. Moreover, the Jewish observances in which Nicodemus and Joseph participated were not false and impious as are the popish services that provoke God's wrath. The two of them later also proved their loyalty to Christ when they claimed his body. According to Eusebius, the "Nicodemites" who use Nicodemus to cover their dissimulation ought rather to imitate his faith and heroism than allege the infirmity of the saints for their own weakness. Nor can Naaman's case excuse Temporiser's "synful hypocrisie," because Naaman was a new convert from idolatry, not a Christian long instructed in the faith.[5] These arguments finally convince Temporiser, who admits that none of his scriptural precedents will justify the hypocrisy of the "Nicodemistes."

In a marginal comment the translator urged his countrymen to depart from papistical superstition by flight or exile lest they fall into despair, which was inevitably "the end of dissimulacion." Among dreadful examples of desperation he mentioned the notorious history of the Italian "Frauncis Spera" as an instance of God's justice on those who acted against the testimony of their conscience.[6] Through the references to it by Calvin and others, Spiera's case had obviously become widely known in Protestant circles.

Musculus' dialogue was followed by a translation of a previously published condemnation of dissimulation by the Italian Protestant exile Celio Secundo Curione, framed as advice to the brethren who

[4] Ibid., sigs. Biiii–v, Diiii.
[5] Ibid., sigs. Eii, Ev, Fii–v, Giiii.
[6] Ibid., sig. Gv.

remained in Babylon and who wished to know whether it was lawful to communicate or be present at "the Babilonicall papisticall services, the hart beyng absent and alienated from all supersticion and vayne religion." Curione rejected such practices and their reasons, including the claim that it was lawful to dissimulate for a good and profitable end: the main end must always be Christ's glory and the salvation of brethren, and "neither hath God any nede of our lyes, and dissimulacions." For those too weak to profess the faith openly he recommended refraining from papal services plus Bible reading and prayer in private houses.[7]

Most Protestant authors who dealt with the question of dissimulation in the 1540s and 1550s handled the subject with the same biblical examples, the same arguments and defenses, and the same refutations. Calvin had laid down the main lines of the attack on Nicodemism, and other writers appear to have added little to the substance of his criticisms, although they usually showed themselves less harsh, more compassionate, and more sensitive to the difficulties of believers who conformed to Catholic rites.

One prolific writer and propagandist concerned with Nicodemism was Pierre Viret (1511–1571), an influential minister in Lausanne for more than twenty years and a longtime friend and colleague of Calvin.[8] In treating the situation of the followers of the gospel under Catholic rule, he addressed a variety of readers. A long casuistical work of 1547 advised crypto-Protestant noblemen, courtiers, and officials through a detailed exposition of the book of Esther, a text also favored by the Marranos.[9] In two other works of the 1540s, however, he appears to have aimed at a wider audience.

The first was an appeal to believers not to yield to idolatry; it was

[7] Curione's letter is printed at the end of ibid. It was also included in the French translation of *Proscaerus* and was first published in Italian in 1552; see Droz, "Musculus," pp. 248–255.

[8] Robert D. Linder, *The Political Ideas of Pierre Viret* (Geneva: Droz, 1964), pp. 181–191, contains an account of Viret's career and a bibliography of his writings but does not discuss his works dealing with Nicodemism. In 1559 a collection of five of his treatises against dissimulation and participation in Catholic ceremonies was published in Geneva under the title *Traittez divers pour l'instruction des fideles qui resident & conversent es lieus & pais esquels il ne leur permis de vivre en la pureté & liberté de l'evangile.* This volume includes the texts discussed below.

[9] *Remonstrances aux fidèles qui conversent entre les papistes: & principalement à ceux qui sont en court, & qui ont offices publiques, touchant les moyens qu'ilz doivent tenir en*

later published in an English translation by a Puritan who judged that it was still necessary for Christians even in the reign of Elizabeth.[10] In this tract Viret expressed a very strong sense of the pollution resulting from popish ceremonies and frequently resorted to the sexual imagery of whoredom and adultery to convey the defilement believers must incur. He identified fear as the predominant motive for conforming. Thus he pictured the "wise men," "proctors and advocates of the flesh," who taught others "to confess Iesus Christ privately, but deny him openly" and who "tell the faythfull that if they dissemble not, they should put themselves in great danger, & others with them." These same wise spirits "woulde not lose one heire of their head for the gospell." Not only did they not dare to utter a word in favor of the truth, but they "will consent to the death of the innocent, and if it be needful . . . will condemne them themselves for feare of being suspected."[11]

Viret found the reasons such people gave for their position frivolous and weak. They were based on the disjunction between heart and mouth, belief and utterance, and grounded in the familiar precedents of Naaman, Paul, and Nicodemus. Viret confuted them with the standard argument that Christ must be confessed openly in body as well as in spirit, for God would not tolerate deceit and could not dwell in the heart if the devil was in the tongue. Besides exonerating Naaman and Paul from all charges of dissimulating, he turned the example of Nicodemus against those who sought to use it to justify their feigned conformity. Although Nicodemus was blameworthy and weak in first coming to Christ secretly by night, at least he did not blaspheme or deny Christ openly by day. Moreover, after the crucifixion he found the courage to reveal himself publicly as Christ's disciple. Like Calvin, therefore, Viret allowed that there could be true and good "Nichodemians" who followed Nicodemus' later example of faith. "Would God," he exclaimed, "that wee had many such Nichodemians that were so fearful, that they would shewe themselves alwayes at neede."[12]

In dealing with the predicament of the Protestant faithful under

---

leur vocation, à l'exemple des anciens serviteurs de Dieu, sans contrevenir à leur devoir, n'y envers Dieu, n'y envers leur prochaine (Geneva).

[10] Epistre envoyeé aux fidèles conversent entre les chrestiens papistiques (n.p., 1543); I cite the English translation by "F. H. Esquier," who was probably Francis Hastings, a younger brother of the earl of Huntingdon, An Epistle to the Faithfull, Necessary for All the Children of God; Especially in These Daungerous Dayes (London, 1582).

[11] An Epistle, sigs. D3, B2, E2, G4.

[12] Ibid., sigs. A, B2-3, C3-4, F4-G2, G4.

persecution, Viret made sympathetic allowance for human infirmity. Observing how hard it was for the flesh to undergo danger, he admitted that he too might be weak and frail in the same circumstances. Yet the question was not what he would do, but rather what should be done and "what wee owe to God." The answer for him, as it was for all Protestant leaders, was either flight or martyrdom. Rather than submit to idolatry, followers of the gospel should flee, despite fear of loss of goods, or else die like the apostles and martyrs who would not forsake Christ.[13]

Viret not only moderated his censure of believers under Catholic rule but wrote as someone who identified with them in their plight. If they could not attain to the high degree of confessing Christ openly, he urged that they become

> secret schollars with Nichodemus . . . And if we shewe not ourselves so openly, yet at the least, let us do no dishonour to Jesus Christ, nor consent unto his adversaries in partaking at the table of divels, & if . . . for feare of losing our goods . . . & lives, we be constrained too much to dissemble, and communicate with idolators, let us not iustifie, but condemne our selves . . . let us acknowledge our over great infirmitie & the over burning love that we beare to our selves . . . more than to Jesus Christ & his word . . . let us pray to God that he will encrease our faith . . . and let us confesse our . . . sinnes, and ask him for mercie . . . let us weepe and waile under this heavie burthen, and . . . this great tyrannie of Antichrist which presseth us so sore . . . [14]

He concluded with a final comfort to the tormented conscience of dissemblers who feared that they were guilty of the sin against the holy ghost, the dread undefined transgression that terrified Christians. He reassured them that in communicating with idolatry they sinned only from weakness, not from malice. But he warned them not to defend their infirmity lest they aggravate their sin.[15]

Another of Viret's writings against Nicodemism, *Admonition and Consolation to the Faithful Who Are Thinking of Departing from among the Papists to Avoid Idolatry,* probed the crucial question of flight and exile.[16] In counseling flight he revealed a much clearer awareness than

[13] Ibid., sigs. G4, C–C2.
[14] Ibid., sig. G4.
[15] Ibid.
[16] *Admonition et consolation aux fideles, qui deliberent de sortir d'entre les papists pour eviter idolatrie* (Geneva, 1547).

Calvin of its practical and psychological obstacles. Starting from the premise "that it is wonderfully difficult [and] almost impossible, to live among the papists, without communicating in their idolatries, or without great danger to one's life," he proceeded to discuss departure from idolatry as a necessity, even though "very hard for the flesh to do." His essential theme was the temptations of Satan which must be overcome in going forth from "Egypt."[17]

The greatest of these temptations, according to Viret, was the fear of falling into poverty. How will we manage and how will we live, the faithful asked themselves when they envisaged abandoning their possessions to go to a strange land. Those accustomed to easy living or engaged in occupations without heavy labor were especially assaulted with such fears by Satan, who knew well how to tempt the servants of God as he did Christ and the saints. Viret expressed pity for the anguish of believers in these circumstances: "They cannot remain among the idolaters without idolatrizing, or . . . danger of losing their goods and their lives. They cannot idolatrize without offending God, nor offend God without danger of eternal damnation and loss of soul and body."[18]

Viret stressed that Christians owed their greatest debt to God, to whom they should pray for the strength to resist idolatry. If they could not confess Christ openly, they should at least not deny him. Believers ought to withdraw from idolatry in the same way that Lot left Sodom and the Israelites Egypt. If the family could not go and it was impossible to remain without danger to life, then it was better to leave family behind than for all to perish together. If wife and children refused to leave, it was better that they perish themselves, as did Lot's wife under God's anger. But if God gave the entire family the heart to depart, then it was usually possible to take along a portion of one's goods in order to subsist. Believers must beware, however, lest their worldly possessions become a cause of perdition, for there were some who were afraid to go unless the could take all their wealth with them. In preparing for flight, they should remember Christ's promises, which did not include repose or mountains of gold. They must be ready for the Lord's discipline and the cross in the places where they sought refuge.[19]

Another temptation Viret mentioned was the fear of dying of

[17] Ibid., pp. 3–4.
[18] Ibid., pp. 4–8.
[19] Ibid., pp. 10, 12–13, 15–16.

hunger. For this he offered the consolation that God would provide for his servants, whom he had promised not to abandon. The faithful should accordingly not torment themselves with cares and worries, but only trust in God and do their duty. The final snare against which Viret warned the faithful was the heresies of the anabaptists, spiritualists, libertines, epicureans, and atheists. The devil used these apostates to draw people to himself, and believers needed to guard against suffering persecution for an error. Viret also cautioned against other kinds of seducers and impostors who professed apparent signs of holiness as followers of the gospel only in order to rob the faithful of their purses and goods.[20]

Viret's focus on moral and practical considerations conveys a lively impression of the real difficulties believers faced in deciding whether to flee persecution. Family dissensions, loss of property, the specter of poverty and even of hunger often stood in the way of their decision. Although religious emigration and exile were a conspicuous feature of the Reformation, it is also not surprising that many crypto-Protestants ignored the preaching of writers such as Viret and persisted in their religious dissimulation.

The fears that induced Protestants to dissimulate rather than emigrate also caused them to forsake their faith. In France the Huguenots had benefited by the royal edicts of toleration which punctuated the first years of the long religious civil war begun in 1562. But in August and September 1572 the terror of the massacre that began on St. Bartholomew's Eve made many French Protestants return to the Catholic church. Theodore Beza reported of his coreligionists in its aftermath that "the defection has been and continues to be incredible."[21] In Rouen, where the Huguenot community numbered more than 16,000, from 300 to 500 or more were killed in the four days of slaughter in September 1572. In the following days and weeks many of the survivors brought their children to the parish churches for rebaptism and underwent a ceremony of abjuration in the cathedral, including adoration of the host, the abhorred idolatry denounced by Calvin and all the ministers of the Reformed religion. At least 3,000 submitted to a formal act of reconciliation with the Roman church. At

[20] Ibid., pp. 19–21, 26–27, 65–70.
[21] Quoted in Philip Benedict, *Rouen during the Wars of Religion* (Cambridge: Cambridge University Press, 1981), p. 123. The rest of this paragraph is based on ibid., chap. 5, which contains a detailed account of the effects of the massacre on the Reformed church in Rouen.

the same time a considerable number chose instead to emigrate to England. Of the many abjurations, some were doubtless genuine, the effect of both disillusionment that God had abandoned their cause and of intimidation. It is just as likely, though, that some were feigned. At other times when their faith was banned French Calvinists had dissembled their beliefs by attendance at Catholic worship, so it is probable that in 1572 a certain number did the same thing by choosing apostasy over martyrdom.

Protestants in England under Mary Tudor went through an analogous experience from 1553 to 1558 after the restoration of Catholicism and revival of the heresy laws. At least 800 Protestants left the kingdom, and more than 300 suffered death as martyrs. Although a number of underground congregations came into existence, the great majority of English Protestants conformed to the restored Catholic church. *The Temporysour,* the English translation of Musculus' *Proscaerus,* was issued by a Marian exile to dissuade his fellow believers from hypocritical participation in popish rites. John Bradford, a Protestant minister burned at the stake in 1555, bitterly denounced the professors of the gospel who showed themselves untrue to God. "They pretend outwardly popery goyng to Masse with the papistes and tarying with them personallye at theyr Antichristian and idolatrous servyce: but with their harts (say they) and wyth theyr spirites they serve the Lord." Bradford denounced this plea as a "mongrel's excuse" used by weak Protestants to preserve their worldly possessions.[22]

A prominent example of submission to Catholicism was Sir William Cecil, future principal minister of Elizabeth I. Cecil conformed outwardly to preserve his political career and escape prosecution for heresy. This Protestant but worldly-wise politician even took part in the diplomatic mission that escorted Cardinal Pole back to England to preside over the kingdom's absolution and return to the Catholic fold. Perhaps he remembered the example of Naaman the Syrian, who in performance of his duty to his sovereign bowed in the temple of the idol Rimmon. Cecil's good friend, Sir Nicholas Bacon, another stalwart Protestant who became a minister of Elizabeth, likewise conformed during this dangerous time.[23]

[22] Quoted from a letter by Bradford in *Strype's Memorials of Archbishop Cranmer,* 4 vols. in 3 (Oxford, 1848–1854), appendix, 3:523.

[23] David M. Loades, *The Reign of Mary Tudor* (London: Benn, 1979), pp. 332, 335, 340, 388; Conyears Read, *Mr. Secretary Cecil and Queen Elizabeth* (London: Jonathan Cape, 1955), pp. 102–104.

The intense concern expressed by Protestant writers in the mid-sixteenth century over religious dissimulation reflected the severe ordeals Protestant minorities experienced under Catholic repression during these years. The main discussions occurred among the Calvinists and Swiss reformers because they had the closest contacts with the Protestant communities "under the cross." Among the best-known Protestant thinkers to examine the question was Peter Martyr Vermigli, the former disciple of Juan de Valdés. Vermigli renounced Catholicism in 1542 and became a noted Protestant theologian and teacher. After a stay in Strasbourg, he moved to England in 1547 during the reign of Edward VI to become Regius professor of divinity at Oxford and an influential figure in the English Reformation. Forced to return to the continent after Mary's accession, he spent most of his remaining years in Zurich, where he died in 1562. His tract to dissuade Protestants in Marian England from conforming to Catholicism was published in English in 1555.[24] Included with it was a sermon against participation in popish worship by the Zurich reformer Henry Bullinger. Much of Vermigli's treatise, together with a casuistical discussion of various questions relating to truthtelling, was later incorporated in his vast theological survey, *The Common Places*.[25] Its treatment of dissimulation and lying added another authoritative voice to the chorus of disapproval against Protestants who deceitfully submitted to Catholic idolatry.

One chapter in this work posed the question "Whether it be lawfull for Christians to dwell among Infidels," including the issue of attending idolatrous ceremonies. In replying in the negative, Vermigli aimed at effecting the greatest possible separation between followers of the gospel and Catholics. To Protestants forced to be present at popish rites the only allowable alternatives were flight or martyrdom. He designated as Nicodemites those who saw no harm in dissimulating their faith by outward conformity. Both the arguments he attributed to them and his refutation of their use of the examples of Naaman, Paul, and other scriptural instances were essentially identical with those of Calvin and other Protestant theologians.[26]

[24] *A Treatise of the Cohabitacyon of the Faithfull with the Unfaithfull* (n.p.); according to Carlos Eire, "Calvin and Nicodemism: A Reappraisal," *Sixteenth Century Journal*, 10, no. 1 (1979), this work was derived from Vermigli's commentary on the book of Judges.

[25] *Loci Communes D. Petri Martyris* (1563); *The Common Places . . . of Peter Martyr* (London, 1583).

[26] *Common Places*, pt. 2, chap. 4, pp. 309–323.

Vermigli moved to wider ground in the chapter "Deceipt or Guile" in relation to the Ninth Commandment, against bearing false witness. After reviewing classical definitions of *dolus* (deceit) and *dolus malus* (fraud) in sources such as Cicero and Roman law, he distinguished good from evil guile, the former being harmful to no one. Thus nurses and physicians use guile with babies and the sick, and David feigned madness to save himself from the Philistine king Achis (1 Samuel 21:13). Though presenting scriptural justifications for guile against enemies of God and the public weal, Vermigli held that an oath must preclude all guile. Similarly, he barred any equivocation in oaths and other promises: "iust and godlie men ought both to use simple and plaine words, and . . . so live with a good conscience."[27]

Vermigli also weighed the use of guile against idolatry and heresy. Here he took the strict position that a good intention could not justify an evil action and maintained, with Augustine, that the Old Testament did not authorize lying with a good intention. Hence in the oft-cited case of Jehu, he refused to acquit him of pernicious lying even though his purpose was to destroy the worshipers of the idol Baal (2 Kings 10:19). This example afforded Vermigli the opportunity to warn the faithful against pleading scriptural arguments to pollute themselves with idolatry by abjuration or attending mass.[28]

Touching briefly on dissimulation, Vermigli commented that it may be either good or bad, depending on whether it was intended to deceive or only to keep counsels secret. The latter kind he ascribed to David and to Christ, who sometimes dissimulated, not to lie, but to keep his identity secret so that he could fulfill his mission of suffering for mankind's salvation. This led Vermigli to the question whether good and godly men may lie. His answer followed the lines laid down in Augustine's classic treatises on lying. Like Augustine, he permitted no latitude even for helpful lies, concluding that whatever their intention they were intrinsically iniquitous and injurious to human society.[29]

Vermigli pursued the issue of Nicodemism further in a later discussion of the case of Naaman. The importance he accorded it suggests that it may have been the most frequent example quoted by the "Libertines" and the "Nicodemites of our time," who held that they need not confess their faith before persecutors because "it is enough to thinke

[27] Ibid., chap. 13, pp. 534–547.
[28] Ibid., pp. 539–540.
[29] Ibid., pp. 541–547.

well in the hart, although outwardlie, true godlinesse be dissembled." His scrutiny of the text led him to reaffirm his earlier judgment that the "cunning" and "subtle" reasons of the Nicodemites provided no justification for submitting to idolatry. By accompanying his king to bow in the idol's temple, Naaman did wrong and set a bad example, and knowing this he sought the prophet Elisha's pardon. "Howsoever we excuse his idolatry," Vermigli stated, "we cannot defend his shamefull dissimulation." In striking contrast with the compliance of Naaman, he pointed to the notable action of the German Protestant princes at Augsburg in 1548, who escorted the emperor Charles V to mass but left him at the church door.[30]

A final topic related to Nicodemism which Vermigli examined was the question of flight, which formed part of his discussion of the Christian virtue of fortitude and overcoming the power of fear for the sake of righteousness.[31] As we have seen earlier, he strongly recommended flight to his followers in Lucca. One of the compositions appended to *The Common Places* included further reflections on flight in an epistle to a friend. Here too he defended flight as licit and censured those who refused to leave the place of persecution so that they might remain comfortably at home with their wealth, "retaining still their usuall . . . dissimulation in the affaires of religion."[32] We do not know whether Vermigli's exhortations spurred many believers to quit their homes in the cause of religion. They provide additional evidence, however, of the great importance the spiritual leaders of the Reformation attached to flight and exile in appealing to the conscience of crypto-Protestants to cease their deceitful conformity to idolatrous rites.

Nicodemism was also practiced by certain Protestant sects. The fragmentation of Protestantism began almost as soon as the Reformation itself. During the 1520s Luther confronted sectarianism in the turbulent Zwickau prophets at Wittenberg and the agitation of the radical preacher Thomas Müntzer. The same years witnessed the emergence of the anabaptist movement and other groups largely independent of Luther in their inspiration. All the beliefs and communities born of the Reformation that regarded the orthodox churches, whether

[30] Ibid., pt. 3, chap. 11, pp. 263–266.
[31] Ibid., chap. 12, pp. 271–290.
[32] "An Epistle of Maister Peter Martyr to a Friende of His, Touching the Flying Awaie in Time of Persecution," ibid., p. 72.

Lutheran, Calvinist, Swiss, or Anglican, as alien to themselves constituted the heterodox, dissident, radical wing of the Reformation.
Among the latter were also the extreme religious individualists who
could not find a home in any denomination and held that no true
church existed on earth. Included within this body were of course
many tendencies and creeds. It was in particular the spiritualistic doctrines embraced by some of the sects that gave them an inner affinity
for religious dissimulation. To be sure, heterodox Christians could
embrace spiritualism without necessarily endorsing dissimulation. On
the other hand, if a sect approved the use of dissimulation, spiritualism
was likely to have provided a ground for the practice.

We have already touched on some of the spiritualistic beliefs
denounced by Calvin in his battle against Nicodemism.[33] Spiritualism,
which was sometimes also associated with libertinism, comprised a
constellation of ideas not invariably present together but of which the
following were apt to be typical: indifference to or disbelief in sacraments, dogma, and ritual; rejection of predestination and acceptance of
free will; elevation of the spiritual Christ present in believers over the
historical Christ of the New Testament; the allegorizing of scripture
in the name of the supremacy of the spirit against the letter; the
consequent conception of the inspiration of the holy spirit as a source
of religious truth far more authoritative than the deliverances of
churches and ministries; the perfection or deification of believers
through their participation in Christ's spirit or that of his prophets;
antinomianism or emancipation of the spiritual person from external
ordinances and even, for certain spiritualists, from the moral law.[34]

Lacking faith in either Catholicism or the visible churches of
Protestantism, spiritualists were persecuted by both as heretics, blas-
phemers, and unbelievers. Understandably, their devaluation of the
external and dogmatic side of religion made it easy for some of them
to attempt to evade persecution by means of dissimulation. They
would pretend conformity to the prevailing ecclesiastical order while
in fact forming a community apart whose members, enfranchised by
the spirit, secretly adhered to a heterodox creed. This was part of
Calvin's indictment in his treatise of 1545 against the spiritual libertines, whom he attacked for misusing the word *spirit*. Among the sins

[33] Above, Chapter 4.

[34] For a useful analysis of spiritualism see George H. Williams, *The Radical
Reformation* (Philadelphia: Westminster Press, 1962), and his introduction to *Spiritual and Anabaptist Writers* (Philadelphia: Westminster Press, 1957).

he attributed to them was "duplicity of heart and language."[35] He charged that they used deceit to do whatever seemed pleasing to men and conformed without scruple to the superstitions of the papists because they regarded all external things as subject to the Christian's liberty. Pierre Viret made the same accusation. According to him, the spiritualists, whom he also called libertines, held to a doctrine of lying based on Old Testament examples such as Abraham and Isaac. They considered it permissible "to lie, simulate, and dissimulate . . . and . . . abjure the whole Christian religion" in dealing with those who were not of their sect, whom they regarded as dogs undeserving of the truth.[36]

Spiritualist groupings of this kind came into being around charismatic personalities who assumed the role of prophets and whose disciples formed a clandestine religious society disguising its principles from the world under a cover of outward conformity. One of these prophets was David Joris, whose chequered career and its posthumous dénouement afford a striking illustration of the link that could exist between spiritualism and dissimulation.

A native of Delft and glass painter by occupation, Joris was one of the numerous folk caught up in the sectarian fervor of the first years of the Reformation. In 1528, because of an outrage he committed against the eucharist, he was whipped, had his tongue bored, and was sentenced to three years' banishment from Delft. He then became prominently involved in the anabaptist movement, which was gaining followers in the Low Countries. As a visionary and millenarian, he shared the apocalyptic expectation of an earthly new Jerusalem which aroused many anabaptists to a pitch of frenzy at the beginning of the 1530s. This belief culminated in the catastrophic revolt at Münster in 1534, when anabaptists seized control of the Westphalian city and tried by force to establish a millennial kingdom of the saints. The revolt and its bloody suppression caused a decisive shift in Joris' outlook. In its aftermath he became a spiritualist, rejecting the use of the

---

[35] *Contre la secte phantastique et furieuse des libertins qui se nomment spirituelz*, in *Opera*, ed. Johann Baum, Eduard Cunitz, and Eduard Reuss, 59 vols. (Brunswick, 1863–1896), 7:col. 170.

[36] *De la communication que ceus qui cognoissant la verité d'evangile ont aus ceremonies des papistes* (1547), reprinted in *Traittez divers*, pp. 229–231. The allusion to dogs is derived from Jesus' saying in Matthew 7:6: "Give not that which is holy unto dogs, neither cast ye your pearls before swine, lest they trample them under their feet, and turn again and rend you."

sword and envisaging salvation and the heavenly kingdom as a purely
inward and spiritual possession. Still convinced of the imminence of
the end of the world, he proclaimed himself the prophet of the last
age and the third David, in succession to Christ as the second. He
alone, he believed, held the key to scripture, a book sealed with seven
seals and to be opened only by the man spoken of in Revelations 2:3
who possessed the key of David.[37]

In turning to spiritualism, Joris was strongly influenced by the ideas
of Sebastian Franck, an Erasmian humanist and a mystic who was the
greatest spiritualist thinker of the time. No one went further than
Franck in negating the institutional basis of religion and identifying
Christianity exclusively with the spirit's power in the individual
believer. According to Franck, after the time of the apostles a true
church had ceased to exist, and from then on churches, ministries,
preaching, and sacraments became superfluous. Faith for him was a
purely inward illumination of the spirit governed only by the eternal,
invisible word of God. He considered Catholics, Lutherans, and
Calvinists as all equally mistaken in clinging to an external religion.
Rejecting any kind of dogmatism, he was deeply tolerant and opposed
to religious strife and violence. Christianity as he conceived it had
nothing to do with membership in visible churches. True Christians
constituted rather an invisible church of spiritual persons scattered
among heathen and unbelievers, often persecuted as heretics, and not
to be united till the end of the world.[38]

Although Franck never defended the licitness of dissimulation, his
religion of the spirit sundered from all forms of external observance
could easily lend itself to such a purpose. He did, moreover, stress the
necessity of discretion and accommodation in a corrupt world that
hated and persecuted true prophets as heretics. Thus in a letter
explaining his ideas to an anabaptist preacher, he cautioned against let-
ting his words be seen by "canaille and swine." Not only did many by

[37] For Joris' career and ideas, see Roland Bainton, *David Joris Wiedertaüfer und
Kämpfer für Toleranz in 16. Jahrhundert* (Leipzig: Heinsius Nachfolger, 1937); Alas-
tair Hamilton, *The Family of Love* (Cambridge: J. Clarke, 1981), pp. 17–23;
Herman de la Fontaine Verwey, "Trois hérésiarches dans les Pays-Bas du XVI
siècle," *Bibliothèque d'Humanisme et Renaissance,* 16, no. 1 (1954); Williams, *The
Radical Reformation,* pp. 381–386, 483–484.

[38] Bainton, *David Joris,* pp. 13–14, 30–34. The main study of Franck remains
Alfred Hegler, *Geist und Schrift bei Sebastian Franck* (Freiburg in Breisgau, 1892).
See also Rufus Jones, *Spiritual Reformers in the 16th and 17th Centuries* (London:
Macmillan, 1914), chap. 4.

untimely talk bring themselves to the gallows, he declared, but Christ forbade giving holy things to dogs, who might turn and rend the giver. Citing Paul's advice to adapt to the time, he advised that "one should speak prudently and where it fits in. For everything has its time." This was not in itself Nicodemism, but its implications clearly led in that direction.[39]

With his transition to spiritualism, Joris shifted his conception of God's kingdom from the world to the individual soul. Ascribing the highest authority to his own utterances, he taught that regeneration was a purely interior, spiritual process and that heaven and hell lay within rather than outside man. His claim to be a divinely inspired prophet attracted many anabaptists who felt disillusioned and cast adrift following the Münster revolt. Soon he and his disciples began to encounter persecution. In 1538 and 1539 his mother and more than fifty of his followers were executed in Delft. Another disciple later paid with his life for his involvement in the dissemination of Joris' principal work, *The Wonder Book*.[40] He himself became a hunted man forced to travel from place to place, seeking refuge from supporters who risked their lives on his behalf.[41]

In 1544, accompanied by his wife, eleven children, and a group of disciples, Joris left the Netherlands with an abundance of possessions and settled in Protestant Basel under the assumed name of Johann van Brugge, representing himself as a merchant who had become a refugee for the gospel. There he passed his remaining years, living affluently on contributions received from disciples, who accepted him as the messiah. Following his arrival he and the adults in his company were obliged to swear obedience to the city and to subscribe its confession of faith. He presumably did so without any scruples of conscience, since he regarded all creeds and ceremonies with the same indifference as mere externalities. In due course he was given citizenship. To all outward appearance he was a rich and respected burgher of independent private means.

[39] Sebastian Franck, *A Letter to John Campanus*, in Williams, *Spiritual and Anabaptist Writers*, p. 160. Ginzburg, *Il Nicodemismo*, chap. 5, notes the implications for dissimulation in Franck's ideas and implausibly suggests Otto Brunfels' influence.

[40] Herman de la Fontaine Verwey, "The Family of Love," *Quaerendo*, 6, no. 3 (1976), 229. Joris' *T'Wonder-boek* was published in 1542 in Deventer. Calvin denounced its extreme obscurity of language and allegorizing as a sign of deceit.

[41] See G. K. Waite, "Staying Alive: The Methods of Survival as Practiced by an Anabaptist Fugitive, David Joris," *Mennonite Quarterly Review*, 61, no. 1 (1987).

During his many years in Basel Joris continued to produce his obscure, mystical works, which he arranged to have printed in Dutch in the Netherlands. He also kept up an extensive correspondence with followers in the Netherlands, France, and Germany. To avoid discovery he sometimes sent verbal communications through emissaries and instructed his correspondents to use false names and addresses. A proponent of religious toleration, he became a friend of Sebastian Castellio, a professor of Greek in Basel and Calvin's adversary in the controversy over Servetus' execution. During Servetus' trial Joris composed a plea to the council of Swiss cities protesting his persecution, although it was probably never delivered. Under the pseudonym George Kleinberg he may also have contributed a portion to Castellio's treatise against persecution.[42]

Before Joris' death disputes arose within his family and among his disciples, some of whom had come to regard him as a hypocrite, which threatened him with exposure. Despite this danger, and notwithstanding a few suspicions by outsiders, he preserved the secret of his identity until he died in 1556, when he was buried with all religious honors in the Basel church of St. Leonard. Three years later, continuing dissension among his followers finally led to his denunciation by his son-in-law. The investigation launched by the civic magistrates established that the man they had known as Johann van Brugge was the notorious heresiarch Davis Joris. He was accused of keeping concubines and other immoralities, as well as of many blasphemous beliefs. His body was ordered exhumed and consigned to the flames for heresy along with his writings. His disciples were compelled to make a public abjuration of their errors and subscribe again to the city's confession of faith. In view of the Nicodemism they had learned from their master, their recantation and oaths could well have been another manifestation of deceitful conformity.[43]

The history of David Joris and his sect makes plain how, in addition to the motives of fear and prudence, the dualism implicit in the spiritualist divorce of spirit from letter offered ingress to a doctrine of

---

[42] Joris' letter is printed in Bainton's edition of Castellio's *Concerning Heretics* (New York: Columbia University Press, 1935), pp. 305–309; his possible contribution to the latter is discussed in ibid., pp. 10–11.

[43] Bainton, *David Joris,* contains an appendix of documents. An anonymous English tract apparently published in Basel in 1560, *David Gorge Borne in Holland, a Very Blasphemer of Our Messias Iesu Christ,* includes some curious details.

dissimulation. A more significant example of the same phenomenon appears in another spiritualist sect centered in the Low Countries, the Family of Love, which, unlike the Jorisists, attracted some distinguished minds and was more successful in preserving its clandestinity.

A native of Westphalia, Hendrik Niclaes, the founder of the Family of Love, was noted to have been precociously religious and subject to visions as a child. He was first converted to Protestantism by the teachings of Luther. Attracted by the piety of the sectarians, in 1531 he moved to Amsterdam, where he carried on a prosperous business as a merchant and associated with the anabaptists. Although his relationship to them is unclear, he probably subscribed to their belief in the imminent approach of the new Jerusalem, which reached its explosive climax in the revolt at Münster. While in Amsterdam he also began to conceive of himself as a prophet or messiah. During this period he was arrested for heresy but was released after convincing his interrogators of his unimpeachable orthodoxy. His release seems puzzling in view of his close connections with anabaptism and suggests that he may already have possessed a rationale for dissimulation.[44]

Niclaes' path to spiritualism was probably influenced by the teachings of Joris as well as of Sebastian Franck. As in the case of Joris, his evolution reflected the recoil from violence which occurred in the anabaptist movement after the traumatic events at Münster. In 1540 he had a vision instructing him to found his sect and set down God's truth in writing. A further revelation commanded him to depart from the persecution in Amsterdam and go to Emden, in East Friesland, where he settled in 1541. Here he lived for nearly twenty years, during most of the time a highly regarded merchant of unsuspected Protestant orthodoxy. Meanwhile he was secretly penning a succession of tracts and winning disciples to his sect, which he named the House or Family of Love. Though small in terms of numbers, the Familists in due course extended from Germany and the Netherlands into France and as far away as England. With the help of supporters, he also created a propaganda network for the underground distribution of his books, which were published both in Low German and in translations.

[44] Alistair Hamilton, *The Family of Love* (Cambridge: James Clarke, 1981), p. 30. Hamilton's is the most detailed modern study of the Family of Love. See also Jean D. Moss, *"Godded with God": Hendrik Niclaes and His Family of Love* (Philadelphia: American Philosophical Society, 1981); Fontaine Verwey, "The Family of Love"; Bernard Rekers, *Benito Arias Montano (1527–1598)* (London: Warburg Institute, 1972), chap. 4 and passim.

His first printer, located at a safe distance from him in Deventer, was Dirk van den Borne, who also printed Joris' *Wonder Book.* His works appeared without mention of the place of publication and were signed only with the initials "H. N." Niclaes claimed they stood for "Helie Nazarenus," Elijah the Nazarene, a prophet of God. Others interpreted them as "Homo Novus," the new Christ or messiah.

Despite Niclaes' secrecy, rumors about the Family of Love and attacks on him by Protestant ministers eventually forced him to leave Emden in 1560. Thereafter he disseminated his ideas and directed his followers from a variety of places, his movements carefully concealed. The notorious exposure of Davis Joris would have made him especially cautious. In Cologne, where he apparently spent the last ten years of his life, he left no trace of his presence.[45]

Niclaes strove to give the Family of Love a hierarchic structure of elders, bishops, and priests somewhat analogous to the Catholic system, although it is doubtful that he succeeded in developing this order very far. The members of the hierarchy, insofar as they actually existed, remained invisible and unknown. In 1573 a revolt within the sect against his egocentric domination led to a schism when his closest disciple, Hendrik van Barrefelt, broke away as a new prophet. The latter called himself "Hiel," the life of God, and won the devotion of the most important members in the Netherlands, who accepted him as their master. This offshoot or second Family of Love formed a close-knit circle that continued to hide its heretical opinions with the same methods of dissimulation and secrecy.

Familism exhibited some of the classic hallmarks of the spiritualistic type of religion. Niclaes brushed aside the literal and historical sense of scripture as a dead letter, finding its true meaning solely in the spiritual knowledge revealed to him by God. He pictured humanity as having fallen away after Christ's appearance into a corruption and formalism from which the spirit had disappeared. He proclaimed himself the prophet of the last age of time, bearing a message of regeneration to save men and lead them to the land of peace before the final judgment. The most distinctive feature of his message was its emphasis on believers' perfectionism. By experiential communion with the spirit within, Niclaes taught, men become "godded" or deified. Just as God appears in man through the spirit, so man in the same way can be unified with God. This perfectionist doctrine naturally

---

[45] Fontaine Verwey, "The Family of Love," pp. 240–241.

provoked charges of immorality. Enemies accused the Familists not only of sexual libertinism but also of holding themselves freed from sin and not bound by the moral law.

In contrast to Sebastian Franck, Niclaes assumed that only his disciples belonged to the community of the elect. He regarded his sect as the invisible church, its members an elite emancipated from outward observances. In accordance with this conception, he was completely indifferent to the split between Catholics and Protestants and treated the dogmas and ceremonies of both as irrelevant to the welfare of believers. In *The Glass of Righteousness* (ca. 1562), probably his most important work, he declared that "not in anything that is visible or feelable, nor in any . . . services or ceremonies which are observed with men's hands in contention . . . consisteth either Salvation or condemnation before God, nor can they bring vantage or damage at all unto souls."[46] He also taught that subjects ought to submit to secular authority and not use religion as a pretext for disobedience. That people should sacrifice their lives rather than conform to ceremonies seemed actually sinful to Niclaes. In a letter probably written during the reign of Mary Tudor, he tried to dissuade two young Englishwomen from martyrdom for refusal to participate in Catholic services.[47] God wanted them to live and be well, he told them, forsaking only the man of sin hidden in the heart. Thus the Familists, whose real religion lay in the teachings of their sect, were instructed to conform to all churches and profess whatever creed the state imposed.

In the Netherlands the initiates of Familism consisted of a small number of humanists, scholars, merchants, and artists who sought an inner repose and detachment from the confessional conflicts of their time. Niclaes' doctrines offered them a retreat into an interior liberty that allowed them to feign conformity to either Catholicism or Protestantism while embracing a personal faith equally indifferent to both.

A key figure in the Family of Love was the printer Christophe Plantin (1520–1589), whose affiliation with the sect was discovered

[46] Quoted from Henry Niclaes, *An Introduction to the Holy Understanding of the Glasse of Righteousness* (Cologne, 1575), chap. 16, sec. 35, in Rufus Jones, *Studies in Mystical Religion* (London: Macmillan, 1923), p. 438.

[47] This letter by Niclaes was first published in an attack on Familism by the English Protestant minister Henry Ainsworth, *An Epistle Sent unto Two Daughters of Warwick from H. N. the Oldest Father of the Familie of Love* (Amsterdam, 1608), p. 51.

only in the late nineteenth century.[48] Plantin first worked in the Paris book trade but migrated to Antwerp in 1548, possibly from fear of an impending heresy prosecution. He eventually became the greatest printer and publisher in the Netherlands, his press's emblem, the golden compasses, known throughout Europe. He had manifold relationships, personal, religious, and business, with Familism. Although how he came to meet Niclaes has never been established, the latter used his press and provided him with vital financial support during the earlier part of his career. From 1555 to 1562 he printed secretly a number of Niclaes' works, including *The Glass of Righteousness.* Through his contacts with members and sympathizers of the sect in France and elsewhere he also played a crucial role in the distribution of the prophet's writings and in other Familist affairs.

In 1562 Plantin fell into trouble for publishing a book by Calvin in contravention of the heresy edicts. Although he pleaded that his employees had printed the book without his knowledge or permission, he left the country temporarily for Paris while his property was confiscated and sold for debt. With the assistance of Niclaes, his goods were collusively purchased by two Antwerp merchants, one of whom, Cornelis van Bomberghen, was probably a Familist. Despite the fact that Bomberghen was to become known as a Calvinist, this did not preclude an affiliation with the Family of Love. The next year Plantin succeeded in clearing himself and recovered his business in a partnership he formed with Bomberghen and several of the latter's relations who also had ties with the sect.[49]

When schism divided the Familists, Plantin transferred his allegiance from Niclaes to the successor prophet Hiel, whose works he also printed. Although he remained faithful throughout his life to the spiritualist doctrines of the sect, its Nicodemism inevitably stamped his conduct with opportunism and deceit. These were reinforced by his determination to ensure the survival and success of his business in perilous times.

In 1566 the outbreak of revolt in the Netherlands inaugurated a long, terrible resistance against the policies and rule of its absentee sovereign, Philip II of Spain. Plantin, opposed to every form of fanaticism and

[48] Leon Voet, *The Golden Compasses*, 2 vols. (Amsterdam: Van Gendt, 1969), 1:21n. For Plantin's association with the Family of Love and heresy, see ibid., esp. pp. 21–30; Colin Clair, *Christopher Plantin* (London: Plantin, 1960), esp. chap. 2; Hamilton, *The Family of Love*, esp. pp. 43–48, 64–70.

[49] See Voet, *Golden Compasses*, 1:34–48.

intolerance, remained uncommitted, indifferently serving all parties according to circumstances. During the earlier period of the revolt he maintained his credit with the Spanish authorities by repeated protestations of Catholic orthodoxy and loyalty to the regime. He enjoyed the patronage of Cardinal Granvelle, Philip II's minister, and of Gabriel de Zayas, a royal secretary with whom he corresponded regularly in Spain for many years. Through these influential connections he gained the king's support for one of the greatest enterprises of contemporary scholarship, the Polyglot Bible, which Philip decided in 1568 to entrust for publication to Plantin's firm.

On the other hand Plantin also had numerous relationships with the Calvinists and rebels in the Netherlands. In the later years of the revolt he wrote poems to its leader, William of Orange; published Calvinist works and rebel tracts; and became printer to the States General, the body that temporarily replaced the Spanish government in the Netherlands. For a brief time he even removed to Leiden to serve the university, a Calvinist stronghold, as its printer.[50] Yet he lived long enough also to welcome the Spanish reconquest of Antwerp in 1585 and the restoration of Philip II's rule in the southern Netherlands by the duke of Parma, the king's governor general.

His spiritualism made it easy for Plantin to be a *politique* who placed peace above confessional loyalties and saw no reason to undergo martyrdom for a belief. The rationale of his Nicodemism was elitism, which he expressed clearly in a conversation with Hadrian Saravia, a Dutch minister, in Leiden. Plantin said that there had always been many religions hostile to each other, all of them involving simulation and dissimulation, "but they are not to be despised . . . since they are all useful to feebler minds. The common people have need of such elementary aids, since they cannot grasp the heavenly and divine in any other way. There is only one piety, which is simple and without simulation. The world has many religious people, but very few pious ones." He observed further that while ceremonies were necessary for common folk, they were superfluous to the more perfect. The latter should nevertheless use these forms and not despise them lest they offend weaker brethren who required outward worship.[51]

[50] Ibid., pp. 55–114; Hamilton, *The Family of Love*, pp. 69–70.

[51] Saravia reported these statements in letters written twenty years later, in 1608, to Archbishop Bancroft of Canterbury; the Latin text and English translation are printed in Rekers, *Benito Arias Montano*, pp. 156–157, 102–103.

Plantin's friends who were Familist disciples included the geographer Abraham Ortelius and Justus Lipsius, one of the foremost classical scholars of the age. It has been suggested that Peter Brueghel, the friend of Ortelius and greatest of the Low Countries painters of the sixteenth century, may also have been a member of the sect; but of this there is no evidence.[52] Ortelius and Lipsius, both heirs of the humanist tradition, adapted the spiritualist piety they derived from Niclaes and Hiel to their own general outlook. Repelled by denominational dogmatism and religious war, they fashioned a refuge for themselves in political quietism and inward withdrawal. As witnesses of the revolution in the Netherlands they wished only to stay clear of its passions and partisanship. Their tolerant, nondogmatic religion verged on skepticism by comparison with the orthodoxies of their day. Nicodemism, with its approval of external conformity in religious matters, was an essential feature of the attitude of noncommitment they sought to cultivate. When Ortelius contemplated the conflicts around him, he regarded the Catholics, Huguenots, and Dutch rebels as three different diseases, each wanting to dominate rather than bow beneath God's merciful hand. He strove to make himself indifferent to the blows of fortune and, according to a critical friend, valued a "safe tranquillity" beyond all else. For him Christianity consisted neither in saying nor in doing but in the inward possession of Christ.[53]

Lipsius developed a full-fledged moral and political philosophy of which dissimulation was an inseparable element. He betrayed a quintessential Nicodemism in his prudential shifts between Catholicism and Protestantism. Born a Catholic, he was educated by the Jesuits and in the Catholic university of Louvain, where he became a professor. From there he went to the Lutheran university at Jena, then back again to Louvain, then to the Calvinist university of Leiden, and finally once more to Louvain. He probably became a Familist through his friendship with Plantin. He cared nothing for creeds and rituals and, while affirming his loyalty to Christ, once said that "all religions and no religion are one and the same to me."[54] He was content to avoid trouble by external conformity.

[52] According to Charles de Tolnay, *Pierre Bruegel l'ancien*, 2 vols. (Brussels: Nouvelle Societé d'Editions, 1935), 1:9–10, Brueghel shared the libertine and tolerant religious beliefs of Plantin and Ortelius.

[53] Hamilton, *The Family of Love*, pp. 50–51, discusses Ortelius' beliefs.

[54] Quoted in Jason L. Saunders, *Justus Lipsius: The Philosophy of Renaissance Stoicism* (New York: Columbia University Press, 1955), p. 19n.

In 1584 Plantin published Lipsius' treatise on moral philosophy, *On Constancy*, which expounded a Christianized neostoicism impervious to external goods and evils.[55] Familist spiritualism, with its emphasis on inward indifference and outward conformity, blended well with this doctrine. The constancy Lipsius advocated had nothing to do with loyalty to principles. It consisted rather of an inner equilibrium to be achieved by moderation of the passions and independence of the adversities of fate or fortune. The work viewed the patriotism, pity, and suffering in response to the woes afflicting the Netherlands as delusions of the soul. While not denying social obligations, it aimed chiefly at inculcating the duty of the individual toward himself so that, having subdued the affections of the mind, he could attain tranquillity. Lipsius outlined a strongly privatistic moral code, one that could serve as a guide in stormy times for those who desired to build an inner bastion against the religious and ideological divisions of the age. For this reason his neostoic creed exerted a strong influence on contemporary intellectuals.

Lipsius' political ideas were in accord with his moral detachment and Nicodemism. As we saw earlier, his edition of Tacitus in 1574, followed by his commentary on the Roman historian in 1581, helped to launch the vogue of Tacitism, with its endorsement of dissimulation for reasons of state. His subsequent political treatise, *Six Books of Politics or Civil Doctrine*, which Plantin published in 1589, provided an influential argument in support of reason-of-state doctrines.[56] As a handbook for princes, it recommended the conventional virtues of justice, piety, and goodness. At the same time it also approved the use

---

[55] *De Constantia Duo Libri* (Antwerp, 1584); I have used the English translation of 1594, *Two Books of Constancie*, ed. Rudolf Kirk (New Brunswick, N.J.: Rutgers University Press, 1939). The revival of stoicism, to which Lipsius made a major contribution, is discussed by Saunders, *Justus Lipsius*; see also Nannerl Keohane, *Philosophy and the State in France* (Princeton: Princeton University Press, 1980), pp. 129–133; Gerhard Oestreich, *Neostoicism and the Early Modern State* (Cambridge: Cambridge University Press, 1982). Jean Jehasse, *La renaissance de critique* (Saint-Etienne: Université de Saint-Etienne, 1976), chaps. 2–5, includes an extended discussion of Lipsius' work and his religious and political attitudes which also touches on the question of his sincerity. None of these writers is aware of Lipsius' affiliation with the Family of Love.

[56] *Politicorum sive Civilis Doctrinae Sex Libri* (Antwerp, 1589). I have used the English translation of 1594, *Six Bookes of Politickes or Civil Doctrine;* for the points noted in the text, see bk. 4, chaps. 3, 4, 13, 14; bk. 6, chap. 6. Oestreich, *Neostoicism*, chap. 3, contains a good account of Lipsius' political thought.

of "mixed prudence," or deceit by rulers for public ends. It distinguished three kinds of deceit: light, middle, and great. Lipsius justified the cultivation of the first kind, which included dissimulation; he was willing to tolerate the second, which came near to vice, when profitable to the commonwealth; and he condemned only the third, consisting of pure treachery and malice, as opposed to both virtue and the laws. He contended that dissimulation was necessary in a state, agreeing with Machiavelli that a prince must be a dissembler who could play the fox as well as the lion. His political quietism led him to condemn any resistance to authority and to favor absolutist rule, which would suppress internal dissensions and maintain order and peace. For the same reason he held that only one religion should be tolerated in a kingdom and that those who publicly dissented from it should be punished. He counseled, however, that people who differed privately without manifesting their disagreement ought to be left alone and not made subject to any inquisition. He was also consistent in his preference for noncommitment, advising private individuals to avoid taking sides in a civil war.

His religious changes and conformism gained Lipsius a reputation for duplicity. Some of his contemporaries concluded that he was a hypocrite concerned solely for his own interests.[57] The Dutch minister Saravia, who knew him in Leiden, spoke disparagingly of Familists such as Lipsius and Plantin, noting that in the religious persecution in the Netherlands, "while the faithful followers of Christ were suffering all manner of affliction, men of that sort had nothing to fear. When all the pious were fleeing into exile, they remained safe in the peace and quiet of their homes."[58] Dirck Coornhert, town clerk of Harlem, another tolerant spiritualist but one who opposed the neutralism and secretiveness of the Family of Love, was no less critical. He described Lipsius as a "heathen-Machiavellian" and charged that he approved the persecution of Protestants after returning to the profession of Catholicism at Louvain. Pierre Bayle, who wrote of Lipsius a century later in his famous *Dictionary,* also stressed his inconstancy and opportunism.[59] These negative comments were an inevitable con-

---

[57] Hamilton, *The Family of Love,* pp. 101–102.

[58] Printed in Rekers, *Benito Arias Montano,* pp. 102, 157; I have slightly modified the translation.

[59] Pierre Bayle, *Historical and Critical Dictionary,* trans. Pierre Des Maizeaux, 2d ed., 5 vols. (London, 1734), s.vv. "Koornhert" (3:673, n. C), "Lipsius" (3:841–843); Oestreich, *Neostoicism,* p. 63. Although he was a profoundly tolerant

sequence of Lipsius' acceptance of the legitimacy of dissimulation. In both morals and politics, he was willing to bow to power while rationalizing his submission by an inner neutrality and detachment.

Another of Plantin's intimates affiliated with the Family of Love was the Spaniard Benito Arias Montano, a Catholic priest, Erasmian humanist, and eminent Hebraist and biblical scholar. In 1562 Arias Montano was one of the theologians sent to the Council of Trent. On his return he became a chaplain to Philip II, who esteemed him highly. Philip then named him to oversee the editorial work on the Polyglot Bible, which Plantin had been commissioned to produce under the monarch's patronage. In 1568 Arias moved to Antwerp to join a team of scholars for this purpose. There in the next few years he was secretly converted to Familism through his association with Plantin's circle.[60]

The Polyglot Bible, which was already well advanced when Arias began his labors on it, was completed in 1571 but was not well received in Spain, where there was hostility to Erasmian humanism and opposition to its methods of biblical scholarship. Conservative Spanish theologians attacked it for its departures from the Vulgate and for undue reliance on Jewish and talmudic sources. A papal commission in Rome also found many shortcomings in it. Several treatises Arias had contributed to the Polyglot's final volume of scholarly apparatus were suspected of cabalistic tendencies. Although the papal commission eventually approved the work, it did so with various reservations. In part because of his Hebraic interests and approach to the Polyglot, it has been suggested that Arias may have been a *converso* or Marrano. There appears to be no evidence, however, that he had any Jewish ancestry.[61]

---

spiritualist, Coornhert remained a Catholic and apparently never resorted to Nicodemism. Influenced by Sebastian Franck and a moderate in all things, he disbelieved in a visible church and regarded all churches as equally valid; see Olga Rinck-Wagner, *Dirck Volkertszoon Coornhert 1522–1572 mit besonder Berücksichtigung seiner politischen Tätigkeit* (1919; repr., Vaduz: Kraus, 1965); Hamilton, *The Family of Love*, pp. 102–107. His spiritualist ideas and dedication to tolerance, which led him to criticize both Calvinism and Lipsius, are further discussed by Jones, *Mystical Religion*, chap. 7; and Joseph Lecler, *Toleration and the Reformation*, 2 vols. (London: Longmans, 1960), 2:271–286.

[60] Rekers gives an account of Arias Montano's life and describes his connection with Familism in the Netherlands in *Benito Arias Montano*, chap. 4.

[61] See ibid., chap. 3, for an account of the Polyglot Bible. Marcel Bataillon, *Erasmo y España*, 2d ed. (Madrid: Fonda de Cultura Económica, 1966),

One immediate result of Arias Montano's conversion to Familism was his efforts to influence the Spanish government toward conciliation and clemency in the Netherlands. Even though he had no sympathy with the revolt, he favored respect for provincial privileges and a lessening of repression. For a time before his departure from the provinces he served as a political adviser to Don Luis de Requesens, the governor general appointed in 1573, to whom he recommended this policy. He became a devout disciple of the prophet Hiel as well as a close friend of Familists in the circle around Plantin. His Nicodemism permitted him to conform to Catholicism while secretly subscribing to the heretical doctrines of the sect.[62]

In 1576 Arias returned to Spain with the hope of devoting himself to his studies. Instead, he was ordered by Philip II to become librarian of the Escorial, the great palace-monastery the king was building in the Sierra de Guadarrama away from Madrid. Here, in the very residence of this most orthodox and intolerant of monarchs, he continued his close relationship with his Familist friends in the Netherlands. From Luis Pérez, a Marrano banker of Antwerp who belonged to the sect, he received Spanish manuscript translations of Hiel's writings which served as a vital inspiration to him. Plantin also sent him frequent letters touching on religion and dispatched books by Hiel in separate sheets. These works arrived in parcels directed in care of the royal secretary, Gabriel de Zayas, who was unaware of their contents. Arias and Plantin used a code to refer to the Familist prophet, calling him *amicus, poeta,* or simply *ille,* and terming his writings "poems" or "Gallic letters." More than once Arias warned Plantin to use caution in his letters on account of censorship.[63]

During his years at the Escorial Arias formed a nucleus of spiritualist disciples among the Hieronymite monks of the royal monastery of San Lorenzo. As he was permitted by the Inquisition to read any books

---

pp. 738–747, discusses Arias' biblical scholarship in relation to Erasmianism. Albert Sicroff, *Les controverses des statuts de "pureté de sang" en Espagne du XVe au XVIIe siècle* (Paris: Didier, 1960), pp. 269–270, reiterates the view of Américo Castro and others that Arias was a *converso* and connects this with a "Jewish ascendancy" in his approach to the Polyglot. Arias' Jewish ancestry and Marranism are convincingly denied by Angel Alcala, "Tres notas sobre Arias Montano. Marranismo, Familismo, Nicodemismo," *Cuadernos hispanoamericanos,* 296 (1975), 349–357; see also Rekers, *Benito Arias Montano,* p. 3n.

[62] Rekers, *Benito Arias Montano,* chaps. 2, 4.

[63] Ibid., pp. 33, 80, 90–91, 99.

he wished without restraint or expurgation, he was free to pursue his ideas under a cover of Catholic scholarship. He was a venerated teacher to the monks to whom he communicated his interior religion and the writings of Hiel. One of his converts was Fray José de Sigüenza, a humanist scholar and future historian of the Hieronymite order, who became a fervent spiritualist. In 1590 Arias left the Escorial to devote his remaining years to biblical and other studies. Through Sigüenza and others the influence of his spiritualism persisted in Spain for a while. By the early seventeenth century, however, it gradually faded away, as did also the Familism of the Netherlands after the passing of Plantin and his friends.[64]

In reflecting on Arias Montano's career, one is struck by its apparent puzzles and contradictions. Was he truly a hypocrite and deceiver? Was there a complete split between his inner and outer religious life? Or did he deceive himself and remain in his own eyes a faithful Catholic? And did he contrive to harmonize intellectually his Catholic conformity with his spiritualist beliefs? There seems to be no way to answer these questions. Like a number of other thinkers who resorted to dissimulation in an era of intolerance and persecution, Arias' mind and basic convictions remain an enigma that the historian cannot penetrate.

In England the Family of Love probably originated in the arrival of Dutch refugees from the persecution in the Netherlands. During the 1570s a number of Niclaes' writings, probably printed in Cologne, appeared in English. The translator of some of these was Christopher Vitel, a carpenter by trade and member of the sect, who may have traveled abroad and met Niclaes in Holland or Cologne. The small number of members of the few scattered communities of English Familists belonged in the main to a much lower social level than did the sect's adherents in the Netherlands. They consisted of traders, artisans, tenant farmers, and laborers, some of whom were illiterate. A few yeomen of Elizabeth I's guard were also reported to be Familists. Besides the spiritualism they had absorbed through Niclaes' teaching, they had picked up a mixture of anabaptist and other heresies. Thus they rejected the trinity and denied that Christ was equal with God, practiced rebaptism, and thought no one should be baptized before the age of thirty. They refused to observe the sabbath or to say "God

[64] Ibid., chap. 5.

save," affirming that all things were ruled by nature, not directly by God. They were also unwilling to bear weapons. Subscribers to a moral antinomianism derived from Niclaes' perfectionism, they maintained that whatever they did by the inspiration of the spirit could not be evil. The righteous, they believed, were without sin.[65]

When the authorities detected members of the sect they noted not only their heretical tenets but also their Nicodemism and justification of dissimulation. In 1561 two Familists were interrogated by Sir William More, a Surrey justice of the peace. According to their deposition, they went to church in conformity with the law "although inwardly they did profess the contrary." To all questions from outside their sect they declared that they were not bound to answer truly but only as best pleased their questioner. They deposed further that they "may be subtle and lie for the Holy Ghost is subtle." They admitted to the use of equivocation, having

> certain shifts . . . to answer every question that shall be of them demanded with deceiving the demandment. As for example: if one be demanded how he believeth in the Trinity, he will answer, "I am to learn of you," and so provoke the demandment to show his opinion therein, which done, he will then say, "and I do believe so," by which words he meaneth he believeth the demandment, such as he thinketh, but not that he thinketh so.[66]

Ministers of the Elizabethan church who wrote against the Family of Love invariably mentioned its members' approval of dissimulation. An anti-Familist work of 1579 adduced Niclaes' incomprehensible "dark speaking" and his supplanting of "the true and grammatical sence" of scripture by a "bastardly broode of Allegories" as proofs of his intention to deceive.[67] The Reverend John Rogers, author of another attack, claimed to be well informed about the Familists through his acquaintance with members of the Dutch refugee church who had known Niclaes, as well as from reading the latter's books and conversations with adherents of the sect. He associated Niclaes with Joris as the founder of the heresy. According to him, Familists were

[65] Moss, *"Godded with God,"* pp. 23–26 and chaps. 2–5, deals with English Familism, as does Hamilton, *The Family of Love,* chap. 6.

[66] Moss, *"Godded with God,"* app. 1, prints the text of this deposition, which also includes a statement of Familist beliefs.

[67] John Knewstub, *A Confutation of the Monstrous and Horrible Heresies Taught by H. N. and Embraced of . . . the Familie of Love* (London, 1579), pp. 5a, 85a.

unwilling to discuss their beliefs with outsiders because of fear. One of the maxims he attributed to them was "to denie before men all theire doctrine, so that they keepe the same secrete in their hearts." He noted their practice of attending church while maintaining secret conventicles forbidden by law. In Mary Tudor's reign, he declared, they "perswaded many [to go] to Masse" and added that they "do the lyke" in Flanders.[68] Another hostile account said that Niclaes had given permission to his English followers to be present at idolatrous services and to keep their consciences secret to themselves. According to this writer, they justified the concealment of their beliefs by Jesus' injunction in Matthew 7:6, "Give not that which is holy unto dogges, neither cast your pearles before swine."[69]

By 1580 the Familists had gained such notoriety that a royal proclamation was issued against them. This stated that they met "secretly in corners" and held "privy assemblies of . . . simple unlearned people" to whom they taught their heresies. Besides other wicked doctrines, it cited their belief that they might deny anything by oath or otherwise when questioned by a magistrate. Some of the sect's members who were arrested under his proclamation formally recanted their opinions, including the proposition they ascribed to Niclaes that it was lawful to lie and dissemble to those not of their religion. Given that they had held this belief, however, their recantation itself could have been simply another manifestation of dissimulation.[70]

Familism survived in England as a thin underground stream to surface once more during the mid-seventeenth-century revolution against the Stuart monarchy and established church. Further translations of Niclaes' writings appeared in the 1640s and 1650s, and Familist ideas mingled with the spiritualism and antinomianism of the kindred sects that emerged in this era of comparative religious tolerance and battle for liberty of conscience. Various sectarians such as the Ranters, who like earlier heretics were given to spurious recantations, openly expounded a spiritualistic Christianity, scandalizing orthodox Protestants with their dangerous heresies. Although Familism gained new

[68] John Rogers, *The Displaying of an Horrible Secte of Grosse and Wicked Heretiques, Naming Themselves the Familie of Love* (London, 1578), sigs. Aiiii–v, Diiii; idem, *An Answer unto a Wicked & Infamous Libel* (London, 1579), sig. Gii.

[69] William Wilkinson, *A Confutation of Certain Articles Delivered unto the Familye of Love* (London, 1579), sigs. Iiii, Siii.

[70] The proclamation and recantations are printed in Moss, *"Godded with God,"* apps. 2–4.

disciples, it failed to live down its reputation for duplicity in the eyes of its adversaries. This was one of the many sins for which it stood condemned in an examination of spiritualism written by Samuel Rutherford, a leading Scottish Presbyterian minister. Rutherford, who had a wide knowledge of spiritualist doctrines, traced their origins back to early Christian heresies. In surveying their history, he mentioned many authors, including Juan de Valdés. Like other critics, he linked Niclaes with David Joris. Against the spiritualists' rejection of externals and their insistence only on what was in the heart, he cited Calvin's indictment of Nicodemism. He also recalled from the letter to the Galatians Paul's rebuke of Peter for dissimulation. The Familists, he declared, "will esteeme any religion indifferent" and "conforme to all popish ceremonies, to Arminianisme, Popery, or what else is, or shall be by law established." In his uncompromising Calvinism, Rutherford, like all previous opponents of Nicodemism, judged spiritualism to be "a Religion for the times and the flesh."[71]

[71] *A Survey of the Spirituall Antichrist* (London, 1648), pt. 1, pp. 62, 64, 164, 169, 351. For Familism in the earlier seventeenth century and the English revolution, see Moss, *"Godded with God,"* pp. 58–63; Hamilton, *The Family of Love,* pp. 135–141; C. Hill's discussion of the Familists in *The World Turned Upside Down* (London: Maurice Temple Smith, 1972) does not mention their Nicodemism or their doctrine of dissimulation.

CHAPTER 7

Nicodemism and Catholic Recusancy
in England

With Elizabeth I's accession in England in 1558, Catholicism was once more proscribed, and Protestantism based upon a state church was reestablished as the sole legal religion. Unlike contemporary Catholic sovereigns, Elizabeth never instituted any heresy prosecutions or conducted a general inquisition into religious beliefs. Her government did, however, demand conformity to the national church by all subjects. The Act of Uniformity of 1559 decreed one form of public worship for the entire realm and made attendance at church services on Sundays and holy days compulsory on pain of a shilling fine for every absence. A rule in the prayer book whose use was imposed by this act also enjoined participation in communion three times a year. A statute of 1581 raised the fine to twenty pounds a week for four successive absences from church. Statutes of 1587 and 1593 further increased the pressure for church attendance. At the same time the Act of Supremacy of 1559 required all ecclesiastics and temporal officials to swear an oath acknowledging the queen as supreme governor of the church and in all spiritual causes. Besides these measures, a number of other penal laws ordaining additional disabilities against Catholic priests and laymen were passed in the reigns of both Elizabeth and her successor, James I.[1]

As a result of the 1559 and subsequent legislation, English Catholics suffered under the same regime of compulsory conformity that oppressed the Protestant subjects of Catholic rulers on the continent. The Catholic who refused to attend the established church was guilty

[1] Penry Williams, *The Tudor Regime* (Oxford: Clarendon Press, 1979), chap. 8, surveys the measures for the enforcement of Protestantism and conformity in Elizabeth's reign.

of the crime of recusancy. It is true that the laws against recusancy, whose execution depended to a considerable extent on local initiative, were often laxly enforced, especially during the earlier years of Elizabeth's reign. In the aftermath of Pope Pius V's famous bull of 1570 excommunicating and deposing her, however, the treatment of Catholics became much more rigorous. Beginning in the late 1570s a growing number of English missionary priests trained in seminaries abroad were sent to minister to and reclaim Catholics in England, thus adding to the government's fears and causing it to harden its policy. The statute of 1581, with its stringent penalties for recusancy, laid a very severe burden on Catholics. Throughout the last twenty-five years of Elizabeth's rule, Protestant England's conflict with the Counter-Reformation and the armed power of Spain, in addition to the danger of treason and assassination at home, made Catholics constantly suspect and subject to periodic persecution.

The recusancy laws subjected English Catholics to a permanent ordeal of conscience. Refusal to conform to the Protestant state church could bring hardship and even ruin. They could conform only by some rationalization for compliance entailing a degree of deception. The phenomenon of Nicodemism and religious dissimulation thus inevitably made its appearance. Far from being limited exclusively to Protestantism and its heterodox offshoots, Nicodemism was a no less characteristic feature of English Catholicism.[2] Its prevalence became an acute concern to Catholic ecclesiastical authorities, who sought to encourage religious resistance and stamp out the practice of conformity, which endangered the survival of the faith. There can be no doubt that the permanent compulsion exerted by the recusancy laws was one of the main reasons for the gradual decline of Catholicism in England to the status of a minority creed between the middle and the end of the sixteenth century.

During at least the first dozen years of Elizabeth's reign, most Catholics seem to have attended services of the established church.

---

[2] Historians of the English Catholics under Elizabeth and the Stuarts have failed to recognize the relationship between Catholic conformity and Nicodemism. Of recent works, Elliot Rose's *Cases of Conscience* (Cambridge: Cambridge University Press, 1975), which contains a discussion of Catholic casuistry on church attendance, does not mention Nicodemism. P. J. Holmes, *Resistance and Compromise* (Cambridge: Cambridge University Press, 1982), the best treatment of Catholic casuistry and literature on the question of conformity, refers to Nicodemism only once (p. 3).

This was due chiefly to the fact that few of the priests surviving from Mary Tudor's time, who were dwindling in number and were of course forced to minister in secret, gave a strong instruction to Catholic consciences in favor of recusancy. Church-papists, as conformists were called, went to the official church to avoid the penalties of the recusancy laws. For doing so, they found various excuses. Many chose to regard their attendance as an act of political obedience rather than one of religious adherence. Some of the prayers and scriptural readings they heard in worship would also have been used in Catholic services and might thus seem to make little religious difference.[3]

Catholic noblemen and gentlemen led the way as conformists. One of the best-known examples was Lord Montague, a Catholic peer who was permitted by the priest living in his household to attend the Anglican church provided he did so from obedience to the queen and without approving the service.[4] Sir Edward Coke, who had been Queen Elizabeth's attorney general, stated with reference to the Catholic gentry that "from the year 1 Eliz. unto 11. all Papists came to our Church and service without scruple. I myselfe have seen [Sir Thomas] Cornewallis, [Sir Henry] Beddingfield, & others at Church: so that then for the space of ten years, they made no conscience nor doubt to Communicate with us in prayer." Coke contended that the decline of this practice stemmed from the papal bull of excommunication of 1570, following which Catholics began to refuse conformity.[5] Catholic writers, who strove to minimize the influence of the bull because of the troubles it brought upon the English Catholic community, did not accept this explanation but nevertheless also admitted the earlier prevalence of conformity. In 1580 the Jesuit Robert Parsons, the fore-

---

[3] Philip Hughes, *The Reformation in England,* 3 vols. (London: Hollis & Carter, 1954), 3:247–248; Arnold O. Meyer, *England and the Catholic Church under Queen Elizabeth* (New York: Barnes & Noble, 1967), p. 30; see also John Bossy, *The English Catholic Community 1570–1850* (London: Oxford University Press, 1975), chap. 6.

[4] Hughes, *Reformation in England,* 3:248 and n. For Montague's Catholicism, see Roger Manning, *Religion and Society in Elizabethan Sussex* (Leicester: Leicester University Press, 1969), pp. 159–161; according to Manning, Montague ceased to attend Protestant services after 1589 upon being told by a later spiritual director that his conformity was sinful.

[5] Coke made this statement during the trial of the Gunpowder conspirators in 1606; *A True and Perfect Relation of the Proceedings at the Several Arraignments of the Late Most Barbarous Traitors* (London, 1606), sig. H2. Bedingfield and Cornwallis had both been officials and privy councillors in the reign of Mary Tudor.

most English Catholic controversialist, wrote that at the beginning of the queen's reign, "when the danger of this schism was not very well realized, for ten consecutive years practically all Catholics without distinction used to go to [the heretics'] churches."[6]

In the period to which Parsons referred, widespread uncertainty prevailed among Catholics as to whether their spiritual guides considered attendance at Protestant services a permissible evil or not. In 1562 the Spanish ambassador in England, Bishop de Quadra, commented on the painful perplexity of Catholics who sought his advice on the question. He observed that the case of the English Catholics was a novel one not covered by the canons against communication with heretics, since in England Catholicism was forbidden by law. While opposed to church attendance, he was reluctant to condemn those who complied with the recusancy laws, lest they be driven to desperation. The prayers, he pointed out, some of which derived from the former Catholic service, contained no false or wicked doctrines. Setting aside therefore "the sin of dissimulation" and the harm that came of a bad example, de Quadra opined that being present at the English service was not an evil in itself. His response, accordingly, was to console those who conformed by minimizing their offense, while encouraging others who had so far held firm to persist in their resistance.[7]

In adapting to their situation of enforced conformity Catholics resorted to the same evasions and subterfuges as did crypto-Protestants and the Spanish Marranos. They were the typical methods and excuses of Nicodemism. To avoid the Anglican communion service they would absent themselves from home at Easter or allege that they were out of charity with a neighbor and hence unfit to receive communion. The priest Gregory Martin, one of the first to write against conformity by Catholics, listed various devices and pretexts, all of which he deplored as mortal sins, through which "a man doth communicate with heresie, and deny his faith by many indirect and covert wayes . . . by wilful presence." They included the taking of communion with a protestation "as far as it agreeth with the word of God" and "seeming to receave although he do not"; also, "giving his name to the vicar as having received" and "conceving a new

---

[6] *Letters and Memorials of Father Robert Parsons, S.J.,* ed. Leo Hicks (London: Catholic Record Society, 1942), 58.

[7] Charles Bayne, *Anglo-Roman Relations 1558–1565* (Oxford: Clarendon Press, 1913), prints and discusses this letter, pp. 174–175, 293–295.

sense when his wordes import falshood & must needes sound consent to the hearers." Some Catholics went to church but succeeded
in avoiding taking communion. Others brought their Catholic
prayer books to read during the service. Gentlemen would take
Catholic communion at Easter in their private chapels and then say
afterward that they had received according to the Anglican rite. It
was reported of Sir Thomas Cornwallis, whom Coke described as a
conformist, that during "service tyme when others on their knees
are at praiers, he will sett contemptuously reading on a booke (most
likely some Lady psalter or portasse) which have been found in
his pue."[8]

In a letter written in 1590 to the general of the Jesuit order in
Rome, Henry Garnet, provincial of the English Jesuits, summed up
the "dissimulations" of which Catholics were guilty at an earlier time.
"Multitudes nominally Catholics," he stated, were in fact "traitors"
and "deserters" to their religion; "exterior dissimulation was not even
thought to be wrong, provided interiorly a man's faith was sound."
Catholic students in the universities pretended to be heretics, mar-
riages were celebrated by heretical rites, and the sacrilegious Protestant communion "partaken by all." Catholics held it acceptable if,
after participating in heretical services, they attended Catholic ones,
thus serving both Baal and Christ.[9]

In 1562 a petition from Catholic noblemen concerning the licitness of church attendance was forwarded to Pope Pius IV. Without
mentioning the question of communion it inquired if being present
at the English service was permissible, and cited the danger to
Catholics of imprisonment for recusancy. The pope apparently
referred the petition to the Congregation of the Inquisition. The
inquisitors delivered a negative reply. They declared that the petitioners wished to escape persecution by passing themselves off as
heretics, and quoted the words of Jesus, "whosoever shall be
ashamed of me and of my words, of him shall the son of man be

---

[8] Gregory Martin, *A Treatise of Schisme, Shewing, That Al Catholikes Ought in
Any Wise to Abstaine Altogether from Heretical Conventicles* (London, 1578), sig. Ciiii;
Bossy, *The English Catholic Community*, p. 122; Patrick McGrath, *Papists and Puri-
tans under Elizabeth I* (New York: Walker, 1967), p. 107; Bayne, *Anglo-Roman
Relations*, pp. 160–161; a portasse was a portable breviary.

[9] Quoted in Philip Caraman, *Henry Garnet 1555–1606 and the Gunpowder Plot*
(New York: Farrar, Straus & Giroux, 1964), pp. 109–110.

ashamed" (Luke 9:26). The petitioners' duty was to obey God, and this was especially necessary in the case of nobles and magnates, whose actions could occasion scandal.[10]

The subject of Catholic conformity was also referred in 1562 to a committee of theologians at the Council of Trent. It is unclear in exactly what form the question was submitted, but in any case it received only informal consideration, never being placed before the council lest the ensuing publicity lead to greater persecution of English Catholics. There are several different versions of the opinion of the fathers at Trent. According to the first published mention of the episode by Gregory Martin in 1578, it banned attendance at Protestant services as absolutely illicit. According to an account by the Jesuit Parsons, even though the Catholic church had always prohibited participation with heretics, certain English noblemen nevertheless asked the Council of Trent whether they could go to church while attending the queen, when they bore the sword of state and the like, as in the case of Naaman the Syrian. In answer the committee of theologians decided that for such a cause only, pertaining exclusively to temporal things, they might be present at the English service. According to another account, by Garnet, the committee pronounced churchgoing unlawful, "and this was occasioned for that Calvin himselfe held it not lawfull for any Protestant to be present, not only at our Masse, wherein perhaps they may say there is idolatry, but not at our Evensong, being the same with theirs."[11]

The opinion of the fathers at Trent, which definitely condemned conformity, though perhaps with a reservation for noblemen obliged to accompany the queen to church, could not have been widely known and thus had little effect at the time.[12] During the 1560s a number of Catholic clergy also attempted to combat submission to the recusancy laws. In 1566 Lawrence Vaux, a Lancashire priest, circulated a letter to Catholics warning that those who brought their children

[10] Bayne, *Anglo-Roman Relations,* pp. 164–165, 177; the petition and reply are printed in ibid., pp. 290–291, 296–297.

[11] Martin, *Treatise of Schisme,* sig. Cv; Robert Parsons, *A Brief Discours Contayning Certayne Reasons Why Catholiques Refuse to Goe to Church* (East Ham, 1580), fols. 24–24v; Garnet made this statement at his treason trial for complicity in the Gunpowder Plot; *A True Relation,* sig. X–XI; see also the account of this episode at the Council of Trent in John Pollen, *The English Catholics in the Reign of Queen Elizabeth* (London: Longmans, Green, 1920), p. 100.

[12] Holmes, *Resistance and Compromise,* p. 84.

for baptism or were present at the services or communion of the English church did not walk in a state of salvation. Neither would the pope, he said, grant any dispensation or exception for any of the laity who entangled themselves in schism by participating in the English church's sacraments or services. "He that will flatter and dissemble," wrote Vaux, "is an enemy to God," and he stressed the peril of hell to those who continued in the schism of conformity.[13]

Catholics who went to the services of the established church were considered guilty of schism, an offense defined as a reserved sin, for which only a priest endowed with special authority was able to grant absolution. One who had this authority could also convey it to others. In the 1560s, however, few priests possessed such authority. In 1567 two well-known clerics, Thomas Harding and Nicholas Sander, both exiles in Louvain, obtained authorization from the pope to absolve Englishmen who attended heretical services, provided they desisted and returned to Catholic worship exclusively. Writing to Rome, they reported that disagreement had arisen as to whether laymen could be absolved who merely attended Protestant services but refrained from communion. They accordingly sought a statement from the pope that abstention not only from communion but also from all attendance at the English church was required for absolution. Father William Allen, who in 1568 founded the Douai seminary for the training of English youth as missionary priests, was another who acquired authority to absolve for schism.[14]

Such isolated measures did little to deter Catholic submission to the recusancy laws. During the 1560s there was still no generally known, authoritative condemnation of conformity. Meanwhile, Catholics were able to persist in their dissimulation, either ignoring counsel to the contrary or persuaded that their spiritual teachers were willing to tolerate it as an unavoidable evil.

A treatise on images by Nicholas Sander, published in 1567 in Louvain, was apparently the earliest work by an English Catholic writer to denounce conformity. In his preface Sander reprehended Catholics for going to the "false congregations" of the Protestants. He criticized

[13] Hughes, *Reformation in England*, 3:249–259; Christopher Haigh, *Reformation and Resistance in Tudor Lancashire* (Cambridge: Cambridge University Press, 1975), pp. 249–250.

[14] J. J. Scarisbrick *The Reformation and the English People* (Oxford: Blackwell, 1984), p. 144; the letter of Harding and Sander is printed in Meyer, *England and the Catholic Church*, pp. 475–478.

the distinction, a commonplace of Nicodemism, between heart and body which some pleaded as a defense: "it divideth one man in twain, setting the heart in one cumpanie, and the bodie in an other as though anie man could go to church except his hart caried his bodie thither." Determined to dispel illusions, he declared that "whereas there is a rumour . . . that this going to schismatical Service is or may be wincked at, or dispensed in the Catholikes, of certaintie it is not so." He pointed to the sin of those "who by dissembling . . . theyr faith, have provoked many others to schisme and heresie," and asserted that "the key cold demeanour" of Catholics proved that God was just in punishing them with heresy when he saw that "for feare of a small temporall losse, they can be content to put in hazard their everlasting salvation."[15]

A decade later Gregory Martin, a biblical scholar and theologian, published a more sweeping condemnation of church attendance in a tract dealing with schism.[16] Though bearing the imprint of Douai, 1,250 copies of the book were actually printed on an underground press in London by William Carter. The latter was executed in 1584 for his part in its publication. Martin's work marshaled an array of arguments against conformity taken from the Bible, church fathers, and Christian history. Among scriptural texts he did not include the example of Nicodemus but gave considerable attention to the precedent of Naaman the Syrian.

Explaining why Catholics conformed, Martin declared that "who knoweth not that colde Catholikes come to Churche in England upon this false principle: We must obeye a lawe." This justification based on the duty of obedience was the specious plea of "dissembling Catholikes" who submitted to a false religion "for feare of smal dammages." No less strongly did he reject the view, also held by "many colde Catholikes," that denial of the faith was "an indifferent thynge" as long as the heart inwardly possessed true belief, even though out-

[15] *A Treatise of the Images of Christ, and of His Saints* (Louvain, 1567), sigs. Ai–ii, Aiiiia, Aiiiic.

[16] *A Treatise of Schisme;* A. C. Southern, *Elizabethan Recusant Prose 1559–1582* (London: Sands, 1950), pp. 351–352, 452–453, gives details about its secret printing. For English Catholics' writings on recusancy and other subjects, I have drawn on Southern; Peter Milward, *Religious Controversies of the Elizabethan Age* (London: Scolar Press, 1977); idem, *Religious Controversies of the Jacobean Age* (London: Scolar Press, 1978); and Antony Allison and David M. Rogers, eds., *A Catalogue of Catholic Books in English Printed Abroad or Secretly in England 1558–1640* (London: Dawson, 1968.)

wardly the mouth of necessity denied. He noted that the case of Naaman was a favorite text with "noble men that gladly would yeelde a litle to please their prince, so they might do it by example of Scripture and the authoritie of a prophet." As Martin interpreted the episode, however, Elisha did not approve of Naaman's request for permission to attend his king in the idol's temple. When the prophet bade Naaman go in peace, he meant rather that the latter should do well. Furthermore, Naaman was only newly converted from idolatry and might have fallen back had he not been allowed to perform his customary service to his master. But the permission given him was designed only for babes and young Catholics, not as strong meat for those already confirmed in the faith with an understanding to discern good from evil. The right way to adore God, said Martin, was to have no commerce with heretical temples.[17]

To the plea that the apostles permitted certain things as indifferent, including eating meats offered to idols, he objected that actions could not be indifferent in themselves if they caused scandal and injured weaker believers by inducing them to follow a bad example. He also commented on the defense that going to the heretics' prayers was only a small thing, while to forsake parents, wife, and children, was "very much," so that "if presence only will excuse the matter, it seemeth more expedient to yeelde." This argument he stigmatized as plain sin, a rationalization for betrayal condemned by the many examples of martyrs who remained steadfast in their faith.[18]

Unlike Sander and Martin, most clerical opponents of Catholic Nicodemism tempered their condemnation of conformity with a measure of realistic recognition of the hard situation in which the laity found itself.

At the college of Douai founded by William Allen, later moved to Rheims on account of the revolutionary disturbances in the Netherlands, the seminarians preparing for the English mission received instruction in casuistry to assist them in their guidance of conscience in the confessional. The casuistical manuals they studied naturally included cases of conscience posed by the recusancy laws. The teaching in these cases treated reasonable fear of the danger of death or of heavy persecution as a just or reasonable ground for occasional

---

[17] *Treatise of Schisme,* sigs. Av, Cv, Fv.
[18] Ibid., sigs. Fv, Kv1.

conformity. Accordingly, while pronouncing it sin to frequent the churches of heretics, the judgment held that a Catholic who did so from reasonable fear was not thereby excommunicated and could participate in Catholic services and the mass.

In other cases related to recusancy, composed for the seminarians by William Allen and the Jesuit Robert Parsons, a priest was allowed to admit to confession Catholics who went to the heretics' churches out of necessity. One of the justifications cited for this view was the precedent of Naaman. Generally, the Allen-Parsons cases explicitly held that "if a man cannot avoid going to church without endangering his life or his family, he may lawfully go."[19] In a letter of 1592 addressed to Catholics in England, Allen, who had been made a cardinal a few years earlier, bade priests not to teach or defend the opinion that it was lawful to communicate in Protestant services. Yet along with this instruction he also urged them to use compassion toward the laity who were occasional conformists because of fear or the need to preserve themselves and their families. Though calling the practice unlawful, he said that those who were guilty should not be dealt with harshly and should be absolved if they confessed their infirmity. Even if they repeated their offense they should not receive a more severe penance than was assigned to other sins, and perhaps even a lesser one when all circumstances were considered; "be assured," he stressed, "that the way of mercy is safer than the rigor of justice."[20]

This attitude contrasted sharply with Calvin's uncompromising severity toward the crypto-Protestants who submitted to Catholic idolatry. One explanation of the contrast lay in the difference between Calvin's moral rigorism and the more humane and flexible principles of Catholic moral theology in the direction of conscience. But another reason was that the spiritual leaders of Elizabethan Catholicism still hoped to reverse the English Reformation and restore the Catholic church to power. Hence while always insisting upon the obligation of nonconformity, they were also willing to concede a minimal accommodation to the recusancy laws if required for Catholic survival and especially for the survival of the nobles and gentlemen on whom the future of English Catholicism so greatly

[19] P. J. Holmes, ed., *Elizabethan Casuistry* (London: Catholic Record Society, 1981), pp. 20, 39, 75–76; this volume contains the text of the Douai-Rheims and Allen-Parsons cases of conscience, which date respectively from the later 1570s and early 1580s. They are discussed in idem, *Resistance and Compromise,* chap. 8.

[20] Quoted in Thomas Knox, *Douai Diaries* (London, 1878), pp. xxiii, xlvii.

depended. Indeed, the Allen-Parsons cases strongly emphasized the need for noble and wealthy Catholic families to retain their high position in the interests of the faith in order to be able to do it service after the queen's death.[21]

The same reasons probably also account for the very significant fact that in combating church attendance Catholic authorities never recommended flight in order to escape persecution. The subject of flight and exile was never discussed by Elizabethan Catholic casuists. They did not want Catholics to emigrate but to remain in England holding fast to their religion till it came into its own again.

In 1580 the first Jesuit missionaries, Robert Parsons and Edmund Campion, landed in England to pursue their hazardous work among the English Catholics. Campion was caught within a few months and executed for treason; Parsons, continually hunted by the government, was forced to return to the continent in little more than a year. An exceptionally prolific propagandist, a lively writer and hard-hitting controversialist, the exiled Parsons (1546–1610) was to play a vital political and intellectual role in the history of English Catholicism until his death.[22] No one defended the Catholic cause more effectively or forcefully on numerous topics of difference with Protestant adversaries. His career also reflected in a high degree many of the religious and political forces of the Counter-Reformation as they came to bear on English affairs. His membership in the Society of Jesus, his close relations with Rome, his connections with the Spanish monarchy, and his influence in the training and direction of the English mission priests gave his activities and outlook a broad international character. At the same time, his political strategy, which came more and more to identify Catholic interests with the power of Spain, and the opinions he put forward on various disputed questions, were also to provoke the bitter enmity of some of the English secular priests and other Catholics who disliked and distrusted the Jesuits.

As part of his underground activity during his brief time in England, Parsons made strong efforts to intensify the campaign against Catholic conformity and to remove all doubts about the unlawfulness of attending Protestant services. To that end he discussed the question

[21] Holmes, *Elizabethan Casuistry,* p. 75; see also ibid., pp. 3, 5.

[22] DNB, s.v., contains a concise account of Parsons' career. Though referred to in all histories of Elizabethan Catholicism and discussed from various perspectives in numerous monographs, Parsons' life remains one of the major desiderata of Elizabethan biography.

at a meeting in London with some priests and laymen.[23] He also addressed the problem directly in *A Brief Discours Contayning Certayne Reasons Why Catholiques Refuse to Goe to Church,* often referred to as *Reasons for Refusal.* It was published under the pseudonym John Howlet and with a false Douai imprint on a secret press Parsons had established outside London. Further editions appeared in 1599, 1601, and 1621, the two former also the product of a secret press and bearing a false Douai imprint.[24]

Parsons opened his tract with a clever dedication to the queen expressing the loyalty and obedience of Catholics and pleading for toleration on the ground that it was wrong to force conscience. At the same time, with no apparent awareness of inconsistency, he justified compulsion against heretics, because they had received the true faith and corrupted it. Most of the work, however, consisted of a set of arguments to dissuade Catholics from church attendance. Parsons declared that those who went to church knowing it to be wrong were damned; but his purpose was to address the other sort of Catholics who thought that "for some wordly respecte," such as saving their offices, dignities, and liberty, they might be present at church and who considered too scrupulous those who refused to conform. In passing he remarked that the problem was solely one of Catholics who advocated attendance, not the taking of communion or the Oath of Supremacy—"for as for swearinge, and receavinge, I thincke no Catholicke this day in Europe thincketh it lesse than damnable."[25]

He listed a number of reasons against churchgoing supported by scriptural, patristic, and historical examples: it could infect with heresy even those well grounded in religion; it caused scandal by inducing others to sin, offending the conscience of faithful Catholics and arousing the contempt of Protestants; it signified a direct denial of one's religion; it was schism and a violation of the unity of the Catholic church; it entailed dissimulation and thus treason to God and breaking of faith; it meant loss of all the benefits of the Catholic religion. Protestants themselves, he noted, set an example by being recusants in Catholic countries. As for the external constraint of the law, he refused to countenance this as an excuse, since yielding was nonetheless a voluntary act.[26]

[23] Pollen, *English Catholics*, pp. 334–336.
[24] Allison and Rogers, *Catalogue of Catholic Books*, p. 115.
[25] *A Brief Discours*, fols. 4–6.
[26] Ibid., fols. 21–22.

Parsons blamed especially the "fond" and "unwise" Catholics who preferred men's glory to God's. These were the "dissemblers" who had persuaded themselves in troubled times that they could preserve their conscience and hold their peace while still acting against conscience because what they did amiss would not be laid upon them at the day of judgment "but upon the Prince and Magistrats" who compelled them against their will. He likewise spurned the plea of those who said, "I am there in body, but I consent not . . . in harte," because all consorting with heretics' services was sin. Many, he pointed out, yielded to the blandishments of magistrates that if they conformed outwardly they might retain their consciences and be reputed good subjects. For him this excuse was nothing but "damnable dissemblinge," of which "many thousand now in England" were guilty. Another deception he condemned was "procur[ing] any other to affirme or swear for him falsely, that he hath bene at Church, received the Communion, or the like."[27]

Parsons laid particular weight on the inconsistency of Protestants in compelling Catholics to attend church against their conscience. He cited the fact that anabaptists refused to go to Lutheran churches, Lutherans to antitrinitarian assemblies, English Puritans to the established Protestant church, and Protestants in other countries to the Catholic church. Protestants therefore violated their own principles, he concluded, in forcing Catholics to dissimulate by attending church.[28]

This claim provoked a sharp rejoinder from Protestant controversialists. One churchman asserted that the prince and magistrates did not want papists to come to church as hypocrites and dissemblers but to hear and be instructed. Parsons' argument, he said, could be

> retorted upon his own necke. The Protestants [sic] recusants in other countries are not allowed by the papists . . . to alleadge their conscience for their refusal, but are eyther compelled to conforme . . . to Popery, or else are cruelly put to death. No more shoulde the pretence of conscience excuse the papists, but that they shoulde receive the same measure which they meate to others, and of ye cup which they mingled to other, be made to drink a double portion them selves.[29]

[27] Ibid., fols. 22–23v, 37–37v, 66.
[28] Ibid., fols. 52–52v.
[29] William Fulke, *A Brief Confutation of a Popish Discourse* (London, 1581), p. 56; for other replies to Parsons, see Milward, *Religious Controversies of the Elizabethan Age,* p. 52.

The sole exception Parsons admitted in his general prohibition was conformity for some known and particular temporal purpose. This was the sense in which he construed the case of Naaman. Having been permitted by Elisha to accompany his king into the idol's temple, Naaman did not act in a way that caused scandal; moreover, he was a recent proselyte and novice, "and . . . many things are tolerated with novices, which afterwards are taken away." Thus Naaman was not guilty of idolatry but had only served his king.[30] Parsons' interpretation of this crucial precedent would presumably have applied only to Catholic nobles attending the queen to church. It was thus consistent with the position on recusancy taken in the manuals of casuistry used in the training of English mission priests.

The rigorous alignment of Catholic teaching against conformity to Protestant worship was further reinforced by the annotations in the English version of the Bible made by scholars at the Douai-Rheims seminary. The Rheims translation of the New Testament, published in 1582, contained several notes referring to dissimulation in religion. On the subject of recusancy an annotation to the second epistle of John bade Catholics to avoid all consorting or conversation with heretics even in worldly affairs and pronounced any communication with them "in spiritual things . . . a great damnable sin."[31] The Douai translation of the Old Testament, which did not appear until 1609, included an extended comment on the case of Naaman. After pointing out that those "in mind and iudgement Catholiques" used Naaman as an excuse to go to Protestant services, it stressed the differences "between this mans case and ours." Naaman's presence in the idol's temple, it explained, was not seen at the time as a revolt against the true religion, nor did it cause scandal to others, who were then all infidels. The situation was quite otherwise in a Christian country where there was controversy over the true religion. In the latter circumstances, "al that . . . repaire to the same assemblies for publique service of God, are reputed to be of the same religion or els dissemblers." Whereas Naaman might have been thought disloyal had he refused to accompany his king,

> in our case, verie few do such temporal service about the king in church: and such as doe carrie the sword, scepter, or the like, are

[30] Parsons, *A Brief Discours*, fols. 63–64.
[31] *The New Testament . . . Translated out of the Latin Vulgate . . . and First Published by the English College of Rheims* (New York, 1834), p. 295.

accounted of that religion, which is there practiced, except they do manifest the contrarie, as this man did, and our men commonly do not. Yea if anie do say they are Catholiques, and yet goe to the Protestantes church, they are counted of that rank.

The annotation further contended that, unlike Naaman, the Catholics who attended Protestant services thereby gave a "distinctive signe" of their conformity, and of participation in that religion which these dissemblers knew in their conscience to be false. The conclusion it drew was that Naaman's example "doth in no sorte warrant their going to the heretical church" and that "none can goe without incurring grevous sinne, and eternal damnation."[32]

For all the weight Catholic authority exerted against church attendance, not all its clergy shared this judgment, and several priests openly challenged prevailing opinion. The most influential of these dissenters was Alban Langdale, chaplain to Lord Montague and deprived former archdeacon of Chichester. It was he who as Montague's spiritual counselor had permitted him to attend the established church. Langdale composed a concise reply to Parsons' *Brief Discourse* which Parsons reported was "secretly spread abroad in wrytten hand" and had persuaded some principal Catholics, including Lord Paget, that it was licit to go to church. It was likely, he believed, "to make greate motion coming togeather with the storme of persecution."[33]

Langdale announced his opinion in his title, "A Treatise to Prove That Attendance at the Protestant Church Was in Itself No Sin, and Therefore Might Be Lawfully Submitted to for the Purpose of Avoiding a Persecution So Intolerable at Present, and Threatening to Grow Much More So.[34] Starting with the claim that the situation of English Catholics was without precedent, he dealt with the problem from several angles. Thus he argued that the prohibition against Catholic conformity depended on human, not divine, law and could there-

[32] *The Holy Bible Faithfully Translated out of the Authentical Latin . . . by the English College of Doway* (Douai, 1609), pp. 771–772.

[33] Quoted in Southern, *Elizabethan Recusant Prose,* pp. 437, 460, which also discusses Langdale's authorship of this reply. For Langdale, see *DNB,* s.v.

[34] Langdale's tract is among the Elizabethan state papers and is noted in *Calendar of State Papers Domestic in the Reign of Queen Elizabeth 1547–1580* (London, 1856), p. 69. My account is based on Southern, *Elizabethan Recusant Prose,* pp. 142–143; and Holmes, *Resistance and Compromise,* pp. 91–93. Rose discusses it, *Cases of Conscience,* pp. 75–77, but is unaware of Langdale's authorship.

fore be justifiably broken in cases of necessity such as just fear of death, prison, or loss of goods. He denied that church attendance was a betrayal of the faith, since it was not generally regarded as "a signe distinctive" between Catholics and Protestants. Not only did "puritans" refuse to go to the established church, but Protestants themselves did not consider it "a speciall marke," because they knew that there were many Catholics ready to die for their faith who nonetheless went to church. To Langdale's mind attendance was commonly interpreted solely as a sign of the difference "betweene a true subiect and a rebbel." Moreover, Catholics who were present but neither participated in prayers nor knelt nor received communion signified their dissent as plainly as though by speech. He therefore concluded that if "the bare going be but in his owen nature a thinge indifferent," it was licit. Among biblical justifications for this position he adduced both the examples of Nicodemus, whom Christ did not reject despite his not showing himself openly, and of Naaman, who served his king in the idol's temple without mortal sin.

Another spokesman for conformity was Thomas Bell, a seminary priest who after a ten-year ministry in England converted to Protestantism in 1592. Although none of his writings in favor of church attendance has survived, his arguments may be inferred from the replies aimed against them. He too invoked the case of Naaman among his precedents and maintained that presence at church was merely a sign of obedience to the queen. He introduced a novel element in recommending that, before going to church, Catholics make a declaration that they attended not because they believed in the services or sacraments but only as a sign of their allegiance to the prince.[35]

Bell's opinions troubled other clergy and brought an answer from the provincial of the English Jesuits, Henry Garnet (1555–1606), whose anonymous *Apology against the Defence of Schisme* was secretly printed on a London press in 1593. After spending some years in exile on the continent, Garnet had returned to England from Rome in 1586 to serve in the English mission and thereafter took a leading part in the Catholic struggle. His *Apology* was the fullest, widest-ranging attack of the time on the theory and practice of Catholic Nicodemism. Together with another anonymous tract he published on the subject,

[35] See Haigh, *Reformation and Resistance,* pp. 280, 289; Holmes, *Resistance and Compromise,* pp. 95–97.

A Treatise of Christian Renunciation, also secretly printed in the same year, it was the final salvo in the Catholic battle against conformity during the Elizabethan period. The two works also shed considerable incidental light on the daily hardships and duplicitous conduct of Catholics oppressed by the recusancy laws.[36]

In the *Apology* Garnet reviewed a number of scriptural passages pleaded by proponents of conformity. One was the example of Jehu, who feigned belief in the idol Baal in order to slay its worshipers (2 Kings 10:19). Of this precedent he recalled that Jerome in his dispute with Augustine had approved of Jehu's action and used it to defend Peter's dissimulation against Paul's rebuke in Galatians 2:11–14. Garnet, however, held that Jehu was guilty of "wicked dissimulation." As to the difference between the two apostles, he noted that Augustine and most other divines had censured Peter's conduct. Nonetheless, he added the significant proviso that there were "lawfull dissimulations."[37]

He then took up the case of Naaman, arguing that the latter did only temporal service to his king and "civil reverence," not religious reverence to idols. Accordingly, he granted that a Catholic might accompany his prince to the church of a contrary religion as a lawful temporal duty. This example, he cautioned, however, was only for courtiers and could not be used to "inferre any formall presence in going to the Church with hereticks to be lawfull." Later he also stressed that those compelled as attendants to go to heretical services were conscience bound "to leave the court if they may without manifest daunger of incurring the Princes disgrace."[38]

Garnet denied that the duty of obedience to princes entailed church attendance in compliance with the law. Human ordinances contrary to God's law should not be obeyed, and, as the recusancy statutes commanded participation in a false religion, they were unlawful. He likewise denied the claim that church attendance was not a voluntary action because it proceeded from fear; only violent external coercion could deprive acts of free will. He also rejected the excuse that church attendance was done with a good intention, such as to pray Catholicly or to save families, goods, and lands. This pretext he dismissed as "most

[36] Garnet's authorship of these two works is established in Antony Allison, "The Writings of Fr. Henry Garnet, S.J. (1555–1606)," *Biographical Studies,* 1, no. 1 (1951). For his life see Caraman, *Henry Garnet.*

[37] *An Apology against the Defence of Schisme* (London, 1593), pp. 26–29.

[38] Ibid, pp. 30–32, 55.

frivolous" and a rationalization that would justify the "maintenance of all . . . wickednes."[39]

From his own knowledge Garnet gave an interesting picture of the many subterfuges Catholics used that to his mind were nothing but sinful dissimulation: devices such as making others think they went to church, saying that they had gone or would go, or going on grounds of obedience without intending a religious signification. There were also those who went "but pray not there: or pray by them selves," or who "by their own procuring or consent are put in the booke of communicants," which meant that they were listed as complying. Then there were others "such as gette license" from the archbishop of Canterbury's ecclesiastical court "to be married where they will," or who "send their children to be christened by [Protestant] ministers, or say the minister christened them." There were those as well "which are married by a Catholicke Priest with the [Protestant] communion booke . . . that it may seeme they be married conformably: [and] those which having secret Pewes or closettes looking into the Church, cause some other to go thether, that them selves may be deemed present." All who were guilty of these ruses, Garnet asserted, "have not lied to me but unto God." He would not admit that his doctrine was too scrupulous. Because the way was strait and combat inevitable between Christ and the world, "treacherous dissimulation, false worshippings, dublenesse, deceite," must be "farre from those hartes which embrace Christian verety." The only safe and easy way for Catholics, he exhorted, was to avoid all association with schism and heresy.[40]

In a later section of the *Apology* he contended that conformity was incompatible with such virtues as faith, peace, and truth. His hatred of Protestantism was as extreme as Calvin's for Catholicism. Terming Calvinism a religion "compacted of excrements," he admonished that those who took their bodies to Calvinist and heretical churches could not have their souls in the Catholic church. In denouncing dissimulation in religion as a violation of truth, he referred to Augustine's treatise on lying. He noted, however, that Augustine's strictures against lying did not apply to certain evasions by means of silence or "lawfull equivocations" in the case of Catholics examined by civil authorities. This significant qualification foreshadowed a theme that he discussed extensively in a later work.[41]

Garnet also examined the controversial topic of distinctive signs in

---

[39] Ibid, pp. 41–46.
[40] Ibid, pp. 61–65.
[41] Ibid, pp. 95–96, 112; see below, Chapter 9.

religion, which had figured in the arguments of both Langdale and Bell. The position he took was that princes had no power to ordain such signs as expressions of obedience. In his view, signs such as ceremonies could not be indifferent in their nature but were intrinsic to one's religious affiliation and identity. Attendance at heretical services was accordingly as clear a sign of heresy and schism "as the devout going of a Catholicke to Masse in a catholick congregation, hath a profession of Catholicke faith, and of Catholicke unity."[42]

The main motive for Catholics' church attendance, according to Garnet, was "the feare of being esteemed a hollow and dissemblinge subiect." Hence to discredit both priests and laity, the Catholics' adversaries charged them with Pius V's bull of 1570 against Elizabeth; indeed, Catholics were accused of being accessories to the bull only "because they are not conformable in this one action of coming to . . . divine service." Yet the bull appeared, he observed, before many Catholics then alive had been born or reached years of discretion. He himself, he claimed, had never read it, nor did he know what it said. Moreover, every Catholic in England bore the same dutiful and cordial affection to his sovereign since the bull, "as if any such thing had never come forth."[43]

Garnet's words on this delicate and vital subject appear heartfelt and sincere. Nevertheless, it is impossible to avoid the suspicion that in professing his ignorance of the papal bull, this learned and well-informed Jesuit may have been employing the "lawfull equivocation" that he had mentioned earlier and was afterward to defend at length in another treatise.

The final part of Garnet's book sought to prove from canon law and other authorities that the Catholic church had always forbidden communication with heretics. From the variety of arguments contained in its pages, the *Apology* seems to have been intended equally for both priests and laity. In contrast, Garnet's *Treatise Of Christian Renunciation* was addressed primarily to lay readers. Quoting many extracts and examples from sacred writers and history, it appealed to Catholics to take up the cross in constancy to the faith. It stressed "how often the question of going to hereticall Churches hath bene tossed in our countrey." Yet despite "the generall resolution" of many learned and reverend priests, certain private persons who had made gods of their bellies and worshiped Mammon still followed the pernicious custom

[42] Ibid, pp. 131–139.
[43] Ibid, pp. 144–145.

of frequenting heretical conventicles; even worse, they defended their wickedness and "allure their frendes and subiectes to the same iniq-uitie." Garnet connected the controversy with a certain division among the clergy. As he perceived it, the apologists for conformity ascribed the opposing doctrine to those whom they called "the young clergy," the missionary priest ordained abroad who had been sent back to England to sustain Catholicism in its travail of persecution. Garnet vigorously defended this "young clergy," to which he himself belonged, as "more wise, more learned, more vertuous than these reverend men thinke them selves" who were called old clergy.[44] Although in the end he denied any distinction between the two, his comments exposed a conflict of opinion on the vital question of con-formity between the older generation of priests from Queen Mary's days and the new generation of seminary-trained secular priests and Jesuits educated under the direct inspiration of the Counter-Reforma-tion.

As an appendage to his tract Garnet criticized the practice of attending church with a protestation. This expedient, proposed by Thomas Bell, consisted of a privately expressed disavowal of belief in the Anglican service or sacraments. The advocates of conformity who adopted it claimed that it had been allowed by Gregory Martin. There was, however, nothing in Martin's *Treatise of Schisme* authorize this device.

Garnet maintained that no protestation could excuse presence at Protestant services, which was an act of sin and schism in its own nature. He related how after the recusancy statute of 1581, Martin, then president of the English college at Rheims, had submitted the proposition of going to church with a protestation to the Sorbonne, which judged it altogether unlawful. Martin also submitted it in Rome to the distinguished canonist Cardinal Toletus, who likewise condemned it. Garnet further referred to a letter of Gregory XIII stating that because the sin of going to heretical services was the result of fear, it deserved compassion and was more easily absolved. Some Catholics had then seized on the letter to permit church attendance as a sin to be pitied and absolved or even regarded as no sin at all. Other subtle persons took the pope's opinion to mean that it was only a venial sin from which no life could be free and therefore not a cause of eternal damnation.

[44] *A Treatise of Christian Renunciation* (London, 1593), pp. 13–18.

All these views Garnet repudiated as sheer sophistries. He was willing to concede that a protestation could be licit in those instances in which presence at church did not signify compliance with a false religion, as in the case of Naaman. Otherwise, though, he held consistently that participation in heretical worship was a "greevous mortal sinne" and that the pope had said no less.[45]

Garnet's writings provide an exceptionally detailed description of Catholic Nicodemism and its rationale and methods. His concentration on the problem indicates that well into the 1590s dissimulation to escape the recusancy laws was still persistently practiced by many Catholics in England. Looking back from the end of the century, Robert Parsons also commented on the controversy waged over church attendance. It had lasted many years, he said, and the issue was consulted by learned men in Rome and Paris but never ended "untill by tyme and by practise, zeal and authority of priests comminge from the Seminaries beyond the seas and by good Catholike men at home, the matter hath bin cleared and the negative part fully established to the confusion of heresy and edification of all forrayne nations."[46]

But if the theoretical battle had been won, as Parsons thought, Catholic participation in Protestant services had not stopped. In refuting the duplicitous doctrines of the defenders of conformity, Parsons, Garnet, and other clerics deployed all the resources of Catholic casuistry and moral exhortation. Yet notwithstanding all their efforts, under the compulsion of the recusancy laws numerous Catholics evidently continued to go to church while still believing they were faithful to their religion.

There was a close and ironical resemblance between the Catholic clergy and their hated Protestant counterparts in the combat each waged with Nicodemism. On either side of the deep religious divide preachers implored and commanded believers in similar tones and with similar reasons to shun deceit and hypocritical conformity. Both stressed the themes of loyalty to Christ and the peril of damnation in dissembling one's faith. Both focused on the leading cases in the scriptures, such as Naaman, Jehu, and Paul's rebuke of Peter's dissimulation in Galatians 2:11–14. Neither party would tolerate the separation between heart and mouth, between interior belief and outward con-

[45] Ibid, pp. 150–166.
[46] "Domesticall Difficulties" (1599–1600), in *The Memoirs of Father Robert Persons, Miscellanea,* ed. John Pollen (London: Catholic Record Society, 1906), pp. 61–62.

duct, which was one of the pillars of Nicodemism. It is true that Catholic authorities granted a limited latitude for conformity on the ground of reasonable fear which Calvin himself never permitted, and that they expressed more compassion than he toward the sin of participation in a false religion. In essential respects, however, their positions were indistinguishable, being a reflection of the same religious principles and a response to the same temptation to deceit which persecution inflicted on their Christian flocks.

CHAPTER 8

Casuistry, Mental Reservation, and Dr. Navarrus

Casuistry has disappeared into the limbo of discredited sciences along with judicial astrology, phrenology, spiritualism, and other once-flourishing intellectual pursuits. Save perhaps in a few quarters of the Catholic church, it has become obsolete if not extinct as a method of dealing with moral problems. Yet the countless writings devoted to casuistry from the later Middle Ages down to the seventeenth century and beyond, as well as the exceptional intellects of the men who were its masters, are proof of the high importance it formerly possessed in the culture and religion of Europe.

The science of casuistry consists in application of the general rules of morality to concrete situations in which the particular circumstances involve conflicting duties and create doubt or confusion as to what is right or licit to do. Inescapable in moral life, situations of this sort give rise to cases of conscience which it is the casuist's function to resolve. In the Catholic church the rules the casuist applies are derived from moral theology, itself deemed a science. Within the Catholic context, the science of casuistry is also concerned with the degree of fault or sin to be assigned to the transgression of a moral rule in particular cases.

This purely nonevaluative characterization of casuistry conforms to definitions given by both Catholic and Protestant scholars.[1] Casuistry,

---

[1] See the articles "Cas de conscience" and "Casuistique" by Edmond Dublanchy in *Dictionnaire de théologie catholique,* ed. A. Vacant, E. Mangenot, and E. Amann, 18 vols. (Paris: Letouzey, 1930–1972); William Whewell, *Lectures on the History of Moral Philosophy in England* (London, 1852), pp. xxviii–xix; and Kenneth Kirk, *Conscience and Its Problems* (London: Longmans, Green, 1933), chaps. 3–4. Albert Jonsen and Stephen Toulmin, *The Abuse of Casuistry* (Berkeley:

however, has another and pejorative meaning as well. Like the ancient sophists who taught the art of persuasion and were consequently accused of showing how to make the worse case seem the better, thus giving to their name and the term *sophistry* a lastingly disparaging connotation, casuistry has been widely regarded as a species of ingenious and plausible reasoning designed to circumvent some rule of moral conduct.

Nothing contributed more to fasten this stigma upon it than Blaise Pascal's famous satire, *The Provincial Letters*. Devoutly Catholic and theologically an adherent of Jansenism, Pascal wrote as a rigid moralist to expose those of his religion who undermined Christian morality by false principles of casuistry. His particular target was the Jesuits, whom he denounced for their casuistical teaching, charging that they sanctioned a lax morality and cloaked a "human politic prudence under the pretence of divine Christian prudence." Despite the corruption it allowed, they promoted this teaching, he believed, in order to seduce and obtain control over the consciences of believers who sought their spiritual direction. While one of his chief bêtes noires was the doctrine of probabilism approved by the Jesuits, he also singled out other casuistical doctrines for condemnation, among them equivocation and mental reservation. He cast blame not only on French casuists but also on many foreign authorities, not all of them Jesuits, such as the Italian Sylvester Prierias, the Portuguese Emanuel Sa, and the Spaniards Gabriel Vazquez, Francisco Suarez, Tomás Sanchez, Luis Molina, Gregory de Valencia, Antonio Escobar y Mendoza, and Martin de Azpilcueta, who were among the most eminent casuists, canonists, and moral theologians of Catholic Europe.[2]

Some years before Pascal, another noted Jansenist controversialist, the theologian Antoine Arnauld, known as "the great Arnauld," had also published an indictment of Jesuit casuistry. His *Moral Theology of the Jesuits* (*Théologie morale des Jesuites*) directed its main fire against the Frenchman Father Bauny's *Somme des péches* but referred likewise to the

---

University of California Press, 1988), surveys the history of casuistry and attempts to rehabilitate it as a method of dealing with moral problems. According to the authors, by reason of its particularity and attention to the diversity of circumstances it is superior to the abstract universalism of modern moral philosophy. They give a definition of casuistry on p. 256.

[2] Blaise Pascal, *Les provinciales* (1656–57). I have used the translation by A. J. Krailsheimer, *The Provincial Letters* (Harmondsworth: Penguin Books, 1967), letters 6–7.

opinions propounded by Spanish doctors of the order. Along with other scandalous doctrines, Arnauld declared that "contrary to the Eighth Commandment" against bearing false witness, the Jesuits "authorize the doctrine of equivocation and mental reservation, which they have introduced, and . . . practice perfectly on all occasions."[3]

The brilliant wit and outstanding literary qualities of Pascal's satire achieved an enduring success in convincing the world of the laxity of Jesuit moral teaching.[4] Although there were many attacks upon the Jesuits from within and outside the church during the later sixteenth and seventeenth centuries and after, *The Provincial Letters* delivered a permanent blow not only to the order's reputation but to casuistry itself. In England the book was promptly issued in a translation by Henry Hammond, an Anglican clergyman, whose preface alluded to the Jesuits as patrons of "dissimulation and sycophancy."[5] Pascal's polemic could only have served to confirm the widespread English opinion that the Jesuits were untruthful and unscrupulous and the casuistry of the Catholic church little more than a system for the perversion of morals. This was a belief that went back to the struggle of Elizabeth I's government against the Counter-Reformation. As we shall see in the next chapter, the Jesuits were prominent among the missionary priests who came from abroad to inspire Catholic resistance and were also the first to introduce the doctrine of mental reservation into England and defend it against its critics. That they became objects of fear and distrust to Protestant Englishmen was thus understandable.

The pejorative conception of casuistry which dates from the late sixteenth and the seventeenth centuries has persisted ever since. Thus, the author of the article on casuistry in the great *Dictionary of Catholic Theology* (*Dictionnaire de théologie catholique*) felt obliged to respond to some nine objections leveled against it, including the accusations that it is opposed to the integrity of the Christian spirit and is fatally flawed by subtleties and chicanery. Similarly, a lengthy article in the

---

[3] Antoine Arnauld, *Théologie morale des Jesuites* (1643), in *Oeuvres*, 43 vols. (1779; repr., Brussels: Culture et Civilisation, 1964–1967), 29:74, 81.

[4] Pascal undoubtedly exaggerated and caricatured the casuists' faults; see Malcolm Hay, *The Prejudices of Pascal* (London: Neville Spearman, 1962); Jonsen and Toulmin, *Abuse of Casuistry*, chap. 12.

[5] Blaise Pascal, *Les Provinciales; or, The Mysterie of Jesuitisme, Discovered in Certain Letters* (London, 1657), quoted in Paule Jansen, *De Blaise Pascal à Henry Hammond. Les provinciales en Angleterre* (Paris: Vrin, 1954), p. 31.

same work on laxism and the opposition it encountered from Pascal
and others is at pains to distinguish laxist principles from the science
of casuistry in its proper nature.[6]

During the mid-nineteenth century another notorious controversy
involving casuistry erupted when the English writer and Protestant
clergyman Charles Kingsley accused the great Catholic apologist,
John Henry Newman, of lying and duplicity. As one of the intellectual leaders of the Oxford movement during his days as a Protestant,
Newman shocked the entire Anglican church by his conversion to
Catholicism in 1845. Though unquestionably a man of rectitude, he
had a subtle and complex mind that sometimes chose to use the principles of "economy" and "reserve" in communicating religious truths.
These principles, which resembled the methods of accommodation for
which Erasmus and the defenders of Nicodemism had praised the
apostle Paul, consisted in withholding the truth till the time was
opportune and in adapting and limiting it to the capacity of its
hearers.[7] The resulting impression of lack of candor and veracity helps
to account for Kingsley's attack. But the latter in any case was merely
a reflection of the deep-seated prejudice and suspicion of Catholic
deceitfulness harbored by English Protestants for three centuries.

Kingsley charged Newman with reliance on the teachings of the
moral theologian Alfonso Liguori (1696–1787) in connection with his
principle of "economy." The works of Liguori, who was canonized
in 1839 and later recognized by the pope as a *doctor ecclesiae,* represented the culmination of Catholic casuistry in their influence within
the church. Opposed to rigorism in the confessional, he permitted
practices that critics equated with lying and dissimulation.[8] "How can
I tell," Kingsley wrote,

> that I shall not be the dupe of some cunning equivocation, of one of
> the three kinds laid down as permissible by the blessed Alfonso de

[6] "Laxisme," in *Dictionnaire de théologie catholique;* the principal section on the
"querelle du laxisme" is by Emile Amann.

[7] Robin Selby, *The Principle of Reserve in the Writings of John Henry Cardinal
Newman* (Oxford: Oxford University Press, 1975). Though sympathetic to
Newman, Selby shows how doubts of his candor and honesty might arise.

[8] See J. I. von Döllinger and Franz Reusch, *Geschichte der Moralstreitigkeiten in
der Römisch-Katholischen Kirche seit dem 16. Jahrhundert,* 2 vols. (Nördlingen, 1889),
chap. 6; Henry Lea, *A History of Auricular Confession and Indulgences in the Latin
Church,* 3 vols. (Philadelphia, 1896), chap. 21.

Liguori and his pupils, even when confirmed by an oath, because then we do not deceive our neighbor, but allow him to decieve himself? . . . It is admissible, therefore, to use words and sentences which have a double signification, and leave the hapless hearer to take which of them he may choose.[9]

Newman replied to Kingsley's impeachment in his *Apologia pro Vita Sua,* which vindicated his reputation. Casuistry necessarily figured among the subjects he discussed, with two appendixes devoted to the principle of economy and to lying and equivocation. According to Newman, the former was founded upon Jesus' words "Cast not your pearls before swine." He explained that it meant either concealing the truth, stating it partially, or presenting it in "the nearest form possible to a learner or inquirer, when he could not possibly understand it exactly." While recognizing the abuse to which it was liable, he justified the principle and denied that he had ever misused it.[10]

Touching lying, he observed that "the theory of the subject is surrounded with considerable difficulty." In certain extreme cases he held that it would be lawful to lie, an opinion, he pointed out, that was shared by such great Protestant writers as John Milton, Jeremy Taylor, and Samuel Johnson. Moreover, almost all authors, Catholic and Protestant, "admit that when a just cause is present, there is some kind or other of verbal misleading, which is not sin." In the same connection he pointed to the difference of opinion among Catholic experts concerning equivocation and mental reservation. Here he recorded his disagreement with Liguori's approval of equivocation even when confirmed by oath, averring that on this matter he preferred other guidance. Nonetheless, he defended the casuistical practices of the Catholic church. Because moral theologians were compelled to deal with multitudes of sick and sinful souls who needed direction, they had to consider special cases. Their works were accordingly intended for the confessor, not for the preacher, and hence did not provide the best insight into Catholic doctrine. Newman compared manuals of casuistry to works on pathology which failed to show the harmony of the human frame. Suggesting

[9] Quoted in J. H. Newman, *Apologia pro Vita Sua* (1854) (London, 1892), preface, p. xiii; see also Josef Altholz, "Truth and Equivocation: Liguori's Moral Theology and Newman's *Apologia," Church History,* 44 (1975).
[10] *Apologia,* Note F, pp. 343–347.

the catechism as a better source, he cited its emphasis on the duty of veracity as evidence of the supreme importance assigned to truth in Catholic morality.[11]

Liguori's teachings in the realm of casuistry appeared near the end of a tradition that began in the early church. Even before this, Stoic philosophers had applied casuistry to morals and invented sophisticated devices to render morality easy, including means for relaxing the rules against lying and dissimulation.[12] The church fathers, however, were the earliest Christian casuists. Thus, when Cyprian, bishop of Carthage, examined in *The Lapsed* (*De Lapsis*) the conduct of believers who yielded to idolatry under persecution and assigned them penances for their sin, he was dealing with a fundamental case of conscience. Similarly, on the problems relating to dissimulation, Augustine's two classic works on lying may be described in part as major casuistical treatises.

The subsequent development of casuistry into a formal science in Christian Europe was closely connected with the history of the confessional and the sacrament of penance. During the earlier Middle Ages, clerical writers compiled numerous penitential books containing questions for sinners and lists of sins with their appropriate penances. Later, a momentous decree of the Fourth Lateran Council (1215) required that all Christians take confession at least once a year, thereby providing an important stimulus for the further evolution of casuistry. The decree stated that the priest confessor must be prudent, intelligent, and, like an experienced physician, pour wine and oil into the wounded conscience. He must take care, it said, to know the circumstances of the sin and sinner in order to understand what advice to give and the remedy to apply. It compared the confessor to a judge who has to deliver penitential judgments, and sternly prohibited him from revealing anything heard in confession. Through the confessional, casuistry was bound up with both canon law and moral theology, an association that caused it to be termed *jurisprudentia divina*.[13]

[11] Ibid.

[12] Kirk, *Conscience and Its Problems,* pp. 138–149, discusses the casuistry of the Stoics.

[13] Döllinger and Reusch, *Moralstreitigkeiten,* 1:9–10; Walter Ullmann, *The Growth of Papal Government in the Middle Ages* (London: Methuen, 1955), pp. 374–381; canon 21 of the Lateran Council on annual confession is printed in Heinrich Denziger, *Enchiridion Symbolorum,* ed. Karl Rahner, 31st ed. (Freiburg im Breisgau: Herder, 1960), p. 437. For an account of some of the main penitential

In the thirteenth century casuistical treatises began to appear in the form of *summae casuum* intended for confessors. One of the earliest and most important was the *Summa on Penance* (*Summa de Poenitentia*) of the Spanish canonist and general of the Dominican order, Raymond of Peñafort. These compilations multiplied in the following centuries, reaching fruition in such famous works as the Dominican Sylvester Prierias' *Summa of Summas on Cases of Conscience* (*Summa Summarum de Casibus Conscientiae*), also called the *Sylvestrina*, in 1514. It is probably impossible to overestimate the influence of the *summae* on the priesthood's direction of conscience and thus on the lives of believers.[14]

During the later sixteenth and the seventeenth centuries the expansion of casuistry continued, resulting in an enormous mass of manuals, commentaries, and treatises. A glance at the lists of authors, by no means complete, contained in the articles on casuistry and probabilism in the *Dictionnaire de théologie catholique* or in the third volume of Johannes von Schulte's monumental history of the literature of the canon law, shows with what momentum the literature of casuistry increased. Von Schulte's list of Spanish writers alone, most of them postmedieval, comprises 160 names and yet fails to mention such distinguished figures as Domingo de Soto, Juan Azor, and Gregory de Valencia.[15]

In this period works of casuistry proliferated with an ever-denser growth of arguments, distinctions, and hypothetical cases. In vying with one another to overthrow opinions and establish new ones, casuists multiplied rather than allayed doubts; their elaboration of cases enclosed the entire moral life of Catholics in a network of solutions. In his *Moral Solutions* (*Resolutiones morales*) the Sicilian theologian Antonio Diana dealt with about 20,000 cases and provided no less than 6,595 solutions. For such keen and subtle minds, the more diffi-

---

books, see John McNeill and Helena Gamer, *Medieval Handbooks of Penance* (New York: Columbia University Press, 1938).

[14] Johannes Dietterle, "Die *Summae Confessorum* . . . von ihren Anfängen an bis zu Silvester Prierias," 3 pts., in *Zeitschrift für Kirchengeschichte*, vols. 24, 28 (1903, 1907); Thomas Tentler, *Sin and Confession on the Eve of the Reformation* (Princeton: Princeton University Press, 1977), chap. 2; Pierre Michaud-Quantin, *Sommes des casuistique et manuals de confession au Moyen-Age (XII–XVIe siècles)* (Louvain: Editions Nauwelaerts, 1962); and Fred Broomfield's introduction to *Thomae de Chobham Summa Confessorum* (Louvain: Editions Nauwelaerts, 1963).

[15] Johannes von Schulte, *Die Geschichte der Quellen und Literatur des Canonischen Rechts von Gratian bis auf Gegenwart*, 3 vols. (Stuttgart, 1875–1880), 3:715–717.

cult, bizarre, and extreme were the cases they analyzed, the greater their satisfaction, since the better they could exercise their ingenuity.[16]

Among Protestants, casuistry was rejected as the introduction of human inventions and perversions into Christian morality. Protestant ministers offered spiritual counsel on many questions, of course, and the works of Calvin and other reformers on the moral dilemmas associated with Nicodemism were partially related to casuistry. Having abolished the sacrament of penance, however, and eliminated the entire Catholic penitential system along with the conception of a mediatorial, sin-absolving priesthood, Protestantism was forced to leave the ultimate judgment of moral questions to scripture and the individual's conscience.[17] As a result, it did not produce a large literature of casuistry. In England religious writings devoted to moral problems were plentiful, but only a small number of Protestant clergy, beginning with William Perkins in Elizabeth's reign, and including William Ames, Jeremy Taylor, and Richard Baxter, wrote systematic casuistical treatises. They were careful, however, to limit the pretensions of casuistry and, as we shall see in the next chapter, showed themselves highly critical of the kind practiced by the Catholic church.

The indictment of casuistry as a technical display of dialectical ingenuity resulting only in moral confusion and laxity adduced various doctrines as proof. The nineteenth-century scholar Henry Charles Lea, who examined the subject in his history of auricular confession, cited occult compensation as one example. According to this doctrine, a person could steal from a debtor if necessary in order to recover a debt. Lea traced its extension to many kinds of theft that were justified as the recovery of a claim, including permissibility for servants to steal from masters if they had not been paid or considered themselves underpaid. Among the teachings associated with occult compensation was the opinion of a sixteenth-century casuist that someone unable to collect a debt might steal it and afterward deny under oath that he had done so, adding the mental reservation, "illicitly." Another opinion held that a thief prosecuted for occult compensation could defend himself by perjury using mental reservation.[18]

---

[16] Thomas Deman, "Probabilisme," in *Dictionnaire de théologie catholique,* p. 491.

[17] Whewell, *Lectures,* p. xxxi.

[18] Lea, *Auricular Confession,* 2:394–397; the first of the opinions cited is attributed to Emanuel Sa, the second to Martín de Azpilcueta, Dr. Navarrus, who is discussed later in this chapter.

Probabilism, however, remains the best known of the doctrines for which casuistry incurred discredit. Coined in the seventeenth century, the term referred to the theory of those moral theologians and casuists who admitted a probable opinion as a legitimate rule of conduct even though on a disputed or doubtful point there existed an opposing opinion recognized as more probable. The doctrine of probabilism thus held that in a situation of doubt it was licit to follow a less or the least probable opinion. Connected with it was the distinction between *probabilitas intrinseca,* a probability resting on inner conviction, and *probabilitas extrinseca,* a probability dependent on the opinion of those accepted as expert or learned. Any opinion having the support of an authority was regarded as probable, even though perhaps less probable than other opinions.[19]

The problem of differing opinions in doubtful cases had been discussed in the Middle Ages by a number of scholastic thinkers, including Aquinas, and in the sixteenth century by a line of prominent theologians at the university of Salamanca, including Francisco Vitoria, Melchior Cano, and Domingo de Soto. None, however, would authorize the position that it is permissible to act in accord with a less probable opinion. In general, all of them adhered to the theories either of tutiorism or of probabiliorism, namely, that when there are conflicting opinions, the safer or more probable one is to be followed. By the late sixteenth century, however, moral theology had generated such a tangle of opinions concerning the Christian's duty to God and his fellow men that it was becoming impossible for confessors to find their way through its mazes in order to determine which were the safer or more probable. Casuists had likewise evolved opinions as interpretations of the precepts of the gospel which were replacing these precepts themselves in the guidance of the confessional. Along with these developments, casuistry was also modifying the conception of sin by ascribing much greater importance to the state of the moral agent's mind and conscience than to the nature of the act itself.

These were the general circumstances in which probabilism made its appearance. Its initiator was another Salamanca professor, the Dominican Bartolomé Medina, in a 1577 commentary on the *Prima Secundae* (part one of the second part) of Aquinas' *Summa Theologiae.* With certain qualifications he propounded the view that in cases of

---

[19] See Deman, "Probabilisme"; Döllinger and Reusch, *Moralstreitigkeiten,* chap. 1; Lea, *Auricular Confession,* chap 21.

two probable and contradictory opinions on a question, one might act on the less probable and less safe. For an opinion to be probable, it was not enough that specious reasons could be produced on its behalf or that it had defenders; it needed to be asserted by wise men and confirmed by the best arguments.[20] The doctrine thereafter went through further evolution and various refinements at the hands of many authors. Although it never lacked for opposition from rigorist theologians and at times from the papacy itself, it came to be very widely accepted in the earlier seventeenth century. Among its consequences was the additional stimulus it provided to casuistry. Once the theory became established that between two probable opinions on the sinfulness of an action, the less probable one favoring liberty from obligation might be followed and that the teaching of a single doctor sufficed to render an opinion probable, casuists had a strong reason to devise new arguments against previous views. Their inventiveness was challenged to discover plausible grounds for the probability of opinions which would accommodate penitents and those seeking guidance by mitigating or removing the sin of particular acts. Similarly, because of the multiplication of opinions and controverted questions, the inability of confessors to determine the true or more probable solution to cases of conscience made them all the more dependent on the principle of probabilism.

After Medina, the first Jesuit to defend probabilism was Gabriel Vazquez, a professor at Alcalá, in a 1597 commentary on the *Prima Secundae* of Aquinas' *Summa Theologiae*. According to Vazquez, probabilism was now the common view of the weightiest theologians of the time. At first the authorities of the Society of Jesus rejected the doctrine for its laxity. But although Jesuits were neither its founders nor by any means its sole advocates among the religious orders, they soon became most closely identified with it as its most strenuous supporters. Although it was taught in France and elsewhere, most of the moral theologians who developed it were Spanish Jesuits. Spain was not only the country of its origin, but the land where the greatest masters of casuistry were to be found.[21]

Apart from lending itself easily to abuse, what gave probabilism its

<hr/>

[20] Cf. Deman, "Probabilisme," pp. 457–468; Döllinger and Reusch, *Moralstreitigkeiten*, 1:29; Lea, *Auricular Confession*, 2:303; Kirk, *Conscience and Its Problems*, pp. 391–392.

[21] Deman, "Probabilisme," pp. 470–473; Döllinger and Reusch, *Moralstreitigkeiten*, 1:30–33; Lea, *Auricular Confession*, 2:304–305.

exceptional importance was that it served as a higher-order principle within the realm of casuistry to license the acceptability of other opinions on all aspects of moral duties. Its most remarkable feature was that it enabled people to act in any matter simply by following the opinion of an approved authority. They did not need to feel a personal conviction of the opinion's truth or rightness or even make an attempt to form their own judgment. The confessor was similarly free; and if a penitent took the laxer course based on a probable opinion, how could he be condemned? Pascal, who was apparently the first European thinker to be concerned with the theory of mathematical probability, in his *Provincial Letters* said about probabilism in morals, "I am not satisfied with probability . . . I want certainty." The concept of *probabilitas extrinseca,* however, created a separation between the mind of the moral agent and the rules on which he acted. Opinions were treated as divorced from the mind, not as beliefs to be embraced, and the consent of authorities replaced interior moral conviction.[22]

Another doctrine that contributed nearly as much as probabilism to the disrepute of casuistry was mental reservation. Associated with it was equivocation, the aim of both being to conceal or dissimulate the truth without incurring the sin of lying. Equivocation entailed the use of words or expressions with a double meaning different for the speaker than for the hearer, whereas mental reservation signified a false statement completed by an unexpressed addition in the mind which made it true. Pascal mentioned both in his *Provincial Letters.* He reported a conversation with a Jesuit who had described the difficulty of avoiding lying, "especially when one would like people to believe something untrue." To get around it, he recommended the doctrine of equivocation as "marvelously helpful" because it allowed one "to use ambiguous terms, conveying a different meaning to the hearer from that in which one understands them oneself." If no equivocal terms could be found, one could resort to what the Jesuit called "the new doctrine of mental reservation." It took the form, he explained, of swearing that one had not done something, although one had done it, by inwardly understanding that one did not do it on a certain day or before one was born or some similar circumstance retained in the

[22] Ian Hacking, *The Emergence of Probability* (Cambridge: Cambridge University Press, 1975), chaps. 7–8; Pascal, *Provincial Letters,* letter 5; Deman, "Probabilisme," pp. 467, 469; Döllinger and Reusch, *Moralstreitigkeiten,* 1:30–32, 37, 475–476; Lea, *Auricular Confession,* 2:351.

mind. By the addition of this mental reservation, not communicated to the hearer, the statement was made true and the lie avoided. According to the Jesuit, this method "is very convenient on many occasions, and is always quite legitimate when necessary or useful to health, honor, or property." Against the objection that it permitted lying and perjury, he cited the authority of the Jesuit Tomás Sanchez' *Treatise on Morality (Opus Morale)*, on the Ten Commandments.[23]

It was not to Sanchez, however, but to an even more celebrated Spanish author that the doctrine of mental reservation owed its full development. This was Martín de Azpilcueta, otherwise known as Dr. Navarrus, one of the most renowned moral theologians, jurisconsults, and casuists of his time. Now virtually forgotten, Navarrus was widely known for his many theological and canonistic writings, which were accorded great authority within the church. Born in 1492 of a noble family of Navarre, he derived his nickname from his patriotic attachment to his homeland. In 1512, when the kingdom of Navarre was conquered by Ferdinand of Aragon and annexed to Castile, Navarrus' family had allied itself with the native house of d'Albret, which had sought the assistance of France. His family's stand in behalf of the independence of Navarre probably affected his subsequent career and attitude toward the Spanish monarchy.[24]

---

[23] Pascal, *Provincial Letters,* letter 9; Tomás Sanchez, *Opus Morale in Praecepta Decalogi, sive Summum Casuum Conscientiae* (Paris, 1615). Equivocation and mental reservation *(restriction mentale)* are discussed briefly in "Mensonge," in *Dictionnaire de théologie catholique;* "Mental Reservation," in *Encyclopedia of Religion and Ethics,* ed. James Hastings, 13 vols. (New York: Charles Scribner, 1908–1927); and Lea, *Auricular Confession,* 2:401–407, who comments that mental reservation as "allowable perjury and mendacity afforded an ample field of casuistical ingenuity" (p. 401). Döllinger and Reusch deal concisely with the subject mainly in relation to the teaching of Alfonso Liguori; *Moralstreitigkeiten,* 1:443–445. Other accounts include Archibald Malloch, "Equivocation: A Circuit of Reasons," in *Familiar Colloquy. Essays . . . to Arthur Barker,* ed. Patricia Bruckmann (Ottawa: Oberon Press, 1978); idem, "Father Henry Garnet's *Treatise of Equivocation,"* *Recusant History,* 15, no. 6 (1981); Jonsen and Toulmin, *Abuse of Casuistry,* chap. 10; and J. P. Sommerville, "The 'New Art of Lying': Equivocation, Mental Reservation, and Casuistry," in *Conscience and Casuistry in Early Modern Europe,* ed. Edmund Leites (Cambridge: Cambridge University Press, 1988).

[24] On the life and works of Martín de Azpilcueta, Dr. Navarrus, see *Dictionnaire de droit canonique,* ed. R. Naz, 7 vols. (Paris: Letouzey, 1935–1965), s.v.; Mariano Arigita y Lasa, *El Doctor Navarro: Don Martín de Azpilcueta y sus obras, Navarros illustres* (Pamplona: J. Ezquerra, 1895); Emile Dunoyer, *L'Enchiridion Confessariorum de Navarro* (Pamplona: Pontificio Istituto "Angelicum," 1957); also von

Trained in civil and canon law, he was educated first at Alcalá and then at Toulouse, where he went in 1510 and later also taught. After becoming a priest, he entered the order of Augustinian canons regular in Navarre. From 1524 to 1538 he was professor at the university of Salamanca, eventually occupying the highest chair in canon law. In 1538, with the approval of Charles V, he was appointed to the same chair at Coimbra, where he was much favored by the king of Portugal, John III, and his wife.[25]

In 1549 Navarrus published a casuistical *Handbook for Confessors and Penitents (Enchiridion, sive Manuale Confessariorum et Paenitentium)*, which became his most popular work. The first Spanish version, *Manual de confesores y penitentes,* was printed in 1553. Between its first appearance and 1625, eighty-one editions of the *Enchiridion* were issued, as well as another ninety-two revisions, abridgments, and translations into Spanish, Portuguese, French, and Italian.[26]

Retiring to Spain in 1555, Navarrus was offered and declined various preferments, including membership of the Supreme Council of the Inquisition, at the invitation of its president, Don Fernando de Valdés, archbishop of Seville.[27] While his reasons for refusing this high office are unknown, it is possible that he disapproved of the Inquisition's methods, and this may perhaps also partly explain the latitude his casuistical teaching permitted to dissimulation. In any event, he soon became involved with the Holy Office in the trial of Bartolomé de Carranza, archbishop of Toledo, primate of Spain, the most famous case in the tribunal's annals and a watershed in Navarrus' own career.

Carranza was made archbishop in 1557 after serving as a valued religious adviser to Charles V and Philip II and as one of Spain's theologians at the Council of Trent. In 1559, on the basis of his previous writings and statements, he was arrested by the Inquisition on the charge of Lutheran heresy. The accusation was apparently the result of a vendetta led by Valdés, archbishop of Seville. By Philip II's command, Navarrus was appointed to act as one of Carranza's counsel. The case developed into a protracted conflict over whether the Inquisition, an organ of Spanish royal power, or the papacy had jurisdiction over the archbishop. Carranza was kept in close confine-

---

Schulte, *Die Geschichte des Canonischen Rechts,* 3:715–717; and *Operum Martini ab Azpilcueta Doct. Navarri,* 3 vols. (Rome, 1590), vol. 1.

[25] Arigita, *El Doctor Navarro,* chap. 6.

[26] See Dunoyer, *L' Enchiridion,* pt. 2.

[27] Arigita, *El Doctor Navarro,* p. 208.

ment and subjected to various indignities. The trial dragged on till 1567, when, at the insistence of Pope Pius V, who otherwise threatened Philip with excommunication, the case was transferred to Rome. There Carranza was finally condemned in 1576 for a number of errors, suspended from his see at the pope's pleasure, and sentenced to seclusion in a monastery and various penances. He died the same year.[28]

Navarrus was always convinced of Carranza's innocence. He was arrested in his own house at the Inquisition's order because he publicly stated this belief.[29] During the proceedings he sought an audience with Philip II and also submitted to him a memorial describing the injustices inflicted on the prelate. There can be little doubt that he incurred Philip's disfavor because of these exertions. A modern Spanish historian has commented on the case that "in this atmosphere of villainy there was at least one just man—Doctor Martin de Azpilcueta, known as Doctor Navarro, who sacrificed his career in Spain for the sake of defending the unfortunate archbishop faithfully and well at his trial."[30]

In 1567 Navarrus, then seventy-five, followed Carranza to Rome, although after the transfer of jurisdiction to the papacy he was no longer involved in the proceedings. He remained in Rome for the rest of his life, a decision that must surely have reflected his feelings about the archbishop's treatment by the Inquisition. In this period he became a theologian and canonist in the Apostolic Penitentiary at the behest of Cardinal Carlo Borromeo, then head of this office of the papal curia and one of the outstanding leaders of the Italian Counter-Reformation.

[28] See the accounts of Carranza's trial in Marcelino Menéndez y Pelayo, *Historia de los heterodoxos españoles,* 8 vols. (Santander: Aldus, 1946–1948), vol. 4, chap. 8; Henry Lea, *A History of the Inquisition in Spain,* 4 vols. (New York: Macmillan, 1922), 2:45–84; and, with references to Navarrus' role, Arigita, *El Doctor Navarro,* chaps. 11–13. The case is described from the papal side in Ludwig von Pastor, *The History of the Popes from the Close of the Middle Ages,* 40 vols. (London: Herder, 1891–1953), vols. 16–18 passim; J. I. Tellechea Idígoras, *El Arzobispo Carranza y su tiempo* (Madrid: Ediciones Guadarrama, 1968). Marcel Bataillon, *Erasmo y España* (Madrid: Fonda de Cultura Económica, 1979), pp. 516–522, 710–714, and passim, discusses Carranza's ideas in connection with Erasmian reform and its suppression in Spain.

[29] Von Pastor, *History of the Popes,* 16:329.

[30] Gregorio Marañon, "El proceso de Arzobispo Carranza," quoted in Henry Kamen, *The Spanish Inquisition* (New York: New American Library, 1965), p. 160; Arigita, *El Doctor Navarro,* p. 312; Navarrus' memorial to Philip II is printed in ibid., app. 10; Lea, *Auricular Confession,* 2:71, believed that Navarrus' defense of Carranza probably destroyed his career in Spain.

The Penitentiary dealt with ecclesiastical censures, marriage dispensations, and many problems connected with the sacrament of penance. Navarrus occupied this position, which enhanced the reputation of his writings throughout the church, until his death in 1586.

During his residence in Rome Navarrus enjoyed the respect and friendship of the several popes under whom he served. In 1570 Pius V would have made him a cardinal, but the project was blocked by the intervention of Philip II. On account of this episode Navarrus wrote a defense of himself in the form of an epistle to his friend the duke of Alburquerque, governor of Milan. Among the stories told of Navarrus is that Gregory XIII visited him with several cardinals and then stood for an hour conversing with him on the street outside his house.[31] The strength and originality of his character are apparent from the portrait of him in his old age by Philippe Galle, the Flemish engraver, which was printed as the frontispiece to the Roman edition of his works. The piercing gaze and sunken cheeks, great beaked nose, and jutting, determined chin give evidence of an independent, forceful personality, as well as of the lifelong intellectual labor to which he dedicated himself on behalf of the church.[32]

Navarrus' writings ranged from ascetic and liturgical works to canonistic commentaries and treatises on moral theology and casuistry. His *Enchiridion,* a handbook for confessors, was his most comprehensive survey of moral questions, including several touching on dissimulation in relation to the sacrament of penance. Ten of its chapters addressed each of the Ten Commandments. In his discussion of the Second Commandment, against taking God's name in vain, and of the Eighth, against bearing false witness, he dealt briefly with several problems of lying and dissimulation. On the question whether an oath should be taken according to the intention of the judge who administered it or of the person who swore it, he concluded that it must be according to the judge's intention if the latter was acting within his competence. But if he exceeded his competence or proceeded unlaw-

[31] Arigita, *El Doctor Navarro,* p. 404, who also prints Navarrus' defense in app. 15. The story about Gregory XIII is taken from von Schulte, *Die Geschichte des Canonischen Rechts,* 3:716.

[32] The portrait, included in the 1590 Roman edition of Navarrus' works, is reproduced in Arigita and in Bataillon, *Erasmo y España.* Navarrus' funeral monument, in the Roman church of San Antonio dei Portoghesi, includes a bust reproduced in Dunoyer, *L' Enchiridion.*

fully even if competent, or likewise if a private man extorted an oath by force or importunity, then one could swear according to one's own intention, even though the oath was false according to the intention of the person to whom it was sworn. For support of this opinion Navarrus referred to his commentary on the chapter "Humanae aures" in Gratian's *Decretum*. He also mentioned a story of the use of equivocation by Francis of Assisi, one that was often cited by casuists of the period in connection with lying. According to the story, Francis saw a man fleeing from a murderer, who then came upon the saint and demanded if his quarry had passed that way. Francis replied, "He did not pass this way," pointing toward the sleeve of his cassock, thus deceiving the murderer and saving a life while shunning a lie.[33]

In dealing with the prohibition against false witness, Navarrus followed Augustine's and Aquinas' analyses of the lie and left no doubt that *simulatio* and *hypocrisis* in either words or actions were mortal sins. He left considerable freedom, however, for the protection of secrets. In certain cases he justified not revealing a secret even when one was sworn to say what one knew. In such instances, the person questioned might answer without fear of perjury that he did not know, "mentally understanding that he did not know so as to be obliged to reveal it" *(intelligendo intra se, illud se non ita scire, ut detegere teneatur)*. On this controversial point he noted the disagreement of several authors and again cited his commentary on "Humanae aures" to reinforce his position.[34]

The treatise to which Navarrus referred, *A Commentary on the Chapter Humanae Aures, XXII. q. V, on the Truth of an Answer Expressed Partly in Speech and Partly Reserved in the Mind, and concerning the Good and Bad Art of Dissimulation*, was the one in which he expounded his doctine of mental reservation.[35] In it he discussed the passage from

---

[33] *Enchiridion*, in *Operum Martini ab Azpilcueta Doct. Navarri*, 1:99 (chap. xii, nos. 8–9). Navarrus' reference to his commentary on "Humanae aures" could not have appeared in early editions of the *Enchiridion*, since the commentary was not published until 1584 (see note 35). I have been unable to find the source of the story about St. Francis in the early lives and legends.

[34] Ibid., pp. 167–169, 283 (chap. xviii, nos. 3, 8, 61).

[35] *Commentarius in cap. Humanae Aures, XXII. qu. V. De Veritate Responsi; Partim Verbo Expresso, Partim Mente Concepti. & De Arte Bona & Mala Simulandi* (Rome, 1584). I cite the text from *D. Martini ab Azpilcueta Navarri I. U. D. Praeclarissimi Commentaria*, 3 vols. in 2 (Venice, 1588), vol. 1. In this and subsequent editions I have seen, the commentary's title differs slightly from that of the first edition and lacks the words "& De Arte Bona & Mala Simulandi." The survey of Navarrus'

Gregory the Great's *Moralia,* "Humanae aures," which Gratian had incorporated in his canon law collection, the *Decretum.* The text in Gratian stressed the distinction between heart and mouth, intention and speech, inner and outer:

The ears of men judge our words as they sound outwardly, but the divine judgment hears them as they are uttered from within. Certainly he is one that knows who explains from the words of another his will and intention; for he ought not to consider the words but rather the will and intention, because the intention should not serve the words, but the words the intention.

On this passage Navarrus built his rationale for the licitness of mental reservation and dissimulation.

In the commentary's dedication, addressed to Pope Gregory XIII, Navarrus explained that it stemmed from questions put to him about "Humanae aures" at the Jesuit College of Valladolid. After quoting the text from Gratian, he stated the *casus* or *argumentum:* a man, N., privately tells a woman, "I take you as my wife," but with no intention of doing so; when asked under oath by a judge whether he has said these words, he replies that he did not say them, mentally understanding *(subintelligendo mente)* that he did not say them "with the intention of taking the woman as his wife." Navarrus then posed three questions arising out of the case. First, was N.'s answer to the judge a lie in the presence of God? Second, even if it was licit for him to lie, did he commit perjury in the presence of God? Third, even if he neither lied nor perjured himself, did he nevertheless sin for some other reason?[36] (The type of marriage contract premised in this case, known as *de praesenti,* was based on a verbal exchange between the parties. Later in his discussion Navarrus pointed out that such an instance would now have been rare, since the Council of Trent had

---

writings in "Azpilcueta," in *Dictionnaire de droit canonique,* fails to mention the commentary on "Humanae aures" and its pivotal importance for the development of the doctrine of mental reservation. The brief treatment of mental reservation in "Mensonge," in *Dictionnaire de théologie catholique,* likewise contains no mention of Navarrus. Lea discussed the doctrine, *Auricular Confession,* 2:401–407, but was unaware of Navarrus' contribution and did not refer to his commentary on the subject. Malloch, "Equivocation," gives a concise account of Navarrus' commentary. Both Jonsen and Toulmin, *Abuse of Casuistry,* chap. 10, and Sommerville, "New Art of Lying," mention the work but do not examine its detailed arguments and conclusions.

[36] *Commentarius,* fol. 218v.

recently decreed that a matrimonial contract was not valid unless made in the presence of the parish or another priest and witnesses.[37] This point, however, did not affect the issues and conclusions in the case.)

On the first question, Navarrus declared that N. did not lie either before God or in the forum of conscience: not before God, because the divine majesty knew and understood the true sense in which the man uttered the words; not in conscience, because a lie, according to Augustine, was the signification of what is false. At this point Navarrus introduced the central argument of his entire discussion. It rested on the basic distinction, taught by all the "logicians" *(dialectici)*, between several different kinds of speech, which could be either purely mental, purely vocal, purely written, or mixed *(oratio mixta)*. Accordingly, mixed speech should be judged true or false by a consideration of all of its parts, both expressed and tacit. Thus, in the statement "God is an angel," if the first two terms were vocal and the third written or mental, the whole was false and heretical, although the vocal part was true and Catholic. Contrariwise, the entire statement "God is not an angel," in which the first three terms were vocal and the fourth mental, was true and Catholic, while its vocal part was false and heretical. By the same reasoning, the answer N. made to the judge was a mixed speech, partly vocal and partly mental, and true as a whole although the vocal part was false. And since God understood the entire speech, N. spoke the truth before God and in his conscience.

For proof of this opinion, Navarrus referred to the innumerable instances of mixed speech in scripture and secular literature. "The wicked shall not rise in the judgment" (Psalms 1:5), for example, included the mental understanding "to eternal glory"; the whole was thus true and *de fide* but the vocal or written part false and heretical. Another precedent, repeatedly cited in treatments of lying, was Christ's answer to his disciples that he did not know the day of the last judgment (Mark 13:32; Matthew 24:36). The Lord's speech would have been false, according to Navarrus, if separated from his mental understanding that he did not know it "so that it is appropriate to reveal it to them."[38]

Navarrus termed this kind of speech "amphibology" *(amphibologia)*

---

[37] Ibid., fol. 222v (q. 3, no. 4).
[38] Ibid., fols. 219–219v (q. 1, nos. 1–4).

and justified its use in a variety of situations. As further evidence of its validity, he adduced the authority of all who held that if a confessor was asked whether a penitent had confessed a certain sin to him, he might properly answer that it was not confessed, mentally understanding "so that he is bound to tell it." The mental reservation made the statement true of which the spoken part alone was false. His conclusion to the first question, therefore, was that N. did not lie to the woman in the words he spoke to her with the mental reservation that he did not say them with the intention of taking her in marriage. He further concluded that "no one who for the just sake of safety of mind or body, of piety, utility, or other necessity, or of virtue or any good action, uses amphibology in this manner either lies or commits the sin of lying."[39]

With regard to the second question, whether N. perjured himself before God, Navarrus defended the use of amphibology as an avoidance of perjury. Among other reasons he mentioned the received opinion concerning an example that figured widely in casuistical analyses of the lie. In this case a person is asked under oath if he comes from a certain town reported to be infected by the plague. Although he does come from there, he knows that it is actually free of plague. Hence he may justly respond that he does not come from this town, adding the mental reservation "which has the plague." This reply, Navarrus held, satisfied the question in the presence of God and also accorded materially with the questioner's intention, which was to bar entrance to anyone arriving from a plague-stricken place. On this ground he reaffirmed his judgment that for the sake of safety of mind, body, honor, or any virtuous act, it was permissable to use amphibology and equivocation *(verbis amphibologicis & duplicibus)*. In behalf of this position he recalled Jerome's approval of dissimulation as "useful" *(utilem)* in the example of David, who feigned madness before Achis king of Gath, an action that would have been sinful had not David done so with the mental reservation that he was not obliged to reveal his sanity publicly. He also quoted Aquinas' opinion that an accused was not bound to admit the truth to a judge proceeding unlawfully, and asserted that in such circumstances an accused who resorted to amphibology did not commit perjury. Whether to a judge, a superior, or even to a spiritual superior to whom one had sworn obedience, Navarrus maintained that a respondent might employ

[39] Ibid., fols. 219v–220 (no. 4 and conclusion).

amphibology and equivocation for just cause and that in doing so he spoke the truth before God and brought no wrong to anyone. As a corollary he observed that when an accused exercised his right not to admit the truth, he did so without "evil deceit" *(dolo malo)* or lying, but by prudence and "good deceit" *(dolum bonum)*. This last distinction undoubtedly harked back to the one Roman jurists made in the *Digest* between *dolus* or *dolus malus,* the deceit used to cheat or defraud another, and *dolus bonus,* the justified shrewdness directed against an enemy or robber. On these grounds, in Navarrus' view, when the man N. prudently used mental reservation to make his speech true, he was not guilty of perjury.[40]

Navarrus then turned to the third and last question of the commentary: whether N., even if not a liar or perjurer, nevertheless sinned for other reasons. Rather than resolving this issue, he contented himself with pointing out that while he had proved that N. was not guilty of lying or perjury, the latter might have sinned in other ways, such as by deceit and cunning, which were vices contrary to true prudence, or by lust in copulating with a woman not his lawful wife, contrary to the natural and divine law against adultery in the Decalogue.[41]

After distinguishing good from evil deceit in various problems related to promises and contracts of marriage, Navarrus summed up with fourteen conclusions based on his discussion of all three questions. First, he claimed to have shown a "new method" *(novus modus)* of excusing the most truthful patriarchs of the Old Testament from the charge of lying. At this point he reviewed the familiar biblical precedents, discussed by Augustine and so many others, of Abraham's statement that Sarah was not his wife and similar apparently false speeches by Jacob, Isaac, and Joseph. In each case, according to Navarrus, a mental reservation made their statements true. Thus, when Abraham denied that Sarah was his wife, his saying could be excused by his having added the mental reservation for just cause that she was not his wife "so that he is bound to say so publicly."[42]

Navarrus' second conclusion stated that there existed a double art of

[40] Ibid., fols. 220v–222 (q. 2, nos. 9–10, 12, 15); for Jerome's endorsement of "utilem simulationem," incorporated by Gratian in the *Decretum,* from which Navarrus cites it, and Aquinas' opinion, see above, Chapter 2; for the distinction in the *Digest* between *dolus bonus* and *dolus malus,* see Adolf Berger, *Encyclopedic Dictionary of Roman Law* (Philadelphia: American Philosophical Society, 1953), s.v.

[41] *Commentarius,* fols. 222v–223 (q. 3, nos. 1–2, 6).

[42] Ibid., fols. 223–223v (no. 7).

simulation and dissimulation. One was the bad kind lacking just cause, which did not care whether it lied in words or in actions. The other art was the good kind and also what Jerome called useful. Entailing no lie, it was practiced solely for just cause and without evil deceit or vulpine cunning. Those who used the bad art were guilty of sin. Those who "prudently and for just cause" said or did something that "separately signifies a falsehood but is made true by a mental understanding, do not lie and use good prudence without evil deceit or cunning."[43]

From this Navarrus drew the further conclusion that people erred who either praised or condemned all simulation and dissimulation. Only those who practiced the bad art were to be condemned; those who practiced the useful art deserved praise. And it followed as well that all who simulated or dissimulated without just cause sinned venially, and that they sinned mortally if they did harm thereby to their neighbor.[44]

The next three conclusions affirmed the licitness of mental reservation and of answering according to one's own intention rather than that of the interrogator in a variety of circumstances. All presupposed a respondent questioned unjustly by a judge or by someone with an evil intention instead of the intention he ought to have.

In his remaining comments Navarrus moved to even wider ground. By means of this doctrine, he claimed, "we can avoid innumerable sins negligently committed in saying something without a mental reservation that joined with it would be true." Thus, if asked whether one had money to lend, or a certain book, or news, one could reply, "I don't have it" or I don't know," escaping sin by mentally understanding "so that I am obliged to lend or give or tell it."[45]

Then applying his doctrine to politics, he observed that "a certain monarch" whom fame reported as never lying and contenting all who spoke and treated with him even in great affairs, was one who made use of this "good art." With its help this king returned pleasing replies, licitly saying what was false but rendered true by a mental understanding. This was more easily done, Navarrus added, by monarchs who acknowledged no superior and were less obliged to make answer to others. To excel in this art, he also pointed out, it was

43 Ibid., fol. 223v (no. 8).
44 Ibid. (no. 9).
45 Ibid. (no. 13).

necessary to be serene and in control of one's passions, reserved and of few words, as was the ruler he had mentioned who was such a master of it. He then mentioned "another great monarch" who, because of a "secret flaw" in his son and heir, withdrew him from the study of letters, saying that he did not want his son skilled in any Latin save the apothegm "He who does not know how to dissimulate does not know how to rule" *(Qui nescit dissimulare nescit regnare)*. Navarrus added that in an opinion he had once given at the command of a great prince who hated all dissimulators, he had explained that this apothegm of the aforementioned monarch should be understood as signifying "the good art of simulation and dissimulation," the kind Jerome called useful, which was free from lying when used for just cause, and not the wicked kind employed without just cause consisting of base deceit, vulpine cunning, and lies.[46]

Whom did Navarrus have in mind in these veiled examples connecting his justification of mental reservation with the kindred doctrine of reason-of-state? While we cannot be sure, the characteristics he ascribed to the unnamed ruler in the first allusion seem to point strongly to Philip II. The second allusion derived from a well-known story told of Louis XI of France, one apparently traceable to the latter's minister, the historian Philippe de Commines. The king was reported to have made this statement concerning dissimulation in connection with the education of his son, the future Charles VIII. The identity of the third prince, to whom Navarrus said he explained the true meaning of the apothegm in favor of dissimulation, I have been unable to guess, unless it is perhaps the king of Portugal, whom he had also served.[47]

After this remarkable application of mental reservation to politics, Navarrus devoted his two final conclusions to the dissimulation of

[46] Ibid., fol. 224 (nos. 11–12).

[47] Arigita, *El Doctor Navarro*, p. 260, also suggests that Navarrus referred to Philip II in his example of the monarch who used "good dissimulation." Louis XI's citation of the maxim *Qui nescit dissimulare . . .* was mentioned by many Spanish theorists of reason-of-state in the sixteenth and seventeenth centuries; see J. A. Fernández-Santamaria, *Reason of State and Statecraft in Spanish Political Thought, 1595–1640* (Lanham, Md.: University Press of America, 1983), pp. 97, 118, 125, 132. I have been unable to find this story about Louis XI in Commines's *Memoires* or to discover a classical origin for the maxim. It is cited as a medieval proverb by Hans Walther, *Lateinische Sprichwörter und Sentenzen des Mittelalters in alphabetischer Anordnung*, 6 vols. (Vandenhoeck & Ruprecht: Göttingen, 1963–1967), vol. 4, no. 24329.

religious belief. Here he rejected any inference that a Catholic could use mental reservation to dissimulate his faith or to simulate being a heretic. In explanation, he stated that while mental reservation might be used for just cause without lying or perjury, one who adopted it might notwithstanding be guilty of many other sins, since it could be applied to ends and amid circumstances that were mortally evil. Such was the case, he declared, of a Catholic who pretended to be a heretic or infidel. Hence a Catholic could not dissimulate his faith and was obliged to confess it whenever the honor of God required it, as well as for the confirmation of the faith of his neighbor and to avoid scandalizing others. Navarrus did concede that a Catholic might conceal his faith if he could do so without overthrowing the honor of God and injuring the faith of others. Nevertheless, a Catholic interrogated about his religion sinned mortally if he replied that he was not a Catholic or denied his faith in any tacit way.[48]

With these dicta Navarrus reached the end of his commentary, which closed with a submission of all his opinions to the highest judgment of the supreme pontiff and sole vicar of Christ, the pope.

It is impossible to guess Navarrus' reasons for publishing his commentary on "Humanae aures." Although its point of departure was a case of matrimonial contract, it covered many other topics and approved the resort to mental reservation and equivocation over an indefinitely broad area. From one angle it exemplified a humane flexibility in its concern to protect the rights of persons under unjust questioning. From another angle, however, it constituted a striking instance of the effectiveness with which casuistry could produce a sanction for practices that were inherently deceitful even though they were alleged not to violate the moral ban against lying. In his justification of mental reservation, Navarrus was apparently most preoccupied with its use in legal proceedings in order to permit accused and other parties to defend themselves against unlawful and invasive interrogation. Whether this could in any way have reflected his attitude toward the Inquisition's procedure we can only wonder. Generally speaking, he laid down a basic distinction between good and bad dissimulation. Within the limits of just cause, which served throughout as his criterion, he also commended mental reservation in the affairs of common life. He extended it likewise to politics, on which his teaching over-

[48] *Commentarius*, fol. 224 (q. 3, nos. 13–14).

lapped with the idea of reason-of-state. To the question of dissimulation in religion he paid only slight attention. English Jesuits, however, were shortly to devote extensive consideration to its legitimacy
in this domain as well. On account of the Jesuits' close association
with it, the doctrine of mental reservation presently became the subject of widespread controversy in England, with reverberations on the
continent because of the hostility there toward the Jesuits.

Navarrus' commentary did not include a formal analysis of the lie.
Nevertheless, it clearly assumed as its primary definition that the lie
was an enunciation contrary to the speaker's mind rather than a false
statement made with the intention to deceive. Augustine, though
including both conceptions, propounded the latter as his formal definition. Peter Lombard's *Sentences* likewise incorporated the two for-
mulations. Aquinas, although he retained Augustine's definition,
highlighted the alternative one in characterizing speech against one's
mind as the formal essence of the lie. It is this apparently innocuous
conception that informed Navarrus' defense of mental reservation; for
when the lie was conceived simply as speech not in accord with the
speaker's mind, the questioner or interlocutor seemed either to disap-
pear or to become completely irrelevant. All that counted in Navarrus'
view was the conformity of speech, including the portion not
expressed, to the meaning in the speaker's mind. That this meaning
must be inaccessible to the questioner or hearer made no difference.
Thus the communicative relationship existed only between the
speaker and himself and the speaker and God, who of course knew the
reserved mental part and therefore understood the true meaning of his
utterance.

While Navarrus was far from the first to reflect on the device of
reserving a meaning in the mind to evade the sin of lying, he was
apparently the first to elaborate it so fully and to base its justification
on the notion of "mixed speech."[49] Hence he was able to claim that
he had devised a "new method." It was usual, however, for moral
theologians and canonists dealing with lying and perjury to consider
both the different senses of words and according to whose intention,

---

[49] The French Jesuit Théophile Raynaud cited a long line of authorities in his
defense of the doctrine of mental reservation. He traced the term *mentalis restrictio*
to the fourteenth-century theologian Petrus de Palude; *Disputatio de Veritate
Morali, cum Mendacio & Locutionibus Aequivocis ac Mente Restrictis Comparata*, in
Opera Omnia, 19 vols. (Lyons, 1665), 14:105. On Raynaud, see also below,
Chapter 9.

the questioner's or respondent's, an oath or statement should be understood. In the case of equivocation, the fact that a word could have several publicly accepted meanings made it possible for a speaker to intend it in one sense while allowing a questioner to suppose it was intended in another. An early example in the literature of casuistry of this trick of speech to avoid a breach of truth or conscience appeared in the *Summa de Poenitentia* of the noted thirteenth-century theologian Raymond of Peñafort. Raymond held that a man who was asked the whereabouts of an innocent fugitive who had taken shelter in his house from a murderer could reply, "Non est hic," an expression that could mean either "He isn't here" or "He doesn't eat here." The emphasis in cases of this sort fell on the use of ambiguous expressions and a concealed sense in circumstances in which there was no moral obligation to reveal the truth or else a moral obligation to conceal it. Raymond claimed that his opinion was justified by countless precedents in scripture.[50] It may well be that the main root of the concern sustaining such devices lay in the imperative need to safeguard the secrecy of the confessional against intrusive questions from whatever source. Protection against unjust questioning by religious superiors in ecclesiastical visitations was probably also a background factor.

In his defense of mental reservation Navarrus enlisted the opinions of Jerome, Gregory the Great, Aquinas, Duns Scotus, and more recent scholastics such as Gabriel Biel, John Major, and Sylvester Prierias.[51] Biel, for example, one of the foremost theologians of the fifteenth century, reviewed the subjects of lying and perjury at length in his commentary on Peter Lombard's *Sentences*. After referring to the text of "Humanae aures" in relation to matrimony, he wrote that "words pronounced externally do not oblige without an interior consent. Who therefore does not inwardly intend to oblige himself is not obliged in the presence of God." He also allowed that a statement made with a mental understanding might not be a lie if it was not contrary to the speaker's mind.[52] The Dominican Prierias' *Sylvestrina* was probably the best-known *summa* of moral theology in its time. In

---

[50] Raymond of Peñaforte, *Summa de Poenitentia*, quoted in Julius Dorszynski, *Catholic Teaching about the Morality of Falsehood* (Washington, D.C.: Catholic University Press, 1948), p. 25; and in Gregor Müller, *Die Wahrhaftigkeitspflicht und die Problematik der Lüge* (Freiburg in Breisgau: Herder, 1962), p. 177.

[51] *Commentarius*, fols. 220, 221v (q. 1, no. 7; q. 2, nos. 11–12).

[52] *Epitome et Collectorium ex Occamo circa Quatuor Sententiarum Libros* (1501; repr., Frankfurt, 1965), bk. 3, distinctio 39, q. 1, sig. Riiv; Biel treated lying, perjury, and

connection with oaths he invoked "Humanae aures" to permit
swearing according to one's own intention in cases of unlawful or
unfair questioning, rather than that of the person to whom the oath
was sworn. Thus, in an example used by many other casuists, he permitted a woman wickedly required by her husband to swear whether
she had committed adultery to swear what was true according to her
own understanding though false according to the hearer's. Under the
topic of lying, he noted that an inexpedient question might be
answered with a mental reservation. One of the precedents he used
was Jesus' reply to his disciples that he did not know the day of
judgment, mentally understanding that he did not know it to reveal it
to them *(subintelligendo ut revelandum)*. Prierias pointed out, however,
that one must beware of this kind of concealment if it caused scandal
or if an obligation existed to confess the truth. To withold the truth in
such cases would be mortal sin.[53]

Navarrus also drew on the great sixteenth-century humanist scholar
Andrea Alciati, celebrated for his historical and philological studies of
Roman law, to support his argument for mixed speech that was partly
vocal and partly mental. In his treatise *On the Meaning of Words* dealing
with legal language, Alciati had included a discussion of amphibology,
which he defined as arising from the ambiguity either of a single word
or of a conjunction of words.[54]

In his commentary, Navarrus also referred in passing to his disagreement with several noted sixteenth-century authorities. One of
these was the Dominican professor of theology at Salamanca,
Domingo de Soto, who in his *On Justice and Law (De Iustitia et Iure),* a
treatise based on Aquinas' *Summa Theologiae,* had touched on equivocation and mental reservation in a survey of oaths. Soto stated that
Jerome's recommendation of dissimulation as useful applied only to
the *simulatio* that was employed without falsehood. He permitted
amphibology, or equivocation under unlawful questioning, provided
the words used did not have an artificial meaning and were not a lie.
In general, he condemned "mental restriction" as deceitful. The sole
exception he allowed was when a response made with a mental reser-

---

oaths in ibid., dists. 28–39. Raynaud, *Opera Omnia,* 14:156, also cites Biel on
mental reservation.

[53] *Summa Summarum que Sylvestrina Dicitur* (Strasbourg, 1518), "Juramentum,"
chap. 3, no. 2; "Mendacium," chap. 6, nos. 1–4.

[54] "Amphibologia," in *De Verborum Significatione Libri Quatuor* (Lyons, 1530),
bk. 4.

vation was such that the interrogator could not fail to be aware of the latter. This would be the case, for example, in a question about the confessional, to which the answer given was "I don't know," coupled with the mental reservation "so as to tell you." This reply would not be a lie because the reserved clause, though unspoken, would be apparent to the questioner. Soto interpreted Jesus' reply to his disciples that he did not know the day of judgment as another instance of the same kind.[55]

Another writer from whom Navarrus recorded his dissent was Juan Ginés Sepúlveda, a humanist, jurist, and historiographer to Charles V who he said had been his fellow student at Alcalá. Sepúlveda was known for his defense of war and the military life against the criticisms of Erasmus as well as for his controversial arguments in favor of the inferiority and subjection of the Indians in the New World.[56] Sepúlveda's short tract on the giving of testimony in secret offenses was striking for its criticism of mental reservation and other species of dissimulation.[57] Cast in the classical form of a dialogue, the work was dedicated to the count of Cienfuentes, Charles V's ambassador in Rome. Its subject, as Sepúlveda explained in the preface, was the contention between honesty and utility, a matter that had been debated in Rome before the count by learned men amid much disagreement. The count, he said, had also solicited his own view, and later he was moved to write on the question when, on returning to Spain after twenty-two years in Italy, he saw theologians instilling erroneous opinions about it into the ears and minds of students. The two speakers in his dialogue were Philetus and his teacher Theophilus, who represented the author. The nineteen short chapters of the treatise covered some of the same topics associated with lying, dissimulation, and the observance of secrecy and withholding of the truth in

---

[55] *De Iustitia et Iure* (Salamanca, 1556), pp. 457a–458b; Navarrus, *Commentarius,* fol. 220; Soto also dealt with the same subject in a short treatise, *De Ratione Tegendi et Detegendi Secretum* (Salamanca, 1541).

[56] *Commentarius,* fol. 220, and *Enchiridion,* p. 283 (chap. xviii, no. 61); on Sepúlveda see Bataillon, *Erasmo y España,* 421–425, 632–633; J. A. Fernández-Santamaria, *The State, War and Peace. Spanish Political Thought in the Renaissance 1516–1559* (Cambridge: Cambridge University Press, 1977), chaps. 6–7; Anthony Pagden, *The Fall of Natural Man* (Cambridge: Cambridge University Press, 1982), chap. 5.

[57] *De Ratione Dicendi Testimonium in Causis Occultorum Criminum Dialogus* (Valladolid, 1538). I have used the text in *Joannis Genesium Sepulveda . . . Opera,* 4 vols. (Madrid, 1780), vol, 4.

particular circumstances that were commonly examined by canonists and casuists.

One of the early chapters dealt with whether words should be taken in their common meaning in answering questions, as well as with the definition of the lie as speech contrary to one's mind. Philetus said that if questioned by a judge about a secret offense, he would answer that he knew nothing, subjoining in his mind "that he ought to reveal to the judge." He denied that he would be guilty of lying and perjury in this case, since he did not speak against his mind. In reply Theophilus asked who taught Philetus such a fine subterfuge for perjury. By this method, he pointed out, he himself would not be lying if he said he had never seen Spain, adding the mental understanding "for the past twenty-two years." Quoting Augustine's definition of the lie as a *falsa significatio* made with the intention to deceive, he asserted that words must be used in their common and customary meaning. He concluded, therefore, that Philetus' answer would undoubtedly have been a lie, despite the hidden mental reservation.[58]

Subsequent chapters canvassed the problem of lying from several different angles. Sepúlveda also discussed the text of "Humanae aures" and the method of "puerile amphibology," meaning both equivocation and mental reservation, as a way of abolishing the lie. Philetus suggested that Theophilus must regard as foolish Gregory's saying that we should consider the speaker's mind and not his words. Theophilus commented, however, that Gregory's dictum must be interpreted without deceit or malice as good and honest men would understand it. Hence he declared that lying could not be evaded by amphibology, even with the addition of a thought unknown to others. Philetus replied that although lying was odious to him, it would be right for him to use mental reservation to save a friend about whom he was being questioned. He insisted that this would not fall under Augustine's strictures against the lie, since his intention would not be to deceive but to help a friend. Theophilus rejected this reasoning, however, contending that it was not enough for the mind to conceive the truth unless one returned an answer to the question asked in which the entire meaning was expressly stated. Nor, he added, could any situation of danger make a false statement involuntary, for even to avoid danger lying remained a voluntary act.[59]

[58] *De Ratione Dicendi*, chap. 5.
[59] Ibid., chaps. 6–7.

Later, when Philetus asked what good men should do to escape lying and perjury without betraying a friend, Theophilus declared that no pretext justified an evil action and that right reason must be the interpreter of all laws. He stressed the concordance of right reason with natural law and Christ's teachings, and observed that in a conflict of obligations the stronger one was binding unless it led to sin. Although Philetus again pleaded that exceptional circumstances should permit responding to a question with a mental reservation, Theophilus rejoined that perjury was never justifiable and that in some cases death was preferable to the commission of evil acts.[60] In the final chapter he named several theologians who confirmed his own position. No doctor before Gabriel Biel, he claimed, had openly ventured to excuse the giving of false testimony in another's case.[61] On this point Navarrus took issue with Sepúlveda, citing various earlier commentators who had expressed a view similar to Biel's.[62]

Although Navarrus had developed the rationale of mental reservation far more fully than any of his predecessors, Sepúlveda's dialogue shows that its legitimacy was already being taught in Spain earlier in the sixteenth century. Its intensive treatment in Navarrus' commentary, however, gave the doctrine an unprecedented prominence. While it remained for the English Jesuits who adopted Navarrus' teaching to advocate its use in conditions of religious persecution, contemporary theologians in Catholic countries were concerned mainly with its application to other contexts in which it might be licit not to disclose secret or incriminating information. Some of them also took a different approach from Navarrus to mental reservation.

Among the commentators to consider equivocation and mental reservation after Navarrus was the Spanish Jesuit Juan Azor, a professor first in Alcalá and later in Rome, who discussed the subject in a large treatise on questions of conscience in relation to the Ten Commandments.[63] Examining oaths and vows under the Second Commandment, he expressed partial disagreement with Navarrus. He objected that the latter's rule based on "Humanae aures" in favor of keeping a reserved meaning in the mind was so general that it would be impossible under it for any response to be a lie. Whatever a person was

[60] Ibid., chaps. 8–11.
[61] Ibid., chap. 19.
[62] *Commentarius*, p. 220.
[63] *Institutionum Moralium in Quibus Questiones ad Conscientiam . . . Pertinentes Breviter Tractantur*, 3 vols. (Lyons, 1600–1612).

asked, whether about what he did, saw, or knew, he could answer without lying. To rectify this defect, Azor propounded certain rules of his own on mental reservation. The most important was that it should not be employed if no injury was threatened. He regarded it as licit in appropriate circumstances, as when a priest was asked to divulge something heard in confession or an accused was unlawfully questioned by a judge. Otherwise he condemned it as wicked. He discussed the matter again in connection with the Eighth Commandment. In a chapter on amphibology which reviewed various justifications for ambiguous speech, he posed the doubt whether mental reservation was licit in the common conversation of men. His answer pronounced it permissible provided it did no one an injury or was not a denial of charity. Failing these conditions, he called the practice unlawful because "it could excuse all lying" and would undermine all charity and human conversation between neighbors.[64]

The neoscholastic philosopher and jurist Francisco Suarez, a Spanish Jesuit who became a professor at the Roman College of the Jesuits and later occupied the highest theology professorship at Coimbra, was another thinker to deal with equivocation and mental reservation. In an analysis of oaths in his commentary on the *Secunda Secundae* of Aquinas' *Summae Theologiae,* he devoted three chapters to the subject of amphibology in its several aspects.[65] Suarez endorsed some of Navarrus' opinions and, like him, held that a lie consisted of speech contrary to the mind. He was thus able to recognize various ways in which a speaker could take advantage without sin or perjury of ambiguous language to swear an oath in his own sense rather than in that of the imposer's or hearer's. What conformed to the mind of the speaker, he pointed out, need not always conform to the mind of the hearer.[66] Though approving the use of amphibology in the form of mental reservation, he did not accept Navarrus' argument for it in terms of mixed speech. Written, vocal, and mental speech, he maintained, belonged to different orders of signification and therefore could not combine to make a single proposition. Since a mental sign signified only to the conceiver, it was not an apt sign for someone else. Likewise, vocal speech, which was a "sensible sign" ordained to signify to others, could not be aptly joined to a mental or interior sign.

[64] Ibid., vol. 1, bk. II, chap. 4, pp. 1064–66; vol. 3, bk. 13, chap. 3, pp. 906–907.
[65] *Tractatus Quintus de Juramento et Adjuratione,* bk. 3, chaps. 9–11, in *Opera Omnia,* 24 vols. (Paris, 1859), vol. 14.
[66] Ibid., chap. 9, pp. 694–696.

On this ground he asserted that if anyone could speak or write what he wished by conceiving a mental sense not in the words themselves, it would be contrary to all human faith and as harmful to human society as outright lying.[67]

Despite these objections, in a chapter titled "Whether it is licit to swear with an amphibology conceived only in the mind," Suarez proceeded to show how mental reservation could be lawfully practiced. First, he affirmed it as probable that it pertained to human free will to make use of compounds of speech in expressing the mind. Next, he described several methods by which this might be done in order to utter true statements without mixing different orders of speech. For instance, one could finish a speech with an expression inaudible to others, as in swearing "I did not do it," completed by the inaudible murmur "today." Or one could declare, "I swear," then say to oneself the words "that I am saying," concluding aloud with "I did not do it." Or in yet another way, one could utter a sentence without vocalizing the end, as by stating "I did not do it," but not speaking the final word "today." He found a precedent for such usages in the much-quoted sayings of Jesus that he did not know the day of judgment or on another occasion that he would not go up to the feast of tabernacles, though he afterward went (John 7:8-10). Suarez explained that in these examples Christ did not lie because he added a mental understanding to his words.[68]

Having made this argument, however, Suarez stressed that amphibology must be employed cautiously and only for just and necessary cause; otherwise it would be a serious fault and a grave sin if accompanied by an oath. It was licit only when someone was unjustly required to disclose or to swear something that was wrong to reveal. In a just interrogation, on the other hand, or if one voluntarily offered to speak, one must speak simply and with a sense comprehensible to the listener.[69]

Suarez conceded that amphibology, which he called "a kind of dissimulation," was the same as lying if resorted to without just cause or necessity. This led him to consider why it was not therefore a lie in any kind of circumstances, given that "a lie does not cease to be a lie because of a just end." He replied that when necessity supervened,

[67] Ibid., chap. 10, pp. 697-698.
[68] Ibid., pp. 698-699.
[69] Ibid., chap. 11, p. 699.

amphibology was absolved from lying because it propounded words in some true sense even if not understood by the hearer; furthermore, the speaker did not intend to speak or swear falsely, and what he said had a true sense that was the only one he intended. Hence on a strict view the speaker neither lied nor spoke falsely. Suarez cited "Humanae aures" on this point to bolster his conclusion that "the intention distinguishes the action." Finally, he acknowledged that while amphibology need not be a lie in a strict sense, it could entail other sins, such as cunning, imprudence, and injustice, if misused. Dissimulated speech without justification, he observed, might not lack truth and yet still be repugnant to human faith and entail pernicious deceit that would be mortal sin if done with harm to one's neighbor.[70]

Suarez' discussion of mental reservation is striking for the tortuous reasoning and hair-splitting distinctions with which he both defended and qualified its use. The tenuous arguments by which he sought to differentiate it from lying might well seem to be an exercise of misplaced ingenuity. Other contemporary Jesuit theologians who treated the doctrine added their own twists to its rationale. Gregory de Valencia, a noted compatriot and friend of Suarez, who was professor at Ingolstadt for many years before ending his career in Rome, expounded it in his commentary on Aquinas' *Summa Theologiae*. He approved amphibology generally and allowed a wide latitude to an accused unjustly interrogated. In permitting mental reservation in such a case, he held that someone who used it to deceive another person spoke or swore truthfully, although it was not the truth the other person wanted to hear. The resulting deceit was therefore due not to the speaker but to the hearer, who simply understood the statement in his own sense.[71] The Belgian Jesuit Leonard Lessius, theology professor at Louvain, also sanctioned mental reservation. According to his view, if someone had no obligation to reveal his whole mind when questioned, then he was also not obliged to express all of his words, but might voice some and add the other part tacitly. This would not be lying, Lessius claimed, because the speaker did not intend to affirm only the vocal part, but rather the latter in conjunction with the reserved part, together with which it was true.[72]

70 Ibid., pp. 700–701.

71 *Gregorii de Valentia . . . Commentariorum Theologicarum,* 4 vols. (Lyons, 1619), 3:1043–44, 1405–06 (disp. V, q. xiii; disp. VI, q. vii).

72 *Leonardi Lessii e Soc. Iesu in Academia Lovaniensi Sacrae Theologiae Professoris. De Iustitia et Iure* (1605) (Paris, 1628), p. 626 (bk. 2, dubitatio ix, no. 47).

Some of the most respected and influential moral theologians of their time thus followed Navarrus in maintaining the licitness of mental reservation, while adding their own contributions to the stock of reasons in its favor. Although they all sought to hedge it with safeguards against abuse, they still left ample scope for its employment. By the first decade of the seventeenth century the doctrine of mental reservation had become an established part of the casuistical teaching of Catholic Europe. It is therefore not surprising that its acceptance began also to encounter increasing opposition from critics within and outside the church who denounced it as indistinguishable from lying.

CHAPTER 9

England and the Controversy over Mental Reservation

The story of mental reservation in England begins with the Catholic missionary priests and in particular with the Jesuit poet and martyr Robert Southwell (ca. 1561–1595). Casuistry was an essential part of the missionaries' instruction. At the Douai-Rheims seminary founded by William Allen, the seminarians studied Navarrus' *Enchiridion* for confessors twice a week. Cases of conscience composed for their guidance also treated Navarrus as a leading authority.[1] The Jesuit *Ratio Studiorum,* the plan of education for the Society's colleges, likewise assigned casuistry an important place in the curriculum. It provided for a professor of cases of conscience and required that casuistical problems be handled by means of questions and answers, with the professor pointing out the probable opinions. The students were expected to spend two hours every Saturday in disputations on cases of conscience.[2] The English College in Rome, which Allen established in 1579 as another training ground for mission priests, followed the Jesuit system and would therefore have also provided for the teaching of casuistry. As the seminarians of the English College went for some of their classes to the Roman College of the Jesuits, they would have heard lectures by famous Jesuit theologians. The Englishmen would

[1] Thomas Knox, ed., *The Letters and Memorials of William Cardinal Allen* (London, 1882), p. 66; P. J. Holmes, ed., *Elizabethan Casuistry* (London: Catholic Record Society, 1981), p. 1. Idem, *Resistance and Compromise* (Cambridge: Cambridge University Press, 1982), chap. 10, discusses Catholic priests' use of casuistry in England.

[2] Edward Fitzpatrick, ed., "Rules of the Professor of Cases of Conscience," in *St. Ignatius and the Jesuit Ratio Studiorum* (New York: McGraw-Hill, 1933), pp. 165–167. The *Ratio* was formally issued in 1599 but reflected earlier practice.

not only have read Navarrus, but most likely would also have been aware of his presence in Rome and perhaps even have seen him there before his death in 1586. It was at the English College that Robert Southwell both studied and served as a tutor for five years before embarking on his missionary career. He came to Rome after a period at Douai, where the Jesuit Leonard Lessius was one of his professors and where he also discovered his vocation for the Society of Jesus. In Rome he was ordained to the priesthood and completed his Jesuit training. From there he set out in 1586 on his religious enterprise in England.[3]

We have already encountered, in connection with English Catholic recusancy, the cases of conscience which William Allen and the Jesuit Robert Parsons drew up for the exercises in casuistry at the Douai-Rheims seminary. These cases also dealt with problems of dissimulation and equivocation, especially in relation to the safety of priests. One of the questions they broached was whether a priest could change his clothing, appearance, or name to conceal his identity. The answer considered such changes permissible on the ground that "pretence . . . is lawful" and cited Christ's pretense to his disciples at Emmaus that he would go further (Luke 24:28). Though cautioning that a priest should not dissimulate if it caused scandal or when interrogated by lawful authority, it denied that Elizabethan officials ever had a legitimate right to question priests. The argument also treated the use of "pious equivocation" as different from lying. It justified responding to questions by means of equivocation, contending that responsibility for the resulting deceit would rest not with the respondent but with the questioner, who by taking the answer in his own sense deceived himself. The opinion concluded generally that one could keep silent about the truth or hide it as long as one did not directly deny it.[4]

[3] Pierre Janelle, *Robert Southwell the Writer* (New York: Sheed & Ward, 1935), chap. 1; Christopher Devlin, *The Life of Robert Southwell, Poet and Martyr* (New York: Farrar, Straus and Cudahy, 1956), chaps. 2–6; Henry Foley, *Records of the English Province of the Society of Jesus*, 7 vols. in 8 (1875–1883; repr., New York: Johnson Reprint, 1966), 1st ser., 1: 302–318. Arnold Meyer, *England and the Catholic Church under Queen Elizabeth* (London: Routledge & Kegan Paul, 1967), pp. 92–121, gives a concise account of the English continental seminaries, especially Douai and the English College in Rome. The latter and the Roman College under Jesuit direction, which became the papal university authorized by Gregory XIII, are also discussed in Ludwig von Pastor, *The History of The Popes from the Close of the Middle Ages*, 40 vols. (London: J. Hodges, 1891–1953), vol. 19, chap. 6.

[4] Holmes, *Elizabethan Casuistry*, pp. 63–66; see also ibid., pp. 54–55.

Another case held that a priest must not deny his faith or lie when questioned, but could otherwise use any means he wished, whether equivocation, silence, or returning the question, in order to avoid replying. Further topics included the obligation of oaths and promises exacted from Catholics under interrogation or in prison. In these cases the answers distinguished various circumstances in which such undertakings would not be binding and might be licitly evaded by "mental reservation" and "sophistical swearing."[5]

Many of these opinions were grounded in the basic assumption of the human right of self-preservation. The preamble to the cases by Allen and Parsons laid down that the conservation of life is enjoined by divine and natural law, and that when human law and the holy canons of the church conflict with the former, they lose their force. It concluded that "the law of the Church can never of itself oblige a man to put his life in danger." The scope of this principle, although certain qualifications were noted lest the faith and religion be damaged, afforded ample room for the methods of dissimulation the casuists permitted.[6]

The cases the English seminarians studied presupposed the severe persecution of Catholics by heretics, and differed in this respect from the casuistical manuals written by theologians for Catholic countries. They also cast light on the hard lot of the priests engaged in the reconversion of England. A pathetic glimpse appears in a case that inquired if a priest might lawfully celebrate mass on an unconsecrated altar or without relics or holy vestments. The answer permitted him to do so, recognizing that there might be no alternative. It commented that

> although the law of the Church is to be obeyed where serious necessity does not force us to do the contrary, the spiritual distress and suffering of the priests in England must be considered. They live amid so many difficulties and dangers and amid so much desolation and have hardly any human consolation, and as a result their devotion to the celebration of the mass is in some ways a sort of necessity for them, for it prevents their spirits being entirely overwhelmed, as they would be if they were deprived of the use of the holy sacrifice.[7]

Southwell journeyed to England in the summer of 1586 in the company of his friend and fellow Jesuit Henry Garnet. Catholic mis-

[5] Ibid., pp. 52, 77, 124, 125–126.
[6] Ibid., p. 62.
[7] Ibid., pp. 81–82.

sionary priests at the time were exposed to the utmost danger from the penal laws, under which some had already been executed for treason. Besides earlier legislation and royal proclamations denouncing seminary priests and Jesuits as traitors and making it treasonable to be reconciled or to reconcile another to the church of Rome, a statute of 1585 threatened death to all English subjects ordained abroad as priests who remained in England longer than forty days. Any person who received or aided them was likewise to be punished by death. By virtue of this law, simply to be a priest or Jesuit in England became treason. Under the circumstances, the men sent to rescue their country from heresy had to exercise their spiritual functions in secret. They were forced to dress as laymen, use false names, and pretend to various occupations. They had to move for safety from one place to another, find refuge in Catholic households willing to risk receiving them, and secure hiding places for themselves in the event of search. They had to be prepared to respond to dangerous questioning and to be ready for arrest at any moment.[8]

Notwithstanding these perils, Southwell eluded capture for six years, while Garnet remained at liberty until 1606. During the later years of Elizabeth's reign, the great majority of priests in England were seculars, and the Jesuits never amounted to more than a handful. In 1598 the number of secular priests exceeded 300, in contrast to only 15 Jesuits.[9] Garnet, who was appointed in 1587 as the superior or provincial of the English Jesuits, wrote in the same year to the general of the Society in Rome, Claudio Aquaviva, concerning the priests' perplexity over the licitness of denying their identity: "It is no small question among us whether when a priest is asked by a magistrate if he is a priest or not, he is allowed expressly to deny it. To some this denial appears tantamount to denying Christ." Two years later he reported that a meeting of Jesuits had decided that although priests may never directly deny their priesthood, they could place the burden of proof on their accusers and

---

[8] The act of 1585 against Jesuits and seminary priests, 27 Eliz. c. 2, is printed in Geoffrey Elton, *The Tudor Constitution,* 2d ed. (Cambridge: Cambridge University Press, 1982), pp. 433–437; see also Meyer, *England and the Catholic Church,* pp. 145–149, 204–208. The narrative of the Jesuit John Gerard, *John Gerard. The Autobiography of an Elizabethan* (London: Longmans, Green, 1951), contains a vivid description of the life of a priest in conditions of persecution.

[9] Thomas Knox, ed., *Douai Diaries* (London, 1878), p. lxiv; Thomas Law, ed., *The Archpriest Controversy,* 2 vols. (Westminster: Camden Society, 1896–1898), 2:xix. Of the secular priests, forty to fifty were old Marian clergy, the rest being missionaries who had been ordained abroad.

use every form of evasion short of actual denial. In a subsequent letter he told Aquaviva that the priests now believed that it was lawful to deny their priesthood on the basis of an opinion given by the Roman theologians.[10]

The English government was led to this persecution in self-defense. In its view the papal excommunication of the queen in 1570, and England's mortal combat with Spain and the Counter-Reformation, made every Catholic suspect, in particular the priests. The latter were feared as agents of treason and thus became victims of the irreconcilable conflict between the theocratic claims of the papacy and the total allegiance the national royal state demanded of them. Even if they avoided any involvement in politics and were willing to recognize the temporal supremacy of the monarch, the presumption of disloyalty still clung to them. These circumstances alone can explain the fate of a man such as Southwell. Although he had written a powerful protest against the government's persecution of Catholics and the torture of priests to force them to accuse themselves, he was never a party to any plots or accused of a criminal act.[11] In 1592 he was finally captured, betrayed by the daughter of a family in whose house he had often secretly lodged and celebrated mass. In prison he was brutally tortured to elicit information about his opinions, friends, and contacts. But apart from admitting that he was a Jesuit priest and professing his loyalty to the queen, he refused to say anything, not even as to the color of the horse he had ridden on a certain day. After three years of imprisonment, he was tried in 1595, condemned, and executed as a traitor.[12]

It was during his trial that the issue of equivocation and mental reservation first came up. Anne Bellamy, Southwell's betrayer, confessed his instruction to her that when questioned she might lawfully deny knowing where a priest lay hidden even though she knew. The attorney general, Sir Edward Coke, pressed the point, charging him with teaching Bellamy the wicked doctrine according to which if required to say whether she had seen Southwell at her father's house, she could swear in the negative with the mental reservation "not with the intention to tell you." Southwell nevertheless defended the prac-

---

[10] Philip Caraman, *Henry Garnet 1555–1606 and the Gunpowder Plot* (New York: Farrar, Straus, 1964), pp. 54–55, 116–118, 134.

[11] Robert Southwell, *An Humble Supplication to Her Maiestie* (wr. 1591, pub. 1600), ed. R. C. Bald (Cambridge: Cambridge University Press, 1953).

[12] I have used both Janelle, *Robert Southwell,* and Devlin, *Life of Robert Southwell,* for these and other facts about Southwell's life, imprisonment, and death.

tice, maintaining that it was agreeable to the word of God and supported by the church fathers, the civil and canon law, and the policy of all Christian nations. To prove his position, he asked what Coke would do if the French king were to invade England, forcing the queen to flee for her life, and he alone knew of her whereabouts. If questioned, would not Coke deny any knowledge of where she was even under oath, using a mental reservation? If he refused to swear when silence indicated knowledge, then, Southwell stated, he would be neither the queen's good subject nor friend. On hearing this argument, the chief justice of the court commented, "yf this Doctrine should be allowed, it would supplant all Justice, for we are men, and no Gods, and can iudge but accordinge to [men's] outward actiones and speeches, and not accordinge to their secrette and inward intentions."[13]

Another Jesuit, John Gerard, who was arrested in 1594, likewise defended equivocation and mental reservation to his captors. In his autobiography he described how he was tortured and later asked to name the Catholics he knew. On refusing he was taxed with the same evil doctrine as Southwell. Gerard insisted to his interrogators, however, that equivocation differed from lying, being simply the concealment of truth where there was no obligation to reveal it. It was not for use in ordinary human relations, but a shield against those who questioned without authority to compel men to accuse themselves. Christ himself practiced it, he claimed, in telling his disciples that he did not know the day of judgment and again when he said he would not go up to the feast in Jerusalem, although he intended to go. These statements were never charged against Gerard in a judicial trial, because after three years of imprisonment he managed an extraordinary escape from the Tower.[14]

In reply to Catholic accusations of unjust persecution, the government maintained the official position that it did not inquire into the consciences of Catholics or punish them for their religion, but was concerned solely with the political menace they presented.[15] While this was in a measure true, its hatred of the Catholic church and the

[13] Janelle, *Robert Southwell*, pp. 67, 81–82; the latter's account of Southwell's trial is based on a contemporary manuscript, "A Brefe Discourse of the Condemnation and Execution of Mr. Robert Southwell"; for the quotation see p. 291.

[14] *John Gerard*, pp. 125–127.

[15] This was the burden of the official declaration published in 1583 and probably written by the queen's chief minister, Lord Burghley, *The Execution of Justice in*

intermixture of religion and politics during the period make it impossible to exonerate the Elizabethan state from the charge of grievous persecution of its Catholic subjects. In the apology he published in 1584 on behalf of the English Catholics, William Allen noted the government's claim that "none is asked by torture, what he believeth of the Mass or Transubstantiation or such like." To this he justifiably rejoined,

> it concerneth religion no less to demand and press us by torture, where, in whose houses, what days and times we say or hear Mass, how many we have reconciled, what we have heard in confession; who resorteth to our preachings, who harboureth Catholics and priests; who sustaineth, aideth, or comforteth them; who be they that have their children or pupils in the Society or Seminaries beyond the seas; where such a Jesuit or such a priest is to be found; where Catholic books are printed, and by whom, and to whom they be uttered in England? Which things being demanded of evil intent and to the annoyance of the Catholic cause, God's priests, and innocent men; no man may by the law of God and nature disclose.[16]

Among the government's inquisitorial methods of dealing with priests was to subject them to the "bloody questions," as Catholics termed them, that were meant to entrap them into divulging their opinions concerning the pope's authority over rulers and what side they would take in the event of a papally sponsored invasion. There was no ground in English common law to put such questions. In 1581 interrogatories of this kind were administered to thirteen imprisoned priests, including the Jesuit Edmund Campion, who was executed later in the same year. The accused men offered various replies. Two rejected outright the papal claim to depose the queen. Campion declined to say anything save that he did not meddle with such questions. Others responded with evasions and refusals. One priest professed loyalty but pleaded ignorance whether the pope could discharge subjects from obedience, claiming that the question was "too high and daungerous for him to answere." A second "prayed to be asked no such questions as may touch his life." Others said in regard to a possible invasion that "when that case shall happen" they would "make

---

England; see Conyers Read, *Lord Burghley and Queen Elizabeth* (London: Jonathan Cape, 1960), pp. 251–254.

[16] *A True, Sincere and Modest Defence of English Catholics* (1584), 2 vols. (London: B. Herder, 1914), 1:21. Allen's book was a response to *The Execution of Justice in England*.

answer, and not before," or they would pray that "the right may have place." Most of the number tried to protect themselves against the questions as best they could without disavowing the pope's deposing power.[17]

From 1573 to the end of Elizabeth's reign, in 1603, her government executed 128 priests, 7 of whom were Jesuits. Fifty-nine laypeople also suffered death for being reconciled to the church, for harboring and helping priests, or for other religion-related offenses. Another 42 priests and laymen perished in prison.[18] Most English Catholics remained loyal subjects who wished for nothing more than to combine political allegiance with continued fidelity to their religion. Under the life-threatening dangers they faced, however, some at least had more than sufficient reason to seek refuge in dissimulation. Mental reservation, which had come into public notice during Southwell's trial, was merely the most sensational and controversial of the methods Catholics adopted for withholding the truth from hostile questioners. In 1598 the Jesuit provincial Henry Garnet composed a treatise on equivocation which upheld the legitimacy of mental reservation. The first discussion of the subject by an English casuist, its purpose was the defense of Southwell, to whom the work was dedicated. After circulating in manuscript, copies of the treatise came into the hands of the government in 1605 during investigation of the Gunpowder Plot.[19] Garnet's foreknowledge of this Catholic conspiracy to assassinate James I and the members of Parliament cost him his life and added to the ill repute of his teaching. Even Shakespeare referred to the doctrine and its connection with the plot. In *Macbeth*, written in

[17] Reproduced from a contemporary document in Charles Dodd, *Church History of England*, ed. Mark Tierney, 5 vols. (London, 1839–1842), vol. 3, app. 3. Allen commented bitterly on the bloody questions in *A True . . . Defence*, 1:78–80; see also Holmes, *Resistance and Compromise*, p. 45; Meyer, *England and the Catholic Church*, pp. 157–160.

[18] Dodd, *Church History of England*, 3:161–170.

[19] Garnet's manuscript was first published as *A Treatise of Equivocation* (London, 1851), with a preface by David Jardine, who was unaware of its authorship. Antony F. Allison, "The Writings of Father Henry Garnet S.J. (1555–1606)," *Biographical Studies*, 1, no. 1 (1951), showed that it was attributable to Garnet. Archibald Malloch, "Father Henry Garnet's Treatise of Equivocation," *Recusant History*, 15, no. 6 (1981), discusses the work in its historical context. Caraman, *Henry Garnet*, includes remarks on equivocation in chap. 16 and app. E; see also Holmes, *Elizabethan Casuistry*, pp. 121–123.

1606, he inserted a scene for comic relief in which a character played on the word *equivocator* as someone "that could swear in both the scales against either scale; who committed treason enough for God's sake, yet could not equivocate to heaven."[20]

The original title of Garnet's work underscored its character as an examination of a case of conscience concerning lying: *A treatise of equivocation wherein is largely discussed the question whether a Catholicke or any other person before a magistrate being demaunded uppon his oath whether a Prieste were in such a place may (not w^{th}standing his perfect knowledge to the contrary) without Periury and securely in conscience answere, No, wth this secret meaning reserved in his mynde, that he was not there so that any man is bound to detect it.* Later, however, the author crossed out this title and substituted one better suited to his aim of proving that mental reservation made it possible to avoid lying: *A treatise against lying and fraudulent dissimulation . . . published for the defence of innocency and the instruction of ignorants.*

Garnet (1555–1606) was well equipped to tackle his subject. An excellent scholar, he had studied and taught at the Roman College of the Jesuits before going on the English mission. During his many years in England, he would also have been able to obtain access by various means to Catholic manuals of moral theology and other writings. In his dedication he stated that even though Southwell had convincingly alleged examples in behalf of equivocation, the idea was still "much wondered at" by both heretics and Catholics; hence he thought it needful to discuss it. The ensuing disquisition drew on a variety of authorities and cited the sayings of Jesus and other scriptural cases that had become standard precedents in every treatment of dissimulation. Most of all Garnet relied on Navarrus' commentary on "Humanae aures." From Navarrus he adopted the conception of mixed speech as capable of forming a single true proposition of which a part was reserved in the mind. Hence someone who replied, "I knowe not" with the mental reservation "for to tell you" would be speaking the truth. In the same way, someone unjustly examined by a magistrate could licitly answer, "I did not hear masse," mentally reserving the statement "so that I can be lawfully charged therfor, or accused by any."[21]

Garnet went on to note two types of equivocation, one of which

[20] Act a, scene 3, lines 9–13; see Henry Paul, "Garnet's Doctrine of Equivocation," in *The Royal Play of Macbeth* (New York: Macmillan, 1957).

[21] *A Treatise of Equivocation*, pp. 9–11, 15, 18, 24.

used words in different senses, the other consisting of a mental reservation. While a number of schoolmen, he said, had permitted the former, a few, of whom Soto was the first, disallowed the latter as a lie, although Navarrus and other famous authorities approved it. To resolve the disagreement on the question, he turned for support to the doctrine of probabilism. No Catholic, he asserted, could without arrogant temerity condemn his opinion in favor of mental reservation as improbable or, seeing that it was probable, call its practice sinful. Accordingly, when there were two probable opinions,

> a man may without sinne follow either, if it may be done without preiudice of our neighbour; and if one be lesse probable than the other, yet so long as it is within ye compasse of probability, wch it is if it have 2 or 3 grave autours (as ours hath very many), then may a man be bound under sinne . . . to chuse ye lesse probable in case a superior comaund or our neighbour may be otherwise notably [damaged].

To enforce his argument he made the point that liars had no need "to dispute of ye lawfull use of equivocation, they taking a readier way to serve their turne, by plaine untruthes and evident perjuries."[22]

Apart from mental reservation Garnet examined several other ways to conceal the truth without a lie, such as by words true in one sense but false in another and by answering questions obliquely or with ambiguous expressions. Since both Christ and holy persons employed all these methods, he pronounced them lawful in certain times and circumstances, especially for English Catholics, who "live for the most parte amongst . . . violent and continuall adversaryes." In defining the conditions for any form of equivocation, he deemed it permissible only for the sake of health of soul or body, piety, charity, just profit, or necessity. These provided a wide excuse, but he likewise stressed that equivocation needed a sure ground lest it tend to the dishonor of God or injury of a neighbor, and that it would be a mortal sin to use it in the profession of faith.[23]

Garnet devoted considerable attention to the legitimacy of equivocation in circumstances connected with oaths. His basic assumption throughout was that Catholics as the victims of unjust persecution were entitled to use mental reservation and other deceptive methods in their own defense. One of his arguments involved the casuistical distinction between the immediate and final intentions of a questioner

[22] Ibid., pp. 29–31, 44–47.
[23] Ibid., pp. 48–51, 53, 59–60.

and was illustrated by the well-known case of someone required to state on oath whether he came from a certain place infected by the plague. In Garnet's view, such a person might reply that he did not come from there even if he did, because he knew it had no plague and his answer therefore satisfied the final intention of the questioner, which was to exclude people who might be plague carriers. Similarly, Catholics asked under oath by a judge about other Catholics could withhold the truth, as Catholics were not traitors and to apprehend the latter was the final intention of both the judge and the law. Garnet further maintained that to protect themselves, Catholics would be justified in equivocating in an oath whether it was enforced or taken voluntarily. Even in the case of an oath containing an explicit renunciation of equivocation, he held that it was allowable to swear it with a mental reservation. In this instance, a lie would at most be a venial sin, whereas no lie could be as sinful as divulging the truth to the harm of other Catholics. In such a matter, he added, even plain lies without a true reserved meaning did not so offend God by their falsity that he would not reward Catholics for their fidelity.[24]

Garnet's treatise concluded with a statement of approval from the superior of the English secular priests, George Blackwell, praising it for its learning, piety, and help in instructing and consoling afflicted Catholics. The notoriety it presently acquired was a result of its association with the Gunpowder Plot. Although the government never learned who its author was, it discovered a copy of the treatise in a search of the chambers of Francis Tresham, one of the conspirators. Later Tresham was proved to have resorted to mental reservation under questioning when he falsely denied that he had seen or communicated with Garnet for sixteen years. During their trial, Attorney General Sir Edward Coke charged the conspirators with "perfidious and periurious Equivocating" allowed and taught by the Jesuits "not onely . . . to conceale or denie an open trueth, but Religiously to averre, to protest upon salvation, to swear that which themselves know to be most false, and all this by reserving a secret and private sense inwardly to themselves, whereby they are by their Ghostly fathers perswaded, that they may safely and lawfully delude any question whatsoever." Coke exhibited and discussed the treatise, which he denounced as "a very labyrinth to lead men into error and falshood."[25]

[24] Ibid., pp. 81, 84–87, 97–99, 102–105.
[25] These statements appeared in the official government account, *A True and*

Garnet himself was tried separately in March 1606 for complicity in the Gunpowder Plot. Coke labeled him a "Doctor of Dissimulation and Destruction" and spoke of equivocation as a lying and blasphemous doctrine. Although the law of nature, he declared, had joined heart and tongue in marriage, the discord between them had produced a speech conceived in adultery which had bred the bastard offspring of equivocation. Garnet, admitting that he and Tresham had used equivocation, defended the practice. The Catholic church, he told his prosecutors, condemned all lying in the cause of faith and religion but permitted equivocation when there was no obligation to disclose the truth and as a protection against self-accusation under questioning. Even on the scaffold, Garnet was bidden by an official to make a full confession and "not . . . Equivocate." He replied that "It is no time now to Equivocate" and that he had already revealed all he knew. According to the official government account, he also stated, "I am sorie that I did dissemble . . . but I did not think they had had such proof against me, till it was shewed mee."[26]

Garnet had sought to define the conditions in which mental reservation would be licit, and in doing so he provided Catholics with an arsenal of reasons for its use. While it is impossible to ascertain whether or not its practice was widespread, it may well have been frequent, as a case heard in Ireland suggests. In 1613 an Irish grand jury was charged with perjury before the Irish privy council's Court of Castle Chamber for refusing to present a true bill against persons accused to it of recusancy. The jurymen, Catholics themselves, pleaded that it was against their conscience to charge any of their own faith with recusancy and stated that they had taken their oath with "a special reservation or exception to theire mindes" of all things that should touch their conscience or religion. In censuring them the court showed itself knowledgeable about mixed propositions that permitted a secret reserved meaning to evade lying. It called the practice a recent innovation that, if accepted, would make it impossible for anyone ever to be guilty of lying. It noted, moreover, that in contrast to Catholics, the Protestants persecuted under Mary Tudor had never been found to use equivocation, but answered truly and directly though at the price

---

Perfect Relation of the Proceedings at the Several Arraignments of the Late Most Barbarous Traitors (London, 1606), sigs. I, I1.

[26] Ibid., sigs. T4, V5–6, Y3–4, Fff3.

of their lives. The court resolved that the commonwealth "cannot possibly stand if this wicked doctrine bee not beaten downe and suppressed," for if it took root, there would be no faith, truth, or trust, commerce and contracting would cease, and civil society be dissolved.[27]

The connection of mental reservation with the Jesuits and the Gunpowder Plot provoked a barrage of attacks by English writers.[28] Even before the plot, George Abbot, a fellow of an Oxford college and future archbishop of Canterbury, had stressed its dangers in some lectures on moral questions which denounced its use by Southwell and portrayed the new doctrine, unknown in former centuries, as pure lying.[29] Not only Protestants but Catholic secular priests wrote these polemics. The English seculars' bitter enmity to the Society of Jesus at the end of Elizabeth's reign stemmed from their opposition to the Jesuits' political ideas in favor of the papal deposing power and resistance to the queen, and likewise to their resentment at the Jesuits' attempt to dominate the English mission. After Clement VIII in 1598 appointed George Blackwell as archpriest or superior of the seculars and instructed him to consult on every important matter with the Jesuits, a group of more than thirty seculars who regarded Blackwell as no more than a Jesuit tool appealed to Rome against him. From these Appellants, as they were named, and their lay sympathizers came some of the fiercest anti-Jesuit propaganda.[30]

In 1601 one of the Appellants, Christopher Bagshaw, published a diatribe against the Jesuits and Robert Parsons as traitors and liars. Besides accusing them as agents of the king of Spain, he indicted them for their duplicitous practice of equivocation and mental reservation. He described how, if a priest was asked whether he would support the queen in case of a papal invasion, the Jesuits approved the answer that

[27] See Anthony Petti, ed., *Recusant Documents from the Ellesmere Manuscripts* (London: Catholic Record Society, 1968), pp. 245–254.

[28] Peter Milward, *Religious Controversies of the Jacobean Age* (London: Scholar Press, 1978), pp. 82–86, contains a bibliography of the controversy.

[29] George Abbot, *Quaestiones Sex* (Oxford, 1598), "Epistle to the Reader" and chap. 1.

[30] See Thomas Law, *A Historical Sketch of the Conflicts Between Jesuits and Seculars in the Reign of Queen Elizabeth* (London, 1889); Arnold Pritchard, *Catholic Loyalism in Elizabethan England* (Chapel Hill: University of North Carolina Press, 1979), chaps. 7–10; and Holmes, *Resistance and Compromise,* chap. 17. Peter Milward, *Religious Controversies of the Elizabethan Age* (London: Scholar Press, 1977), pp. 116–124, gives a bibliography of the publications in the Appellant controversy.

he would take the queen's part with the mental reservation "if the pope will commaund us so to doe," thus deceiving the questioner. As a result of this, Bagshaw complained, the belief had arisen that "Catholicks are not to be trusted in anything they say." Hence when charged with any treason by the authorities,

> we have no way left unto us to acquit our selves from it. For be our answers never so direct and true (as honest men ought to answer their Christian brethren, and so much more the Civill Magistrate) our adversaries may say unto us, that we keepe this or that to our selves, which (as they can frame it) is sufficient to hang us . . . Whereby you see unto what a gulph of danger and discredit this double dealing of the Fathers with their heathenish position hath brought us poore secular Priests, and othermore honest and single harted Catholicks.[31]

A pamphlet by William Watson, another Appellant, repeated these accusations, equating the Jesuits' practice of mental reservation with "secret concealed treason." While admitting equivocation to be justifiable in some circumstances, he pronounced it absolutely wrong if used to answer a magistrate's questions relating to the safety of the queen and country. The Jesuits, he said, believed that everything should be according to the time and nothing according to the truth. They had perverted Paul's words that he was made all things to all men so that they could swear and forswear as suited their interest. Since they could answer one way and mean another, it was impossible for anyone not a Jesuit "to knowe a Iesuits heart."[32] Another tract by one of the Appellants' lay supporters described the Jesuits as guilty of

> lying legierdemaines, & dishonest dealings . . . consisting of mentall evasions in their speech . . . half-fac'd tearmes, tergiversations . . . whole and demie-dublings, the vulpecular fawne . . . holding it law-full to be forsworne in too manie cases . . . of all which they have an Arte . . . whereby they take away . . . not onlie all good religion from amongst men, but also even morall honestie.[33]

[31] *A Sparing Discoverie of Our English Iesuits and of Fa. Parsons under Pretence of Promoting the Catholike Faith in England* (London, 1601), pp. 7–8, 11–12; for Bagshaw's authorship see Milward, *Religious Controversies of the Elizabethan Age*, p. 119.

[32] *A Decacordon of Ten Quodlibetical Questions concerning Religion and State* (London, 1602), pp. 32, 66–67. For Watson's authorship, see Milward, *Religious Controversies of the Elizabethan Age*, p. 119.

[33] Anthony Copley, *An Answer to a Letter of a Iesuited Gentlemen* (London, 1601),

These were typical shots in the furious campaign waged by some English Catholics against mental reservation and other Jesuit teachings. Of the Protestants the most prominent opponent was Thomas Morton, a leading anti-Romanist cleric who was rewarded for his services to the English church by a succession of bishoprics ending with appointment in 1632 as bishop of Durham. Morton's first pamphlet after the uncovering of the Gunpowder Plot, *An Exact Discoverie of Romish Doctrine in the Case of Conspiracie and Rebellion* (1605), was an arraignment of mental reservation along with other nefarious Catholic precepts and principles. He amplified his treatment in succeeding works such as *A Full Satisfaction,* whose aim, as its title page proclaimed, was to expose the two Romish doctrines of "hainous Rebellion, and more then Heathenish Aequivocation." Several of these writings were produced as replies to Catholic opponents, notably Robert Parsons. Morton's discussion throughout these tracts was repetitive and offered no arguments against mental reservation which could not have been found in the works of Catholic authors themselves. He was acquainted with the literature of casuistry, citing Navarrus and other experts, and had also read Garnet's *Treatise of Equivocation* and the collection of cases of conscience drawn up for the English seminarians by Allen and Parsons.[34]

Morton denounced mental reservation as "lying falsehood" and blamed priests for using it to deny their priesthood and to misrepresent the truth in other ways. He dismissed the concept of mixed speech as an error because a secret or reserved meaning could not express or signify. Even eminent Catholic authorities such as Soto, known as the "subtile Doctor," and Azor, "your owne great Moralist," considered mental reservation as equivalent to lying and to perjury when used with an oath. He likewise aimed a blow at the doctrine of probabilism. After observing that the Jesuit Emanuel Sa had justified mental reservation even though a more probable opinion

---

pp. 92–93; for Copley's authorship, see Milward, *Religious Controversies of the Elizabethan Age,* p. 119.

[34] *A Full Satisfaction, concerning a Double Romish Iniquitie* (London, 1606). Part 3, sec. 2, is titled "A Confutation of Aequivocation." To have read Garnet's treatise, of whose authorship he was of course unaware, Morton would have had to be given access to a copy by the government to aid him in his polemics. He referred to the treatise and to the Allen-Parsons cases, which he called "The Resolution of English Cases," in the dedicatory epistle to *A Full Satisfaction.*

opposed it, he commented that the Jesuits "have another winding in this their Labyrinth, that Many times the less probable opinion is to be followed." In a review of scriptural cases, he contended that Jesus neither equivocated nor intended to deceive when he denied knowing the day of judgment. In reality, Christ's *nescio* meant that he did not think it fit for his disciples to know, and this was the clear sense in which they understood him. The undetectability and danger of mental reservation, Morton declared, dissolved "the naturall policie of all kingdomes" and compelled the English government to put priests to the rack to extract the truth.[35]

In his largest discussion of the subject, a laborious rejoinder to Parsons covering various popish teachings, Morton went over his previous arguments and several additional ones advanced by Parsons. Here he cited Sepúlveda's disapproval of mental reservation and engaged in a battle of interpretation about the opinions of other Catholic authors. Thus Soto, "never alloweth any other Equivocall sense, which is wholly infolded in the clause of Reservation, but that only which the outward speech it selfe may . . . carrie in the common use, according to the apprehension of the discreet hearer." To the suggestion that he himself would rely on mental reservation to refuse a request for a loan from an unreliable borrower, Morton replied that such an answer would be a lie. Against the biblical precedents its proponents invoked to approve amphibology in the form of mental reservation, he reiterated his judgment that "the Scripture alloweth not the Romish reservation." If "this new manner of Mentall Equivocation" were to take hold, he warned, lying would become unnecessary because mental evasion would be as secure and easy as any lie.[36]

From abroad as well came Catholic works against Jesuit morality which were published in England in translation. These had already started to appear a few years before, as in the anti-Jesuit pamphlets by the noted French jurist and champion of Gallicanism Etienne Pasquier.[37] In 1609 a tract translated from German inveighed against the Jesuits for their use of equivocation and mental reservation and also surveyed Navarrus' commentary on "Humanae aures." Navarrus, it

---

[35] *A Full Satisfaction*, pp. 47, 56, 59–60, 73–75, 97.

[36] Thomas Morton, *The Encounter against M. Parsons* (London, 1610), bk. 1, pp. 203–206, 216–217; bk. 2, pp. 36–38, 128–129, 171.

[37] *The Iesuit Displayed* (London, 1594); *The Iesuites Catechism* (London, 1602).

claimed, had composed his work "in favour, and on behalfe of the most famous Societie of Iesus."[38] Continental anti-Jesuit propaganda intensified as a result of the assassination in 1610 of Henri IV of France, an act their enemies attributed to the Jesuits' influence. The monarch's assassin, François Ravaillac, was thought to have been inspired by the famous justification of tyrannicide expounded by Juan de Mariana, a Spanish member of the order, in his political treatise *De Rege* (1599). The murder of the French king could thus be seen as akin to the criminal Gunpowder conspiracy in which Garnet had been inculpated. The Sorbonne and the Parlement of Paris condemned Mariana's book and the doctrine of equivocation. Hostile writers asserted that it was impossible to trust Jesuits' words or oaths because of their readiness to lie and answer questions with a mental reservation. Father Coton, Henry IV's Jesuit confessor, published a declaration to refute these accusations, which was promptly printed in English. His statement elicited a reply, *Anti-Coton,* also quickly translated. The latter accused the Jesuits of regicide and other misdeeds and, referring to Garnet's use of equivocation, condemned their subtle tricks to conceal their plots against the sacred persons of princes. The Jesuits' disavowals deserved no credence, said the writer, because they did not hesitate to forswear themselves by mental reservation.[39]

From the continent also came an apology for Garnet published by a Jesuit theologian with the approval of the general of the Society of Jesus, Claudio Aquaviva. The author, Andreas Eudaemon-Ioannis, who wrote in reply to Sir Edward Coke, ranged over various controverted doctrines ascribed to the Jesuits and firmly supported Garnet's opinion in favor of the legitimacy of equivocation and mental reservation. He considered them justified both by scripture and by the law of nature, which decreed that no one was bound to accuse himself. In rebutting the charges against his fellow Jesuit, he returned the accusa-

[38] *Aphorismes; or Certaine Selected Points of the Doctrine of the Iesuits* (London, 1609), p. 21. The original edition of this work appeared in Augsburg.

[39] For the reaction to the king's murder and the subsequent attacks on the Jesuits, see Roland Mousnier, *L'assassinat d'Henri IV* (Paris: Gallimard, 1964), chap. 4; and Edouard Piaget, *Histoire de l'établissement des Jésuites en France* (Leiden, 1893), chap. 8. Milward, *Religious Controversies of the Jacobean Age,* pp. 19–28, lists the English publications connected with Henry IV's assassination. Coton's *Lettre declaratoire de la doctrines des pères Iesuites* (Paris, 1610) was published the same year in English in *The Letter of a Catholike Man beyond the Seas.* The reply, *Anti-Coton* (Paris, 1610), appeared in English with the same title in 1611; the references to it in the text are from pp. 17, 20–21.

tion of lying and perjury not only against Coke but also against Luther, Calvin, and other Protestant reformers.[40]

In response to such writings, several other Protestant champions took up the quarrel against mental reservation and its Jesuit patrons. John Donne, who may have assisted Morton in several of his writings, published a satire on the Jesuits which, among their other sins, pictured them as dissemblers and liars. To the doctrine of free lying propounded by many authors and never banned by the church, Donne said they had added another, "lesse suspitious" but extremely useful, namely, "Mentall Reservation and Mixt propositions."[41] Thomas James, Bodley's librarian at Oxford, stigmatized the members of the Society as Machiavellians and dissemblers who would take any oath "according to the lawes of their mentall evasions and equivocations . . . which permits them any dissimulation." Because they had bewitched so many Catholics with their teaching, it had become impossible, he commented, to rely on a Catholic's word. Ironically, to support his portrayal he drew on the denunciations of the Jesuits by the secular priests.[42] Similar attacks came from two more Oxford dignitaries, Robert Abbot, Regius professor of theology, and John Prideaux, the rector of Exeter College, both of whom included an indictment of equivocation and mental reservation in their catalogues of the Jesuits' and Garnet's wicked deeds.[43]

Another Protestant controversialist was Isaac Casaubon, a noted French emigré scholar, who described equivocation as a newly invented science identified with the Society of Jesus and developed especially in England. He distinguished the Jesuit device of mental reservation from the "reticence" and "dissimulation" that he said were "ofttimes necessary in this wretched life." He regarded mental reservation, however, and its rationale of mixed speech as simply a method of lying. Scoffing at the view that mental reservation was licit under questioning by a magistrate but not in the intercourse of private

[40] R. P. Andreae Eudaemon-Ioannis e Societate Iesu ad Actionem Proditoriam Edouardi Coqui Apologia pro R. P. Henrico Garnet (Cologne, 1610), pp. 19–20, 29–30, 34, 39, 49–53.

[41] Ignatius His Conclave (London, 1611), Facsimile Text Society (New York: Columbia University Press, 1941), pp. 76, 77.

[42] The Iesuites Downefall (Oxford, 1612), pp. 17–18, 20.

[43] Robert Abbot, Antilogia adversus Apologiam Andreae Eudaemon-Ioannis Iesuitae (London, 1613); John Prideaux, Castigatio Cuiusdam Circulatoris (Oxford, 1614), likewise a reply to Eudaemon-Ioannis.

life, he termed it a strange new theology. He brought up Garnet's admission of equivocation to underscore the conclusion that the doctrine of mental reservation conduced to the overthrow of princes and the destruction of human society.[44]

Even Sir Walter Raleigh touched upon the subject in his vast *History of the World,* published in 1614 during his long imprisonment in the Tower. In discussing Joshua's dealings with the Gibeonites and the necessity to keep faith, he spoke of the "cunning perfidiousness and horrible deceit of this latter Age, called Equivocation." He praised Joshua for shunning the help of "Mental Reservation" and condemned the "God-mocking" practice of reserving a secret meaning in swearing oaths as a dissolution of the trust binding parents and children, masters and servants, and princes and subjects.[45]

One of the principal contentions in all these Protestant polemics was that mental reservation was a recent invention, a departure from the Christian past newly devised for the Jesuits' nefarious purposes. This was among the main points in another anti-Jesuit work that appeared late in the controversy. Its author, a London clergyman, Henry Mason, called Jesuit equivocation a new art "unheard of before these latter dayes." He made a distinction between "logicall Equivocation," defined as ambiguous speech, and "Jesuiticall Equivocation." While considering the first as lawful when there was a just cause to conceal the truth, he condemned the second, which relied on mental reservation and mixed propositions, as plain lying, and claimed that equivocation had never been traditionally understood to include this method. In tracing its origin, he explained that its groundwork had been laid by the later schoolmen and casuists, who had never dreamed what would result. He cited the disapproval of Soto and Sepúlveda to prove that as recently as their time, "which was about some 60 yeeres ago, there was still little or no speache of any Equivocation by mentall reservation . . . as the Romanists now fancie." It was Navarrus, the pope's "reader of cases at Rome," who in his commentary on "Humanae aures" first "broached this new arte," building on earlier arguments in favor of ambiguous speech. The Jesuits then took it from him, "which afterward they polished with great dexterity and care." Mason held that their doctrine actually destroyed the true nature of

---

[44] *Isaaci Casauboni ad Frontem Ducaeum S.J. Theologum Epistola* (London, 1611), pp. 108–111, 119–121.

[45] *The History of the World* (London, 1687), pp. 185, 186 (pt. 1, bk. 2, chap. 6).

equivocation by changing its meaning to justify lying under cover of the truth. It could serve to protect treason, to counterfeit miracles and apparitions, and to forge false and slanderous reports. It permitted the concealing of any truth or inculcation of any untruth "in ordinary dealings and course of life." If mental reservation were valid, he stressed, no one could ever be convicted of lying except by his own confession.[46]

Among the immediate consequences of the Gunpowder Plot was a further series of punitive measures against Catholics. Most severe was a statute of 1606 commanding recusants under heavy penalties to take the Anglican sacrament annually and imposing a new oath of allegiance on them in which the question of equivocation and mental reservation also figured. The oath required them in the first place to declare in the most comprehensive terms their loyalty and recognition of James I as rightful king and their disavowal of the deposing power of the pope as an impious, heretical, and damnable doctrine. In addition, it obliged them to swear that they made these statements according to their plain and common meaning "without any equivocation or mental evasion or secret reservation whatsoever." The oath's framers were so much concerned about equivocation that in an earlier version, not retained in the final wording, the swearer was made to say that he was "bounde in conscience by the worde of God, to speake the truth sincerely and unfaynedly according to the asking and understanding of you, that doe examine me." By the act of 1606 anyone over the age of eighteen indicted for recusancy was bound to take the oath, and in 1610 it was extended to many other categories of subjects.[47]

The oath of allegiance precipitated an international controversy while fomenting new dissensions among English Catholics and adding fresh fuel to the disputes between them and the English gov-

[46] "Address to Parishioners," in *The New Art of Lying Covered by Iesuites under the Vaile of Equivocation* (London, 1624), pp. 7–9, 26–29, 30–33, 55–59, 69, 88–89, 99–100.

[47] The statutes imposing the oath of allegiance and its extension in 1610, 3 & 4 Jac. I, c. 5, and 7 & 8 Jac. I, c. 6, are printed in Joseph R. Tanner, *Constitutional Documents of the Reign of James I* (Cambridge: Cambridge University Press, 1930), pp. 86–94, 105–109; an earlier draft of 1605 with other precedents for the oath is given in Roland G. Usher, *The Reconstruction of the English Church*, 2 vols. (New York: Appleton, 1910), 2:310–320.

ernment. Many of the Catholic laity were willing to subscribe it purely as a test of civil loyalty. Blackwell, the superior of the secular priests, urged the seculars and other Catholics to take it and also did so himself. Pope Paul V, on the other hand, denounced the oath as contrary to the faith, warning that Catholics who complied would endanger their salvation. The great Jesuit theologian in Rome, Cardinal Robert Bellarmine, likewise attacked it as impugning the papal primacy and criticized Blackwell for endorsing it. In the oath's support James I himself took up the pen. The king defended its necessity in the wake of the Gunpowder conspiracy as a means to distinguish good subjects from traitors and to effect a separation between loyal Catholics and those carried away by fanatic zeal to engage in treason and rebellion for religion.[48]

Blackwell was in prison when the oath of allegiance was administered to him. To ensure that his disavowal of the papal deposing power was genuine and without any form of secret reservation, his examiners interrogated him closely on his attitude. Probably they feared that he would use a mental reservation even when disclaiming its use, thus annulling his disclaimer. If he could do this, then it is hard to see how any answer he gave could ever have been considered satisfactory. Garnet's treatise, after all, had said that it would be at most a venial sin to use mental reservation even in an oath containing a renunciation of the practice.

Among those opposed to the oath of allegiance was Robert Parsons, the best known of the English Jesuits. He denied a Protestant adversary's accusation that one of his reasons for condemning the oath was its declaration that it was to be taken without equivocation. To this he countered that "no Equivocation was, or is to be admitted in any Oath concerning Religion or our profession thereof." Since papal primacy was an integral part of the Catholic faith, he claimed that Catholics who swore the oath must have done so with certain exceptions in favor of the pope's indirect power in relation to rulers, which they

---

[48] *A Large Examination Taken at Lambeth of M. George Blakewell* (London, 1607) includes Blackwell's defense of the oath and Bellarmine's criticism. James I's *Triplici Nodo, Triplex Cuneus, or an Apologie for the Oath of Allegiance* (London, 1607) also contains the two papal breves condemning it. Charles McIlwain, ed., *The Political Works of James I* (Cambridge, Mass.: Harvard University Press, 1910), pp. lv–lxxx, discusses the literature of the oath controversy and reprints James's *Apologie*. Milward, *Religious Controversies of the Jacobean Age,* pp. 89–119, contains a bibliography of the controversy.

would have expressed clearly, thereby excluding all equivocation. This was his charitable view, he explained, of those of his faith who had yielded to subscribe.[49]

Although Parsons repudiated equivocation and mental reservation in relation to the oath of allegiance, he was their most strenuous defender in the controversy engendered by the Gunpowder Plot. Oxford trained, a colorful personality and bold propagandist, leader, and organizer, Parsons wielded a prolific pen that made him the most prominent representative of Catholicism in its disputes with its English opponents. Not only was he the repeated target of Protestant attacks; he was also hated by many of the secular priests for his Hispanophile policies and dominant influence in the English mission. To his enemies he seemed the incarnation of the image they had formed of the Jesuits as blackhearted traitors, intriguers, and advocates of lying. In 1580 he and Edmund Campion had been dispatched as the first of the Jesuit missionaries to England, where he made many converts and established an underground press for the publication of Catholic literature. Then and later he took a leading part in the campaign to dissuade Catholics from attending Protestant services in compliance with the recusancy laws. After Campion's capture he made his escape to the continent, never again to return to his country, although he continued to be involved in all the great affairs affecting English Catholicism. He was a confidant of Cardinal William Allen, a political expert consulted by the papal and Spanish courts, and a power in the English seminaries. He traveled widely, living in Rome, then for nine years in Spain, and again in Rome, where in 1597 he became rector of the English College. Parsons' one goal was the restoration of Catholicism, and to this end he carried on an incessant literary activity. Of his many writings the one that aroused the greatest storm was his tract on the succession to Elizabeth, in which he maintained the right of the people to depose the ruler and alter the succession for just cause and the sake of true religion, and advanced the claim of Philip II's

---

[49] *The Iudgment of a Catholicke English-Man Living in Banishment for His Religion* (St. Omer, 1608), p. 18; *A Discussion of the Answere of M. William Barlow* (St. Omer, 1610), pp. 30, 93, 97. A work in favor of the oath of allegiance by an English Benedictine, Thomas Preston, written under the pseudonym Roger Widdrington, supported it on the basis of probabilism and stated that "very few Lay-Catholikes of any name, or worth with us doe refuse to take the Oath"; *A Theologicall Disputation concerning the Oath of Allegiance* (London, 1613), sigs. a3–c. See *DNB*, s.v., for a survey of Parsons' career.

daughter, the Infanta Isabella, to the English throne.[50] Parsons likewise undertook the task of vindicating the licitness of equivocation and mental reservation against the assaults of Thomas Morton and other Protestant controversialists.

In responding to an attack on the Jesuits by the Appellants, Parsons had commented, "He that sticketh not at lies, never needeth to use Equivocation."[51] This statement expressed the essence of his position that the methods of dissimulation permitted by Navarrus and other casuists were not lies but legitimate means of withholding the truth. His main discussion of the subject appeared in *A Treatise Tending to Mitigation towardes Catholicke Subiectes in England,* written as a confutation of Morton's earlier polemics. A work of over 550 pages, it was crammed with authorities—Aristotle, the Bible, Augustine and other church fathers, canonists, and theologians, as the controversial style of the age required. Intended as an argument for the toleration of Catholics by the English government, it covered a number of issues, including the loyalty of Catholics, but its largest theme was equivocation, with which it dealt at much greater length than did Garnet's treatise. While composing it, Parsons said, he had not seen Garnet's work; only when he reached the end did a copy "at this very instant" come into his hands.[52] He followed up this book with another on the subject two years later.[53] Between them these two compositions contained the fullest contemporary treatment of equivocation by an English Catholic author.

In the *Treatise Tending to Mitigation* Parsons explained that he wished to distinguish "lawfull and unlawfull Amphybologie or Equivocation" and to prove that equivocation was not a new doctrine invented by the Jesuits, as the ignorant believed, but had been discussed for centuries in theology and law. He likewise wanted to show that it did not destroy human intercourse, since "we doe except from the license of Equivocation the common conversation of men in contracts, bargaines, and other like affaires, whereby any dammage or preiudice may grow to another man."[54]

[50] Robert Parsons, *A Conference about the Next Succession to the Crowne of England* (Antwerp, 1594), which appeared under the pseudonym R. Doleman; Thomas H. Clancy, *Papist Pamphleteers* (Chicago: Loyola University Press, 1964), pp. 62–70.

[51] *A Briefe Apologie, or Defence of the Catholike Ecclesiastical Hierarchie* (Antwerp, 1601), quoted in Clancy, *Papist Pamphleteers*, p. 178.

[52] *A Treatise Tending to Mitigation* (St. Omer, 1607), pp. 369, 553.

[53] *A Quiet and Sober Reckoning with M. Thomas Morton* (St. Omer, 1609).

[54] *A Treatise Tending to Mitigation*, sigs. A3, D2.

Parsons insisted that Catholics always condemned lying and preferred plain and simple speech, contrary to what calumniators said. Equivocation, however, or amphibology, as he also termed it, was not lying, but a privilege permitted by human, natural, and divine law for the defense of innocence and the concealment of secrets. Far from being an innovation of the Jesuits, it had been received as true and lawful doctrine for four centuries. Had it been wrong, it could not have won universal acceptance as permissible in certain conditions. To uphold his claim of its antiquity, he enumerated an array of writers from Aquinas and other scholastics down to the moral theologians and casuists of his own time. While some of these, he observed, disagreed about aspects and applications of equivocation and were more strict and scrupulous than others, all approved its lawfulness in certain conditions. To his opponent Morton, he put the same case that Southwell had posed at his trial: what if the queen's life were in danger and Morton commanded to say where she was? Would he not have used equivocation or "doubtful speech" to delude her enemies? Many other such cases could occur, he pointed out, in which lying would be a sin, silence a confession of knowledge, and lawful evasion the only recourse. In the same way problems could arise that made equivocation necessary in relation to oaths and secrecy when judges and magistrates questioned unjustly and beyond their powers. As further evidence, he quoted sayings by Paul and Jesus such as the latter's statement to the Jews when they demanded a miracle, "Destroy this temple, and in three days I will raise it up" (John 2:19–22). Although Jesus had meant by his speech the temple of his body in reference to his resurrection, his hearers understood it as the temple of Jerusalem. Such examples showed that "sometimes of necessity wee must admit some use of equivocation without lying, for otherwise many places of the Scriptures and other holy men's writings & doings cannot be well understood or defended."[55]

Parsons listed two kinds of equivocation, mental reservation and ambiguous speech. The former, he held, while not comprised in Aristotle's concept of a doubtful or ambiguous sense, belonged to equivocation in its wider meaning. To bring out its character, he suggested that it would be more appropriately called "amphibology" because of its combination of mental and verbal speech. Internal or mental speech, he maintained, was not only possible, but capable of uniting

[55] Ibid., pp. 275–277, 279, 282–286, 288–290, 292–294.

with verbal speech to form a single proposition. Since he also conceived the lie as an utterance contrary to the speaker's mind, it followed that statements made with a mental reservation would be true.
As an illustration he used the model case of a man who replied to an
unjust questioner, "I am no priest," adding the mental reservation "so
as I am bound to utter it to you." This answer, which conformed to
the speaker's mind, was not a lie and could be affirmed without sin in
certain conditions. Hence someone questioned against law and equity
could frame any proposition true in his own sense, and this sort of
"deceit and dissimulation" would be licit. Such speech would be a
concealment of the truth, not a falsehood. The intention of the
reserved clause would not be to deceive, but to defend against the
injurious questions of an unjust judge, "I speaking a truth . . .
according to my meaning, though he taking it otherwise is deceaved
therby, but without any fault of mine." He also compared such reservations with the rhetorical figures of reticence—"what shall I say
more"—and of aposiopesis—"what shall I complain more"—locu-
tions that together with the implied unspoken part constituted a
single proposition of mixed speech.[56]

To buttress his view, Parsons avouched both "the very instinct of
nature" and a roster of luminaries, not only Jesuits but Dominicans
and others, including some "of the Spanish nation," all of whom
sanctioned equivocation in certain circumstances. Among the names
cited were Prierias, Cajetan, Paludanus, Lopez, Bañes, Toletus, Sa,
Suarez, Azor, Gregory de Valencia, and Molina. He also adduced further scriptural examples. The case of John the Baptist, who said no
when asked by the Jews if he was a prophet, was exactly analogous to
the model case of the man who denied being a priest. Since John
actually was a prophet, he must have answered with a mental reservation (John 1:21). Similarly, Jesus' statement "I do not judge any man"
(John 8:15) would have been false without a mental reservation,
Christ having been appointed as judge of the quick and the dead. In
the best-known precedent, in which Jesus told his disciples that he did
not know the day of judgment, Parsons interpreted the answer as "an
amphibologicall and equivocall mixt proposition, conteyning a
mentall reservation of our Saviour, not expressed in wordes." As an
additional argument, he observed that dissimulation was lawful even
though a listener formed a false meaning, provided its end was not to

[56] Ibid., pp. 317–318, 326–332, 339–342, 344–346.

deceive but something good and profitable. For God and nature had not left men devoid of a refuge in reason to preserve secrets without lying. The law of nature thus allowed man to use "amphibologicall speech that hath a true meaning in the speakers understanding," if it was done "not to deceave or hurt, but to defend himself."[57]

In looking further at the conditions that made mental reservation licit, Parsons stressed that a respondent was obligated to answer truthfully and in the questioner's sense when interrogated by a lawful judge or superior proceeding lawfully. But if a judge exceeded his authority or acted illegally, then he ceased to be a judge, and a defendant was free to employ all lawful means to avoid injury. This led Parsons to consider whether in such circumstances a defendant could answer a question by a direct denial even under oath. Though noting the disagreement of Soto and Sepúlveda, he endorsed the opinion in Navarrus' commentary on "Humanae aures," supported by numerous other doctors, that a defendant could directly deny an accusation with a mental reservation that God would understand. As Parsons summarized the accepted teaching, a person unjustly pressed to divulge a secret that he was unable to do without injury or public damage, could lawfully answer in word or oath according to his own true meaning, even though the hearer was thereby deceived, and this would be neither lying nor perjury.[58]

In his final remarks, Parsons exhorted Catholics not to use equivocation except for lawful reasons and in cases of just necessity. Again he justified the English priests willing to sacrifice their lives who used equivocation to avoid injury and save those who sheltered them. While fully supporting their conduct, he also pointed out, however, that if a priest believed equivocation would cause scandal or fail to gain him liberty, then it might be better if he confessed his priesthood. In all these affairs, Parsons observed, truth and justice were the two virtues that must govern.[59]

Parsons' second treatise, *A Quiet and Sober Reckoning with M. Thomas Morton,* was an even longer reply in his running debate with Thomas Morton, and largely a rehash of his previous arguments. He taunted Morton with his presumption in trying to match his own unfledged knowledge with the ranks of the great Catholic learned for

---

[57] Ibid., pp. 355–357, 363–364, 378–381, 397–398, 403.
[58] Ibid., pp. 416, 419–420, 426–428, 437.
[59] Ibid., pp. 545, 549–550.

a thousand years and "to come forth as it were in hose and dublet & challenge the whole Church of God." The only new point brought forward on dissimulation was the lie of Ananias and Sapphira to the apostle Peter, for which God struck them dead (Acts 5:3–10). Morton had cited this episode as an example of divine punishment of mental reservation. Parsons answered, however, that Sapphira was guilty of unlawful equivocation in order to deceive and did not speak the truth in her own sense, whereas unjustly questioned priests used lawful mental reservation to avoid lying.[60]

In spite of their repetitiousness and length, Parsons' treatises were able works of controversy. He was a lively writer and ingenious debater, even if he undertook a heavy burden in trying to demonstrate that mental reservation did not violate the moral law against lying. As Garnet's treatise not only remained unpublished but also was much shorter, Parsons' works constituted the most detailed exposition and defense of the doctrine of mental reservation in English. They supplied an anthology of authors, texts, and opinions from which probably even his opponents quarried. Their main arguments were taken from Navarrus' commentary on "Humanae aures." But whereas Navarrus had paid little attention to the problem of religious dissimulation, Parsons' overriding concern was to vindicate the legitimacy of religious dissimulation in the case of priests and other Catholics who relied on mental reservation to withhold information and escape detection. This was the central issue between him and his opponents. Since they took his reasoning to mean that mental reservation made lying impossible, they became more convinced than ever that the Jesuits were masters of deceit whose casuistry offered lying the widest conceivable license.

In the years following the polemical exchanges between Parsons and Morton, although anti-Romanist controversies in England continued, discussion centering upon equivocation and mental reservation gradually waned. That Catholics were prone to lying and dissimulation was taken for granted and became one of the common beliefs of popular Protestantism. Thus during the English civil war, an ordinance of Parliament in 1643 required an oath from popish recusants abjuring the doctrines of papal supremacy, transubstantiation, and salvation through works. This was to be sworn without any equivocation, mental reserva-

[60] "Epistle Admonitorie," in *A Quiet and Sober Reckoning*, pp. 97–99, 112–113.

tion, or secret evasion, the words being taken "according to the common and usual meaning of them." Later, the Test Act of 1673 obliged all officeholders to receive the Anglican sacrament and subscribe a declaration against transubstantiation. In 1678 a second Test Act, designed to bar Catholics from sitting in Parliament, ordered all peers and members of the House of Commons to swear their disbelief in transubstantiation, the mass, and adoration of the virgin and saints as superstitious and idolatrous, and to do so "in the plain and ordinary sense of the words . . . as they are commonly understood by English Protestants, without any evasion, equivocation or mental reservation whatsoever."[61] The purpose of the latter, like previous penal legislation, was to compel conscientious Catholics to declare themselves and undergo the disabilities of their religion. Yet it may seem strange or even illogical that if English Protestants believed Catholics were likely to lie, they should place any reliance on an oath the latter might swear, however carefully formulated. Even so, the Test Act remained on the English statute book until 1829.

Outside England, and particularly in France, mental reservation continued to be a subject of contention because of the persistent quarrels within the Catholic church between the Jesuits and their opponents. Navarrus' theory of mental reservation gained widespread support and underwent further development by other theologians.[62] Its acceptance provoked a bitter reaction from Catholics who saw the casuistical principles of the Jesuits as a contradiction of the precepts of the gospel. Jesuits, however, were neither alone nor unanimous in espousing laxist doctrines: theologians belonging to other religious orders also favored them, and there were individual Jesuits who opposed these teachings. Yet so great was the enmity toward the Society of Jesus that it was easy for many in the church to hold its members chiefly or solely responsible for a type of casuistry which licensed the subversion of Christian morality.[63]

In 1625 an English Benedictine, John Barnes, who lived in France

---

[61] Charles H. Firth and Robert S. Rait, *Acts and Ordinances of the Interregnum,* 3 vols. (London: H.M.S.O., 1911), 1:255–256; John P. Kenyon, *The Stuart Constitution,* 2d ed. (Cambridge: Cambridge University Press, 1986), pp. 385–387.

[62] Above, Chapter 8, and see Archibald Malloch, "Equivocation: A Circuit of Reasons," in *Familiar Colloquy. Essays . . . to A. E. Barker,* ed. Patricia Bruckmann (Ottawa, Ont.: Oberon Press, 1978), pp. 135–141.

[63] See "Laxisme," in *Dictionnaire de théologie catholique,* ed. A. Vacant, E. Mangenot, and E. Amann, 18 vols. (Paris: Letouzey, 1930–1972), col. 42.

and had once served as a mission priest in England, published a Latin treatise against equivocation which he then translated into French. His attack was one of the most comprehensive discussions of the subject that had yet appeared, certainly in France. It was a long, learned critique of the views contained in the Belgian Jesuit Leonard Lessius' *De Iustitia et Iure* and in Parsons' *Treatise Tending to Mitigation.* Barnes, who looked upon mental reservation as nothing but lying, blamed the fashionable casuistry in its favor for bringing hatred and persecution upon Catholics living among heretics. In his dedication, addressed to Pope Urban VIII, he justified his work as an attempt to clear Catholics of the charge that their religion constrained them to lie. Similarly, in his preface he pointed out that English Protestants attributed to the entire Catholic church the dishonest assertions of Parsons and other Jesuits.[64]

Barnes surveyed the standard cases in both the Old and New Testaments as well as the opinions of a host of ancient, medieval, and modern writers to sustain his thesis of the unlawfulness of equivocation and mental reservation as a species of lying. His main authority was Augustine, whom he followed closely in refusing any excuse for dissimulation and in denying that the scriptures either lied or permitted lying. He regarded the doctrine in favor of equivocation as merely an invention of weak modern theologians. Likening Lessius to Machiavelli and the ancient Priscillianists, who approved lying for religion, he warned that the claim that God and Christ equivocated opened the way to atheism. No plea of necessity, he contended, whether for the good of the church or the state, could justify equivocation. Not only was the doctrine of mental reservation contrary to truth, justice, and the nature of an oath; it also protected traitors to their country and undermined the obedience of religious to their superiors and the observance of their rule by religious communities. In analyzing amphibological speech, he argued that one of the reasons for its falsity was the inability of the mental part of the

---

[64] *Traicté et dispute contre les équivoques* (Paris, 1625), translated from *Dissertatio contra Aequivocationes* (Paris, 1625). Barnes's life brought him into conflict with his order, the Jesuits, and the papacy. His book was eventually put on the Index, and he himself was arrested in 1627, imprisoned, and brought forcibly to Rome, where he spent the last thirty years of his life in confinement for insanity. For his career and writings, see *DNB,* s.v.; *Dictionnaire de théologie catholique,* s.v.; and Maurice Nédoncelle, *Trois aspects du problème anglo-catholique au XVIIe siècle* (Paris: Bloud & Gay, 1951), chap. 1, which also discusses his treatise against equivocation.

mixed proposition to qualify either as speech or as an answer to an actual question. It was simply a nonlanguage and a deception, since speech had to issue from the mouth and be capable of being heard or perceived by the senses. The mental reservation recommended by Lessius and Parsons was thus a vain effort to establish a truthful dissimulation and a lie without lying. Barnes even devoted several chapters to cases of deception by animals and plants and to delusions of the senses in order to disprove the claim that nature itself sanctioned dissimulation.[65]

Barnes's work drew a quick and much shorter rejoinder from Théophile Raynaud (1588–1663), one of the most renowned French Jesuits.[66] An erudite controversialist, Raynaud charged Barnes with many errors and defended Lessius and the legitimacy of mental reservation on the basis of the scriptures, church fathers, and many later writers. He traced the term *mentalis restrictio* to the fourteenth-century theologian Paludanus (Petrus de Palude) and pointed out that the practice was everywhere now called "mental reservation" *(mentalis reservatio)*. On his interpretation, the familiar case of Jesus' denial to his disciples that he knew the day of judgment was only one of numerous instances in which Christ had spoken with a mental reservation. In refuting Sepúlveda, whose well-known criticism of mental reservation Barnes had mentioned, he commented that although the Spaniard was accomplished in polite letters and not a bad historian, "a theologian he was not." Raynaud packed his pages with the names of the moral theologians, summists, and canonists whose support he claimed for the use of mental reservation. As an alternative to Navarrus' rationale for the doctrine, he proposed a conception of mixed speech which related it so closely to the particular circumstances of the exchange between speaker and hearer that the responsibility for misunderstanding and deception fell entirely upon the latter, who should have been able to complete the spoken with the reserved part of the utterance.[67]

Anti-Jesuitism in France sprang from distrust of the order's close ties

[65] *Traicté et dispute*, chaps. 1, 3–4, 7–8, 10, 14, 18, 32–33, and passim.

[66] *Splendor Veritatis Moralis* (Lyons, 1627). I have used the edition titled *Disputatio de Veritate Morali, cum Mendacio et Locutionibus Aequivocis ac Mente Restrictis, Comparata, in Opera Omnia,* 19 vols. (Lyons, 1665), vol. 14. For Raynaud's career and writings, see *Dictionnaire de théologie catholique,* s.v.

[67] *Disputatio de Veritate Morali,* pp. 105, 137, 153, chap. 20 and passim. See also Malloch, "Equivocation," pp. 139–140.

to the papacy, its political influence, and its moral teachings. The trend gained new momentum at the end of the 1630s with the emergence of the Jansenist movement. Jansenism owed its distinctive religious ideas to the revival of Augustinianism, signalized in the celebrated posthumous work by Cornelius Jansen, bishop of Ypres, *Augustinus,* published in 1640. With its commitment to an Augustinian theology of grace and predestination and its austere principles of morality, Jansenism was deeply hostile to the Society of Jesus. The Jansenists stressed mankind's utter depravity as a result of the Fall and its total helplessness without grace, which God granted to only a handful. Their belief implied that the world was steeped in corruption and the ways of society evil or of no value to the Christian life. The Jesuits, on the other hand, maintained the efficacy of human free will to cooperate with God's grace in obtaining salvation and saw no basic contradiction between the values of the world and those of Christianity. They adapted their spiritual direction to the social position and style of life of their penitents, many of whom belonged to the highest ranks, requiring no great sacrifices from them in gaining an eternal reward.[68]

To a modern critic such as Henri Brémond, in his magisterial history of French religious ideas, the Jansenist outlook was profoundly flawed. Brémond considered the Jansenists' accusations against the Jesuits to be exaggerations and compared Jansenism's excessive rigorism and its pessimism about human nature unfavorably with the "devout humanism," optimism, and charitable flexibility of the Jesuits.[69] From the Jansenist standpoint, however, the Jesuits were patrons of a worldly morality who, by easing the path to heaven, led souls to perdition. The abbé de Saint-Cyran, the founder of the Jansenist movement, believed the Society of Jesus had nothing to do with an authentic Christianity. In 1643 his disciple, the theologian Antoine Arnauld, published a notorious attack on the laxity of their moral theology.[70] Jansenist opposition

[68] Nigel Abercrombie, *The Origins of Jansenism* (Oxford: Clarendon Press, 1936), discusses *Augustinus* and Jansenist and Jesuit theology; Antoine Adam, *Grandeur and Illusion: French Literature and Society, 1600–1715* (New York: Basic Books, 1972), chap. 5, brings out the social implications of Jansenist and Jesuit beliefs.

[69] *Histoire littéraire du sentiment religieux en France,* 11 vols. (Paris: Bloud & Gay, 1929–1933); for the humanism of the Jesuits and a critique of Jansenism, see vol. 1, pt. 1, chap. 1, esp. pp. 11–17, and pt. 3, chap. 1; see also the account of Father Coton, Henry IV's Jesuit confessor, 2:75–131, and the extended discussion of Jansenism in vol. 4.

[70] Abercrombie, *Origins of Jansenism,* p. 173; Adam, *Grandeur and Illusion,* p. 95; for Arnauld's book, *La théologie morale des Jesuites,* see above, Chapter 8.

culminated in 1656–57 in *The Provincial Letters* of Blaise Pascal, whose treatment of Jesuit casuistry in such doctrines as probabilism and mental reservation dealt a devastating blow to the order's reputation. His work incited a fresh outburst of controversy between the Jesuits' enemies and their apologists. A body of priests in Paris and some of the provinces also published a statement denouncing the bad maxims of the casuists, who were in turn defended by Jesuit writers.[71]

Meanwhile, in 1653 Pope Innocent X condemned as heretical five propositions on grace and predestination which were ascribed to Jansen's *Augustinus*. In reacting to the papal censure, the Jansenists were not averse to a little casuistry themselves. Refusing to disavow their beliefs, they adopted the position that although the five condemned propositions were false, they were not contained in Jansen's treatise. They distinguished between the question of right and the question of fact. Though acknowledging the pope's infallibility in regard to the first, on which they professed submission, they denied that he was infallible with respect to the second. They thus maintained in effect that even though the pope could not err in points of faith, he was incapable of determining as a fact whether a proposition was actually contained in a certain book. In 1656, a subsequent papal decree pronounced that the five propositions were condemned in the sense given them by Jansen. Louis XIV's government and the French church mounted an effort to crush Jansenism by requiring all clergy to subscribe a formula expressing adherence to the papal condemnation. Pascal's *Provincial Letters* was also placed on the Index by the Roman Inquisition.[72]

In spite of the pressures exerted upon Jansenism, opposition to Jesuit casuistry remained strong in France. The Sorbonne and the French bishops joined with the Jansenists in the outcry against them. Finally Rome was compelled to take notice of the criticisms, and in 1665 Pope Alexander VII issued a decree, which was extended the following year, against a number of current errors in matters of morals. Its preface lamented the damage to souls caused by the presence of a multitude of opinions alien to the simplicity of the gospel and the evangelical teachings of the church fathers, which had

[71] The article "Laxisme" discusses the quarrel and describes the reaction to *The Provincial Letters*.

[72] Adam, *Grandeur and Illusion*, pp. 97–98; and von Pastor, *History of the Popes*, vol. 30, chap. 5, and vol. 31, chap. 5, describe the measures against the Jansenists and their response.

resulted in a relaxation of Christian discipline and threatened the corruption of Christian life. The censured propositions included extravagant opinions of casuists on a variety of matters—for example, that a husband did not sin in killing his adulterous wife; that a confessor could give a love letter to a penitent in the confessional; and that it was licit for an innocent man to kill a false accuser, witness, or a judge if he had no other way to avoid injury. Two of the condemned errors involved probabilism. One of them stated that an opinion in even a single book by a recent or modern author should be accepted as probable so long as it was established that the Apostolic See had not rejected it as improbable.[73]

In 1679 renewed complaints and criticisms from France and the university of Louvain brought a still more sweeping condemnation of various casuistical doctrines by Innocent XI and the Roman Inquisition. This act was the highwater mark of the papacy's attempt to deal with the consequences of a relaxed casuistry that had its foundation in probabilism.[74] The decree censured sixty-five moral errors, several of which directly concerned the doctrine of probabilism. One of these, for example, held it as probable that a person could judge according to the least probable opinion. Another held that when one acted in accordance with a probable opinion, however weak it might be, as long as it remained within the bounds of probability one always acted prudently. Among other moral errors the papal decree stigmatized were the following: that it was licit to desire the death of one's father because of the rich inheritance it would bring; that a son who killed his father while drunk might licitly rejoice in the fact if he thereby inherited a fortune; that God neither could nor would damn someone who called upon him as witness to a light lie; that it was licit for cause to swear an oath without the intention of swearing, whether in a light or weighty matter; that a gentleman might kill anyone who calumniated him if he had no other means of avoiding such ignominy; that it was not a mortal

[73] The decree is printed in Heinrich Denzinger, *Enchiridion Symbolorum,* ed. Karl Rahner, 31st ed. (Freiburg im Breisgau: Herder, 1960), nos. 1100–1146; see props. 6, 18, 19, 27, 28. For its background see von Pastor, *History of the Popes,* 31:246–260; and "Probabilisme," in *Dictionnaire de théologie catholique,* cols. 530–533, which also prints the preface.

[74] See von Pastor, *History of the Popes,* 32:428–432, whose account is slightly disingenous; and "Laxisme," cols. 72–85, for the background to the papal decree of 1679, which is printed both in the latter and in Denzinger, *Enchiridion Symbolorum,* nos. 1151–1216.

sin falsely to accuse another of a crime to defend one's honor; that copulation with a wife whose husband consented was not adultery; that a servant who helped his master to violate an unmarried girl was not guilty of mortal sin if he did so for fear of notable damage.[75]

Three of the condemned propositions endorsed the practice of mental reservation. The first declared that it was neither a lie nor perjury for someone, whether under questioning or of his own free will, to deny that he had done a thing, even if he had done it, using a mental reservation or some other means. The second stated that one might employ amphibology for just cause whenever necessary or useful for the sake of health, honor, possessions, or any virtuous act in which the concealment of the truth was deemed expedient. The third allowed a man who obtained public office by means of a bribe to deny under oath that he had done so, using mental reservation despite the intention of the imposer of the oath, because no one was obliged to avow a secret crime.[76]

The censure of these last three propositions, especially the second, clearly applied to the opinions contained in Navarrus' commentary on "Humanae aures." That some casuists also relied upon his work to authorize dissimulation in religion was something of an accident. Though certainly aware of the persecution of English Catholics, Navarrus had not made any reference to their plight in advocating mental reservation as a licit method of concealing the truth. His rationale for dissimulation was so broad, however, that it was easy for the Jesuits to extend it to the situation faced by priests and other Catholics in England. Its utilization for this purpose aggravated the scandal surrounding the doctrine and did far more harm than good to Catholic interests.

The papal decree of 1679 was not the last attack on the laxism of the casuists. The flow of criticism continued, and in 1700 the assembly of the French clergy condemned 127 propositions dealing with faith and morals, some involving probabilism and its excesses, and one opinion that stated that "the patriarchs and prophets, the angels, and Christ himself, without mentioning just and holy men, have used equivocation, ambiguous speeches, and mental reservation."[77] Obviously the

[75] Denzinger, *Enchiridion Symbolorum*, nos. 1151–1216, props. 2, 3, 14, 15, 24, 25, 30, 44, 50, 51.

[76] Ibid., props. 26–28.

[77] For the censure by the Gallican church and some of the condemned propositions, see "Laxisme," cols. 58–66; the one on mental reservation is prop. 66.

doctrine of mental reservation persisted despite papal disapproval and other weighty opposition. It was still maintained in the following century in a modified form by Alfonso Liguori, the most influential of later Catholic moral theologians. Though prohibiting purely mental reservation, Liguori sanctioned a practice so close to it as to make it seem a distinction without a difference. In cases of unjust questioning, he held that a respondent could answer with an unspoken afterthought, even under oath. He also commended a form of equivocation in which someone who was asked whether he had knowledge of a secret he was obliged not to divulge, could answer, *Dico non,* meaning "I say the word no," which his questioner, however, was intended to understand as a straightforward reply in the negative.[78]

Such devices, which were supposed to deceive without committing the sin of lying, no longer have a place in the thought of philosophers or religious teachers concerned with moral problems. Man, however, is an animal who seeks to justify his acts. Early modern casuistry in matters such as mental reservation and truthtelling reflected a legalistic conception of morality in which adherence to formal rules of conduct was exaggerated out of all proportion to its importance, while the substance of morality was obscured and lost. If the casuists exercised their ingenuity to devise new ways to express falsehoods without a technical violation of the rule against lying, this was because the Catholic system of morality had become increasingly a legal one of purely mechanical, outward compliance tied to penances and the confessional. The approval of dissimulation in the form of mental reservation by the Jesuits and other moral theologians of Catholic Europe, whether for the sake of religion or for any other cause deemed just or necessary, was one of the inevitable effects of this development.

[78] J. I. von Döllinger and Franz Reusch, *Geschichte der Moralstreitigkeiten in der Römisch-Katholischen Kirche seit dem 16. Jahrhundert,* 2 vols. (Nördlingen, 1889), 1:443–445.

CHAPTER 10

Casuistry and Dissimulation
in English Protestantism

English and continental Protestantism in the sixteenth and seventeenth centuries could show little in the domain of moral theology to match the massive science of casuistry in the Catholic church. While many English religious writers were concerned with the sort of practical divinity that provided moral guidance, only a few theologians, beginning with William Perkins at the end of the sixteenth century, produced manuals of casuistry. On the continent, where Johann Alsted, David Pareus, Frederick Bauduinus, and a few other divines also published casuistical treatises, the number was likewise small.[1] Commenting on this fact, Thomas Fuller noted in the mid-seventeenth century that Protestants were deficient in "case divinity" and that except for one or two recent authors whom they could consult, they had to go to the works of their Catholic enemies "for offensive and defensive weapons in cases of conscience."[2]

It is hardly surprising that the English and other Protestant churches failed to develop a science of casuistry comparable in scope or volume to that of the Catholics. Although diligent Protestant ministers might try to direct their flocks in the path of honest and holy living through sermons, catechizing, books, and private conference,

[1] K. E. Kirk, *Conscience and Its Problems* (London: Longmans, Green, 1933), pp. 203–204, lists sundry Protestant writers on casuistry. It is impossible to agree with his statement that "the output of Reformed casuistry in the seventeenth century is very considerable." Norman Clifford, "Casuistical Divinity in English Puritanism during the Seventeenth Century: Its Origins, Development, and Significance" (Ph.D. diss., University of London, 1957), mentions various writers who offered counsel in cases of conscience, but only a few of them were systematic casuists.

[2] Thomas Fuller, *The Holy State and the Profane State* (London, 1840), p. 69.

morality for them essentially meant following the divine law in the scriptures. Since Protestantism had abolished confession along with the sacrament of penance, its clergy had no authority as judges over conscience. Although they might be consulted as spiritual guides on moral dilemmas and could teach, advise, and warn, morals still depended on the individual's personal convictions and his immediate responsibility to God. Moreover, because of its association with Catholicism and the Jesuits, casuistry was highly suspect as opening the way to immorality. Jeremy Taylor, one of the leading English theologians of the seventeenth century to deal with the subject, expressed the common sentiment in observing that Catholic doctors had made cases of conscience "unstable as the face of the waters and unmeasurable as the dimensions of the moon," with the result that confessors were able "to answer according to every man's humour, and no man shall depart sad from their penitential chairs."[3]

English Protestants were frequently confronted with moral conflicts as a result of the enforcement of conformity by the royal state and established church. At various times under the Tudors and Stuarts certain groups among them faced the threat of persecution and the consequent temptation to dissimulate their beliefs. The imposition of compulsory oaths and subscriptions on Protestant dissenters as religious and political tests occasioned both controversy and evasion. The English theologians who wrote treatises on cases of conscience also touched on some dilemmas connected with dissimulation and truthtelling. The response to such tests and the casuistry of the theologians enable us to see how far the theory and practice of dissimulation figured in English Protestants' experience at this period.

The earliest significant manifestation of religious dissimulation in English Protestantism occurred in Mary Tudor's reign. Edward VI had established Protestantism in 1547 as the state religion. Upon his death and her succession to the throne, Mary restored Catholicism and enforced it through heresy prosecutions, with the result that Nicodemism made its appearance among her Protestant subjects. Alongside the sufferers for conscience whom John Foxe memorialized in his *Book of Martyrs* was the much larger number of believers who

---

[3] Jeremy Taylor, *Ductor Dubitantium, or the Rule of Conscience in All Her General Measures* (1660), in *Whole Works*, ed. Reginald Heber, rev. Charles Eden, 10 vols. (London, 1847–1854), 9:x–xi.

sought safety from persecution in pretended conformity to Catholic worship. Tracts such as Wolfgang Musculus' *Temporysour* and Peter Martyr Vermigli's *Treaties of the Cohabitacyon of the Faithfull with the Unfaithfull* were printed abroad in English and then smuggled into the kingdom to dissuade Protestants from religious dissimulation. Musculus' translator, an exiled Protestant minister, referred more than once in his preface to "the dissimulate hyprocrisie" of his countrymen who "cloke and dissemble" their faith and had made themselves odious in God's sight by their submission to idolatry.[4] The same theme appeared in a lamentation for the state of England penned by Nicholas Ridley, formerly bishop of London, one of the Protestant martyrs under Mary. Ridley exhorted his fellow Protestants to flee the realm to avoid pollution by popish superstition and warned against the sinful excuses they invented for dissembling their convictions.[5] From these appeals to conscience against any compromise with idolatry, it is clear that Marian crypto-Protestants used the same arguments as continental Nicodemites to justify their participation in Catholic rites. They pleaded the examples of Naaman the Syrian, Nicodemus, and Paul and claimed that they conformed only outwardly from fear of death or loss of goods, while inwardly their hearts remained pure.

With Mary's death and Elizabeth's accession in 1558, Protestantism again became the state religion. But along with the Catholic threat, which most concerned the Elizabethan regime, a new sort of religious opposition came into being in the form of Puritan dissent within the established church. Puritanism was a hotter kind of Protestanism strongly intent on the further reformation of religion with or without the crown's consent. Clerical Puritans and their lay adherents condemned the existing church for its retention of many relics of popish superstition. They demanded changes in the liturgy and removal of certain ceremonies. The more radical attacked the system of ecclesiastical government itself as unscriptural and anti-Christian and proposed to curtail the bishops' powers or abolish episcopacy altogether in favor of a presbyterian form of church polity. Conducting a well-orchestrated propaganda campaign, solicitous of influential lay support, and efficiently organized, the Puritan movement challenged the government's authority in both church and state. Puritan clergy disre-

---

[4] Wolfgang Musculus, *The Temporysour*, trans. Robert Pownal (Wesel, 1555), sig. Aiiii.

[5] "A Lamentation for the State of England," in John Foxe, *Acts and Monuments*, ed. Josiah Pratt, 8 vols. (London, 1870), 7:576–577, 579.

garded church ordinances of which they disapproved, persistently engaging in practices of nonconformity contrary to the form of worship prescribed in the official prayer book. In the 1570s some also created an underground presbyterian religious organization in certain localities to implement their scheme of reformation. When moderate measures to secure obedience proved unavailing, the government launched a stronger effort to crush Puritan dissent. The crackdown began in earnest with the appointment in 1583 of John Whitgift as archbishop of Canterbury.[6]

To reduce Puritans to conformity, Whitgift required that all clergy subscribe three articles as a condition of exercising any ecclesiastical function. The first acknowledged the rightfulness of the crown's supremacy over the church and the clergy. The second and third contained a declaration that the church's prayer book, ordinal, and thirty-nine articles of religion were all agreeable to the word of God, plus a promise to observe only the forms authorized in the prayer book in religious services and administration of the sacraments.[7]

These articles created a serious moral problem for Puritan ministers. Though willing to swear to the first article, they could neither assent that the prayer book and articles of religion accorded fully with God's word nor promise conformity to a form of worship which offended their conscience. On the other hand, if they refused subscription they risked expulsion from the ministry.

The sixteenth and seventeenth centuries were the age par excellence of the English state's use of oaths and subscriptions as compulsory tests of belief and obedience. Oaths were traditionally regarded as one of the strongest bonds holding society together. Despite Jesus' command against swearing (Matthew 5:33–37), Christian theologians and jurists had interpreted the prohibition restrictively as applying only to promiscuous and unnecessary swearing, and therefore sanctioned oaths in numerous contexts. Feudal oaths, oaths taken by judges, jurors, and witnesses, by officials and magistrates, and by guild officers and members, were among the many commonly accepted by nearly all Christians. But the device of imposing oaths and subscriptions as testimonials of conformity, even if the requisite formula vio-

---

[6] See Marshall Knappen, *Tudor Puritanism* (Chicago: University of Chicago Press, 1939); Patrick Collinson, *The Elizabethan Puritan Movement* (London: Jonathan Cape, 1967).

[7] Whitgift's articles are printed in Collinson, *The Elizabethan Puritan Movement*, pp. 244–245.

lated conscientious belief, was relatively novel. Such statements were more likely to be extorted through fear of punishment than given voluntarily. This method, destined to be used repeatedly into the next century, began with Henry VIII's repudiation of papal authority and annexation of religious supremacy. An act of Parliament then commanded certain classes of subjects to acknowledge by oath the monarchy's supremacy over the church and religion, an obligation that continued under Elizabeth and her successors. The main burden of such declarations fell upon Catholics, not only in the case of the supremacy oath but also in those of the oath of allegiance imposed after the Gunpowder Plot and the Test Acts of the later seventeenth century. But the state also attempted by the same method to compel conformity by dissident Puritan ministers of the established church. Whitgift's articles were the first major application of subscription for that purpose.[8]

Apart from the subscription thus demanded of them, the machinery of church authority oppressed Puritans with yet another oath that also posed a moral problem. The Court of High Commission, consisting of churchmen and civil lawyers, was the principal organ used by Elizabeth and her successors for the enforcement of the crown's ecclesiastical supremacy. While the suppression of surviving Catholicism among the clergy had been the commission's primary concern, it was also an essential instrument of the government's effort to coerce Puritans into obedience. The commission required those whom it summoned to take an oath before questioning, in which they promised to answer truthfully whatever interrogatories were put to them. This oath, known as the *ex officio* oath because administered to accused at the commission's order in cases begun on its own initiative, was normal procedure in the ecclesiastical courts. Tendered to someone suspected of nonconformity, however, even before he was informed of

[8] For the oath of allegiance and the Test Acts, see above, Chapter 9. An earlier statute of 1571, 13 Eliz. I, c. 12, required subscription by the clergy to "all the Articles of Religion which only concern the confession of the true Christian Faith and the Doctrine of the Sacraments." Relying on this ambiguous phrasing in the statute, Puritans who took the subscription interpreted it in a limited sense as signifying assent only to the doctrinal part of the Thirty-nine Articles, thus assuaging their conscience by means of casuistry. Whitgift's version of 1583 tried to eliminate the ambiguity by specifying acknowledgment of "all" the articles without any further qualification as agreeable to the word of God. Roland G. Usher, *The Reconstruction of the English Church*, 2 vols. (New York: Appleton, 1910), 1:365–371, 373–374, gives an account of the historical background to subscription in the English church.

the charges against him, it placed him in danger of incriminating
himself by his testimony. For this reason, and because it was unknown
in the courts of common law, Puritans and a number of lawyers constantly condemned it as illegal. Despite their opposition, however, the
High Commission continued to use the *ex officio* oath as long as it
remained in existence.[9]

Both the imposition of subscription and the *ex officio* oath presented
Puritan ministers with a heavy stumbling block. In either case compliance meant acting contrary to conscience. English Catholics and
priests in similar circumstances could resort to dissimulation, assured
by their casuists that it was licit to do so because they had no obligation to disclose the truth to heretical magistrates. How did Puritans
deal with comparable scruples in such situations in which they could
be punished for failure to conform?

When tendered Whitgift's articles, a few of the recalcitrant clergy
refused subscription entirely. Most, however, tried to resolve their
scruples by means of casuistry. Thus, they would state their willingness to subscribe, but only with reservations. To this Whitgift
responded that just as an oath in a court of law must be taken in the
sense intended and not according to the private meaning of the party
swearing, so subscription was required "in that meaning which those
that be in authority . . . do set down, and not in that sense which
everyone shall imagine." Because of their persistent resistance, however, many Puritan ministers were eventually permitted to make a
limited or conditional subscription or to subscribe with "a holy and
godly resolution" on certain points. In other instances they were
exempted from subscribing if they promised in writing to adhere to
the prayer book and orders of the church. Of course, when they subscribed with a condition—as, for example, that they did so only "as far
as the law requireth"—their intended meaning was that the law did
not require subscription, hence tacitly reaffirming their belief in the
latter's illegality. Similarly, if they promised to observe the prayer
book, they meant that they would follow only those parts of it conso-

[9] See Geoffrey Elton, *The Tudor Constitution,* 2d ed. (Cambridge: Cambridge
University Press, 1982), pp. 221–226; Roland G. Usher, *The Rise and Fall of the
High Commission,* 2d ed. (Oxford: Clarendon Press, 1968); and, for the resistance it
provoked in connection with the problem of self-incrimination, Leonard Levy,
The Origins of the Fifth Amendment (New York: Oxford University Press, 1968),
chaps. 2–9. The Court of High Commission was abolished by the Long Parliament in 1641 at the beginning of the English revolution.

nant with their beliefs. By means of such casuistical devices, which Whitgift tolerated in order to separate the small core of the most intransigent from the rest, most Puritan clerics were able both to salve their consciences and to avoid expulsion from the ministry.[10]

Whitgift's articles remained in effect by administrative fiat for the rest of Elizabeth's reign, but when James I came to the throne in 1603, about a thousand Puritan ministers petitioned him for reformation of abuses in the church, including a request to be spared subscription. Their statement indicates the sort of casuistry which allowed them to acknowledge the godliness of the prayer book. "Divers of us that sue for reformation," they said, "have formerly in respect of ye tymes, subscribed to the book, some uppon protestation, some uppon exposition given them, some with Condition, rather then the Churche should have been deprived of our Labours and ministerie."[11]

Their request went unheeded, however. In 1604, under the direction of Richard Bancroft, Whitgift's successor as archbishop of Canterbury, the convocation of the clergy enacted a new body of canons which made subscription part of the law of the church. With this new weapon, Bancroft, a bitter enemy of the Puritans, set out once again either to make them conform or to drive them from the church. The canon on subscription left no loopholes. It provided that no one could be admitted to the ministry or an ecclesiastical living without subscribing the three articles *ex animo* and "to all things contained in them."[12]

Pressed to subscribe, Puritan dissidents found themselves in a renewed moral dilemma between violating their conscience or abandoning their ministry. Some declined subscription, protesting that the articles and prayer book included "sondry things which are not agreable but contrary to the Word of God." Others as before expressed a willingness to subscribe but with provisos that permitted them "to interpret the things in the fayrest sense . . . the words of subscription may beare," or they tendered their subscription on the basis of "a comodious interpretation" of the meaning of the articles. As a result of these evasions, by the end of the archbishop's campaign the only clergy to be deprived of their ministry were those who adamantly

[10] Collinson, *The Elizabethan Puritan Movement*, pt. 5, chaps. 2–3, and pp. 249, 254, 264, 266.

[11] Printed in Stuart Babbage, *Puritanism and Richard Bancroft* (London: Society for the Promotion of Christian Knowledge, 1962), p. 44.

[12] Printed in Usher, *Reconstruction*, 2:309.

refused either to subscribe or to conform. These amounted to probably less than 10 percent of the total number who opposed the articles.[13]

Such were the methods Puritan ministers adopted to accommodate their conscience to subscription. Although their casuistry involved some dissimulation, they usually made no secret of it, unlike the English Catholics in similar circumstances, but openly expressed their intention to use a reserved or equivocal meaning in subscribing. These shifts, which enabled them to yield a purely formal submission to the decrees their consciences rejected, go far to explain how it was possible for most of them, despite their nonconformity, to retain their offices in the state church.

The *ex officio* oath administered by the Court of High Commission confronted Puritans with a still more formidable obstacle to conscience. Once they took it, they rendered themselves liable to self-incrimination by their replies to the ensuing questions from the commission's members, which they had sworn to answer truthfully. During the 1580s and 1590s in the course of the government's battle to suppress the Puritan movement and its clandestine presbyterian organization, the commission called many nonconformists before it to submit to interrogation that could lay the basis of a legal prosecution against them.

Under Mary Tudor's persecutions thirty years earlier, many Protestants suspected of heresy had tried to avoid answering questions about their beliefs lest they incriminate themselves.[14] Similarly, since Puritans considered the *ex officio* oath unlawful, one of their tactics before the High Commission was to refuse to take it unless told of what they stood accused. If informed of the matters on which they were to be examined, they might still refuse to swear or answer, contending that accusations against them should be proved by witnesses, not by their own testimony. Thus, in 1590, when the commission tendered Thomas Cartwright, one of the intellectual leaders of the Puritan clergy, "the generall and indefinite oath to answer whatever I should be demaunded touching articles to be objected against me," he refused, declaring that "I estemed it contrary both to the lawes of god, & of the land, to require such an oath, especially of a minister." By taking this stand, as Puritans frequently did, a defendant could halt the

[13] See Babbage, *Puritanism and Richard Bancroft*, pp. 127, 217–219, 226–229; W. J. Sheils, *The Puritans in the Diocese of Peterborough 1558–1610* (Northampton Record Society, 1979), pp. 82–83.

[14] See Levy, *Origins of the Fifth Amendment*, p. 77 and chap. 2, which cites examples from Foxe's *Book of Martyrs*.

commission's proceedings. As a consequence, though, he was also likely to be committed to prison for contempt without bail until he consented to swear and to undergo questioning.[15]

In a tract written to justify the High Commission's procedure, Richard Cosin, a civil lawyer who was one of its members, described the Puritans' method of responding to the *ex officio* oath. He likened their attitude to that of the Catholics, maintaining that "none but Iesuites, Seminary priests, & such like obstinate papists have resisted this othe in hir Majesties time, or have charged it to be ungodly; until these new reforming Innovators did start up: & that both the sorts of them do build upon the selfe same argument." According to Cosin, some Puritans persistently rejected the oath and demanded that witnesses and accusers be produced against them, even when having been told that their accusation was based either on common fame, on some form of presentment, or on the public interest. He viewed this conduct, intended to put a stop to further proceedings, as particularly reprehensible, an attempt "to circumvent . . . by cautels, and frustratorie shifts." Others pretended a willingness to swear but would do it only "with limitation and protestation, that they intend not thereby to be bound, either to accuse themselves, or their brethren." Cosin deemed this excuse analogous to the reasoning of the Jesuits, who also sought to evade questioning about their activities because it was "against nature and charitie." Another of the Puritans' responses was to admit that although they were bound in conscience to reveal their own or their brethren's true crimes and offenses, they had no obligation to disclose those actions which were really good but for which the law and the iniquity of the time could punish them. In Cosin's view this argument allowed every private subject to judge when and how far he should testify his knowledge of any matter. Would it not, he asked, "put a sure buckler into the hands of the Iesuites . . . to holde foorth against the lawfull examination of the Magistrates, touching themselves, or their complices?" If the Puritan innovators did not think of their nonconformity as a crime, neither did Jesuits "condemne their lewde seducing of her Maiesties subiectes as treasonable."[16]

---

[15] Albert Peel and Leland Carlson, eds., *Cartwrightiana* (London: Allen & Unwin, 1951), p. 27; Cartwright was imprisoned for refusing the *ex officio* oath; see ibid., pp. 28–30, for a statement of reasons by imprisoned Puritan ministers for their opposition to the oath.

[16] Richard Cosin, *An Apologie; of, and for Sundrie Proceedings by Iurisdiction Ecclesiasticall* (London, 1593), pt. 3, pp. 32, 179, 181–183.

The Puritans adopted these devices and every other means, Cosin believed, "to cloke their . . . actions" and "flie from the light." They felt they had committed no offense to incur the magistrate's displeasure and hence were not obliged to assist the magistrate. In effect, they said their cause was good even if the magistrate judged otherwise, and, as they were persuaded of their innocency, they would not be instruments of their own or other nonoffenders' detection.[17]

Cosin's defense of the *ex officio* oath stressed the parallel between Puritans and Catholics in their attitude toward interrogation by the government. Moreover, the Jesuits, seminary priests, recusants, and their concealers and harborers were "as assured of the goodness of their cause" as the Puritans were "touching theirs, & their designements."[18] This parallel, which was often drawn by the Puritans' adversaries, was indignantly rejected by a Puritan lawyer, James Morice, in a treatise against the *ex officio* oath. In condemning the oath as illegal because it led either to perjury or to self-incrimination, he denied that it was "first misliked by Iesuites and seminary Priests, and from them derived to others." On the contrary, it had been opposed earlier by English Protestants under Catholic persecution, "true Christians, holie, learned and Religious men, and that for good causes and considerations."[19]

Despite all the hatred dividing them there was a resemblance between Catholics and Puritan nonconformists in their attempts to elude incriminating questioning by royal officials. This similarity was recognized by John Udall, a Puritan minister haled before the High Commission in 1588 on suspicion of complicity in the secret publication of the notorious Martin Marprelate tracts against the bishops. After Udall rejected the *ex officio* oath, one of the commissioners told him his refusal was identical with the answer the seminary priests gave: "for they say, there is no law to compel them to take an oath to accuse themselves." Udall replied that "if it be a liberty by law, there is no reason why they should not challenge it." Although the priests were bad subjects, "until they are condemned by law [they] may

[17] Ibid., pp. 184, 201–202.

[18] Ibid., p. 209.

[19] James Morice, *A Briefe Treatise of Oathes Exacted by Ordinaries and Ecclesiastical Judges . . . and of Their Forced and Constrained Oaths Ex Officio, Wherein Is Proved That the Same Are Unlawfull* (1593), p. 18. Morice's attack on the *ex officio* oath could not be published in England and was probably printed in Middleburg, in the Netherlands, to escape the government's censorship.

require all the benefits of subjects."[20] This comment was most exceptional, for in general the Puritans strongly approved of the severity of the government's measures against Catholic recusants and priests.

Like Jesuits and seminary priests, Puritans took refuge in casuistry to justify their resistance to the *ex officio* oath. They had no doctrine of dissimulation, though, authorizing them to answer falsely even under oath. Instead of mental reservation, they relied chiefly on legal obstruction or tried to propose explicit qualifications as a condition of taking the oath. In their legal objections they had behind them the opinion of Puritan lawyers such as Morice, who maintained that the *ex officio* oath savored of the procedure of the Catholic Inquisition and was contrary to the law of the land.[21]

Occasionally, however, we find evidence that Puritans resorted to a more deceitful kind of casuistry in dealing with the High Commission. Thus, in a consultation about their conduct when summoned before the commission, some ministers decided that it would be justifiable to mislead their examiners without taking the oath if possible, but even under oath if necessary. To the questioning to follow, they concerted such evasive answers as "I did not doe as in the Interrogatory," "I did not to my memory doe etc.," and "I doe not knowe that I did or said any such thing." They also considered how to admit some facts while denying the rest. If a commissioner pressed them to remember, they recommended saying, "I am upon oathe and not you and I pray you to forebeare," or "I am upon oathe, leave me to my conscience. You are to take my answer not directe itt."[22]

A still more noteworthy example of dissimulation to outwit government repression occurred in connection with the Martin Marprelate tracts, which appeared as part of the Puritan campaign against episcopacy. Between October 1588 and September 1589 seven of these seditious satires were secretly printed, several in editions of 2,000 copies. Their author was an anonymous Puritan calling himself

---

[20] Quoted in Levy, *Origins of the Fifth Amendment,* p. 165.

[21] Ibid. Richard Cosin's defense of the High Commission and *ex officio* oath was written as a reply to attacks by Morice and another Puritan lawyer, Robert Beale, clerk of the privy council. Unlike Morice's treatise, Beale's work remained unpublished. On the opposition of the common lawyers to the *ex officio* oath and other features of the commission's procedure, see Levy, *Origins of the Fifth Amendment,* chaps. 6–8; and Usher, *Rise and Fall of High Commission,* chaps. 6–9.

[22] Quoted from a manuscript at Queen's College, Oxford, in Usher, *Rise and Fall of High Commission,* pp. 127–128 and n.

"Martin Marprelate, gentleman." Produced by Puritan printers on a migratory press, all bore false imprints; the first professed to have been "printed oversea in Europe within two furlongs of a bounsing priest." The tracts were widely read and discussed. Although some of the Puritan clergy censured them for their levity, their ribald humor, stinging wit, and scurrilous personal attacks exposed the bishops to deadly ridicule. The government made intensive efforts to stop their publication and apprehend those responsible. While the pamphlets were still appearing, it was discovered that Mrs. Elizabeth Crane, a Puritan, had harbored the press for a short time in her house in Surrey. On being questioned, she refused the *ex officio* oath, saying "she would not be her own Hangman" and "could not in her Conscience be an accuser of others." For this contempt and for harboring the press, she was heavily fined and imprisoned. In the investigations following seizure of the press, royal officials put several of the printers to torture and interrogated other accomplices and suspects in the hope of ascertaining Martin's identity. Despite all its exertions, however, the government never succeeded in conclusively establishing the pamphlets' authorship.[23]

The Marprelate tracts were not only a great propaganda coup but also one of the most significant episodes of secret printing in the history of sixteenth-century religious dissent and its evasion of censorship. Whoever Martin was, either he kept his identity hidden even from his closest associates or else none of them betrayed him. In a careful reexamination of the problem of the tracts' authorship, Leland Carlson has recently made a convincing case that they were written by Job Throckmorton, a member of the House of Commons in the Parliament of 1586 and a zealous Puritan. One of the original suspects, Throckmorton was indicted in 1590 for slandering the queen's government and writing libels against it under the name of Martin Marprelate. Apparently as a result of a technical flaw in the indictment, the proceedings against him were suspended. Nevertheless, he was neither pardoned nor acquitted, but remained on probation till his death in 1601.

In 1594 Throckmorton issued a reply to an attack against him by a

[23] See *The Marprelate Tracts* (repr., Menston: Scolar Press, 1967); William Pierce, *An Historical Introduction to the Marprelate Tracts* (London: Constable, 1908); Leland Carlson, *Martin Marprelate, Gentleman* (San Marino, Calif.: Huntington Library, 1981); Collinson, *Puritan Movement*, pp. 391–396 and passim. My discussion is based in part on Carlson, chap. 2.

hostile churchman in which he denied all knowledge of the tracts' author. To back his claim he affirmed his readiness to take an oath whenever the state required it that "I am not Martin, I knewe not Martin, And concerning that I stand endighted of, I am as cleare as a childe unborne." This explicit disavowal has always been held an obstacle to the assignment of the tracts to him. But given the weight of evidence that Carlson has provided for his authorship, his statement was probably a clever piece of casuistry. He had previously been involved in other clandestine publications under several pseudonyms and was quite capable of resorting to subtle devices to misrepresent the truth. It is noticeable that he did not offer to state in his proposed oath that he was innocent of any part in the writing of the Marprelate tracts or in their financing, publication, or distribution. Although as a religious man of strong beliefs he would perhaps have been unwilling to lie, he might well have sought to avoid technical falsehood by means of equivocation. In that case the words in his proffered oath could be interpreted as follows: "I am not Martin [no, I am Job Throckmorton], "I knewe not Martin [because he is a literary invention, not a real person], And concerning that I stand endighted of, I am as cleare as the childe unborne [of course I did not slander the queen's government, but rather attacked the wickedness of the bishops]."[24]

If Throckmorton employed a form of casuistry to mislead officials and to clear himself, it would not be surprising. Although we are inclined to think of Puritans as rigid moralists, their critics frequently pictured them as hypocrites who dissembled vices such as avarice, lust, and lying under a cloak of godliness. Of these two conceptions, the first is undoubtedly closer to the truth. But the Puritans were compelled to grapple with moral dilemmas in the same way as other people. Although Puritan nonconformists had no systematic rationale to permit deception and were often forthright to their interrogators, they were not averse to casuistry in self-defense. No less than Catholic priests and recusants they believed they were enlisted in a righteous cause and therefore justified in resorting to such methods of dissimulation as they judged licit in order to withhold the truth and defeat the government's attempt to silence them.

[24] See Carlson, *Martin Marprelate,* chap. 4, on Throckmorton's life and writings. With slight changes I have adopted his interpretation of the equivocation in Throckmorton's proffered oath.

The English Protestant theologians who dealt with moral problems were obliged to consider some of the same practical questions examined by Catholic moral theologians and casuists in their manuals, including the perplexities and conflicts of duties involving lying and dissimulation. Before the appearance of systematic works of casuistry in Protestant England, the most important writer to discuss the topic of lying was the reformer William Tyndale (ca. 1490–1536), whose translation of the New Testament made an inestimable contribution to the English Reformation. His treatment was exceptional in its willingness to countenance the lie in certain circumstances, as he made clear in his exposition of the gospel of Matthew.

The text on which he based his comment was Christ's command to his disciples not to swear (Matt. 5:33–37). After showing that Christ did not forbid all manner of swearing and that oaths were permissible in certain cases, Tyndale strongly emphasized that Christians were obliged to keep their word even without an oath. He then went on to say, however, that " to lie . . . and dissemble is not alway sin." One of his proofs was David's feigning madness to the king of the Philistines, an action no more sinful, in Tyndale's view, than his slaughter of the Amalekites. Tyndale defended lying and dissimulation either for charitable reasons or in a holy cause. To lie to someone in order to prevent the hurt or death of a neighbor "is the duty of every Christian man by the law of charity, and no sin; no, though I confirm it with an oath." On the other hand, "to lie for to deceive and hurt, that is damnable only."[25]

Tyndale's commentary went through at least six editions in the sixteenth century, so it must have been fairly widely read. Another work that touched upon the subject was Peter Martyr Vermigli's *Common Places,* a commentary on the scriptures posthumously published in both English and Latin versions in 1583. Vermigli played an important role in the English Reformation while serving as a divinity professor at Oxford during the reign of Edward VI. His discussion of deceit and guile distinguished between good and evil guile; he considered it lawful to use guile against the wicked and the enemies of God and the public weal, but prohibited it in the case of an oath. He drew a similar distinction between good and bad dissimulation, depending on

[25] *Exposition upon the Fifth, Sixth, and Seventh Chapters of Matthew* (1533), in *Expositions and Notes of Sundry Portions of the Holy Scripture* (Cambridge, 1849), pp. 55–58.

whether its aim was only to keep counsels secret or to deceive someone. He granted that Christ sometimes dissimulated for the sake of his mission, as did David by God's inspiration. On the matter of lying he departed from Tyndale's opinion. In deciding whether a good or godly man might lie, his judgment was in accord with Augustine's: he prohibited even lies to preserve a neighbor as harmful to human society. It is doubtful that Vermigli was either clear or consistent in approving guile and dissimulation of the good kind while condemning all lying and insisting on the inviolability of an oath.[26]

Although some biblical commentaries such as Tyndale's and Vermigli's dealt with moral problems, William Perkins (1558–1602), a Cambridge University theologian, was recognized as the first English Protestant writer to examine cases of conscience on a systematic basis.[27] A prolific author, Perkins achieved renown both as an expert casuist and as one of the most influential Calvinist theologians of his time. His preeminent concern was with the doctrine of grace, predestination, and election in its application to the life of the individual believer, and he was highly esteemed for his skill in practical divinity. As an exposition of the Calvinist conception of salvation in its experiential aspect, his works gained an unrivaled popularity. Despite strong Puritan sympathies, he refrained from acts of nonconformity himself. When pressed to state his opinion of the lawfulness of subscription to Whitgift's articles, he declined, preferring, said Thomas Fuller, a near contemporary, "to enjoy his own quiet, and to leave others to the liberty of their own consciences." It seems probable that he regarded the question of subscription as too dangerous a subject to handle.[28]

Perkins dealt incidentally with questions of casuistry in several

---

[26] *The Common Places* (London, 1583), pt. 2, chap. 13; see above, Chapter 6.

[27] For accounts of English Protestant casuistry, see H. R. McAdoo, *The Structure of Caroline Moral Theology* (London: Longmans, Green, 1949); Thomas Wood, *English Casuistical Divinity during the Seventeenth Century: With Special Reference to Jeremy Taylor* (London: Society for the Promotion of Christian Knowledge, 1952); Clifford, "Casuistical Divinity"; Camille Slights, *The Casuistical Tradition in Shakespeare, Donne, Herbert, and Milton* (Princeton: Princeton University Press, 1981), chaps. 1–2; William Whewell, *Lectures on the History of Moral Philosophy in England* (London, 1852), chap. 1.

[28] Thomas Fuller, *The Church History of Britain*, ed. James Nichols, 3d ed., 3 vols. (London, 1842), 3:121. *DNB*, s.v., refers to Perkins' Puritanism and caution. H. C. Porter, *Reformation and Reaction in Tudor Cambridge* (Cambridge: Cambridge University Press, 1958), chap. 12; and R. T. Kendall, *Calvin and English Calvinism to 1649* (Oxford: Oxford University Press, 1981), summarize his theology. Clif-

works. In *A Direction for the Government of the Tongue according to Gods Word,* he stigmatized the belief that a lie was permissible to procure some great good for one's neighbor or country.[29] In another work he indicted Catholics for the sin of perjury in teaching,

> with one consent, that a Papist examined may answer doubtfully against the direct intention of the examiner: framing another meaning unto himselfe in the ambiguitie of his words . . . whereas in the very law of nature, hee that takes an oath should sweare according to the intention of him that hath power to minister an oath: and that in truth, iustice, iudgement.[30]

He also composed a treatise on the nature of conscience which included a discussion of the obligation of laws and oaths.[31]

His chief claim to fame as a casuist, however, was his *Whole Treatise of the Cases of Conscience,* a posthumously published work based on his university lectures.[32] It consisted of three books dealing respectively with man as such, man's relation to God, and man as a member of the three societies of family, church, and commonwealth. In the second book he took up the problem of religious dissimulation which Protestant reformers and the spiritual guides of English Catholics were alike forced to address. The first question he propounded was whether believers were obliged to confess their faith "before the Adversary," meaning, of course, the Catholics. He answered that such confession was necessary, as was granted by "all Divines, save only . . . some pestilent Heretickes." As to when Christians must confess their faith, they were bound to do so either in case of questioning by those in authority such as judges and magistrates or in order to advance God's glory, avoid scandal, and prevent weaker brethren from falling away. Apart from these circumstances, Christians could "lawfully conceal their faith" and even their persons "by changing their habit and attire."[33]

---

ford, "Casuistical Divinity," discusses his casuistry, also briefly treated in Elliot Rose, *Cases of Conscience* (Cambridge: Cambridge University Press, 1975), chap. 11.

[29] In *The Workes of That Famous and Worthy Minister of Christ Mr. William Perkins,* 3 vols. (Cambridge, 1626–1631), 1:443.

[30] *A Reformed Catholike,* ibid, 1:619.

[31] *A Discourse of Conscience,* ibid., vol. 1.

[32] Ibid., vol. 2; first published in 1607, it is reprinted with *A Discourse of Conscience* in Thomas Merrill, *William Perkins, 1558–1602, English Puritanist* (Nieuwkoop: B. de Graaf, 1966).

[33] *Whole Treatise,* pp. 86–87.

Perkins next posed the question at the heart of Nicodemism: "whether it bee lawfull for a man . . . to go to idol-service, and heare masse, so as he keepe his heart to God." On this matter his view was completely negative. Like Calvin he argued that, as God created both soul and body, so God must be worshiped with both lest he be deprived of his due "when we reserve our heart to him and give our bodies to Idols." To confirm this opinion he reviewed the classic proof-text of Naaman the Syrian, as well as several other biblical precedents commonly advanced to justify a pretended outward conformity. He admitted no excuse for dissimulation in the case of Naaman, holding that the latter acknowledged his sin in bowing to the idol Rimmon and that it was for his offense that Elisha pardoned him.[34]

When he came to the subject of oaths, Perkins ignored the particular problems that troubled the conscience of Puritan ministers. He did not examine the licitness of a compulsory subscription requiring assent to propositions contrary to one's belief or of an oath that might entail self-incrimination. He took care, however, to refute the doctrines of equivocation and mental reservation. An oath must be sworn "according to the Minde and meaning of the Magistrate," not the taker's own intention. It must also be sworn without ambiguity but in a simple sense so that the words of the mouth agreed with the thought in the heart. If lacking these conditions, it would not be taken in truth but in fraud and deceit. "Popish teachers," he observed, believed they could swear a doubtful meaning in some cases in time of danger, "when being convented before the Magistrate, and examined, they answer yea in word, and conceive a negation, or No in their mindes." He condemned this "most impious" practice by the rule in scripture "that a man should sweare in truth, judgement, and justice."[35]

In all these questions Perkins' attitude harmonized with the strict opinions of other Protestant authorities. In a discussion of prudence in the third book of his treatise he included some additional comments relating to dissimulation. He recommended certain rules of prudence, one of which prescribed that, consistent with keeping faith and a good conscience, "Wee must give place to the sway of the times, wherein we live." Although it was forbidden to be a temporizer or to change one's religion, "we may and must give place to time, as we give place

34 Ibid., pp. 87–88.
35 Ibid., p. 93.

to the streame." In support of this counsel he mentioned the practice of Paul, who accommodated himself to the Jews and when among the heathen "was constrained to speak as they." The theme of prudence also led him to consider "whether a man may lawfully and with good conscience use Policie in the affaires of this life." *Policy* in Perkins' day frequently meant dissimulation and duplicity and was closely associated with the principles ascribed to Machiavelli.[36] In answer he pronounced policy lawful and not opposed to the Christian religion provided it observed certain caveats, in particular that it did nothing contrary to God's honor and glory or against justice. Among examples he cited Paul's pretense before Ananias to be a Pharisee: "And this was no sinne in Paul, for he spake no more but the truth, only he concealed part of the truth" (Acts 23:6). On the other hand, contrary to many casuists, Perkins condemned David's conduct in feigning madness as a fraud and deceit dishonorable to God. In the same connection he also denounced "that which is called the policie of Machiavel," calling it a violation not only of the written law of God but even of the law of nature because founded on lying, deceit, and injustice.[37]

Another of Perkins' compositions, a commentary on part of Paul's letter to the Galatians, also contained observations on dissimulation. He used the passage in the first chapter, in which Paul stated, "before God, I lie not" (Gal. 1:20), to discuss lying. In analyzing the lie he differentiated, as did other casuists, between lying and concealment of the truth by not disclosing what one knows, and permitted the latter for reasonable cause. He also distinguished lying and dissembling from "faining" or "simulation," which meant to speak "not contrary to, but beside or divers unto that which we thinke." If done for reasonable cause and not prejudicial to truth or against the glory of God or good of one's neighbor, feigning of this kind, according to Perkins, was lawful. Amplifying his conclusion, he claimed that there was "a kinde of deceit, called *dolus bonus,*" which is "a good deceit." This was the sort physicians used with patients and parents with children for their good. No fault attached to it, "for it is one thing to contrary the truth, and another to speake or doe something divers unto it." He went on, however, to insist on the sinfulness of lying even for the sake of others' good. Thus, in the case of the Egyptian midwives who lied

[36] Ibid., p. 116. See Felix Raab, *The English Face of Machiavelli* (London: Routledge & Kegan Paul, 1964), p. 78 and n.

[37] *Whole Treatise,* pp. 116–117.

to save the Israelites' children, although what they did was commendable, the means of lying they chose were not.[38]

In the same commentary Perkins also discussed the famous and controversial episode of Paul's rebuke to Peter for dissimulating. He held that Jerome and other exegetes were mistaken in explaining Paul's reproof as done in show. Rather, it was genuine and was provoked by Peter's sin in simulating conformity with Jewish law. In corresponding fashion to his distinction between good and bad deceit, Perkins then explained that simulation was indifferent in itself and good or evil according to circumstances. Whereas lawful simulation was "only beside the truth, and not contrary to it," unlawful simulation was "something . . . signified or fained against the truth or to the preiudice of any." Christ used the first when pretending to his disciples at Emmaus that he would go further, as did Paul in playing the Jew among the Jews. Peter's simulation, however, was of the second kind because it hurt the gospel and offended the Gentiles. Equally unlawful, Perkins added, was "the practice of sundry men who are Protestants with us, and yet in other countries go to Masse: and . . . of our people, who change their religion with the times."[39]

Although he was the first English theologian to produce a systematic treatise on the examination of conscience, Perkins was not a pathfinder in his teachings. His casuistical works occupied an honored place in the English church because they so well reflected the Protestant mainstream in their moral instruction. They showed strong common sense and refrained from the proliferation of hypothetical cases and subtle distinctions characteristic of Catholic casuistry. Although he was undoubtedly familiar with the casuists of the Catholic church, he did not imitate their method of referring to innumerable authors and opinions, and he rarely quoted or mentioned any work other than the Bible. In distinguishing falsehood from concealment of the truth, he followed a well-established tradition going back to Augustine. In accord with Augustine he also forbade lying even for a good cause. On the other hand, his distinction between good and bad deceit and between lawful and unlawful simulation resembled the opinion of Navarrus and, while far narrower in scope, authorized a latitude for some forms of verbal deception exempt from the sin of

---

[38] *A Commentarie or Exposition upon the Five First Chapters of the Epistle to the Galatians,* in *Workes,* 2:183–184.

[39] Ibid., pp. 198–200.

lying. This was especially evident in his approval of speech "beside" or "divers" to the truth rather than against it, a conception that he did not elaborate or try to clarify. His casuistry was highly practical, however, and just as he commended the use of policy and accommodation to the times within definite limits of principle, so he also permitted a measure of dissimulation under certain moral safeguards.

The tradition Perkins inaugurated in the realm of casuistry was continued by a line of churchmen respected both as theologians and as experts on moral problems. The first was William Ames (1576–1633), a Puritan who had been Perkins' disciple at Cambridge. Other successors were Joseph Hall (1574–1656), an Anglican bishop; Robert Sanderson (1587–1663), divinity professor at Oxford and also a bishop; Jeremy Taylor (1613–1667), another Anglican cleric who became a bishop; and Richard Baxter (1615–1691), a leading minister and the most important writer among the Protestant dissenters from the Anglican church in the later seventeenth century. All these learned men were acquainted with the literature of Catholic casuistry and intended their compositions to provide guidance in cases of conscience which they felt was lacking in the Protestant churches. Their own works covered many of the classic problems of Christian moral theology, including questions of truthtelling and dissimulation. Although Ames and Baxter were Puritans and the rest orthodox Anglicans, their moral teachings were broadly representative of English Protestantism without denominational distinction.[40]

William Ames was forced by his opposition to the English church

---

[40] Besides these writers, Donne and Milton also touched on casuistical questions in several of their works, but they did not influence the tradition of English Protestantism. Donne's *Pseudo-Martyr* (London, 1610), written before his ordination in the Anglican church, was an anti-Jesuit treatise that urged Catholics to take the oath of allegiance and even invoked the doctrine of probabilism. Another casuistical work, his posthumously published *Biathanatos* (London, 1648), justified suicide in certain circumstances. Donne may also have assisted Thomas Morton with some of his polemics against equivocation; see R. C. Bald, *John Donne* (Oxford: Clarendon Press, 1970), chap. 9; A. E. Malloch, "John Donne and the Casuists," *Studies in English Literature*, 2, no. 1 (1962); Slights, *Casuistical Tradition*, chap. 4. In his *De Doctrina Christiana*, not published until 1825, Milton's allowance for lying exceeded that of any other English writer of the century and was so wide that it bordered on laxity; see *Christian Doctrine*, ed. Maurice Kelley, in *Complete Prose Works of John Milton*, ed. D. M. Wolfe, 8 vols. (New Haven: Yale University Press, 1953–1982), 6:760–762.

and persecution by his ecclesiastical superiors to leave England in 1610.[41] For the rest of his life he served as minister to several English congregations in the Netherlands and as divinity professor in the university of Franeker. During this period the books he wrote, including the casuistical treatise *Conscience with the Power and Cases Thereof,* made him one of the most prominent Calvinist theologians of the age. His work on conscience contained five books, the last two of which, conforming to the order of the Decalogue, dealt with man's duty to God and to his neighbor. In its opening pages he lamented the absence of casuistical studies by Protestants, noting how much Catholics had done in that field. Although many of their comments consisted of the "dirt of Superstition," they also had "some veines of Silver" from which he admitted drawing "some things . . . not to be despised."[42]

In his treatment of oaths Ames looked closely at the casuistical devices sanctioned by Catholic moral theologians. Like other Protestant authors, he regarded "Mentall Equivocation" as a "grievous Sinne" that destroyed the nature of an oath by its dissimulation. He held that mixed speech could not constitute a single proposition and that the part reserved in the mind testified to nothing. Accordingly, although such speech was admissible in meditation or in relation to God, it could have no place in testimony before men. In agreement with the Jesuit Juan Azor, whom he cited as further proof, he concluded that the practice of mental reservation was "a direct and manifest lye" that opened the door to "all manner of lyes" by making it impossible for any statement to be false "if we doe but reserve something in minde, according to our pleasure." He was no less opposed to verbal equivocation as contrary to the nature of an oath. A respondent who deliberately answered a question in a sense different from that intended by his questioner was thus guilty of lying. Ames dismissed the claim that someone questioned illegally or wrongfully would be entitled to use equivocation because it was licit to provide for one's well-being. Even in such circumstances, he maintained, a respondent would not be justified in injuring the name of God by lying under oath.[43]

---

[41] See Keith L. Sprunger, *The Learned Doctor William Ames* (Urbana: University of Illinois Press, 1972); Clifford, "Casuistical Divinity"; Rose, *Cases of Conscience,* chap. 11.

[42] "To the Reader," in *Conscience with the Power and Cases Thereof* (London, 1643), a translation of *De Conscientia, et Eius Iure, vel Casibus* (1622).

[43] *Conscience,* pp. 51–53 (bk. 4, chap. 22).

Ames followed the traditional conception of lying in defining it as speech that "dissenteth from the mind." Though opposed to the lie for any reason, he considered it lawful to conceal the truth by silence provided that piety, justice, or charity did not require its disclosure. He also considered it permissible to reveal part of the truth and conceal the rest. Similarly, it was sometimes lawful and without falsehood to use words that, though true, would lead the hearer to conclude something false. In approving these practices, Ames dissociated them from mental reservation and equivocation. He rejected the common examples given by Catholic casuists to show that Jesus sometimes made use of mental reservation. In the most-cited of these, in which Jesus denied knowing the day of judgment, Ames explained that Christ spoke there as man, not as God, and thus did not deceive.[44]

Just as Ames was a more radical Puritan than Perkins in his refusal to compromise with the English church, so he was also a more rigorous moralist. Though permitting several means for concealing the truth, he did not adopt Perkins' distinction between good and bad deceit or lawful and unlawful simulation. His greatest concession to verbal deception was to permit a speaker knowingly to employ ambiguous speech from which the hearer could be expected to derive a false conclusion.[45] Like Perkins, he forbade lying and perjury even in cases of illegal and unjust questioning. Protestant dissidents who desired a licit method of dissimulation to circumvent the oaths or subscriptions imposed on their conscience by authority would have found little encouragement in Ames's casuistry.

Joseph Hall, Ames's contemporary, did not gain an equal reputation as a casuist but touched on an aspect of the problem of oaths which neither Perkins nor Ames had addressed. Successively bishop of Exeter and Norwich, during his long career Hall wrote many books on both religious and secular subjects and became well known as a satirist and moralist as well as a theologian and anti-Catholic controversialist.[46] In

---

[44] Ibid., pp. 269–273 (bk. 5, chap. 53).

[45] Rose, *Cases of Conscience,* comments (pp. 198–199) that this is "as clear a definition of equivocation as anyone could wish and an endorsement of a practice that would be hard to match among Catholics." This observation is a misconception, as is Rose's attribution (p. 198) of laxity to Ames's attitude toward law. In the context of his discussion of the Christian's obligation to truthfulness under the Third and Ninth Commandments, Ames's casuistical teaching left no room for the methods of dissimulation approved by Catholic casuists.

[46] See *DNB,* s.v.

one of his polemics he pointed to the great variations of opinion among Catholic writers. He claimed to find 303 contradictions in their works and devoted a special section to their differences concerning confession in which he frequently cited Navarrus. Among his accusations he termed Catholicism "a religion, that allows juggling equivocation and reserved senses; even in very oaths," of which he gave the teaching of the Jesuits and the Dominican Francisco Vitoria as examples. "O wise, cunning, and holy perjuries," he characterized these practices, "unknown to our fore-fathers!"[47]

Hall's *Resolutions and Decisions of Divers Practical Cases of Conscience in Continual Use amongst Men* exhibited an extensive acquaintance with the canonists and casuists of the fifteenth and sixteenth centuries. Its examination of oaths was noteworthy for rejecting as unlawful an oath compelling self-incrimination as a ground for initiating legal proceedings. "Even the Spanish casuists," he said,

> the great favourers and abettors of the Inquisition, teach that the judge may not, of himself, begin an inquiry: but must be led by something, which may open a way to his search; and, as it were, force him to his proceeding *ex officio;* as public notice, infamy, common suspicion, complaint; otherwise the whole process is void in law.

The fair way in all Christian judicatures, he maintained, "should be, by accuser, witness, and judge; in distinct persons, openly known."[48] Although the Court of High Commission was abolished nine years before Hall wrote these words and he did not specifically refer to its use of the *ex officio* oath, his statement seems to imply a clear condemnation of the commission's practice.

In discussing the rights of an accused he noted the opinion of "the learned Azpilcueta, the oracle of the confessaries," and other casuists which permitted a defendant "to answer with such amphibolies and equivocations as may serve to his own preservation; in which course natural equity will bear him out, which allows every man to stand upon his own defence." Hall did not agree with this endorsement of dissimulation. Like other Protestant authorities, he was willing to

[47] *The Peace of Rome Proclaimed to All the World by Her Famous Cardinal Bellarmine and the No Less Famous Casuist Navarre* (1609), in *The Works of Joseph Hall, D.D.,* ed. P. Hall, 12 vols. (Oxford, 1837–1839), 4:17–18, 23.

[48] *Resolutions and Decisions of Divers Practical Cases of Conscience* (1650), ibid., 7:409.

permit concealment of the truth but not its denial or contradiction, which he rejected as sin.[49]

He also scrutinized the problem posed by Nicodemism of whether a believer could be present at idolatrous services. Again in accord with orthodox Protestant opinion, he deplored such presence as sinful and a cause of scandal that confirmed offenders and grieved faithful Christians. He dismissed the example of Naaman the Syrian as "a poor plea," affirming that the prophet Elisha's valediction to Naaman could provide "no warrant for a Christian's willing dissimulation" of his religion.[50]

A considerably more important figure than Hall among English casuists was Robert Sanderson. A specialist in logic and jurisprudence, Sanderson spent some years as an Oxford academic and then became a parish clergyman and chaplain to Charles I. Such was the king's respect for his wisdom that he was reported to have said, "I carry my ears to hear other preachers, but I carry my conscience to hear Mr. Sanderson, and to act accordingly." In 1642, on the eve of the civil war between the king and Parliament, Sanderson became Regius professor of divinity at Oxford. In this position he delivered a series of lectures on the nature and obligation of conscience and another on the obligation of an oath, both of which went through several editions in the seventeenth century. Because of his refusal to subscribe oaths imposed by the victorious Parliament, he was expelled from the university in 1648. Upon the restoration of the Stuart monarchy in 1660, he was appointed bishop of Lincoln.[51]

In his lectures on oaths Sanderson stated that perjury could not be avoided by dissimulation. Insisting that an oath had to be taken in the common meaning of the words and in the same sense as the person to whom it was sworn, he barred equivocation and mental reservation as a sin. The latter, with its rationale of mixed speech, was an even more pernicious doctrine than the former because it destroyed all faith and certitude between men and licensed every sort of lie. Only if the words of an oath were inherently ambiguous did he allow that it

[49] Ibid., pp. 415–417.

[50] Ibid., pp. 430–431.

[51] *DNB*, s.v. Charles I's remark is mentioned by Sanderson's friend Izaak Walton, "The Life of Dr. Robert Sanderson," in *Lives* (London: Nelson, n.d.). These Oxford lectures, *De Obligatione Conscientiae Decem Praelectiones* (1660) and *De Juramenti Promissorii Obligatione* (1647), are in Sanderson's *Works*, ed. W. Jacobson, 6 vols. (Oxford, 1854), vol. 4.

might be taken in the swearer's sense. For this conclusion he cited the familiar passage from Gregory the Great's *Moralia,* enshrined in Gratian's *Decretum,* that the words should serve the intention and not the intention the words.[52]

One of the weightiest cases of conscience Sanderson ever undertook to resolve was a political test, the declaration of loyalty to the English Commonwealth. Commonly known as the Engagement, this declaration was imposed by an act of Parliament in January 1650 after the execution of Charles I, the abolition of monarchy and the House of Lords, and the vesting of supreme power exclusively in the House of Commons. The act ordered all men of eighteen and older to subscribe in the following words: "I do declare and promise, that I will be true and faithful to the Commonwealth of England, as it is now established without a King or House of Lords." Failure to comply involved considerable penalties, including loss of office and disablement from suing in any court of justice.[53] The Engagement precipitated a widespread political debate concerning the legitimacy of the Commonwealth and whether as a usurping power it could demand obedience from subjects as a duty.[54] Since the Engagement was a solemn promise even though it did not call God to witness, subscription presented not only a political issue but a genuine question of individual conscience. During the preceding civil war Parliament had exacted other oaths and subscriptions. The most important was the Solemn League and Covenant of 1643, a pledge in the name of God to reformation and the defense of religion and Parliament, which was subsequently demanded of all males over eighteen. One of its clauses contained a promise to preserve the king's person and authority and was thus incompatible with the Engagement.[55] Equally incompatible with it were oaths of loyalty sworn to the monarchy before the civil war.

The case of the Engagement was submitted to Sanderson by a perplexed clergyman in doubt whether to take it or not. Anxious about

---

[52] *De Juramenti,* pp. 259, 326–328, 330–331, 334.

[53] Printed in C. H. Firth and Robert R. Rait, *Acts and Ordinances of the Interregnum,* 3 vols. (London: H.M.S.O., 1911), 2:325–329.

[54] See Perez Zagorin, *A History of Political Thought in the English Revolution* (London: Routledge & Kegan Paul, 1954), chap. 5; Quentin Skinner, "Conquest and Consent: Thomas Hobbes and the Engagement Controversy," in *The Interregnum,* ed. G. E. Aylmer (London: Macmillan, 1974).

[55] Printed in S. R. Gardiner, *The Constitutional Documents of the Puritan Revolution,* 3d rev. ed. (Oxford: Clarendon Press, 1936), pp. 267–279.

his obligations to his family, he worried that he would lose his ecclesiastical living if he refused. Describing his moral dilemma, he wrote to Sanderson that,

> as I would not be flattered into a conceit that I may safely, without making shipwreck of a good Conscience, take the Engagement . . . so I would not precipitately ruin myself in my temporal estate by an over-preciseness in refusing what is not repugnant to the Rule of Faith, by which every Christian, and especially a Christian minister, ought to steer his course.[56]

The Engagement presented essentially the same kind of problem that led Catholic casuists to approve dissimulation on the ground of just cause. Sanderson, however, came to a different resolution. After explaining the nature of allegiance, he posited that no one who had taken the oath of supremacy or allegiance to the late king and his heirs, or who believed that sovereignty was rightfully in the latter, could subscribe the Engagement without sinning against his conscience, given that he understood the declaration to mean that supreme power was rightly in the present government and that he had an obligation to obey it. This brought him to the central problem of how the Engagement was to be construed and the two crucial questions: could a subscriber take the Engagement in his own sense, or was he bound to do it in the imposer's; and was it necessary or expedient that he ask before subscribing in what sense he was required to do so?

At the outset Sanderson stated that an oath had to be sworn in the meaning of the imposer as expressed by the words according to the common custom of speech. The opposite view, which he identified with the Jesuits' unlawful doctrine of equivocation, he condemned as a subterfuge resulting in perjury. If such a latitude of construction were to be admitted, men could have no assurance of one another's meanings, and faith would be impossible. Promises and assurances were thus to be understood according to the mind and intention of the person to whom they were given, with the words bearing their usual signification, excluding any secret or reserved meaning. If, however, the imposer's intention was not fully declared and the words of an oath were capable of a double sense binding either to more or to less, then it was not necessary, and might well be inexpedient, for the promiser to inquire which of the two senses the imposer intended. In that event, a subscriber "by the Rule of Prudence" could take just

[56] Printed in Sanderson, *Works,* 5:17–19.

advantage of the ambiguity, without violating any law of conscience, to subscribe in the sense "which shall bind us to the Less."[57]

He then analyzed the Engagement's language to show that it was open to both a higher and a lower construction. It could be understood as a promise of fidelity to the present possessors of supreme power or to the entire English nation as a commonwealth and civil society. It might mean approval of the existing government or merely de facto recognition of its power. It could signify the same fidelity and allegiance as were owed the king or a promise like that which a prisoner made to his enemies. These ambiguities, he held, were attributable to the imposer, not to equivocation by the subscriber, and hence justified understanding the Engagement in its lesser sense. He also suggested that the revolutionary government might even have allowed for this sense in order to make the Engagement more acceptable.

After these arguments, Sanderson summed up his conclusions. First, no one could lawfully take the Engagement who intended to break it or believed that it entailed an unlawful promise or obliged him contrary to his allegiance. Second, one who took it for a temporal benefit but was not persuaded in judgment of its probable lawfulness would be guilty of sin. Finally, one who seriously tried to inform himself of the duties of his allegiance and of the Engagement's probable meaning and was then satisfied that he could take it and perform its obligations as not contrary to his allegiance, so that he might avoid injury to his person, estate, or family, could subscribe the declaration. "Since his own heart condemneth him not," Sanderson declared, "neither will I."[58]

Sanderson's resolution of the case of the Engagement was dated December 1650 and was circulated in manuscript until its publication in 1668. Although we cannot tell its influence, a few people thought it actually defended the Engagement or even justified prevarication. If they did so, they overlooked the cautions and qualifications in his arguments. He himself did not use the liberty he permitted others and refrained from subscribing the Engagement.[59]

His opinion, however, was striking for both its strictness and its realistic flexibility. Despite the consequences of refusing the Engagement, it was hedged with qualifications and made no concessions to dissimulation. Moreover, by prohibiting subscription to the Engage-

[57] "The Case of the Engagement," ibid., pp. 24–25.
[58] Ibid., pp. 34–35.
[59] See the introduction in ibid., 1:xiv.

ment with the intention to break it, Sanderson opposed the position of many royalists who were said to take it purely with the resolution not to keep it.[60] Sanderson forbade all equivocation, yet while eschewing undue subtlety found the Engagement's language ambiguous enough to permit an interpretation of its meaning which might satisfy a scrupulous conscience in subscribing. In reaching this conclusion he placed full responsibility for moral decision on the conscience of the person in doubt. To subscribe without sin, this person had to feel sure in his own mind of the probability of the Engagement's lawfulness and of its consistency with his other obligations. By its reasoning, nevertheless, Sanderson's casuistry showed a way for the conscientious man to overcome his scruples and comply with the Engagement, thus enabling him to avoid the penalties ensuing from refusal.

After Sanderson the remaining English theologians of note who wrote works of casuistry were Jeremy Taylor and Richard Baxter. Taylor, an Anglican and royalist, was appointed in 1660 to the Irish bishopric of Down and Conner. A liberal churchman and advocate within limits of toleration and liberty of conscience, he was a celebrated preacher and distinguished author whose books *Holy Living* and *Holy Dying* became spiritual classics. Baxter, a Puritan and supporter of Parliament in the civil war, was ejected from the English church in 1662 with nearly a thousand other dissenting ministers who refused to accept the official liturgy and episcopacy and were thenceforth condemned to suffer under various legal disabilities. Despite his nonconformity he was, like Taylor, a proponent of toleration and religious concord, as well as one of the most widely read writers of the age. His best-known work, *The Saint's Everlasting Rest,* enjoyed an enduring popularity. Both men were more famed for their other writings than for their treatises on casuistry. Their works were far longer, however, as well as considerably more scholastic in character than those of their Protestant predecessors, and resembled the baroque luxuriance of the *summae* of Catholic casuists in their innumerable citations, their sometimes tortuous reasoning, and the range of cases and contingencies they surveyed.[61]

---

[60] S. R. Gardiner, *History of the Commonwealth and Protectorate,* 4 vols. (London: Longmans, Green, 1903), 1:246.

[61] For both Taylor and Baxter, see *DNB,* s.v. On Taylor's casuistry, see Bishop Reginald Heber's introduction to Taylor's *Whole Works,* vol. 1; Wood, *English Casuistical Divinity,* esp. pp. 103–116; and Sir J. F. Stephen, *Horae Sabbaticae* (London, 1892), essays 9–10. On Baxter's casuistry see Clifford, "Casuistical

Taylor's *Ductor Dubitantium, or the Rule of Conscience in All Her General Measures* comprised over eleven hundred pages of questions of conscience, rules, and explanations. It included many references to Catholic casuists, which he explained on the ground that the scarcity of casuistical divinity in the reformed churches made it necessary to resort to Romanist writers. He was severely critical, though, of the latters' teaching and characterized their doctrine of probabilism as a means "to entertain all interests, and comply with all persuasions, and send none away unsatisfied." In the same vein he decried their luxuriance of opinions and unnecessary propositions as creating such uncertainty that men were left in the dark and religion made into "an art of wrangling." Notwithstanding these strictures, in a complex disquisition on the probable and the doubting conscience he prescribed numerous rules for resolving difficulties in cases of opposing probable opinions.[62]

In the third book of his treatise, Taylor scrutinized questions of lying, mental reservation, and equivocation in relation to the subject of human law. The most striking feature of his discussion was its acceptance of the lie as licit in certain circumstances. Though affirming that men have a right to the truth, he held that this right must sometimes give way to a superior right or reason. Thus, it was lawful to lie to children and madmen, or for the sake of charity and to save the life of a neighbor, friend, or public person. On the other hand, he also maintained that a guilty person was obliged to admit the truth if interrogated justly. He likewise recorded his dissent from the opinion of Navarrus and other casuists who justified lying to escape infamy. It was more sinful to lie, he said, than to admit one's disgrace, especially when questioned by just and competent authority.[63]

In his treatment of mental reservation, he recalled the Jesuits' use of the practice, which he prohibited as lying. Nevertheless, he was willing in certain necessary cases to allow other mental restrictions in speech, such as tacit conditions or concealment of part of the truth. As to equivocation, he pronounced it lawful whenever lying was lawful. Hence in cases of great necessity or charity it was permissible to use

---

Divinity"; F. J. Powicke, *The Reverend Richard Baxter under the Cross* (London: Jonathan Cape, 1927), chap. 3; and N. H. Keeble, *Richard Baxter Puritan Man of Letters* (Oxford: Clarendon Press, 1982), chap. 4.

[62] *Ductor Dubitantium* (1660), in *Whole Works,* 9:v-vi, ix, 201, and bk. 1, chaps. 4–5. In his condemnation of the lax moral teaching of the Jesuits, Taylor referred to Jansenist criticisms and Pascal's *Provincial Letters* as proof; ibid., pp. x-xi.

[63] Ibid., 10:100–114.

language of doubtful signification in order to deceive. In these instances, he argued, in which there was no obligation to reveal the truth, the responsibility for deception in ambiguous speech rested with the hearer if he understood its meaning in a false sense.[64]

In the *Ductor* Taylor also examined the subject of compulsory subscription to articles and forms of confession. Here he touched upon a moral problem of significance to all Protestant dissenters from the national church. His opening comment upheld the right of governments to require subscription of this kind, and further specified that one who subscribed must do it "in that sense and signification of things, which the supreme power intends in . . . commanding it." At the same time, though, he observed that the imposition of oaths and articles was likely to bring more evil than good. Accordingly, Taylor contended that if the latter was required without necessity, then men should not be forced to subscribe but left free to comply or not; otherwise it would be persecution. He followed up this argument with a question that "hath been of late inquired," namely, whether it was lawful "for any man to subscribe what he does not believe to be true, giving his hand to public peace, and keeping his conscience for God." He answered that if subscription meant approval, it would be hypocrisy, "a denying to confess with the mouth what we believe with the heart." For this reason he did not endorse it. As his final resolution he concluded that no church should exact subscription to articles that were not evidently true and necessary to be professed. If the supreme power nevertheless required subscription for temporal reasons, then it should be obeyed, but should always show great consideration for the scruples and ease of peaceable dissenters.[65]

Taylor's attitude toward dissimulation was generally similar to that of his predecessors in its comparative strictness. He explicitly tolerated the lie, but within a narrow compass and solely in order to preserve life or to perform some other compelling moral duty. His discussion of mental reservation in the *Ductor,* however, evinced none of the urgency expressed by Protestant controversialists against the Jesuits and their teachings in the wake of the Gunpowder Plot a half-century before.[66] In the case of subscription to formulas of belief, he showed a

[64] Ibid., pp. 121–124.

[65] Ibid., pp. 447–450.

[66] In a subsequent work, *A Dissuasive from Popery* (1664), Taylor condemned the doctrine of equivocation and mental reservation in stronger terms as destructive of Christian society. He also criticized the Catholic handling of cases of conscience,

striking solicitude for liberty of conscience and a recognition that persecution bred hypocritical conformity. Although he disapproved of
dissimulation to evade subscription, he made equally clear that he
considered compulsion in such a case to be inadvisable and morally
wrong. In this judgment he parted from earlier Protestant moralists,
who neglected the question of forced religious oaths and subscriptions
as a basic problem of principle where truthtelling was at issue.

Richard Baxter's *A Christian Directory* (1673) was an 1100-page catalogue of moral analysis replete with questions, cases, and directions for
conduct. In his opening remarks Baxter praised the contribution of his
predecessors and emphasized the continuing need for cases of conscience so that Protestants would not have to go to Romanists for
guidance.[67] The four parts of the volume treated private duties, family
duties, church duties, and duties to rulers and neighbors, respectively.
Lying and dissimulation were discussed under private duties; oaths
were discussed under church duties.

Like so many previous writers on conscience, Baxter attempted to
distinguish between licit and illicit forms of dissimulation and lying.
Thus, after insisting on the inviolable obligation to truthfulness based
on the agreement of words and mind, he pointed out that no one was
bound to make everything known. To those who had no right to
know one could adapt one's speech by using language they would
misunderstand through ignorance. In such instances the blame for the
deception would rest with the hearers, whose own weakness caused
them to deceive themselves. Baxter also acknowledged that deception
was sometimes necessary for the safety of others or the commonwealth. He was willing to permit deceit for these ends as long as it was
not contrary to charity or justice. The lie itself, on the other hand, he
prohibited entirely. Even to the question whether it was not "contrary
to the light of nature" to suffer the destruction of parent, king, self, or
country rather than save them by "a harmless lie," he returned a
negative. In accord with Augustine he considered the lie so hurtful
that if once tolerated as lawful it would gradually undermine all
human society. Baxter denied that the familiar cases of Jesus' words
that he would go further and David's pretense of madness justified

---

with its distinction of venial from mortal sin, and the pernicious effects of the
doctrine of probabilism; *Whole Works,* 6:245-251, 273-274.

[67] Richard Baxter, "Advertisement," in *A Christian Directory: or, A Summ of
Practical Theologie, and Cases of Conscience,* 2d ed. (London, 1678).

lying. He regarded them as "lawful concealment or dissimulation," noting that "all dissimulation is not evil, though lying be."[68]

Turning to equivocation, Baxter described it as lying if it forsook the ordinary sense of words to deceive a person to whom one owed the truth. Against a robber, a tyrant, or an enemy's life-ensnaring questions, however, he allowed the use of "doubtful words," provided they were "not lies or false in the ordinary usage of these words." Thus he granted permission in certain circumstances to employ inherently ambiguous expressions for the purpose of verbal deception. He took a similar view of mental reservation. If the words in the expressed part were false, no reserved meaning could make them true. Conversely, if the expressed part was true, then to reserve something would be lawful "when it is no more than a concealment of part of the truth, in a case where we are not bound to reveal it."[69]

In his discussion of oaths, Baxter commended the opinions of Sanderson and propounded an elaborate casuistry comprising no less than forty-six rules of his own. To one who took an oath he forbade all equivocation, secret reservations, fraudulent interpretations, and dissembling. Imposed oaths, he likewise maintained, must be taken in the sense of the imposer. He followed this with a sometimes hair-splitting examination of the possible ambiguities in oaths and also gave attention to the question of oaths imposed by usurpers or the supreme power. Without alluding to the English government's use of religious and political tests, he held in general that an oath required by the supreme power was to be taken in the latter's meaning. In the event that an imposed oath had a bad or sinful sense, he considered it lawful to take it in one's own meaning, but one was obliged to make this known. Even oaths sworn from fear were voluntary and therefore binding; otherwise there would be no obligation to suffer for Christ, "but anything might be sworn or done to escape suffering."[70]

In a section on ecclesiastical cases of conscience, Baxter touched on the question whether it was lawful to be present at Catholic mass or worship. Though enjoining abstention from mass, he did allow Protestants who "cannot remove or enjoy better" to let their children undergo Catholic baptism if necessary and to be taught reading, arts and sciences, and common principles of religion by pious and moral

---

[68] Ibid., pp. 354–361.
[69] Ibid., p. 361.
[70] Ibid., bk. 3, chap. 5, pp. 26–29 (separately paginated).

priests. They could also join in pious prayers with Catholics provided they went no further. He thus showed far more tolerance and flexibility than earlier Protestant authorities, and left considerable room for accommodation by Protestants forced to live among papists. However, he warned that they must not participate with Catholics in their sinful worship or "scandalously . . . encourage them in it by seeming so to do." On this last point he cited Calvin's writings against Nicodemism, despite the fact that his own concessions in behalf of Protestant attendance would have been anathema to the Geneva reformer.[71]

What is impossible to establish from the teaching of these English casuists on dissimulation is the extent to which their opinions actually influenced individual behavior. All justified their work by emphasizing the Protestants' need for cases of conscience. Nearly all their casuistical treatises went through at least two editions in the seventeenth century and must therefore have been read, though doubtless more by ministers than by laity. The parochial clergy were expected to equip themselves with some knowledge of case divinity to help them in their pastoral responsibilities, and the more conscientious and competent would probably have done so. Some works of casuistry, such as Sanderson's Oxford lectures, were composed principally for the clergy. Others, however, such as Perkins' or Baxter's, were aimed at a broader readership. Ames said his subject was one to which all men should give their close attention, and Baxter intended his *Christian Directory* for use not only by ministers but also "by the more judicious masters of families" and "private Christians."[72] But how far were the opinions and rules of these Protestant authorities translated into conduct? Of this we can say almost nothing. It is clear, nevertheless, that their guidance respecting dissimulation whether for religion or for any other reason was much stricter than that of their Catholic counterparts. They differed from the latter in placing much tighter restrictions on the licitness of dissimulation and the circumstances that would justify it. In the matter of oaths and questioning by officials they altogether excluded the devices of deception sanctioned by Navarrus and other great Catholic canonists and casuists. Taylor alone accepted the lie as licit under very limited circumstances. Others con-

---

[71] Ibid., p. 91.

[72] Ames, "To the Reader"; Baxter, "Advertisement"; see also Wood, *English Casuistical Divinity*, pp. 31–37.

demned it absolutely, but approved of some other form of verbal deception in cases in which no obligation existed to disclose the truth or the life or safety of others was at stake. Most of them distinguished dissimulation from lying, the former being a concealment of the truth, the latter its misrepresentation by falsehood. Those who discussed the question of Protestant attendance at Catholic services considered all feigned conformity unlawful. Even Baxter, who departed from earlier views in not requiring total separation from papists in religion, strictly prohibited pretended participation in the Catholic mass or worship. Protestant casuists recognized the practical exigencies and moral claims that sometimes made dissimulation necessary and excusable. But they were more concerned than the Catholic advocates of equivocation and mental reservation to limit its effects, and showed a higher regard for truthfulness as an essential religious and moral obligation.

CHAPTER 11

Occultism and Dissimulation

When we peer deeply into the intellectual and moral life of sixteenth- and seventeenth-century Europe, we must be struck by how intensely aware its writers and thinkers were of the phenomenon of dissimulation. They showed a far stronger interest in it than did preceding generations and seemed at times to feel its presence as a pervasive or even overwhelming reality. Many of them viewed the world they lived in as filled with duplicity. One of the signs of this intensified awareness was the unprecedented amount of attention theologians and moral guides gave to the problem of religious dissimulation. Still another was the widespread acceptance of the principle of reason-of-state by casuists, political theorists, and politicians. Whether in relation to public or to private affairs, the idea that people commonly went masked and habitually dissimulated their true beliefs came readily to contemporary minds. Nicodemite justifications of feigned conformity among Protestants, Catholics, and sectarians, the sanction extended by casuists to the notorious practices of equivocation and mental reservation, and the approval of "policy" or duplicity by rulers and statesmen, all served to confirm the notion that dissimulation and lying had reached new heights and were more prevalent than ever before.

Elizabethan and Jacobean playwrights such as Christopher Marlowe, John Webster, and George Chapman expressed a deep fascination with the powerful effects of deceit and hypocrisy. Shakespeare frequently exploited the theme of the false presentation of self, and his Machiavellian villains, Richard III, Iago, and Edmund, are consummate dissimulators. When Hamlet's mother asks why he seems to mourn so long for his father, Hamlet's answer, "Nay . . . I know not 'seems' " and "I have that within which passes show," may be taken as attesting the revulsion he feels toward a court world full of falsity. In Tudor England, political men were obsessed with secrecy and ever fearful of dissimulation and deceit in their dealings with others, a state of mind a modern scholar has described as "cultural paranoia." Similarly, both the literature and politics of Restoration England in the later seventeenth century reflected an exceptional preoccupation with the use of deception and disguise and their penetration.[1] Francis Bacon, a perceptive reader of Machiavelli who dwelt much on the art of self-concealment, analyzed the nature of the phenomenon in his essay "Of Simulation and Dissimulation." In his coolly objective view, evincing little moral disapprobation, there were three degrees of "this hiding and veiling a man's self." The first was "Closeness, Reservation, and Secrecy"; the second, dissimulation, "when a man lets fall signs and arguments, that he is not that he is"; and the third, simulation, "when a man industriously and expressly feigns and pretends to be that he is not." Among the advantages of simulation and dissimulation were "to lay asleep opposition," "to surprise," and "to reserve to a man's self a fair retreat." Although Bacon did not wholeheartedly recommend either, he concluded that it was best "to have openness in fame and opinion; secrecy in habit; dissimulation in seasonable use; and a power to feign, if there be no remedy."[2]

Parallels to such remarks abound in the literature of the sixteenth and seventeenth centuries. The duc de La Rochefoucauld observed in his *Maxims* that sincerity was an openness of heart to be found in very few; what "is usually seen is subtle dissimulation designed to draw the confidences of others."[3] In his *Zodiac of Life* (ca. 1531), a much-reprinted and translated moral-didactic work, Marcello Palingenio declared that dissimulation was everywhere regarded as the greatest prudence and endorsed the well-known apothegm that "not to know

[1] *Hamlet*, act 1, scene 2; cf. Lionel Trilling, *Sincerity and Authenticity* (Cambridge, Mass.: Harvard University Press, 1972), p. 13; for "cultural paranoia," Lacey B. Smith, *Treason in Tudor England: Politics and Paranoia* (Princeton: Princeton University Press, 1986; J. R. Jones, *Country and Court: England, 1658–1714* (Cambridge, Mass.: Harvard University Press, 1978), pp. 2–3. S. N. Zwicker, *Politics and Language in Dryden's Poetry: The Arts of Disguise* (Princeton: Princeton University Press, 1984), p. 6, comments on "the degree to which disguise permeates and defines national life in the Restoration."

[2] *Essays*, in *Works*, ed. James Spedding, Robert Ellis, and Douglas Heath, 2 vols. (New York, 1878), 2:96, 98, 99 (cited hereafter as *Works*).

[3] *Maxims*, trans. Leonard Tancock (Harmondsworth: Penguin, 1981), no. 62.

how to dissimulate is not to know how to live." Particularly note-worthy is the judgment of the profoundly perceptive Montaigne. In his *Essays* he reproached his countrymen as incorrigible liars for whom lying was a form of speech rather than a vice. Pointing to "the new-found vertue of faining and dissimulation, which is now so much in credit," he contended that "dissimulation is one of the notablest quali-ties of this age."[4]

Because the Reformation forced the lines of dogma and orthodoxy to be drawn much more tightly, the relatively tolerant attitude toward intellectual diversity characteristic of the fifteenth century gave way to intensified censorship, book burning, inquisition, and other forms of thought control. Philosophers and intellectuals who strayed into het-erodoxy or unbelief did so at considerable risk. If they wished to avoid the terrible fate of Etienne Dolet, Michael Servetus, Francesco Pucci, Giordano Bruno, Tommaso Campanella, Lucilio Vanini, and other daring speculators who suffered death or imprisonment for their ideas, they were obliged to use indirection and concealment. It would not be surprising, therefore, if some of them also resorted to dissimulation. Although the term was applied very loosely, accusations of atheism became quite common in the sixteenth and seventeenth centuries. Among the guardians of orthodoxy the perception of dissimulation was strengthened by the conviction that some of the men of learning in their midst were hypocrites who pretended to be Catholics or Christians while actually embracing heterodox or irreligious beliefs. To demonstrate that a particular thinker commonly used dissimulation, however, remains a most difficult problem. Although an author might intend to convey a covert meaning under an appearance of orthodoxy, it is hard to be sure of this when we have only the words of his text as evidence. The answer to whether or not he was a dissembler is accord-ingly bound to be elusive at best.

Nevertheless, two major currents of thought in early modern Europe seem to have possessed an inherent proclivity for dissimula-tion: occultism and libertinism. Both harbored dangerous ideas, extending in the case of libertinism to actual incredulity. To associate

---

[4] Marcello Palingenio (Pietro Angelo Mazzoli), *Zodiacus Vitae sive De Hominis Vita,* ed C. H. Weise (Leipzig, 1832), bk. 4, lines 682–687; trans. Barnabe Googe (1576; repr., New York: Scholars' Facsimiles & Reprints, 1947), pp. 56–57 (I have slightly altered the translation); Montaigne, *Essays,* trans. John Florio, 3 vols. (London: Dent, 1910), "Of Presumption," 2:373; "Of Giving the Lie," 2:393; "Of Profit and Honesty," 3:13.

the two with dissimulation is not to suggest that every occult or libertine philosopher was necessarily a dissembler. The fact remains, however, that both of these philosophies possessed an innate and avowed
tendency toward secrecy and concealment which might easily also
lead to lying and deception. In this and the following chapters we
shall look at each of them in turn through the examples of a number
of notable individual thinkers in order to discern the features that gave
the two an affinity for such methods.

Belief in the existence of a hidden knowledge containing higher
truths unattainable except by the penetration of certain mysteries goes
far back in Western thought. Not only was this notion characteristic
of some of the religious and philosophical cults of Greco-Roman
antiquity; it also formed an important strand of ancient Christian tradition. In the third century it became the basis of the church father
Origen's enormously influential method of interpreting the Bible.
The greatest of Christian theologians before Augustine despite his
suspect orthodoxy, Origen conceived the sacred writ as possessing an
allegorical sense beyond its evident verbal meaning. The scriptures, he
explained,

> have not only that meaning which is obvious, but also another which
> is hidden from the majority of readers. For the contents of Scripture
> are the outward form of certain mysteries and the images of divine
> things . . . The inspired meaning is not recognized by all, but only
> by those who are gifted by the grace of the Holy Spirit in the word
> of wisdom and knowledge.

He further held that while "all has a spiritual meaning . . . not everything has a literal meaning."[5] According to a modern authority, this
view constituted "the point of departure for all the exaggerations of
medieval allegorism" and the reason that some of Origen's "symbol-
istic techniques became fantastic."[6]

   This conception of a secret or esoteric knowledge was also the leit-
motif of occultism, a mode of thought which achieved an exceptional
popularity and influence in early modern Europe. An amalgamation of
diverse traditions, occultism comprised a variety of doctrines such as

---

   [5] Origen, *De Principiis,* quoted in Johannes Quasten, *Patrology,* 3d ed., 4 vols.
(Westminster: Newman Press, 1964–1986), 2:92–93, with extensive bibliographical references to Origen's doctrine of the several senses of scripture.
   [6] Quasten, *Patrology,* 2:93.

astrology, divination, numerology, alchemy, pneumatology, and the Jewish cabala. One of its main ingredients was hermeticism, the hidden wisdom ascribed to the Egyptian priest Hermes Trismegistus, who was supposed to have lived around or before the time of Moses. In fact the treatises associated with Hermes' name, written in Greek, dated from as late as the second or third century A.D. and represented a mixture of pagan neoplatonic and other mystical and magical beliefs then current in the Roman world. In 1463 the Florentine humanist Marsilio Ficino published a Latin translation of and commentary on the Hermetic corpus. The subsequent widespread revival of hermeticism was reflected in its profound appeal to many thinkers from the Renaissance to the late seventeenth century. The hermetica and other ancient texts of a similar character, such as Orphic hymns, Sybilline prophecies, and Chaldean oracles, were seen by devotees as constituting the *prisca theologia,* or ancient theology. This was understood as the body of teaching derived from remote and venerable sources that in veiled form either prefigured or even included doctrines identical with those of the Christian religion. By means of this interpretation of the *prisca theologia,* occult philosophers could deny that they imported pagan beliefs and practices into the Christian faith and claim that they used them to confirm the truths of Christianity.

These several elements combined into a philosophy that was both speculative and practical. Occultism presupposed an animistic universe full of innumerable unseen spiritual agencies, subtle influences and correspondences between the various planes of being in the cosmos, and invisible sympathies joining earthly to celestial things. To man, created in the divine image, it attributed the ability to call upon and manipulate these unseen forces and influences. Numbers, words, and images were seen not merely as signs, but as entities endowed with mystical properties. To these conceptions occultism united a belief in the survival of a wisdom known to pagan sages of antiquity which could bring spiritual insight and purification to initiates and endow them with a power over things.

The two essential features of occultism were its esoteric character and its close association with magic. The first of these was analogous to Nicodemism and mental reservation in that, like the latter, it effected a separation between what was said and what might be licitly held back or disguised. The secret knowledge the occult philosopher claimed to possess consisted of doctrines intended solely for the initiate. It was to be kept hidden from the multitude lest they misunderstand and misuse it. The philosopher might also use this knowledge to perform operations that produced strange and wonderful effects. In this case he became a *magus* or magician as well. The magic he practiced could be either natural or demonic. The first exerted control over nature to achieve its effects by means of its grasp of the secret properties of phenomena. The second involved commerce with demons and other diabolic beings to accomplish its ends. The line between natural and demonic magic, however, was not always clear, and not all occultist thinkers practiced magic. Some refrained for fear of the dangers it entailed. Nonetheless, magic was an integral part of occultism and had a very great attraction for most of its devotees.[7]

The humanist scholars Marsilio Ficino and Giovanni Pico della Mirandola were the most noted exponents of the occult philosophy in Renaissance Italy. Although as philosophers they dealt with a broad range of topics, both were profoundly esoteric thinkers strongly drawn to a magic whose sources lay in the hermetic tradition and, in Pico's case, in the Jewish cabala. Ficino (1433–1499), a priest and physician, was a practitioner of "good" natural magic who may also have crossed the border into "bad" demonic magic. In his *Three Books of Life* (*De Triplici Vita*) (1489) he described various magical operations.[8] This magic aimed at the operator's own elevation rather than at producing effects on others, and relied for its power on the *spiritus mundi*, or cosmic spirit flowing through the universe, which channeled the

---

[7] On the occult philosophy and its hermetic and other components, see A. J. Festugière, *La révélation d'Hermès Trismégiste*, 2d ed., 4 vols. (Paris: Gabalda, 1950–1954); Frances Yates, *Giordano Bruno and the Hermetic Tradition* (London: Routledge & Kegan Paul, 1964); D. P. Walker, *Spiritual and Demonic Magic from Ficino to Campanella* (London: Warburg Institute, 1958) and *The Ancient Theology* (London: Duckworth, 1972). Eugenio Garin emphasizes the importance of the occult philosophy and magic during the Renaissance and early modern era in "Magia ed astrologia nella cultura del Rinascimento" and "Considerazioni sulla magia," in *Medioevo e Rinascimento*, 3d ed. (Bari: Laterza, 1966). Other helpful accounts are C. G. Nauert, Jr., *Agrippa and the Crisis of Renaissance Thought* (Urbana: University of Illinois Press, 1965); Wayne Shumaker, *The Occult Sciences in the Renaissance* (Berkeley: University of California Press, 1972); Brian Copenhaver, *Symphorien Champier and the Reception of the Occultist Tradition in France* (The Hague: Mouton, 1978).

[8] The actual title of this work is *De Vita Tres Libri*, but I have followed Walker, *Spiritual and Demonic Magic*, on which I have drawn for my discussion of Ficino's magic. Book 3 of *De Triplici Vita*, "De Vita Coelitus Comparanda," is especially important for astral and demonic magic. On Ficino's magic see also Yates, *Giordano Bruno*, chap. 4.

influence of celestial bodies to the spirit of man and the lower world. It called upon stellar and planetary forces and used talismans, images, Orphic songs, and other rites as means to preserve health and prolong life.[9]

Ficino's magical doctrines resembled a sort of astral polytheism, but he defended them as concordant with Catholicism. Nevertheless, he showed some anxiety over the orthodoxy of employing talismans and music. He denied that music contained incantations to summon demons and compel them to produce magical effects. Concerning talismans, he told his reader: "If you do not approve of talismans, which were, however, invented to benefit men's health, but which I myself do not so much approve as merely describe, then dismiss them, with my permission, [and] even, if you wish, on my advice."[10]

The excuse that he merely described without approving this procedure was probably no more than a subterfuge to avert censure. Ficino discussed demonology in detail, showing himself both strongly attracted to it and aware of its dangers. Fearful of being accused of trafficking with demons, he denied that he did so in an *Apologia* for his *De Triplici Vita.*[11] However, D. P. Walker, who studied his magical conceptions most fully, has pointed out that his "apparently non-demonic . . . 'spiritual' practices" may really have been "merely a dishonest camouflage" for the revival of a pagan theurgy involving demonic magic. Whether or not this was so cannot be conclusively determined; yet, as Walker noted, since a Christian could not have openly advocated demonic magic, Ficino would have had to keep it hidden.[12]

We cannot therefore rule out the likelihood that Ficino resorted to dissimulation to disguise the true nature of his magical operations. If this was what he did, it would have been a logical corollary of his esotericism. Despite the fact that he published his ideas on magic, he regarded them as belonging to the domain of reserved knowledge. He intended his magic for an intellectual elite and wished it to remain secret from the ignorant many who would only distort it into idolatry and superstition. In this way he hoped to avoid its dangers.[13] Esotericism for him was thus a form of prudence which may have also lent

9 Walker, *Spiritual and Demonic Magic,* pp. 3–53.

10 Ibid., pp. 42–43.

11 Ibid., pp. 46–52.

12 Ibid., p. 46.

13 Ibid., pp. 51, 53.

itself to dissimulation in order to safeguard higher truths against mis-
interpretation and abuse.

In the case of Ficino's contemporary, the young nobleman and
intellectual prodigy Pico della Mirandola (1463-1499), there is no suggestion of dissimulation. However, his incorporation of occultist
themes strongly influenced subsequent writers. His famous *Oration on
the Dignity of Man,* composed about 1486 as the introduction to a
philosophical disputation to be held in Rome, was steeped in esotericism. It opened with a quotation from Hermes Trismegistus ("A great
miracle, Asclepius, is man"), and extolled both a mysterious occult
knowledge and magic. Pico was obviously convinced that he possessed
this secret knowledge. He cited the opinion of Origen and other
church fathers that besides the written law, God gave Moses "a true
and more occult explanation of the Law" which he was forbidden to
commit to writing or make common. This part he was to reveal only
to a succession of high priests who in turn were to transmit it under a
strict obligation of silence. Jesus likewise communicated many revelations to his disciples which they did not write down lest they become
commonplaces to the rabble. It was thus a divine command that these
"occult mysteries" should be hidden from the people and divulged
only to the initiate. To do otherwise, Pico commented, here citing the
well-known words of Matthew 7:6 which were also used by
Nicodemites, would be to give "that which is holy unto dogs" and
cast "pearls before swine." As further confirmation of this principle,
he alluded to the custom of the ancient Greek philosophers and Egyptians, who preserved their mystic doctrines inviolate from the crowd.
A passionate student of the cabala, he claimed that the cabalistic books
contained the true interpretation of the law as well as many truths of
the Christian religion.[14]

The human creative power Pico celebrated in his *Oration* was partly
that of man as a *magus.* He pointed out that magic had two forms,
demonic and natural, the first of which was entirely dependent on the
work and authority of demons and therefore to be abhorred as monstrous. It was the most deceitful of arts, he said, rightly condemned by
the Christian and all other religions. The second kind, on the other
hand, was nothing else than the perfection of natural philosophy, and

[14] Giovanni Pico della Mirandola, *Oration on the Dignity of Man (Oratio de
Hominis Dignitate),* in *The Renaissance Philosophy of Man,* ed. Ernst Cassirer, Paul
Kristeller, and John H. Randall, Jr. (Chicago: University of Chicago Press, 1948),
pp. 249–252.

all men devoted to the study of divine things approved and embraced it. Whereas demonic magic enslaved men to demonic powers, natural magic gave them lordship over these powers. Abounding in the loftiest mysteries, it contemplated the most secret things and knowledge of nature. In what may have been a criticism of Ficino's magical operations, Pico asserted that anyone who cherished demonic magic "has ever dissembled because it is a shame and a reproach to an author."[15]

In the 900 theses of his proposed disputation, Pico amplified his exalted view of magic in a series of "Conclusions." In contrast to what he termed "modern" magic, which the church deservedly exterminated as diabolical, he maintained that natural magic was licit and not forbidden. This kind of magic united the separated virtues of terrestrial and heavenly things and employed characters, figures, and Orphic hymns in its productions. To these hymns he ascribed the same wonder-working powers as to the psalms of David. Despite describing his magic as "the practical part of natural knowledge," he confessed that "the more secret principles of natural philosophy" showed that "characters and figures can do more in magical operations than material substances." He also stressed the necessity of the cabala, involving the use of Hebrew letters, names, and numbers; without their mystical meaning, he insisted, no magic could possibly succeed. Pico was careful to state that the miracles of Christ were not performed by either magic or the cabala. Nevertheless, he went on to make the remarkable claim that "no science more certainly proves the divinity of Christ than magic and cabala."[16]

This astonishing assertion was one of the theses that got him into serious trouble with the ecclesiastical authorities. A commission of theologians appointed by Pope Innocent VIII found his opinions heretical. Pico replied to the charge in an *Apology* that included a defense of his position on magic. The pope, however, condemned all his theses, forbidding them to be copied, printed, or read. Pico was compelled to make a formal submission, although Innocent's successor, Alexander VI, subsequently absolved him of all charges of heresy.[17]

[15] Ibid., pp. 246–248.

[16] These theses are printed in Giovanni Pico della Mirandola and Gian Francesco Pico della Mirandola, *Opera Omnia*, 2 vols. (1557–1573; repr., Hildesheim: G. Olms, 1969), vol. 1; Pico's twenty-six "Conclusions" on magic and thirty-one further "Conclusions" on the Orphic hymns are on pp. 104–107.

[17] *Apologia*, ibid., pp. 166–181. Yates, *Giordano Bruno*, chap. 5, and Lynn Thorn-

The suspicion of dissimulation is inseparable from occultism, not only because of its preoccupation with the concealment of its esoteric doctrine, but also because of its ambiguous attitude to magic. Pico's career illustrates the animosity aroused even by a magic that he pictured as natural and void of harm. The interest that other occult philosophers betrayed in the dark side of magic seemed to belie the denials they made of having any relationship with demons. They had every reason to be circumspect, moreover, since the prominence of the occult sciences in the culture of the age also aroused strong hostility in various quarters. Many Catholic and Protestant theologians considered hermeticism as nothing more than a form of pagan idolatry and condemned magic as a harmful superstition. Many sixteenth-century humanists and writers likewise disapproved of these pursuits. The French reformer Jacques Lefèvre d'Etaples, though at one time greatly attracted to natural magic, later repudiated it as a dangerous delusion. Erasmus, the foremost biblical scholar of his generation, had no belief in the *prisca theologia,* was indifferent to the cabala, and disliked magic. Apart from this, the Catholic church had long condemned magical arts as evil, and many people were fearful of magic of any sort. Hence occult philosophers' disavowal of all connection with demonic powers may sometimes have been merely a pretense to escape persecution.[18]

One of the most notable figures in the world of occult thought was the German Johannes Trithemius (1462–1516), abbot of the Benedictine monastery of Sponheim until the last ten years of his life. A devout Catholic and vigorous monastic reformer, Trithemius was also an erudite humanist who knew Greek and some Hebrew and built a famous library at Sponheim. Besides writing many religious and historical works, he was deeply absorbed in arcane studies such as astrology, the cabala, and alchemy. One of his books, *On the Seven Secondary Gods,* dealt with the rule of the world by angelic planetary

---

dike, *A History of Magic and Experimental Science,* 8 vols. (New York: Columbia University Press, 1923–1958), vol. 6, chap. 59, discuss Pico's conception of magic and his condemnation.

[18] On these critical attitudes toward occultism and magic, see Walker, *Spiritual and Demonic Magic,* chap. 5, and *The Ancient Theology,* pp. 2–3; Yates, *Giordano Bruno,* chap. 9. Lefèvre d'Etaples never published his treatise on natural magic, *De Magia Naturale* (ca. 1493), probably out of fear, and later rejected its opinions; see Thorndike, *History of Magic,* 4:512–517; and E. F. Rice, Jr., "The *De Magia Naturale* of Jacques Lefèvre d'Etaples," *Philosophy and Humanism: Renaissance Essays in Honor of P. O. Kristeller,* ed. E. P. Mahoney (Leiden: Brill, 1976).

intelligences. Another, *A Defense against Enchantments,* was an attack upon witchcraft. He had a reputation as a necromancer and was reported to have enabled the Emperor Maximilian I to see his dead wife, Mary of Burgundy, as well as phantasms of former emperors, warriors, and heroes. Later writers have explained this feat as done by means of tricks with mirrors and optical illusions.[19]

Trithemius' occult teachings were shrouded in esotericism. A correspondent informed him that his "rare and admirable philosophy" was "so covered over with enigmas" and "arcane words" that he was unable to understand it.[20] His principal contribution to the occult sciences was his *Cryptography (Steganographia),* purportedly concerned with secret writing, which was not printed till 1606 but read widely earlier in manuscript versions. While composing it, he told a friend, a Carmelite monk in Ghent, that he had a great work in progress at which the world would marvel if it were ever published, which, however, it must not be; it would contain "stupendous things," including many "which are not to be divulged publicly."[21] It discussed not only ciphers and methods of encoding but also summoning planetary angels by means of talismans in order to send messages to a recipient without employing words, writing, or messenger. He must have been thinking here of a magic of mental telepathy. By this art, one could not only learn everything one wanted to know about the recipient, but also "everything that is happening in the world."[22]

Trithemius called himself a lover and follower of natural magic and averred that *Steganographia* dealt solely with cryptography. A number of his contemporaries believed otherwise, however. The French Platonist and theologian Charles de Bouelles (Bovillus), to whom he showed the work, denounced it as a manual of demon conjuration fit

[19] *De Septem Secunda Deis* (Nuremberg, 1522); *Antipolus Maleficiorum* (Peapolitana [Peggau?], 1508); Thorndike, *History of Magic,* 6:438–441; Wayne Shumaker, *Renaissance Curiosa* (Binghamton, N.Y.: Center for Medieval and Renaissance Studies, 1982), pp. 92–94; I. P. Couliano, *Eros and Magic in the Renaissance* (Chicago: University of Chicago Press, 1987), pp. 162–163. Klaus Arnold, *Johannes Trithemius* (Würzburg: Komissionsverlag Ferdinand Schöningk, 1971), chap. 10, deals with Trithemius as a magician; N. L. Brann, *The Abbot Trithemius* (Leiden: Brill, 1981), discusses his occult interests passim.

[20] Quoted in Brann, *Abbot Trithemius,* pp. 30, 44.

[21] Quoted in Thorndike, *History of Magic,* 5:524–525; cf. Brann, *Abbot Trithemius,* pp. 18–19.

[22] Walker, *Spiritual and Demonic Magic,* pp. 87–88; quoted in Yates, *Giordano Bruno,* p. 145.

only for the flames. A succession of sixteenth-century writers likewise held that it trafficked in pernicious magic. Others in his own time and afterward defended it as concerned exclusively with cryptography.[23] A recent scholar has concluded that Trithemius' magic was partly demonic and even "more obviously incompatible with Christianity" than Ficino's. It attempted to compel angels and spirits to perform extraordinary acts and was likewise perilous because it was transitive, aiming at effects on others rather than on the operator himself. Moreover, if Trithemius did intend to describe operations involving planetary angels, then the cryptographic part of his book could have provided a convincing alibi.[24]

Whether Trithemius was duplicitous in denying that his was a demonic magic is impossible to say. *Steganographia*'s esoteric intention, however, plus the attendant uncertainty as to its true meaning, themselves create a presumption of dissimulation. In a work on demons which he never completed, he said he would expose the deceptions of the occult sciences.[25] The latter could hardly have been his true opinion; hence if he had wanted to mislead concerning the character of his magical operations, this work itself would have served as a decoy. According to D. P. Walker, Trithemius' protestations that he did not advocate invocations to demons or anything contrary to Christian piety need not have been "downright lies" because he might have considered his own magic to be "good."[26] Nevertheless, given the obscurity and ambiguity of his work, the suspicion of dissimulation cannot be dismissed.

Both the ambiguities and likelihood of dissembling inherent in occultism were strikingly exemplified in the work of Henry Cornelius Agrippa (1486–1535), a friend of Trithemius and the most celebrated occultist writer of the sixteenth century, a man whose interests encompassed the entire spectrum of occult sciences derived from the esoteric wisdom of the ancients and their Christian and Jewish successors. After studying at the university of Cologne, he spent his life as a wandering scholar in France, Italy, Spain, Germany, and the Nether-

[23] Arnold, *Johannes Trithemius*, pp. 183–184; Walker, *Spiritual and Demonic Magic*, pp. 86–87; Thorndike, *History of Magic*, 6:439–440; Shumaker, *Renaissance Curiosa*, pp. 98–99.

[24] Walker, *Spiritual and Demonic Magic*, pp. 86, 89; cf. Yates, *Giordano Bruno*, p. 145.

[25] Arnold, *Johannes Trithemius*, pp. 199–200, describes this work.

[26] Walker, *Spiritual and Demonic Magic*, p. 89.

lands. A practitioner of both law and medicine, he also lectured in several universities and served on occasion as an official and man of affairs but without ever finding the security he sought. Although he reflected the humanism of his time in his longing for spiritual renewal and in his ardent response to the revival of classical antiquity, he gave his main allegiance to occult studies as the repository of an arcane teaching that could raise the mind to the understanding of sublime truths. In consequence, he enjoyed a mixed reputation among his contemporaries: some considered him a pretender and charlatan, others as a great *magus* and profound philosopher.[27] Francis Bacon, himself a student of occult literature, once referred to him as a buffoon, yet included him among important authors deserving serious study. In Christopher Marlowe's *The Tragical History of Dr. Faustus,* he is shown helping Faustus "to practice magic and concealed arts" and described as "honored by all Europe."[28]

Agrippa's fame rested on two works. One, *Occult Philosophy,* was a treatise on the occult sciences with magic as its central subject. The other, *The Vanity and Uncertainty of the Arts and Sciences,* was an uncompromising arraignment of every form of human knowledge as vain and uncertain, extolling the gospel above any human learning and satirizing the vices and follies of many ranks and professions, not least the monks and clergy.[29] Whereas the first exalted the powers of occult thought and magic, the second rejected the mind's ability to know anything. The relationship between these two books itself presents a puzzle that invites suspicion about Agrippa's intentions.

Agrippa showed the earliest version of *Occult Philosophy* to Trithemius, to whom it was dedicated, in 1510. Its first book was printed alone in 1531. Over the following years the work was expanded and shown in manuscript to various friends. The entire work, consisting of three books, was published in 1533. *The Vanity of*

[27] The fullest modern study of Agrippa's life and intellectual evolution is Nauert's *Agrippa,* on which I have drawn for this account.

[28] *The Tragical History of Dr. Faustus,* act 1, scene 1, lines 101, 115–116; F. H. Anderson, *The Philosophy of Francis Bacon* (Chicago: University of Chicago Press, 1948), p. 47.

[29] *De Occulta Philosophia* and *De Incertitudine et Vanitate Omnium Scientarum et Artium,* in *Opera,* 2 vols. (ca. 1600; repr., Hildesheim: G. Olms, 1970), vols. 1 and 2, respectively. I have also consulted *Three Books of Occult Philosophy,* trans. John French (London, 1651), and *Of the Vanitie and Uncertaintie of Artes and Sciences,* trans. James Sanford (1575), ed. Catherine Dunn (Northridge: California State University, 1974).

the Arts and Sciences, composed in 1526, was published in 1531.[30] In the
Vanity, the author retracted his treatise on occult philosophy and all
his esoteric pursuits, even though these undoubtedly remained a vital
interest for him which he never abandoned. In the preface to *Occult
Philosophy,* he touched on his retraction but never explained it.[31] How
could the corrosive skepticism of the former be compatible with the
vast claims for occult knowledge made in the latter?

His biographer, C. G. Nauert, in an effort to resolve this problem
on a purely logical plane, has suggested that there was actually no
contradiction: Agrippa conceived the magical power wielded by man
as dependent not on human reason but on divine inspiration and illumination.[32] An alternative explanation, however, may be that he used
dissimulation in certain parts of the *Vanity* as a defense against the
suspicions and animosity aroused by his magic. Despite his repeated
profession that he was a faithful Catholic ever willing to submit his
judgment to the church, many of his adversaries accused him of
heresy. Some believed he dealt in black magic. The Dominican
inquisitor of Cologne tried to prevent the publication of *Occult Philosophy,* and it was later placed on the Index.[33] He may therefore have
merely pretended to disavow the occult sciences as an alibi in self-
protection. While this explanation can be only conjectural, it is certainly not improbable. At any rate, Lynn Thorndike commented that,
given Agrippa's lifelong belief in magic, his recantation was possibly
"merely an assumed pose." And Frances Yates similarly interprets the
publication of the *Vanity* before *Occult Philosophy* as most likely a
"safety-device" of the sort frequently employed by magicians and
astrologers to fend off theological disapproval by being able to point to
critical statements made by themselves against their own subjects.[34]

The theme of secrecy was basic to Agrippa's thought. He always
stressed that the doctrines of the occult philosophy had to be concealed from the multitude. Like Ficino and Pico, from whose writings
he borrowed freely, he believed that the Mosaic law and the gospel
contained a profound secret meaning revealed only to the few and that
they were part of a single esoteric tradition that included hermeticism

---

[30] Nauert, *Agrippa,* pp. 32–33, 98, 337.

[31] *De Incertitudine,* p. 104; *De Occulta Philosophia,* sig. a3; see Nauert, *Agrippa,*
pp. 98–99, and R. H. Popkin's introduction in *Opera,* 1:xiv–xv.

[32] Nauert, *Agrippa,* pp. 202–203.

[33] Ibid., p. 112; Thorndike, *History of Magic,* 5:136.

[34] Thorndike, *History of Magic,* 5:130; Yates, *Giordano Bruno,* p. 131.

and the cabala. For him magic was the highest and most ancient form of wisdom handed down in secret.[35] In his correspondence there are hints that in his youth he belonged to a quasi-religious secret brotherhood devoted to arcane knowledge and practices, and veiled allusions intimating his connection with some sort of clandestine society appear at a later period as well.[36] In a letter from Trithemius printed at the beginning of *Occult Philosophy*, the abbot, after praising Agrippa's great erudition in penetrating secrets hidden even from the most learned, warned him nevertheless to heed this one precept, namely, to leave common things to the vulgar and to communicate higher truths in secret only to a few intimate friends.[37] Agrippa reiterated in his treatise that occult studies must be shrouded in secrecy and silence lest they become known to irreligious minds. In the same way he insisted that magical operations could not be fruitful unless concealed from all but initiates.[38] In a private letter he explained that the work had an inner meaning other than the literal one whose key was reserved for his closest friends.[39]

His esotericism would thus have furnished Agrippa with a sufficient rationale for dissimulation. If his work harbored a message that led him to dissemble, it was probably related to the character of his magic. He envisaged magic as an approach to divinity and a means of power that could enable men to acquire an ascendancy over nature and over other men through the utilization of an ancient wisdom. Because it was allied with pagan neoplatonism, hermeticism, and the cabala, however, his magic was a risky subject of doubtful orthodoxy.

In the preface to *Occult Philosophy*, Agrippa denied that magic was either harmful, superstitious, or demoniacal, and defended it as a sublime art cultivated by the wisest. Echoing the feeble excuse used earlier by Ficino, he also claimed that his work merely described without approving.[40] What followed was an encyclopedic survey of magic ranging over astrology, divination, numerology, angelology, the

---

[35] Nauert, *Agrippa*, pp. 46–47, 234, 263–264.

[36] Ibid., pp. 17–18; Paola Zambelli, "Umanesimo magico-astrologico e raggruppamenti segreti nei platonici della preriforma," in *Umanesimo e esoterismo*, ed. Enrico Castelli (Padua: A. Milani, 1960), pp. 153–154.

[37] *Opera*, 1: sig. a5–v.

[38] Ibid., pp. 311–314.

[39] Letter to Aurelio Acquapendente, an Augustinian monk and theologian, September 1527; *Opera*, 2:874–875.

[40] *Opera*, 1: sig. a2–v.

cabala, and much other recondite knowledge. Its discussion of the
magical art mingled Christianity with the teachings of pagan and
Jewish occult philosophy in a syncretism that placed them practically
on an equal level. Agrippa described such phenomena as "bindings"
(ligationes), which could make men love or hate and be sick or well,
and could also constrain animals, fire, water, storms, and other natural
events. He spoke of the celestial, intellectual, and divine gifts to be
obtained from both divine and demonic influences, and alluded to
ways to raise up evil spirits and to animate statues by means of an
appropriate demon. Though taking the same path as Ficino's magic,
with its appeal to planetary intelligences, he went considerably further
than the Italian humanist. Invocations to command spirits, the production of various effects through different kinds of seals bearing
celestial images which could be vivified by several kinds of virtues
including the demonic, and operations involving both angels and
demons were among the subjects he treated. He contended that
demons were not diabolical, but rather wise and intelligent spirits.[41]
Throughout his book he linked magic and religion so closely that
they were virtually indistinguishable. Far from limiting itself to the
manipulation of natural forces, his magic sought to tap the powers of
supernatural beings and did not shun the perilous regions of the art.
As both Walker and Yates have described it, it opened the door to the
forbidden and was really demonic.[42]

It therefore seems likely that Agrippa sought to dissimulate by mis-
representing his magic as more innocent than it actually was. At the
conclusion of *Occult Philosophy* he restated his esoteric purpose,
explaining that he had written of magic in such a manner as not to
hide it from the intelligent and prudent, yet without admitting the
wicked and incredulous to its secrets. He bade the former search his
book to gather up its intention scattered in different places: "What we
have concealed in one place, we have made manifest in another so that
it will be apparent to the wise." His work, he added, was designed
only for those of chaste and uncorrupt mind who feared and rever-
enced God.[43]

This sort of mystification was typical of occultist writers. It was one
of the greatest paradoxes of occult philosophy in the era of the

[41] *De Occulta Philosophia*, pp. 68–71, 281–284, 353–354; see also Yates, *Giordano
Bruno*, chap. 7; Walker, *Spiritual and Demonic Magic*, pp. 90–96.

[42] Walker, *Spiritual and Demonic Magic*, p. 96; Yates, *Giordano Bruno*, p. 136.

[43] *De Occulta Philosophia*, pp. 498–499.

printing press that it openly declared its commitment to the deepest secrecy and its possession of precious truths which it pledged to withhold from all but the handful of the enlightened. To protect its esoteric doctrine against misuse, it might have to resort to subterfuges to fool the impious or hostile reader. From this characteristic arises its puzzling obscurity as well as its propensity in some instances to deceive. In Agrippa's case the presumption of dissimulation is considerable. He might have dissimulated to conceal the true import of his magic; or he might even have done so by pretending that he had incorporated a secret message in his pages. In the final analysis, as still a further indication of his deceit, we can never be sure of Agrippa's meaning, veiled as it is by its esotericism.

The penchant for secrecy, with its deliberate obscurity and possible implication of dissimulation, runs like a thread through all of occultist literature. It is found in Paracelsus, Jerome Cardan, John Dee, and other celebrated astrologers, physicians, alchemists, and hermeticists who sought to gain dominion over the forces of nature by means of magic.[44] Robert Bostocke, an Elizabethan disciple of Paracelsus and the alchemists, defended their use of obscure language on the ground that "secretes are to be reveyled onely to the Godly, and . . . the wise," not to the ungodly, foolish, and unthankful hypocrites. A French admirer of Paracelsus, Jacques Gohory, gave a similar justification of the practice. On the other hand, Francis Bacon, a critic of the pretensions of alchemy, severely censured Paracelsus as a liar and impostor who corrupted both religious and human truth.[45] Yet perhaps even Bacon had not entirely freed himself of the addiction to concealment characteristic of occult philosophy in the grand project he had conceived for the reformation of knowledge.

Bacon's keen interest in dissimulation may have been related in part to the influence of the political realism of Machiavelli, to whom, he wrote, "we are much beholden" for showing "what men do, and not

[44] See Paolo Rossi, *Francis Bacon from Magic to Science* (London: Routledge & Kegan Paul, 1968), pp. 28–30; R. J. W. Evans, *Rudolf II and His World* (Oxford: Clarendon Press, 1984), pp. 196–197; Peter French, *John Dee* (London: Routledge & Kegan Paul, 1972), pp. 80–81.

[45] Bostocke, quoted in Allen Debus, *The English Paracelsians* (New York: Franklin Watts, 1966), p. 62; on Gohory, who wrote under the pseudonym Leo Suavius, see Walker, *Spiritual and Demonic Magic*, pp. 101–102; Thorndike, *History of Magic*, 5:636–640. Francis Bacon, *The Masculine Birth of Time (Temporis Masculus Partus)*, translated in Benjamin Farrington, *The Philosophy of Francis Bacon* (Liverpool: Liverpool University Press, 1964), p. 66.

what they ought to do."⁴⁶ His essay "On Cunning" focused on the technique of deception among councillors and politicians and contained only faint expressions of disapproval. The same interest was present in some of the curious memoranda he drew up for his own guidance concerning ways to insinuate himself in the favor of the great. These notes reveal the most secretive side of his labyrinthine personality and must be read in the context of his experience as an aspiring politician amid the intrigues and faction of the courts of Elizabeth and James I.⁴⁷

Bacon was also well versed in the literature of occultism. His master idea of the domination of nature to relieve man's estate as the chief end of scientific knowledge was heavily indebted to the magical tradition in hermeticism, alchemy, and other aspects of occult thought. He interpreted the myths and fables of the ancients as an allegorical repository of a hidden wisdom and, like Trithemius, also devoted himself to the study of cryptography.⁴⁸ Although his philosophical project for the reform of learning departed from the occult tradition in holding that the pursuit of knowledge must be a collaborative and public enterprise, a fascination with esotericism seems to have survived in his thought.

Bacon touched in various places on the principle of withholding higher truths from the unfit. In *The Advancement of Learning* (1605), he referred to it as "the enigmatical method" to prevent the vulgar "from being admitted to the secrets of knowledges, and to reserve them to selected auditors, or wits of such sharpness as can pierce the veil."⁴⁹ In *Valerius Terminus* (1603), whose subtitle, *Of the Interpretation of Nature with the Annotations of Hermes Stella,* indicates its hermetic associations, he spoke similarly of transmitting knowledge "by publishing part and reserving part," or "publishing in a manner whereby it shall not be to the capacity nor taste of all, but shall as it were single and adopt [the]

⁴⁶ *The Advancement of Learning,* ed. W. A. Wright (Oxford: Clarendon Press, 1900), p. 201; Bacon discusses dissimulation with classical examples in relation to politics in ibid., pp. 240–242.

⁴⁷ "Of Cunning," *Essays,* in *Works,* 2:153–158. The memoranda are printed in James Spedding, *The Life and Letters of Francis Bacon,* 7 vols. (London, 1868–1874), vol. 4, chap 2.

⁴⁸ Rossi, *Francis Bacon,* chap. 1 and p. 80. The enlarged Latin version of *The Advancement of Learning, De Dignitate et Augmentis Scientiarum,* contains a discussion of ciphers; *Works of Francis Bacon,* ed. James Spedding, Robert Ellis, and Douglas Heath, 14 vols. (London, 1857–1874), 2:420–426.

⁴⁹ *The Advancement of Learning,* pp. 171–172.

reader."[50] He was fully aware that this esoteric method could lend itself to fraud and deceit. Although the ancients had used it at their discretion, it had later been "disgraced . . . by the impostures of many vain persons who have made it a false light for their counterfeit merchandises."[51] Nevertheless, he did not feel that this fact discredited it. It was not to be laid aside, but used rather "both for the avoiding of abuse in the excluded, and the strengthening of affection in the admitted."[52]

Bacon's supreme ambition was to clear away error and to redirect men's minds by reconstructing the entire basis of knowledge. Although the ends of astrology, alchemy, and natural magic were noble, their theory and practice were full of vanity and errors "which the great professors . . . have sought to veil over and conceal by [their] enigmatical writings."[53] He was convinced that he had discovered a new method of investigating nature which would assure the progress of knowledge and yield great fruits for the improvement of human life. Moreover, as an intellectual reformer he was eager to see his philosophy gain the support of those in power who could put it into effect. Despite this fact, however, his approval of esotericism argues a reluctance to let his ideas become generally known. James Spedding, his indefatigable nineteenth-century editor and biographer, was led by Bacon's remarks on the subject to pose the question how far he wished to keep his system secret. He marshaled a number of passages from both Bacon's earlier and later writings recommending the communication of his ideas only to select readers. After reviewing the evidence, Spedding concluded that although he was not in favor of secrecy, Bacon did desire that his philosophy be reserved solely to fit and chosen minds so as to prevent misconstruction and abuse.[54]

This conclusion, which there is no reason to dispute, testifies to the persistence of esotericism in Bacon's thought even as an intellectual

---

[50] *Valerius Terminus*, in *Works*, 1:71.

[51] *The Advancement of Learning*, p. 171.

[52] *Valerius Terminus*, p. 71.

[53] *The Advancement of Learning*, p. 36.

[54] In his preface to Bacon's *Novum Organum*, Robert Ellis drew attention to Bacon's unwillingness that his peculiar method become generally known (*Works*, 1:152–154). Spedding discussed the kind of reserve Bacon had in mind (ibid., pp. 182–189). In his study of the evolution of Bacon's thought from magic to science, Rossi merely mentions Spedding's comments in a footnote (*Francis Bacon*, p. 240, n. 114) and fails to take up the important problem presented by Bacon's statements.

reformer. This esotericism probably reflected not an intention to mislead concerning the nature of his ideas, but a fear of misprision and incomprehension in their reception. As a philosopher he was ambivalent about secrecy. Any reader can confirm the judgment of one of his editors that he sought in some of his works to veil his doctrines by an affected obscurity.[55] If he was critical of the deceit of which he accused the alchemists and other pretenders to a hidden knowledge, he was equally concerned on the other hand to guard his own conceptions by limiting them if possible to worthy recipients. In this respect, at least, Bacon's mind remained under the influence of the esoteric principle that was one of the legacies of occultism.

Besides the dangers of magic, occult philosophers may have had a further inducement to concealment, and hence also to dissimulation, in the character of their religious beliefs. Amid the bitter contentions of the Reformation and Counter-Reformation they were apt to be inwardly indifferent to dogma and ritual. Their quest for illumination from the mystic sources of ancient wisdom often led them to a vision of spiritual harmony transcending the quarrels of Catholic and Protestant. The universalistic tendencies in occultist thought which caused it to overlook denominational distinctions, and the religious syncretism that rendered it receptive to pagan, Judaic, and even Islamic teachings were scarcely reconcilable with the rigid orthodoxies of an age of confessional strife.

Some of these traits may be seen reflected in the career and ideas of John Dee (1527–1608), hermeticist, sage, and *magus,* whose life coincided with the period in which occult philosophy attained its widest influence on European culture. Dee was renowned throughout Europe as a mathematician, astrologer, alchemist, cabalist, and magician and may also have been an early supporter of Copernicus. His mathematical and scientific interests, however, were almost entirely subordinated to his magicohermetic outlook. Despite an unsavory reputation as a practitioner of black arts, he enjoyed the favor of Elizabeth I, who often consulted him on astrological and other recondite subjects. For this deeply pious scholar and close student of the angel magic of Trithemius and Agrippa, religion and magic were inseparable, and the spirit world more real than the world of the senses.[56] Among his

---

[55] *Works,* 1:152.

[56] On Dee's life and his occult and scientific interests, see Paul Kocher, *Science*

works was a description, not published till long after his death, of his communications with spirits. These episodes took place over a period of years during séances in which an assistant, Edward Kelley, served as a medium or scryer, using a magical stone or crystal. When the latter manipulated this object, angels or spirits appeared in it who responded to questions. Although Dee himself never saw these supernatural beings, who spoke to him only through the medium, he was able in these conversations to receive revelations and prophecies as well as divine commands.[57]

In 1583 Dee went abroad in the company of a Polish Catholic prince, Albert Laski, an enthusiast of alchemy. He spent the next six years engaged in occult pursuits in Poland and Bohemia. During a sojourn in Prague he tried unavailingly to win the patronage of the eccentric Emperor Rudolf II, whose infatuation with the occult sciences made his court and capital an intellectual center where the diverse currents of occultism intermingled. Although in England Dee was a conforming Protestant, he took Catholic communion while in Bohemia and had his son baptized by Catholic rites. He was obviously indifferent to the doctrinal distinctions of rival churches.[58] In this respect his attitude resembled the Nicodemism of the spiritualist sects, whose members hid their interior religion of the spirit behind a pretense of conformity to an established church.

Dee's true religion was a far-from-orthodox brand of Christianity shot through with hermetic elements. Veiled in obscurity, its outlines are dimly discernible in his *Monas Hieroglyphica* (1564), the work for which he became best known. Concealed within its enigmatic pages lay a gnosis concerning the significance of the monas symbol, a mysterious alchemical-astrological diagram he had invented to which he attributed magical powers. His treatise was saturated in astrological, alchemical, and cabalistic magic. Its esoteric doctrines seemed to intimate some kind of spiritual transmutation to be effected by means of

---

and Religion in Elizabethan England (San Marino, Calif.: Huntington Library, 1953); French, *John Dee*; Evans, *Rudolf II*, pp. 218–225. Frances Yates presents a sketch of Dee's career and ideas with some exaggerations in *The Occult Philosophy in the Elizabethan Age* (London: Routledge & Kegan Paul, 1979), chap. 8.

[57] The record of these communications with spirits was published along with additional material by Meric Casaubon, *A True & Faithful Relation of What Passed for Many Years between Dr. John Dee . . . and Some Spirits* (London, 1659). The work is discussed in Shumaker, *Renaissance Curiosa*, chap. 1.

[58] See Evans, *Rudolf II*, pp. 220–222; Shumaker, *Renaissance Curiosa*, pp. 36–37.

supernatural forces related to the monas, thereby enabling the adept to attain direct participation in a celestial spirit realm and a mastery of nature. Dee stressed that he intended the work, which was dedicated to Emperor Maximilian II, solely for initiates. He urged the need to keep its rare truths secret, and appealed to its Antwerp printer, Willem Silvius, on no account to let it fall into the hands of common people. Moreover, he prayed to God for forgiveness if he had revealed "so great a secret in published writings," expressing the hope that "only those who are worthy will understand."[59] He undoubtedly conceived his own religion as soaring far above conventional beliefs in its wisdom and insight. The secrecy in which he shrouded its meaning was a form of deception wholly in keeping with the occult foundation of his thought.

The tendencies in occult philosophy impelling it to diverge from orthodoxy found their fullest universalistic realization in the thought of Dee's contemporary, Guillaume Postel (1510–1581). Postel was one of the comparatively few sixteenth-century humanists who combined a knowledge of Hebrew with classical erudition. While in Constantinople in 1536 as part of a French embassy he also learned Arabic and other Eastern tongues. His early works, reflecting his allied philological and religious interests, brought him a unique reputation as the foremost orientalist of his time. In recognition Francis I appointed him as a royal lecturer in the Collège des Trois Langues in 1538, but his troublesome opinions caused him to be dismissed six years later. Postel's lifelong goal was to convert all people to a broadened, tolerant, synthetic Christianity. One of his most important works, *De Orbis Terrae Concordia* (1544), was intended as a practical manual for the conversion of Islam and sought to show the beliefs common to all faiths.

Attracted by its missionary purpose, in 1544 he joined the newly established Jesuit order, only to be expelled soon afterward because of his religious errors and insubordination. At this time he was also ordained as a priest. Several years later while in Venice he met a pious elderly woman known for her charitable works whom he came to regard as a prophetess possessing supernatural powers and wisdom. He eulogized her as his Mother Johanna, the Venetian Virgin, *mater*

[59] Facsimile edition with English translation and introduction by C. H. Josten, *Ambix*, 12, nos. 2–3 (1964), 99–111, 139, 151, 173, 183. Frances Yates, *The Rosicrucian Enlightenment* (London: Routledge & Kegan Paul, 1972), discusses the *Monas* and its influence.

mundi, and the new Eve, certain that she was appointed to play a redemptive role in an imminent new dispensation to the world. After her death, a mystical experience convinced him that she had returned in her spiritual body to unite herself with him. In his numerous publications he presented himself as the prophet of a new age in which all things would be restored to their original perfection. Because of his questionable orthodoxy he was forbidden to teach in Paris. In Venice his works were banned and the Venetian Inquisition accused him of heresy. As a result, he was imprisoned in Rome from 1555 until 1559. Eventually he returned to Paris, where his activities led the Parlement, which considered him insane, to sentence him to a fairly lax confinement in the monastery of Saint Martin-des-Champs. In this place, still pursuing his religious goal in a flow of writings, he passed his remaining years.

Although Postel's complex thought drew on a variety of sources, he was most profoundly influenced by the occult tradition. He belonged to this tradition in virtue of his religious syncretism, his commitment to astrology, whose origins he traced to the Egyptian lore transmitted to the patriarch Abraham, and his conception of the universe as filled with spiritual forces affecting every aspect of human life. He believed completely in the existence of an esoteric truth hidden in sacred writings whose meaning was reserved only to initiates. His closest bond with occultism, however, lay in the cabala, of which he was an avid student and devotee. He translated the *Zohar,* the most important of the cabalistic books, and venerated Hebrew as a holy language holding the key to all knowledge. It was in this language that God and man had originally communicated and in which God taught Adam the names of things. For him the mystical wisdom in the cabala was the source of the highest divine truths foreshadowing the imminent restoration of the lost harmony between God and mankind. He fitted the Venetian Virgin into his philosophy by identifying her with the *shekinah* of the cabala, an emanation of the divine presence and spiritual mediatrix, while conceiving her also as a bride of Christ.

From the cabala and other elements of occult thought, as well as from the prophetic, eschatological, and messianic motifs in Judaism and Christianity, Postel fashioned his distinctive spiritual vision. It expressed an irenicism transcending the discord of warring creeds. Foretelling the restitution of all things to their original perfection, it looked toward the reconciliation of the religious differences separating humanity. Judaism, Islam, and Christianity were to be united in an expanded, fully spiritualized Christianity independent of dogma. The belief in universal concord through the revelation of a common religion based on the identical teachings that had always inspired all prophets, philosophers, *magi,* and founders of faiths, constituted the essence of Postel's religious outlook.[60]

While this dream of harmony was the core of his message in his published works, there were other aspects of his ideas about which he was more secretive. Postel, one of the most unconventional and visionary minds of the sixteenth century, lived the latter part of his life in the repressive atmosphere of the Counter-Reformation. To acknowledge the influence of some of his sources would have put him at great risk. Thus he never admitted to an interest in Erasmus or Lefèvre d'Etaples, whose Catholic orthodoxy was suspect; nor did he ever mention except with disapproval any of the representatives of medieval and Renaissance heterodoxy from whom he may have borrowed.[61] He also used numerous pseudonyms and circulated many of his writings in manuscript, especially after his confinement in Paris in 1561. One pseudonym that has been traced to him is that of Jehan Boulaese, a name which otherwise remains unknown. M. L. Kuntz has shown that Postel probably assumed it as a cover for some of his clandestine activities in behalf of his imagined new order, to indicate his filial relationship to his beloved Venetian Virgin, Johanna.[62] He likewise adopted various esoteric symbols derived from alchemy to refer to himself and his mission. He hebraized his name as "Postallus," which he said meant "to multiply the dew," and also called himself by its Latin cognate, "Rorispergius" (from *spargere,* "scatter," and *ros,* "the dew"). These pseudonyms signified his conviction that he had been chosen to disseminate God's dew as a spiritual food to humankind. Owing to this and other similarities, it has been suggested that the name and some of the aims of the Rosicrucians, the mysterious secret society whose publications created a sensation by their sudden

[60] For accounts of Postel's career and ideas, see W. J. Bouwsma, *Concordia Mundi: The Career and Thought of Guillaume Postel (1510–1581)* (Cambridge, Mass.: Harvard University Press, 1957); M. L. Kuntz, *Guillaume Postel. Prophet of the Restitution of All Things. His Life and Thought* (The Hague: Martinus Nijhoff, 1981); Lucien Febvre, *The Problem of Unbelief in the Sixteenth Century* (Cambridge, Mass.: Harvard University Press, 1982), pp. 107–122; P. G. Bietenholz, *Basle and France in the Sixteenth Century* (Geneva: Droz, 1969), pt. 2, chap. 6.

[61] Bouwsma, *Concordia Mundi,* p. 32.

[62] Kuntz, *Guillaume Postel,* pp. 152–159.

appearance in the early seventeenth century, may have been indebted to the ideas of Postel and his self-designation as "Rorispergius." The Frenchman was very much concerned to hasten the coming of the world harmony and restitution of all things which he prophesied. The esoteric side of his activities also apparently included an attempt to organize a secret brotherhood of "new men" who would cooperate with him to help bring the new age of divine unity into being.[63]

Postel's beliefs had much in common with the tolerant spiritualism exemplified in the Family of Love, which sought refuge from persecution in Nicodemism. During the later 1560s he took a strong interest as a Hebraist and orientalist in the production of the great Polyglot Bible, whose printer in Antwerp, Christophe Plantin, was secretly affiliated with that underground sect. Postel made many contributions to the edition from Paris, but his participation was concealed because of his suspect reputation. Most of the scholars involved in the work were his friends and disciples. He was aware, moreover, of Plantin's membership in the Family of Love. Although he never joined the sect, he was sympathetic to it and corresponded about it both with the printer and with Plantin's friend the geographer Ortelius, who was also a member.[64]

Among further indications of Postel's heterodoxy were his varied Protestant contacts. Although he greatly disliked the writings of Calvin, who in turn attacked his opinions, he corresponded with the Lutheran Philipp Melanchthon, the spiritualist Caspar Schwenkfeld, and other Protestant figures. Johannes Oporinus, a leading Protestant printer in Basel, published some of his most important works, although he rejected many others by Postel on account of their dangerous tendencies and for fear of displeasing the civic authorities. Protestant Basel, whose intellectual climate as a center of the reformed faith was more liberal than Calvin's Geneva, played a significant part in Postel's life. Through Oporinus he formed valued friendships with a number of the city's scholars and theologians. One of those he might have met during a visit in 1553 was Sebastian Castellio, who

---

[63] Ibid., pp. 134, 149, 165–169, 174–176. On the Rosicrucians and their writings, see Yates, *The Rosicrucian Enlightenment*.

[64] See above, Chapter 6, for the Family of Love and its Nicodemism. On Postel's connection with Plantin and the Antwerp Polyglot and his affinities with Familism, see Alastair Hamilton, *The Family of Love* (Cambridge: Clarke, 1981), pp. 66, 70, 74; Bernard Rekers, *Benito Arias Montano* (Leiden: Brill, 1972), chap. 3; Kuntz, *Guillaume Postel*, pp. 116–117, 162–165.

worked as a corrector in Oporinus' press. Castellio was soon to become known as the author of the famous plea for toleration, *Whether Heretics Should Be Punished,* published in 1554 in protest against Geneva's condemnation of the hunted heretic Servetus. Castellio and Postel were alike in devaluing dogma and exalting charity and love as the means to unite men. Postel himself composed an *Apologia* for Servetus after his execution, which was not published till the eighteenth century but circulated in manuscript.[65]

One of the most intriguing aspects of Postel's thought, likewise rooted in his occultism, was his attitude to Judaism. Here too he was deeply at odds with Catholic orthodoxy. His veneration of Hebrew and the esoteric truths in the cabala gave him a profound respect for the Jewish people, and he was opposed to their persecution or forced conversion. In 1559 during the pontificate of Paul IV he was an eyewitness in Rome to the burning of Hebrew books. He grieved at the spectacle, lamenting that the same destruction was also frequently committed in Germany, France, and Spain, and with it sometimes the destruction of Jews as well. Like that other eminent Hebraist who had worked on the Antwerp Polyglot and belonged to the Family of Love, Benito Arias Montano, he was considered a "Judaizer." After its publication in 1572, one of the reasons for the Polyglot's hostile reception in Rome and Spain was its alleged partiality to rabbinical and Jewish learning. In his reinterpretation of Christianity, Postel blurred its differences from Judaism. Though critical of the Jews for rejecting Jesus as their king, he also spoke of the Jewishness of all men and of Christian Jews, implying a union of the two religions. For him not only were true Christians Jews, but Christianity itself was a culmination of Judaism with the names changed. Among the figures with whom he most closely identified himself was the prophet Elijah. So strong was his dedication to Judaism that it has been conjectured that he even became a convert.[66]

Under the repression he suffered, Postel made several recantations of his opinions, including his notion that the Roman papacy was soon doomed to fall and that he himself was destined to an "angelic papacy" in a reborn church. To the Venetian Inquisition he retracted

[65] Kuntz, *Guillaume Postel,* pp. 47, 107–112; Bietenholz, *Basle and France,* chap. 6 and pp. 140–141; Antonio Rotondò, "Guillaume Postel e Basilea," in *Studi e richerche di storia ereticale italiana del cinquecento* (Turin: Edizioni Giappichelli, 1974); Bouwsma, *Concordia Mundi,* p. 23.

[66] Kuntz, *Guillaume Postel,* pp. 113, 130–133, 168.

this and other opinions as errors, explaining that they were a consequence of his "secret pride and dissimulation."[67] According to François Secret, retraction was "Postel's method." He found dissimulation
inescapable in order to circumvent obstacles to the dissemination of
his teachings and to present his ideas in a better light.[68]

Despite such gestures of pretended conformity, there is no indication that Postel ever embraced a systematic doctrine of dissimulation.
The related theme of secrecy and concealment, however, occupied a
considerable place in his mind, not only because of his deep involvement in occult philosophy but also because of the persecuting orthodoxy against which he was forced to contend. Just as he believed that
scripture held a hidden meaning known only to the initiate, so he
likewise strove to follow the scriptural admonition not to cast pearls
before swine.[69] Rather contradictorily, he wanted at the same time
both to propagate his message of religious reconciliation and the restitution of all things, and to reserve it as a truth whose day had not yet
come. Proclaiming the advent of a new age, he nevertheless tried to
keep his plans for it a secret and to enlist disciples surreptitiously to
assist in its attainment. Postel was both a visionary prophet and a
profoundly esoteric philosopher, an ill-assorted mixture that helps to
explain some of the strange convolutions in his complex structure of
ideas.

A final noteworthy instance of the relationship between occultism and
dissimulation is the renowned French thinker Jean Bodin (ca.
1529–1596), a near contemporary of Postel and similar in his heterodoxy and attraction to Judaism. Bodin's works ranged over many disciplines—law and jurisprudence, history and politics, the sciences and
economics, theology and religion. His most lasting fame, though,
derives from his encyclopedic treatise on comparative politics and
political theory, *Six Books on the Commonwealth* (*De la République*,
1576), in which he formulated his well-known doctrine of absolute
sovereignty. While still an adolescent he became a Carmelite monk

[67] "Mihi semper adfuit comes superbia occulta et dissimulata de Papatu angelico";
Guillaume Postel: Apologies et rétractions, ed. François Secret (Nieuwkoop: B. de Graaf,
1972), p. 205.

[68] See François Secret, "Introduction," in Postel, *Le thresor des propheties de
l'univers* (The Hague: Nijhoff, 1969), pp. 5, 14–16, 26, 27–28; Kuntz, *Guillaume
Postel,* pp. 80–81.

[69] Kuntz, *Guillaume Postel,* p. 169.

and was sent by his order to study in Paris. Obtaining release from his vows before the age of twenty, he went on to study and teach law, practice as an advocate, and serve the French crown as a legal official. During the civil war between Catholics and Protestants which shattered France, he sided with the *politiques,* the party favoring a strong independent royal power and toleration for the Huguenots as the sole means of restoring peace to the kingdom.[70]

Many threads bound Bodin to the occult tradition. Neoplatonism, hermeticism, demonology, and the cabala were major ingredients of his thought. Deeply versed in Hebraic learning, he was greatly influenced by cabalistic and rabbinical literature. He shared the typical occultist belief in the existence of a hidden higher wisdom available only to the few and in the reality of a world of spirits encompassing human life. His intense concern with the power of demons led him to condemn any commerce with spirits as idolatrous and diabolic. In his famous book on witchcraft, *The Demonry of Witches* (*De la démonomanie des sorciers,* 1580), he discussed the activity of demons and denounced their adoration as devil worship. So strongly did he condemn the crime of witchcraft in its renunciation of God that he was willing to dispense with all legal safeguards for the accused in such cases. Nothing less than death at the stake seemed to him sufficient punishment for those guilty of a pact with the devil. Bodin's intellectual authority in this work probably helped to spread the flames of the great European witch persecution, which reached its height between the late sixteenth and later seventeenth centuries.[71]

Throughout his life Bodin was secretly unorthodox in his religion. In 1548, while still a Carmelite, he was charged with heresy but may have recanted, as the outcome of his trial is unknown. In 1562 as a member of the Parlement of Paris, he made a public profession of his Catholicism in compliance with a decree ordering such an oath from

---

[70] See Roger Chauviré, *Jean Bodin Auteur de la "République"* (Paris: Honoré Champion, 1914); Kenneth McRae, "Introduction," in Jean Bodin, *Six Bookes of the Commonweale* (Cambridge, Mass.: Harvard University Press, 1962), pp. A3–A12 (the 1606 English translation of *De la République*); M. L. Kuntz, "Introduction," in Jean Bodin, *Colloquium of the Seven about Secrets of the Sublime* (Princeton: Princeton University Press, 1975), pp. xv–xxviii (a translation of *Colloquium Heptaplomeres de Abditis Rerum Sublimium Arcanis*).

[71] See Kuntz, "Introduction," in Bodin, *Colloquium,* pp. xxx, xxxiv–xxxv; Jonathan L. Pearl, "Le role enigmatique de la Démonomanie dans la chasse aux sorciers," in *Jean Bodin. Actes du Colloque interdisciplinaire d'Angers,* 2 vols. (Angers: Presse de l'Université d'Angers, 1985), 2:405–407.

lawyers. Seven years later, however, he was imprisoned for more than a year as a suspected Protestant until freed by the government's short-lived edict of toleration issued in 1570.[72] Various opinions contained in his correspondence and several of his writings, plus the fact that a certain Jean Bodin was a resident of Geneva in 1552, have been taken as further evidence that he may have been a Protestant. In all probability, however, the man in Geneva was a different person who bore the same name. Moreover, despite the fact that he shared certain Protestant ideas and some of its criticisms of Catholicism, it appears very unlikely that he was any kind of Protestant.[73] Instead, like Postel, he adhered to a peculiar interior religion of his own, neither Catholic nor Christian in nature. For obvious reasons, therefore, he never divulged his true convictions in his lifetime. Notwithstanding his royalism and advocacy of toleration, in 1589, while serving as *procureur du roi* in Laon, he joined the Catholic League, which was in revolt against Henri III and vowed to the extermination of the Huguenots. At that time the League controlled Laon as well as Paris and other parts of France. Bodin not only cooperated with the League but also consented to take its oath. Contemporaries censured his collaboration, which seemed a violation of his principles, attributing it to opportunism and the desire to retain his office. It is much more likely, though, that he acted out of fear and prudence. Had he refused to support the League, he would have been forced to flee or suffer imprisonment and possibly death along with the loss of his property, to the grave detriment of his family.[74]

The various accommodations Bodin made during his life leave little room for doubt that he practiced Nicodemism, assuming a posture of outward conformity in contradiction to his personal beliefs and thereby licensing dissimulation. That he did so may be inferred from several statements in his writings which endorsed the typical Nicodemite separation of inner spiritual conviction from external profession. In his *Method for the Easy Comprehension of History* (1566), he observed that religion itself, which he called "the direct turning of a cleansed mind toward God," was distinct from the faith maintained by

[72] McRae, "Introduction," in Bodin, *Commonweale,* pp. A4–5, A7.

[73] See Chauviré, *Jean Bodin auteur,* pp. 23–25; McRae, "Introduction," pp. A4–5, A7; Kuntz, "Introduction," pp. xix–xx; Pierre Mesnard, "La pensée religieuse de Bodin," in *Fundamental Studies on Jean Bodin,* ed. J. P. Mayer (New York: Arno Press, 1979), pp. 2–11.

[74] Chauviré, *Jean Bodin auteur,* pp. 77–92; McRae, "Introduction," p. A11.

priests and pontiffs under the power of the magistrate. Though agreeing that "the sacrifices and approved rites of the state must be zealously defended," he viewed true religion as an interior possession that could exist "without association in the solitude of one man," who was indeed the happier the more removed he was from the creed of civil society.[75]

Bodin unfolded this theme more fully in his *République* in discussing the problem of factions in the commonwealth. After acknowledging the vital importance of a common religion to the preservation of political unity, he considered the situation in which religious divisions did exist. In this case, he held that the prince should not force people to be of his religion, but try to draw them by persuasion and the power of example. It was impossible, he emphasized, to compel anyone to believe against his will, and the more men were coerced, the more stubborn they became. Accordingly, he advised that if the state permitted only one religion to be publicly professed, then subjects who differed should be allowed to exercise their faith in private. He further recommended, however, that if subjects could not publicly practice the true religion, "which still consisteth in the worshipping of one almightie and everlasting God," then they should nevertheless conform to the religion of the state rather than provoke sedition, so long as their minds still rested "in the honor and reverence of one almightie and everlasting God." To confirm this view, he recalled the classical examples of Baruch, who instructed the captive Jews of Babylon that they should worship the ever-living God with a pure mind when forced to bow to idols, and of Naaman the Syrian, who was pardoned for accompanying his master the king of Syria into the idols' temple, "so that he kept his mind pure and cleane from idolatrie."[76] Both of these precedents are of course familiar to us from their use by Spanish crypto-Jews and defenders of Nicodemism. For Bodin too they were obviously a sanction for pretended conformity. His stance has been likened to that of Marranos who hid their Judaism under the cover

[75] *Methodus ad Facilem Historiarum Cognitionem* (Paris, 1566), translated as *Method for the Easy Comprehension of History,* ed. Beatrice Reynolds (New York: Norton, 1968), pp. 33–34.

[76] Bodin, *Commonweale,* pp. 539–540. These passages were added to the 1586 Latin edition of the *République;* see Diego Quaglioni, "Jean Bodin Nicodemita? Simulazione e dissimulazione religiosa nelle aggiunti latini alla 'république,'" in *Jean Bodin. Actes du Colloque,* vol. 1.

of Catholic worship. This comparison is the more intriguing in light of the disputed suggestion that his mother was a Spanish Jew who taught him Hebrew.[77] What is apparent in any case is that in this principle dissociating inner belief from exterior comportment he possessed a rationale for religious dissimulation by himself and by others in similar circumstances.

No one ever stated more strongly than Bodin how essential was the social contribution of religion to the survival and well-being of the commonweal. To him atheism was the worst of sins and far more harmful in its consequences than superstition. He was compelled to use deception, though, because his ideas were so much at odds with Christianity. Despite the puzzles regarding his religion, its closest affinity was apparently with Judaism. He considered Jesus as merely one in a line of prophets which included most of the Greek philosophers, rather than as a savior and redeemer; and he likewise repudiated the doctrines of original sin, grace, justification, and redemption. A rigid monotheism, needing no church and devoid of intermediaries between God and man, was also a basic part of his creed. Some students of his thought have speculated that he was a convert to Judaism, or have alternatively described him as a Judaizer in the sense of envisaging a universal true religion based on prophetic illumination and on the natural virtues and ethics prescribed in the Jewish law.[78] Others suggest that he inclined toward a philosophical religion similar to deism which was founded on reason and consisted solely of the law of God as the source of all good.[79]

The fullest, least reserved presentation of his religious conceptions was contained in his *Colloquium of the Seven about Secrets of the Sublime*, written around 1593, which marks the final stage of his religious evolution. This work was never intended for publication and was not printed in full until 1857, but it circulated in manuscript among various philosophers of the seventeenth and eighteenth centuries. Its

[77] See Chauviré, *Jean Bodin auteur*, pp. 16–18, 21; M. C. Horowitz, "La religion de Bodin reconsiderée: Le Marrane comme modèle de la tolerance," in *Jean Bodin. Actes du Colloque*, vol 1.

[78] C. R. Baxter, "Jean Bodin's Daemon and His Conversion to Judaism," in *Jean Bodin*, ed. Horst Denzer (Munich: Beck, 1973); Paul L. Rose, *Bodin and the Great God of Nature* (Geneva: Droz, 1980), Introduction and passim. Reynolds, "Introduction," in Bodin, *Method*, p. xxxvi; and Kuntz, "Introduction," in Bodin, *Colloquium*, also note his attraction to Judaism.

[79] Chauviré, *Jean Bodin auteur*, pp. 160–161.

form was that of a dialogue in Venice among seven men of differing faiths—a Catholic, two Protestants, a Muslim, a Jew, an exponent of natural religion, and a skeptic. Although it is impossible to be sure which were Bodin's own opinions or to identify him exclusively with any one of the speakers in the discussion, the general tendencies of the work are unmistakable. Both its title referring to sublime secrets and its emphasis on a secret knowledge underline the importance esotericism held for him as an occult philosopher. When the question arises in the colloquy as to why the ancient Greeks and Hebrews veiled their wisdom in obscurity, and the skeptic Senamus criticizes the practice, the Jew Salomon cites Maimonides to show that this was necessary to keep secret truths from being made common and polluted by profane men. Moses himself, he declares, was unwilling to explain the more secret things revealed to him. The Calvinist Curtius likewise points out that the ancients did not wish to cast pearls before swine or cheapen the most precious wisdom by its accessibility.[80] Throughout the dialogue Salomon interprets the esoteric meaning hidden in scriptural allegories, the cabala, and other writings. Indeed the entire *Colloquium* may be considered as an exposition of the esoteric doctrines of its author.

Of the characters in the dialogue, the Christians, especially the Catholic Coronaeus, are intellectually much less impressive than the others. The dominant personality is the enormously erudite Salomon, to whom as the representative of Judaism all express marked respect. The skeptic Senamus exposes the weakness in all religious beliefs, and for the naturalist Toralba true religion lies solely in loving God and following the laws of nature. The discussion wanders widely without apparent order, examining not only different religious standpoints but also touching on neoplatonism, hermeticism, magic, numerology, demons and angels, the cabala, and many other occult subjects. In all their disagreements, though, the interlocutors remain courteous and firmly linked in fraternal amity. At the conclusion, Salomon deplores Jewish persecution in such acts as the expulsion of the Jews from Spain, while the Lutheran Fridericus quotes the words of Theodoric the Ostrogoth, which Bodin had also cited in the *République,* that it is impossible to command religion "because no one can be forced to believe against his will." Following embraces of mutual love among the seven friends, the final sentence states that thereafter "they held no

[80] *Colloquium,* pp. 90–99.

other conversations about religions, although each one defended his own . . . with the supreme sanctity of his life."[81]

The *Colloquium* is an enigmatic work susceptible of diverse interpretations. The paramount value it assigns to the Old Testament and Jewish teaching would seem to indicate Bodin's preference for Judaism as a religion superior to any other. On the other hand, the work was also a plea for tolerance and condemnation of bigotry, as well as a commentary on the futility of religious controversy. In accord with its tolerant spirit, moreover, it can likewise be read as aspiring toward a universal harmony of religion, a concept similar to the religious universalism of Postel, by whose ideas Bodin may have been influenced.[82] However, the dialogue is also noteworthy for its critical treatment of Christianity and its traditions. Through the comments of Toralba, Senamus, and Salomon it casts doubt on such fundamental beliefs as the divinity of Christ, the trinity, the eucharist, veneration of saints, miracles, eternal punishment, and predestination. It is no less dismissive of religious authority, advancing the claims of reason in place of dogma. Both its skepticism and its arguments in favor of a natural religion were equally corrosive of the Christian faith. These parts of the *Colloquium* were to supply some of the libertine philosophers of the next century with materials for their own critique of revealed religion, credulity, and superstition.

Later Catholic and Protestant authors who read the *Colloquium* in manuscript denounced it for its heretical and irreligious opinions and its partiality to Judaism.[83] Whichever way it was interpreted, it was full of subversive reflections that Bodin would never have been able to publish in print without endangering his life. The principle of esotericism was vital to Bodin, since it allowed him to harbor the most heterodox religious conceptions and still appear a Catholic. We can scarcely doubt that he considered the ideas in the *Colloquium* as a higher kind of knowledge unfit for the many. As with various other occult philosophers, esotericism in his case passed into and provided a sanction for dissimulation. The deception Bodin practiced was further

---

[81] Ibid., pp. 470–471.

[82] Kuntz, "Introduction," pp. lix–lxi; idem, "Jean Bodin's *Colloquium Heptaplomeres* and Guillaume Postel: A Consideration of Influence," in *Jean Bodin. Actes du Colloque,* vol. 2.

[83] Chauviré, *Jean Bodin auteur,* pp. 156–162; Friedrich von Bezold, "Jean Bodins *Colloquium Heptaplomeres* und der Atheismus des 16. Jahrhunderts," in Mayer, *Fundamental Studies.*

grounded in the disjunction he posited between religion as an interior state of mind and as an external gesture of conformity in obedience to the sovereign power. Fated to live in an age of persecution, he veiled his most genuine beliefs, leaving it to later generations to try to puzzle out the true nature of his faith.

CHAPTER 12

Libertinism, Unbelief, and the Dissimulation of Philosophers

Despite the growing secularization of European culture from the Renaissance onward, we inevitably tend to think of the sixteenth and first half of the seventeenth centuries as a period of religious revival. We think of it as the age of the Reformation and Counter-Reformation, as a time of intensified faith and heightened religiosity, as well as the release of new spiritual energies, fanatical intolerance, and the formation of new religious denominations; as an age, in short, in the memorable phrase of Lucien Febvre, "that wanted to believe."[1] But does this mean that amid the resurgence of belief defining this era, the last age of religion in Western history, there was no room for its opposite, for incredulity and irreligion?

In 1942 Lucien Febvre took up this important question in a classic work, *The Problem of Unbelief in the Sixteenth Century (Le problème de l'incroyance au XVI siècle)*. Although it dealt primarily with the religion of the great French writer François Rabelais, it included a provocative, wide-ranging discussion of the possibility of incredulity, rationalism, and atheism in the sixteenth century. In disagreement with the eminent literary historian Abel Lefranc and those who argued that Rabelais was secretly a freethinker and rationalist opposed to Christianity, Febvre maintained that he held the same views as the Catholic evangelical reformers of his generation and was most powerfully influenced by the Christian and biblical humanism of Erasmus. In one of his most brilliant chapters, Febvre showed how profound

[1] Lucien Febvre, "Conclusion," in *The Problem of Unbelief in the Sixteenth Century*, trans. Beatrice Gottlieb (Cambridge, Mass.: Harvard University Press, 1982), p. 455.

was the accord between Rabelais's beliefs and values and Erasmus' philosophy of Christ as the basis of Christian renewal. In the final part of the work, however, he went beyond his original theme to a general consideration of the psychological and intellectual limits of unbelief in the sixteenth century. It was his contention that religion's domination of the mentality and social practices of the age was so pervasive that irreligion was an impossibility. Neither the linguistic nor conceptual equipment of the time, according to Febvre, could offer any foundation for atheism, unbelief, or the rationalistic rejection of religion. Hence, "to speak of rationalism and free thought, when we are dealing with an age when the most intelligent men, the most learned, and the most daring were truly incapable of finding any support either in philosophy or science against a religion whose domination was universal is to speak of an illusion."[2]

Febvre's conclusion did not meet with universal assent by any means. In 1957 Henri Busson, a leading literary and intellectual historian, took strong issue with it in an enlarged edition of *Le rationalisme dans la littérature française de la renaissance (1553–1601)*. Busson contended that like bacteria, which can live in any organism, so incredulity was present even in a believing age. "Not only do we not accept the paradox that incredulity is impossible in the sixteenth century," he stated, but "[we] will affirm rather that it has always existed." The absence from the contemporary language of words such as *rationalism* or *materialism,* he held, did not mean that these states of mind themselves were nonexistent. He pointed, moreover, to the appearance in the sixteenth century of terms such as *atheist, deist, achrist,* and *libertine* and to the availability of earlier coherent systems of negation which served to nourish unbelief.[3]

Likewise severely critical of Febvre were a 1970 study of libertinism in the sixteenth and seventeenth centuries by Gerhard Schneider and a 1977 study of atheism by François Berriot. One of Berriot's main purposes was to portray the ideas typical of irreligion and incredulity through an examination of the numerous contemporary writings directed against atheism.[4] Similarly, in a 1983 reprint of his massive

---

[2] Ibid., p. 353. Febvre's dissent was prompted primarily by Lefranc's "Etude sur Pantagruel," published as an introduction to *Pantagruel* in François Rabelais, *Oeuvres,* vol. 3 (Paris: Champion, 1922–1955).

[3] Henri Busson, "Question préliminaire," in *Le rationalisme dans la littérature française de la renaissance (1533–1601)* (1st ed. 1922) (Paris: Vrin, 1957), pp. 7–13.

[4] Gerhard Schneider, *Der Libertin. Zur Geistes- und Sozialgeschichte des Bürgertums*

monograph on libertinism, René Pintard sought to demonstrate the presence and nature of religious skepticism and free thought in early seventeenth-century France. Although he did not refer to Febvre's view, in his lengthy new introduction Pintard confirmed the existence of significant currents of unbelief whose origins lay in the preceding century.[5]

Febvre's claim was undoubtedly exaggerated. No society has ever been completely unified in its basic ideology; even in a religious age there are always dissenters from the prevailing outlook, no matter how entrenched it may appear to be. If Febvre was right to stress the predominance of belief and to criticize the perception of the sixteenth century as rationalist and freethinking as the worst of errors, this view could in no way license the conclusion that incredulity and irreligion had no place in the intellectual life of the time. These did not need the support of science, since they could draw both on other sources and on always available skeptical modes of reasoning to sustain themselves.

The question of incredulity this controversy poses is not a matter of atheism in the strictly modern sense of the term as a denial of the existence of God. In this sense it was probably rare, and maybe scarcely anybody was an atheist. In contemporary usage, however, atheism had a much broader meaning, covering any kind of nonconformity or immorality. Religious apologists usually failed to make any consistent distinction between it and heresy or theological disagreement. Thus Francis Bacon observed in an essay on atheism that all who "impugn a revealed religion or superstition are by the adverse part branded with the name of atheists."[6] To later sixteenth- and seventeenth-century writers, though, who lamented the growth of atheism, it particularly signified disbelief in scripture or the rejection of doctrines such as the incarnation, the immortality of the soul, and providence, which they considered indispensable to Christianity. In describing atheism in *The*

im 16. und 17. Jahrhundert (Stuttgart: J. B. Metzler, 1970); François Berriot, *Athéismes et Athéistes au XVI siécle en France,* 2 vols. (Lille: Editions du CERF, 1977), 1:5–16, which also cites other scholars who disagree with Febvre; see also the dissent of Jean Wirth, "Libertines et épicuriens: Aspects de l'irreligion au XVIe siècle," *Bibliothèque d'humanisme et renaissance,* 39, no. 3 (1977).

5 René Pintard, *Le libertinage erudit dans la première moitié du XVIIe siècle* (1943), rev. ed. (Geneva: Slatkine, 1983). In 1944 Febvre wrote an appreciative review of Pintard's book which is reprinted as "Aux origines de l'esprit moderne: Libertinisme, naturalisme, mécanisme," in *Au coeur religieux du XVIe siècle* (Paris: SEVPEN, 1968).

6 "Of Atheism," *Essays,* in *Works,* 2:133.

Anatomy of Melancholy (1621), the learned English clergyman Robert Burton associated it with "our great Philosophers and Deists" who esteemed "no man a good Scholar that is not an Atheist" and attributed everything "to natural causes." Mentioning many such thinkers, both ancient and modern, he said that they denied God and all his attributes, maintaining that there was neither heaven nor hell, resurrection of the dead, pain, happiness, or a world to come. To them, religion was a fiction "opposite to Reason and Philosophy, though for fear of the Magistrates . . . they dare not publicly profess it."[7] In 1639 the Dutch Calvinist minister and professor at Utrecht, Gisbertus Voetius, stated in a lecture against atheism that atheists included people who sought to know what was unknowable or forbidden and doubted the reality of miracles and the supernatural.[8] Later in the century Ralph Cudworth, one of the school of Cambridge Platonists and among Thomas Hobbes's strongest critics, associated atheism with materialism: atheists were those who "derive all things from senseless matter." Moreover, they commonly went disguised, "walk[ing] abroad in masquerade," often insinuating their atheism "even when they most . . . profess themselves Theists."[9] Another Cambridge Platonist, Benjamin Whichcote, likewise commented that "the Foundation of Atheism [is] that all being is Body."[10] In one of its principal meanings, then, atheism denoted the type of incredulity antithetical to the tenets of all Christian creeds or even to religion itself.[11]

The presence of incredulity and irreligion generally remains elusive and difficult to prove because persecution subjected their expression to the gravest danger. To try to detect them is accordingly like trying to recognize the identity of a person wearing a disguise or mask. Not until far into the eighteenth century were there any philosophers who

[7] Richard Burton, *The Anatomy of Melancholy*, 3 vols. (London: Bell, 1904), 3:434, 440.

[8] Quoted in D. C. Allen, *Doubt's Boundless Sea: Skepticism and Faith in the Renaissance* (Baltimore: Johns Hopkins University Press, 1964), p. 11.

[9] *The True Intellectual System of the Universe*, 2 vols. (New York, 1838), 1:122–123.

[10] Quoted in C. A. Patrides, *The Cambridge Platonists* (Cambridge, Mass: Harvard University Press, 1970), p. 26.

[11] On the meanings given the idea of atheism in the sixteenth and seventeenth centuries, see Febvre, *The Problem of Unbelief*, pp. 131–146; Allen, *Doubt's Boundless Sea*, chap. 1; Berriot, *Athéismes*; D. P. Walker, "Ways of Dealing with Atheists: A Background to Pamela's Refutation of Cecropia," *Bibliothèque d'humanisme et renaissance*, 17, no. 2 (1955).

openly dared to deny the existence of God. The first avowedly atheistic treatise in this sense was apparently Baron d'Holbach's *Le système de la nature,* published in France in 1770. In England, we are told, the earliest such work, whose author was anonymous, dated from 1782.[12] Over a hundred years before this, the philosopher Thomas Hobbes, though notorious for his heterodoxy, never questioned the principle of theism in propounding his materialist theory of man and the universe. All the same, he showed exceptional courage in publishing ideas so radically opposed to the dogmas of all the Christian churches that he repeatedly incurred the accusation of atheism from his many adversaries. Although despite threats he never suffered any personal harm because of his incredulity, four years after his death some of his works were burned at the order of Oxford University. Benedict de Spinoza (1632–1677), another reputed atheist, was likewise a brave thinker for issuing his treatise in behalf of the freedom to philosophize, *Tractatus Theologico-Philosophicus.* Published anonymously with a false imprint in 1670 but certainly recognized as his by his contemporaries, the book contained a searching critique of the Bible's literal truth which undermined the authority of revealed or supernatural religion. As Spinoza lived in the Dutch republic, however, at the time the only relatively tolerant country in Europe, he was less at risk than Hobbes in expressing such ideas. Nonetheless, in 1674 the Dutch States General prohibited the work along with Hobbes's *Leviathan.*[13]

During most of the early modern era, philosophers who tended toward unbelief feared to disclose their true convictions; they could escape the penalties of their dangerous ideas only by concealment and dissimulation. In a discussion of some well-known English freethinkers of the late seventeenth and early eighteenth centuries such as John Toland, Anthony Collins, and Matthew Tindal, David Berman, a recent historian of atheism, argues that they practiced "the art of theological lying" to cover their genuine thoughts. Berman seeks to show that, despite professing themselves Christians and deists, in reality they were cryptoatheists. As he interprets their writings, the technique they used to subvert supernatural beliefs such as the immor-

---

[12] According to David Berman, *A History of Atheism in Britain: From Hobbes to Russell* (London: Croom Helm, 1988), p. 37 and chap. 5, this was an anonymous *Answer to Dr. Priestley's Letters to a Philosophical Unbeliever* (London, 1782), which he ascribes to Dr. Matthew Turner.

[13] Samuel Mintz, *The Hunting of Leviathan* (Cambridge: Cambridge University Press, 1952), pp. 61–62.

tality of the soul was to give only weak reasons in their favor and strong reasons against them. The purpose of their art of theological lying, he suggests, was threefold: first, self-protection; second, the esoteric communication of their unbelief to those who shared it; and third, the covert insinuation of their opinion to those ignorant of it in order to convert them to the same position.[14]

Although this claim is by no means improbable, it is also one that does not admit of demonstration. Nonetheless, there can be no question that esotericism of this sort was one of the principal methods by which philosophers tried to dissemble their incredulity. The clearest statement on the subject is found in a work by John Toland (1670–1722). Suspected by many as an atheist, Toland was a republican and freethinker, a materialist and pantheist, and an opponent of religious superstition and intolerance whose best-known book was *Christianity Not Mysterious* (1696).[15] His essay on esoteric and exoteric philosophy, "Clidophorus," was remarkable, if not unique, for its exposure of the relationship between esotericism and irreligion.[16] Its observations were no less applicable to the unbelieving philosophers of early modern Europe than to those of antiquity with whom it was primarily concerned.

Composed of thirteen short chapters, "Clidophorus," as its title page proclaimed, was a discussion of "the External and Internal Doctrine of the Ancients: The one open and public, accommodated to popular prejudices and the RELIGIONS establish'd by Law; the other private and secret, wherein, to the few capable and discrete, was taught the real TRUTH stript of all disguises." It opened with a description of how the holy tyranny of pagan priests and founders of fraudulent religions forced the philosophers of most nations to make use of a twofold doctrine in order to serve the truth. While accommodating their popular doctrine to the prejudices of the vulgar and the received religion, they restricted their philosophical doctrine based on truth and the nature of things to trusted friends. To them they confided it

---

[14] David Berman, "Deism, Immortality, and the Art of Theological Lying," in *Deism, Masonry, and the Enlightenment: Essays in Honor of Alfred Owen Aldridge,* ed. J.A.L. Lemay (Newark: University of Delaware Press, 1987).

[15] On Toland see R. E. Sullivan, *John Toland and the Deist Controversy* (Cambridge, Mass: Harvard University Press, 1982).

[16] "Clidophorus" is the second of four essays in Toland's *Tetradymus* (London, 1720). Its Greek title, meaning "key bearer," doubtless refers to Toland's purpose of revealing the key to the esoteric philosophy of the ancients.

only with great precautions and behind closed doors. Among Christians likewise, Toland said, the quarrels of rival sects over verbal trifles and their pretenses to infallibility resulted in hatred, persecution, and inquisition, which in turn gave rise to "ambiguities, equivocation, and hypocrisy in all its shapes" as "necessary cautions."[17]

In the succeeding chapters Toland surveyed the many sages who used a double manner of teaching to conceal their true conceptions, which were far removed from the supernatural beliefs of the popular religion. Among these philosophers were the Egyptians, Zoroaster, and a line of Greek and Roman thinkers from Parmenides and Pythagoras to Plato, Aristotle, Varro, and Cicero. When questioned about the divine nature, they took care not to reveal their true judgment save secretly to very few for fear of the rage and violence of the superstitious. Even Jesus veiled his message in parables and bade his disciples not to cast pearls before swine. The distinction these philosophers made between their external and internal doctrine accounted for the fact that they did not always say the same things on the same subjects. Everywhere, according to Toland, "priests were . . . the cause, why the Philosophers invented their occult ways of speaking and writing," lest they be accused of impiety and be exposed to the hatred and fury of the vulgar.[18]

Finally, Toland pointed out that the esoteric and exoteric doctrine remained as much in use as ever. Because of the danger of telling the truth in religion, it was "difficult to know when any man declares his real sentiments of things." Only if someone maintained the contrary of what was commonly believed and publicly enjoined was there a strong presumption that he had really uttered his mind. The one sure way to have the truth, therefore, was to let people speak freely without being branded and punished for their speculative opinions. Till then truth would be expressed scantily and obscurely if at all, and doctrines professed by many who had no belief in them.[19]

While Toland's treatise did not deal explicitly with dissimulation, it is evident that the esotericism it commended for the avoidance of persecution could easily provide a rationale for lying and deception as well. And as its remarks about the persistence of the double doctrine indicated, the latter's use would have been just as well known to modern philosophers as it was to the ancients. This function of eso-

[17] Ibid., pp. 61, 68.
[18] Ibid., pp. 77–78, 85, 94.
[19] Ibid., pp. 94–96.

tericism was overlooked by Febvre in his discussion of the problem of unbelief. Although his book includes a short section on "Veracity in the Sixteenth Century," it is limited to pointing out that sixteenth-century scientists preferred to keep secret the truths they discovered rather than publicize them.[20] It fails to notice that unbelieving authors might take refuge in esoteric methods as a way of dissembling their convictions. Yet this is a possibility we cannot ignore in looking at some of the thinkers of the period.

In the fifteenth century we hear nothing, apparently, about incredulity or atheism. Toward the middle of the next century, however, writings begin to appear that sound the alarm over various kinds of unbelief and become the forerunners of a multiplicity of similar works published during the late sixteenth and the seventeenth centuries. Concurrently, we also perceive the emergence of a new vocabulary among religious apologists which they apply to impious persons and their conceptions adverse to Christianity—terms such as *atheist, achrist,* and *libertine.*[21]

Convinced of the rising tide of unbelief in his time, one of the first to react was John Calvin. Since he was himself a narrow partisan, he often identified the opinions he condemned with irreligion. However, his comments and those of his coreligionists shed an interesting light on a number of the views that aroused his concern and ire.

In 1542 Calvin received a letter from a friend in Paris supplying information he had sought about certain men who probably belonged to humanist circles. Some of them, at least, were former Protestants who, having abandoned the cause, were well fortified with arguments against evangelical doctrine. His correspondent, who had spoken with them, described them as a race of "achrists." Cultivated in letters and erudite in many disciplines, they acknowledged the New Testament only as the work of a wise author equal to Plato, but certainly not as the creation of God. As for the Old Testament, they denied its sacredness altogether, pronouncing it full of depraved opinions. They considered the divinity of Jesus an invention similar to that of the poets who divinized other eminent mortals, and held that when scripture spoke of him as the son of God it referred only to his divine wisdom. They also scoffed at the notion of eternal punishment, telling the

[20] Febvre, *The Problem of Unbelief,* pp. 414–420.
[21] Henri Busson, "Les noms des incrédules au XVIe siècle," *Bibliothèque d'humanisme et renaissance,* 16, no. 3 (1954).

simple that an all-good God did not create men to condemn them to perpetual flames. Moreover, they were not only pleasure seekers and good livers, but deceitful. They spoke piously with the pious, learnedly with the learned, and superstitiously with the superstitious. In short, they were adept at changing their skins to fit every part.[22]

Although the letter added further details, those I have cited suffice to depict minds that had largely detached themselves from the Christian faith. The account must have made a strong impression on Calvin, confirming all his fears on the subject. Over the next three years, as we have seen, he was concerned even more than usual with the underminers of religion, publishing tracts against the Nicodemites and the spiritual libertines, both of whom he indicted for their dissimulation among other offenses. It was undoubtedly the sort of freethinkers his informant described to whom he alluded in his attack on Nicodemism when he listed among the species of dissemblers the "Lucianists," a reference to the pagan antireligious satirist Lucian, contemners of God who pretended adherence to the gospel while mocking it in their hearts as a fable; as did those who turned Christianity into a philosophy or Platonic idea in their heads.[23]

In 1550 Calvin launched a much fuller attack on such unbelievers in the treatise *Concerning Scandals*. Scandals, he explained, consisted of the things hindering or deflecting men from coming to Christ. Among them he included the proud men of learning instructed in human sciences, whose opinions he reported in some detail. They despised the scripture for its simplicity and its inelegance of language; they denied the divinity of Christ and dismissed the works of God, such as Moses' miracles, as a fable. They also mocked at the credulity of those who believed in doctrines that could not be proved by natural reason. Contemptuous of all religion, they regarded it as a merely human invention. They could see no ground for God's existence and considered the hope of eternal life a notion to divert idiots and a specter to frighten little children. In their view, human souls differed not a whit from those of dogs or pigs. Lacking the fear of God, their morals were tainted; hence they gave themselves up to sensuality, banqueting, and pleasant company. Finally, Calvin connected these

[22] A.-L. Herminjard, *Correspondance des réformateurs dans les pays de langue française,* 9 vols. (Nieuwkoop: B. de Graaf, 1965–66), 8:228–233; see also Busson, *Rationalisme,* pp. 351–354.

[23] *Excuse de Iehan Calvin à messieurs les nicodémites,* ed. Albert Autin (Paris: Editions Bossard, 1921), pp. 219, 223–224.

despisers of God with what he called "atheisme." His use of this term
in French was one of the earliest and conflated actual disbelief in God
with other irreligious conceptions.[24]

Pierre Viret, whom we have previously met as an opponent of
Nicodemism, followed Calvin's line of argument. In "Les libertins,"
one of six dialogues on the effects of permitting religious diversity,
Viret shed further light on contemporary incredulity and the novel
vocabulary it elicited. As he pictured them, "libertines" resembled
"atheists" and "epicureans" and were much further from true religion
than either idolaters or the superstitious, who at least possessed some
seed of religion however corrupted. They were mockers of Christianity found "principally among those who have the most knowledge
of human letters and . . . more intelligent minds in worldly affairs
. . . than do others." Some of them, he pointed out, called themselves
"deists" to have it understood that they believed in some kind of God,
as if they had another deity than the true God of Abraham, Isaac, and
Jacob. They turned all religion into an "academic philosophy" that
could be disputed on all sides as a thing uncertain. Libertines, atheists,
and epicureans alike were characterized by hypocritical conformism.
While contemptuous of religion in their hearts, they accommodated
themselves to any kind, the false or the true, going equally to the
Catholic mass or to Protestant sermons to cover their mockery.[25]

Viret's account gave the term *libertine* a new meaning. In the title of
his tract of 1545 Calvin had coupled libertines with the word *spiritual.*
The object of his polemic was the religious spiritualists who under the
pretext of Christian liberty elevated the spirit above the letter and thus
treated outward observances as a matter of indifference. Condemning
the libertines' antinomianism, impiety, and immorality, he also
accused them of duplicity of heart and language for feigning conformity to idolatry and for allegorizing scripture to suit their desires.[26]

---

[24] *Des scandales,* ed. Olivier Fatio (Geneva: Droz, 1984), pp. 55, 65, 68, 101, 136,
138, 141–143. In France, Busson, "Les noms des incrédules," finds the earliest
occurrence of the Greek word for *atheist* in 1532, of the Latin and French words in
the 1540s. He overlooks the term's appearance in Calvin's *Des scandales.*

[25] "Les libertins," in *L'interim fait par dialogues* (Lyons, 1565), pp. 160–163. Viret
also discussed the libertines in *Instruction Chrestienne* (1564); see the account of this
work in Busson, *Rationalisme,* pp. 489–493; Berriot, *Athéismes,* 2:627–628; Febvre,
The Problem of Unbelief, pp. 31–32.

[26] *Contre la secte phantastique et furieuse des libertins que se nomment spirituelz,* in
Opera, ed. Johann Baum, Eduard Cunitz, and Eduard Reuss, 59 vols. (Brunswick,
1863–1896), vol. 7.

In Viret's dialogue, however, spiritualism dropped from view and the libertine was pictured simply as an unbeliever. Thus libertinism was detached from its earlier context and became synonymous with irreligion. Perhaps it was only a step or two from the first kind of libertinism to the second. Each nevertheless represented a quite different attitude toward religion, even though both may have involved dissimulation.

Of the terms *achrist, Lucianist, epicurean, libertine,* and *atheist,* only the last retained its currency in the sixteenth century and later. *Libertine* came to be used frequently only in the earlier seventeenth century, and *deist* first became common only toward its close.[27] The emergence of the words in this context can only signify the momentous recognition in European consciousness of the growing specter of incredulity as a new danger to the Christian faith.

But who were these achrists, atheists, and libertines, these disbelievers in scripture, the incarnation, and eternal life? Although their orthodox assailants denounced their opinions, we do not find any authors who openly proclaimed their incredulity. Naturally this creates a puzzle in which the question of dissimulation is bound to arise. In *Concerning Scandals,* Calvin mentioned the names of several men as atheists and contemners of Christianity.[28] About two of them, Henry Cornelius Agrippa and Villeneuve (the latter probably a pseudonym of the antitrinitarian heretic Servetus), his accusation was grotesquely mistaken; both were assuredly believing Christians if not in the same sense as himself. Another he named was Rabelais, whom Febvre, however, has convincingly shown to have shared the evangelical outlook of Erasmian Christian humanism. Two more whom he listed were Etienne Dolet and Bonaventure Des Périers, both humanists and men of letters. Concerning the first of these Calvin was probably close to the truth. Quarrelsome and indiscreet, an exceptional classical scholar and known as a fervent Ciceronian, Dolet (1509–1546) incurred a reputation for irreligion and in a famous example of persecution was burned in Paris in 1546 for various heresies, including doubt of the immortality of the soul. A contemporary accused him of "habitually dissimulating" his beliefs about God and the soul; Busson has similarly

---

[27] Busson, "Les noms des incredules"; see also the discussion of the term in Schneider, *Der Libertin,* chap. 1; J. C. Margolin, "Reflexions sur l'emploi du terme *libertin* au XVIe siècle," in *Aspects du libertinisme au XVIe siècle. Actes du colloque international de Sommières* (Paris: Vrin, 1974); Wirth, "Libertines et épicuriens."

[28] *Des scandales,* pp. 137–138.

referred to his "secret thought" antithetical to the dogmas of religion. Setting aside the charge of atheism as an exaggeration, it seems likely that he was one of those "achrists" or "deists" who covertly rejected the Christian faith.[29] In the case of Des Périers (d. ca. 1544), the problem of determining his attitude is even more difficult and is inescapably linked to the possibility of dissimulation.

The work that brought Des Périers's faith into question was *Cymbalum Mundi,* an anonymous satire of 1538 which has always been attributed to him.[30] A witty poet, scholar, and friend of Dolet, he collaborated on the latter's *Commentaries on the Latin Language* as well as on the Protestant Pierre Olivétan's French translation of the Bible. For a few years he belonged to the court of Francis I's sister, Margaret of Navarre, the patroness of literary men and Catholic evangelicals, some of whom Calvin denounced as Nicodemites and renegades to the Reformation. On *Cymbalum Mundi*'s appearance, a royal order promptly censured it for its great abuses and heresies. Its printer was imprisoned, and the Parlement of Paris ordered its suppression, though declaring that it contained nothing contrary to the faith. Des Périers himself went unscathed, possibly because of Margaret of Navarre's protection. His presumed connection in the following year, however, with a second edition of this scandalous work may have been one of the reasons for his subsequent dismissal from her service. He was reported to have committed suicide in 1544 on account of the adversities he suffered after being forced to leave her court.[31]

Although Calvin and numerous other contemporaries, both Catholic and Protestant, considered Des Périers to be an atheist on the evidence of *Cymbalum Mundi,* the latter's intention is far from clear. Consisting of four short, lively dialogues, it professed to be written by Thomas Du Clevier to his friend Pierre Tryocan, names that have been read as anagrams for "Thomas Incredule" (unbelieving Thomas) and "Pierre Croyant" (believing Peter). Its characters include Mercury

[29] On Dolet, see Busson, *Rationalisme,* pp. 112–121; Berriot, *Athéismes,* 1:386–412; Lucien Febvre, "Un cas désespéré? Dolet propagateur de l'evangile," in *Au coeur religieux.*

[30] M.A. Screech stresses in his preface the lack of positive proof of Des Périers's authorship; see Bonaventure Des Périers, *Cymbalum Mundi,* ed. P. H. Nurse (Geneva: Droz, 1983), pp. 15–16.

[31] See Nurse's account of the work and of Des Périers's career in "Introduction," ibid.; Dorothea Neidhardt, *Das Cymbalum Mundi des Bonaventure Des Périers* (Geneva: Droz, 1959), pp. 15–42; Berriot, *Athéismes,* 2:637–640.

and other gods; mortals, several of whom may be based on contemporary personalities such as Martin Luther and Martin Bucer; and some talking dogs. The work is a mixture of erudition, raillery, stories, and comments on human foibles, and it is clear that it is mainly a satire on religion. Noticeable also is the influence of the notorious pagan critics of Christian doctrines and credulity in ancient Rome, Lucian and Celsus. Beyond such features, though, its meaning and even the import of its title remain a puzzle. Some scholars have seen it as an impious allegory contemptuous of all supernatural religion; others argue that it is an attack on Christianity and the church ridiculing the faith in revelation and the divinity of Christ; still others deny that it is irreligious, considering it rather as a critique of the presumptuous dogmatism of Catholic and Protestant theologians alike, or as an evangelical plea for religious quietism in opposition to the noisy controversies that disfigured Christianity.[32]

If these wide disagreements prove anything, it is that the essence of *Cymbalum Mundi* lies in its enigmatic character. In contrast to satires such as Jonathan Swift's *A Modest Proposal,* or George Orwell's *Animal Farm,* its author did not want its meaning to be easily understood. On the contrary, because he took such care to disguise it, we must suspect that it harbored a subversive intention. The likelihood of dissimulation to veil this intention is therefore considerable. If the real sense of the work were religious, intimating, for example, a more inward conception of faith against the wrangling and dogmatism of the theologians, there would have been no reason to disguise it so well. The same thought, after all, was one of the keynotes of Erasmus' teaching. Thus, *Cymbalum Mundi* is likely to be a parable of incredulity. What it seems to have encoded was an anti-Christian, libertine message that, we must presume, the author expected sympathetic and discerning contemporaries would be able to penetrate.

One of the main sources frequently cited to explain the growth of incredulity and libertinism in the sixteenth and seventeenth centuries is the naturalistic Aristotelianism taught in some of the Italian universities, particularly on the subject of the immortality of the soul.[33] The

---

[32] For surveys of the reputation and diverse interpretations of the work, see V.-L. Saulnier, "Le sens du *Cymbalum Mundi* de Bonaventure Des Périers," 2 pts., *Bibliothèque d'humanisme et renaissance,* 13, nos. 1–2 (1951); Neidhardt, *Das Cymbalum Mundi,* pp. 46–47; Berriot, *Athéismes,* 2:633–679.

[33] This is the view of J.-R. Charbonnel, *La pensée italienne au XVIe siècle et le courant libertin* (Paris: Champion, 1919); Busson, *Rationalisme;* Pintard, *Le liber-*

most important figure in the dissemination of this teaching was the
philosopher Pietro Pomponazzi (1464–1525). At Padua and Bologna,
where he was a leading professor, the study of Aristotle was institu-
tionally and intellectually detached from theology and therefore
evolved into a more secular, naturalistic interpretation of Aristotle's
concepts. According to Ernst Cassirer, Pomponazzi's philosophical
orientation was an adumbration of the Enlightenment in scholastic
garb.[34] In a work on the causes of natural effects, he showed himself
skeptical on Aristotelian grounds of the existence of miracles, angels,
and demons, and ascribed the works of nature to the causal deter-
minism of the heavenly bodies as agents of God's will. Although his
method of treating problems was quite scholastic, consisting of a
meticulous analysis of arguments, distinctions, and objections, his conclusions were based on reason detached from the transcendent realm
of faith. The naturalism characteristic of his approach was equally
manifest in his most influential composition, *On the Immortality of the
Soul* (1516).[35]

To later antiatheist authors this work smacked suspiciously of
atheism. The question it addressed was how the attributes of both the
mortal and the immortal could be ascribed to man's nature. After
rigorously examining the opinions on immortality of Plato, Aristotle,
the latter's famous Arabic commentator Averroës, Aquinas, and other
philosophers, Pomponazzi decided that the human soul was so inex-
tricably united with its body even in its highest functions that the
principles of natural reason could in no way sustain the belief in
immortality. In his final chapter he defined the question as a "neutral
problem" in which no natural reasons could be produced to prove the
soul either mortal or immortal. He therefore concluded that since

---

tinage; and Giorgio Spini, *Ricerca dei libertini. La teoria dell'impostura delle religioni nel
seicento,* rev. ed. (Florence: Nuova Italia, 1983), pt. 1, chap. 2.

[34] Ernst Cassirer, *The Individual and the Cosmos in Renaissance Philosophy* (New
York: Harper & Row, 1963), p. 81.

[35] Pomponazzi's philosophy is discussed in ibid., pp. 80–83, 103–109, 136–140;
Paul O. Kristeller, *Eight Philosophers of the Italian Renaissance* (Stanford: Stanford
University Press, 1964), chap. 5; J. H. Randall, Jr., introduction to Pomponazzi,
On the Immortality of the Soul, in *The Renaissance Philosophy of Man,* ed. Ernst
Cassirer, Paul O. Kristeller, and J. H. Randall, Jr. (Chicago: University of Chi-
cago Press, 1948). Pomponazzi's *On the Causes of Natural Effects* (1556) is discussed
by Lynn Thorndike, *A History of Magic and Experimental Science,* 8 vols. (New
York: Columbia University Press, 1923–1958), vol. 5, chap. 6. Allen, *Doubt's
Boundless Sea,* chap. 2, discusses him in connection with his reputation for atheism.

immortality was an article of faith truly proved only by revelation and scripture, the proper course for all Christians was to accept it as infallible. On this ground he held that it must be affirmed as beyond doubt that the soul was immortal.[36]

Pomponazzi's treatise was publicly denounced by other writers as heretical. It appeared just three years after the Fifth Lateran Council had formally proclaimed the soul's immortality as a dogma of the church. Replying to his critics in two further works, Pomponazzi continued to maintain that immortality was contrary to natural principles. Though willing to die for its truth as an article of faith, he said, as a philosopher he could not teach without falsehood that it was demonstrable by reason. No harm came to him because of his opinion, and he remained an eminent professor until his death.[37]

In explaining Pomponazzi's position Busson and others have claimed that he relied on the principle of the so-called double truth, by which a proposition could be true according to faith yet false according to reason; and, moreover, that he used this principle as a hypocritical device to disguise his unbelief. He never spoke of a double truth, however; nor, as Paul Oskar Kristeller has emphasized, do his writings yield any evidence of insincerity to hide his true convictions. His view is perhaps therefore better understood as a defense both of the coexistence of faith and reason and of the independence of philosophy from theology in its own domain.[38] Nevertheless, Pomponazzi's treatise not only strongly influenced subsequent libertine thought in its skepticism concerning immortality but also included an implicit approval of dissimulation on the subject.

One of the arguments Pomponazzi propounded against immortality was that most people choose virtue not for its own sake but out of hope of reward or fear of punishment. Statesmen, therefore, in order to control human wickedness and vice, created the belief in eternal rewards for the virtuous in another life and for the vicious eternal

---

[36] Pomponazzi, *On the Immortality of the Soul*, chap. 15.

[37] Randall, introduction, ibid., pp. 274–276.

[38] Busson, *Rationalisme*, pp. 62–64; Kristeller, *Eight Philosophers*, pp. 84–86; see also idem on the unbelief attributed to Renaissance Aristotelian naturalism in "Le mythe de l'atheisme de la renaissance et la tradition français de la libre penseé," *Bibliothèque d'humanisme et renaissance*, 17, no. 3 (1975). Cf. the careful discussion by Martin Pine, "Pomponazzi and the Problem of 'Double Truth,' " *Journal of the History of Ideas*, 29, no. 2 (1968), who holds that it is necessary to discount Pomponazzi's professions of orthodoxy and that the deepest center of his thought admits only the truth of philosophy.

punishments, "which frighten greatly." Knowing men's proneness to evil and intending the common good, the lawgiver thus "decreed that the soul is immortal, not caring for truth but only for righteousness, that he may lead men to virtue." Nor should he be censured for this, Pomponazzi added, for just as physicians "feign" many things to heal the sick, so the statesman composes fables to keep citizens in the right path. In a related argument he further noted that many men who believed the soul to be mortal had nonetheless written that it was immortal. Such devices, he considered, were necessary as a cure for the inclination to evil of the ignorant many devoted solely to bodily things, who neither knew nor loved the goods of the soul.[39]

These comments were in effect a justification of the use of dissimulation for political and religious ends. They also implied that the Christian belief in immortality might be merely an illusion that lawgivers devised to keep men in order. Beyond this, they permitted the inference that supernatural religion might itself be a political invention of rulers to ensure obedience and order. Underlying them, moreover, was an implicit aristocratic esotericism. The intelligent few who loved virtue for itself did not require the belief in immortality, but ordinary people needed to be deceived by the prospect of eternal reward and punishment if they were to be made good. All these notions sanctioning dissimulation of belief, admittedly of no great prominence in Pomponazzi, were to occupy an important place in subsequent libertine thought.

A number of concurrent intellectual influences contributed to make incredulity a possible alternative for the philosopher during the sixteenth century: the naturalism of the Paduan Aristotelians, the revival of ancient Greek Pyrrhonian skepticism, the ideas of ancient pagan adversaries of Christianity such as Lucian, Celsus, and Julian the Apostate, and the philosophical religion of Cicero, with its rejection of popular superstition.[40] But because any tendency toward unbelief was forced to be circumspect and duplicitous, its detection, as we have seen, is a delicate and complex problem.

Antiatheist authors believed atheists used certain tricks to get their views across. According to the Calvinist minister Voetius, one of their

[39] Pomponazzi, *On the Immortality of the Soul,* pp. 364, 374.

[40] See Busson, *Rationalisme*; Pintard, *Le libertinage*; Berriot, *Athéismes*; J. S. Spink, *French Free-Thought from Gassendi to Voltaire* (London: Athlone Press, 1960), pt. 1.

subterfuges was to pretend to attack atheism by expounding its "Lucianic" tenets and offering only a tepid confutation, thus leaving "certain subtle curiosities" in the reader's mind.[41] The question of the immortality of the soul was generally seen as one of the touchstones of atheism. The Italian physician, philosopher, mathematician, and astrologer Jerome Cardan (1501–1576), whom the orthodox accused of irreligion, wrote a work on immortality in which he cited fifty-four reasons to show that the soul perishes with the body. After planting these doubts, to be sure, he listed a number of arguments in favor of immortality. He finally arrived at a version of the doctrine of the Arab philosopher Averroës that the soul survives insofar as it is part of the universal soul of the world, but otherwise dies. What his real view was is probably impossible to tell. In another work, however, he commented that to subscribe to the belief in immortality was prudent, pious, and free from reprehension. Elsewhere he also declared that on ticklish questions such as the immortality of the soul, "all wise men, even if they do not believe it themselves, agree publicly with the vulgar" *(omnes sapientes, etiam se id non credunt, vulgo plaudant).*[42] Perhaps this provides a clue to his true opinion on the subject.

Gabriel Naudé (1600–1653), who belonged to the inner circle of French libertinism in the earlier seventeenth century, was widely acquainted with Italian thinkers and their works from his studies at Padua and lengthy residence in Italy.[43] He considered Cardan typical of Italian philosophers in giving little credence to the articles of faith and mysteries of the Christian religion. In his judgment, many had "written about the immortality of the soul without believing it, to the point of causing doubt in all their readers." Among his friends was the Paduan professor Cesare Cremonini, a noted Aristotelian of whose duplicity he had no doubt. According to Naudé, Cremonini was an "initiate," a man devoid of all credulity "who well understood the truth but dared not express [it] in Italy." He "concealed his game finely," and "although he had no piety, he wanted to be considered pious." One of Cremonini's favorite maxims was "Think inwardly as

[41] Allen, *Doubt's Boundless Sea*, p. 11.

[42] Cardan, *De Sapientia*, in *Opera*, 12 vols. (Lyons, 1663), 1:550; *De Animi Immortalitate*, ibid., 2:458–465; and *De Sapientia*, ibid., 1:568; quoted in Allen, *Doubt's Boundless Sea*, pp. 51–52, 56–58; on Cardan's incredulity, see Spini, *Ricerca dei libertini*, pp. 29–33.

[43] Pintard, *Le libertinage*; J. V. Rice, *Gabriel Naudé 1600–1653* (Baltimore: Johns Hopkins Press, 1939), chap. 1.

you like, but conform outwardly to custom" *(intus ut libet, foris ut moris est)*.[44] This formula was also congenial, as we shall see, to French libertine thinkers.

Naudé's observations concurred with the general assumption of atheist-hunters that irreligious authors systematically employed concealment and dissimulation to throw the right-minded off the track and prevent detection of their true beliefs. In a book defending the doctrines of providence and the immortality of the soul, the Jesuit controversialist Leonard Lessius pointed to this trait as one of their main characteristics. Although there were many people nowadays, he claimed, who altogether denied any divinity, they kept it secret for fear of the laws and dared to divulge it only to familiars.[45] The French Jesuit François Garasse repeatedly made the same imputation of dissembling in his polemic against atheists and libertines, *The Curious Doctrine of the Advanced Minds of This Age (La doctrine curieuse des beaux esprits de ce temps,* 1624), one of the best-known works of its kind to appear during the period.

Prominent among the authors whom Garasse denounced for denying the immortality of the soul and other impieties was the Neapolitan Lucilio, alias Julius Caesar, Vanini (1585–1619), a wandering priest, monk, theologian, and philosopher who was executed in 1619 for atheism by the sentence of the Parlement of Toulouse. Vanini, whose numerous works included a supposed apologia for religion, *Amphitheatrum Aeternae Providentiae,* and a book of dialogues on the secrets of nature and religious subjects, espoused a radical naturalism derived from both Aristotelian and Epicurean sources. A disciple of Machiavelli, he regarded religion as a political imposture, apparently believing neither in a personal God, the divinity of Christ, or the immortality of the soul, nor in miracles, angels, devils, or prophecies. An inevitable question mark nevertheless hangs over the true character of his ideas, because of the obliquity in their presentation. His *Amphitheatrum,* for example, was ostensibly directed against atheists, Epicureans, Aristotelians, and Stoics. The approach he adopted in this

[44] *Naudaeana* (1701); quoted in Charbonnel, *La pensée italienne,* pp. 60–61, 63–64; and Rice, *Gabriel Naudé,* p. 13. Charbonnel remarks that Cremonini used a sort of "mental reservation" in dealing with conflicts between the truths of Aristotle as he interpreted them and the truths of faith, pp. 270–271. For Italian libertinism in general, see Spini, *Ricerca dei libertini.*

[45] *De Providentia Numinis et Animi Immortalitate adversus Atheos et Politicos* (1613), quoted in Charbonnel, *La pensée italienne,* p. 33.

work appears to have been in keeping with his method of trying to insinuate his incredulity under cover of orthodoxy. While pretending to oppose irreligious principles, he gave them such exposure as to make his intentions suspect. This fact, together with his indiscreet speeches reported by witnesses, cost him his life. "If I were not a Christian," he would write, or "If I were not instructed by the church," and then follow with the statement that in such case he would rather believe the world eternal or some other equally prohibited conclusion. In a dialogue about God, he introduced the arguments of an "atheist of Amsterdam," following which the scandalized interlocutors, Alexander and Julius Caesar, repeated them in their indignation. He used the same devices in dealing with other touchy subjects such as the resurrection of the dead.[46] The relentless Father Garasse threw the spotlight on these subterfuges. In the *Amphitheatrum,* he declared, Vanini spoke as a hypocrite, and in his dialogues as a perfect atheist. He charged the Italian with such ruses as attributing his impieties to a speaker in the dialogue, or to an atheist, or saying that he had heard them somewhere, though in fact they were his own. As he saw it, Vanini followed the common libertine practice of speaking with ambiguities and "sous-ententes" so that if surprised he could disavow his views and protest that he was maliciously accused. That he deserved his horrible end because of his godless beliefs the pious Jesuit controversialist had no doubt.[47]

Nearly all the writers whom antiatheist polemicists singled out for attack were either Italian or French. In England, at least until early in the seventeenth century, there seems to have been little sign of incre-

---

[46] See the dialogues "De Deo" and "De Resurrectione Mortuum," in *De Admirandis Naturae Reginae Deaeque Mortalium Arcanis* (Paris, 1615). Both this work and *Amphitheatrum* include an exposition of numerous arguments against orthodox positions and draw extensively on Pomponazzi, Cardan, Averroës, and Aristotle. *Amphitheatrum,* exercitationes X–XI, sets forth the opinions of the Greek atheist Diagoras. Vanini's ideas and incredulity are discussed by Spink, *French Free-Thought,* pp. 28–42; Allen, *Doubt's Boundless Sea,* pp. 20–21, 69–70, 134–135; Thorndike, *History of Magic,* vol. 6, chap. 47; Spini, *Ricerca dei libertini,* pt. 2, chap. 4; and Tullio Gregory, "Il libertinismo della prima metà del seicento. Stato attuale degli studi e prospettive di ricerca," in *Ricerche su letteratura libertina e letteratura clandestina nei seicento* (Florence: Nuova Italia, 1981), p. 18, who stresses his influence on seventeenth-century libertinism, as does also Busson, *Rationalisme.*

[47] François Garasse, *La doctrine curieuse des beaux esprits de ce temps ou pretendus tels. Contenant plusieurs maximes pernicieuses à la religion, à l'estat, & aux bonnes moeurs* (Paris, 1624), pp. 310–311, 685, 880–887, 1007–08, 1015.

dulity among philosophers and men of letters. Despite an outcry
against the threat of atheism near the end of the sixteenth century,
there were few charges of actual irreligion and abandonment of Christianity directed against specific individuals.[48] In 1593, for example,
accusations of atheism were cast by well-informed witnesses against
Christopher Marlowe (1564–1593), whose plays certainly contain evidence of a naturalistic revolt against the Christian religion. Among
other blasphemies, he was alleged to have called Moses a "jugler" and
Christ a bastard and homosexual. Another opinion ascribed to him
was that "the first beginning of Religion was only to keep men in
awe," a typical libertine argument. His friend the poet Robert Greene
reproved him for his disbelief in God and his adherence to the teachings of Machiavelli, warning that he would lose his soul unless he
renounced his principles. The dramatist Thomas Kyd asserted that
Marlowe gibed at scripture, denied the divinity of Christ, and maintained that many things attributed to divine power could have been
done by men. According to another informant, Marlowe had better
reasons for atheism "than any devine in Englande is able to geve to
prove devinitie." Had he not been killed in a brawl before these
charges could be investigated, he would probably have had to pay for
his opinions.[49]

Sir Walter Raleigh (1552–1618) was one of those with whom Marlowe was said to have discussed his atheistical ideas. Raleigh was
reported to be the master of a "school of atheism." So notorious was
his reputation for incredulity that it eventually gave rise to an official
inquiry. In this instance also dissimulation probably figured as a cover
for heterodoxy.

Raleigh's versatile genius and contempt for convention attracted
him to ideas his contemporaries shunned as perilous. The popular
impression of his atheism was reinforced by his circle of friends,
which included the great mathematician and natural philosopher
Thomas Harriot and the earl of Northumberland, both of whom were
said to be unbelievers like himself. In 1606 Harriot wrote the scientist
Johannes Kepler that he could not philosophize freely in England, and
he refused to publish his discoveries in his lifetime. Of the great

[48] See Michael Hunter, "The Problem of 'Atheism' in Early Modern England,"
Transactions of the Royal Historical Society, 5th ser., 35 (1985), 137–138 and passim.
[49] The full text of these charges is printed in J. W. Shirley, *Thomas Harriot: A
Biography* (Oxford: Clarendon Press, 1983), pp. 181–184; see also F. S. Boas, *Christopher Marlowe* (Oxford: Clarendon Press, 1960), pp. 108–115 and chaps. 14–15.

Elizabethans, moreover, none was more responsive to Machiavelli's conceptions than Raleigh, who found in the Italian thinker a profound guide to the twisted ways of politics and the world. At his trial in 1603 for treason, both his prosecutor, Sir Edward Coke, and the chief justice of the court taxed him with following a Machiavellian policy and holding atheist principles.[50]

In March 1594 rumors about atheistic statements Raleigh was supposed to have made led to an investigation at Cerne Abbas, Dorset, by commissioners specially appointed by the ecclesiastical authorities.[51] Raleigh's brother Carew, his friend Harriot, and other associates were also mentioned in these rumors. Fifteen witnesses, more than half of them clergy, gave depositions as to whether they knew anyone suspected of atheism or of arguing or speaking against or doubting the being of God or his providence or the immortality of the soul, or who said that scripture was not to be believed for its doctrine but only as a matter of "policye or Civell government." One witness, the minister of Sherborne, where Raleigh lived, related how a local shoemaker had told him that despite his preaching that there was a God, a heaven and hell, an immortal soul, and resurrection after this life, there was nevertheless a company of people in the town who said that "hell is noe other but povertie & penurye in this world; and that we dye like beasts and when we are gonne there is no more remembrance of us . . . and such like."

The main evidence came from the Reverend Ralph Ironside, a minister who testified to a dinner conversation at which he was present with Raleigh and some of his companions. We can perceive the direction of Raleigh's mind in the exchange the clergyman reported between himself and the brilliant courtier, writer, seaman, and explorer with his manysided intellectual interests. The discussion focused on the soul, which Raleigh asked Ironside to explain as something very puzzling. When told that it was the spiritual and immortal substance breathed into man by God, he expressed little satisfaction in the answer and contrasted its obscurity with the clarity and demonstrative force of

[50] Pierre Lefranc, *Sir Walter Ralegh ecrivain* (Paris: Armand Colin, 1968), pp. 234, 402–403, and chap. 9; J. W. Shirley, "Sir Walter Ralegh and Thomas Harriot," in *Thomas Harriot Renaissance Scientist* (Oxford: Clarendon Press, 1974); Jean Jacquot, "Harriot, Hill, Warner, and the New Philosophy," in ibid., p. 108.

[51] The documents connected with this investigation are printed in G. B. Harrison, ed., *Willobie His Avisa* (London: Lane, 1926), app. 3; see also Lefranc, *Sir Walter Raleigh*, pp. 379–393; Shirley, *Thomas Harriot*, pp. 189–200.

mathematics. The talk went on to the subject of God, whom the minister defined as *ens ensium,* or the being of beings. "Yea, but what is this
ens ensium?" Raleigh queried. " . . . it is God," the minister reiterated;
but this reply "being disliked as before," Raleigh called for grace to be
said, "for that quoth he is better than this disputacion."

The investigation in Dorset apparently produced no further outcome, and Raleigh emerged from it unscathed, although his reputation for atheism persisted. The whole episode remains somewhat
obscure, possibly because his considerable local importance and the
commissioners' partiality prevented a full exposure of the opinions he
and his friends were reported to hold. But we cannot in any case
overlook the likelihood that he would have relied on dissimulation
to hide his true beliefs. In his *History of the World,* he condemned the
practice of mental reservation.[52] Although this sentiment may have
been sincere, as an experienced courtier and pupil of Machiavelli
Raleigh understood the necessity of politic deception when circumstances warranted: "Wise men" should be "like Coffers with double
bottoms: which when others look into, being opened, they see not all
that they hold."[53] Despite some elusiveness, his writings afford sufficient indication of his skeptical, rationalist, and naturalistic leanings;
and we may surmise that notwithstanding his remaining in some sense
religious, his philosophical and scientific notions led him to doubt
basic Christian dogmas. *The History of the World,* composed in prison
during the years following his treason conviction in 1603, proves that
he was not an atheist: it is premised upon a faith in God as sovereign
ruler of the universe. It also shows, though, his belief in the occult
tradition as the source of a distinctive revelation independent of the
Bible. With this went his acceptance of the esoteric principle of
keeping higher truths secret from the vulgar. Just as Moses had withheld certain knowledge from the Israelites, he noted, so to divulge
such mysteries to the rude multitude would be no better than giving
holy things to dogs or casting pearls before swine.[54] It thus seems
probable that Raleigh's philosophy included skeptical, libertine ideas
that could not have borne the light of day, and that his aristocratic

[52] See above, Chapter 9.

[53] *The History of the World* (London, 1687), p. 602.

[54] Ibid., p. 44; on Raleigh's relation to hermeticism, see Lefranc, *Sir Walter
Ralegh,* chap. 13. E. A. Strathmann, *Sir Walter Raleigh: A Study in Elizabethan
Scepticism* (New York: Columbia University Press, 1951), argues that he was not
an atheist.

esotericism served him, as it did other heterodox thinkers, as a justification to disguise and dissemble his more dangerous beliefs.

From the perspective of early modern states and churches, denial of dogmas such as the immortality of the soul endangered the stability of society, which appeared bound up with acceptance of the teachings of the Christian religion. The insistence of political and ecclesiastical governors on intellectual conformity where religious doctrine was concerned necessarily gave rise to hypocrisy. We are familiar with the religious hypocrisy of Molière's Tartuffe (1664), the stock comic figure who played the pious believer as a cover for his greed, lust, and ambition. We are much less familiar with the intellectual hypocrisy of the philosopher whose conformity provided a cover for incredulity. In this period the mask frequently served as a metaphor for the dissimulation beneath which libertine thinkers hid their opposition to orthodox beliefs and values. One who recurred to this metaphor was the Servite monk Father Paolo Sarpi (1552–1623), famed for his writings against the usurpations of papal and ecclesiastical power. Sarpi attracted the attention of all Europe when Venice employed him as its counselor and theologian in its momentous conflict with the papacy after Paul V laid an interdict on the Venetian republic in 1606 for its defiant curtailment of clerical privileges. In his private reflections he recorded that it was necessary "to remain masked with everyone" *(stare mascherato con tutti)* and to express conventional opinions publicly while privately reserving one's own convictions. Inwardly, he held, one should live and judge according to reason, while speaking and living outwardly in accord with the common opinion. Suspected of being far from orthodox by friends and foes alike, he said of himself, "I am forced to wear a mask, without which no one can survive in Italy." He was convinced that hypocrisy permeated his age. "Everything conceals itself behind the mask of religion," he commented bitterly; even though "in other centuries hypocrisy was not uncommon . . . in this one it pervades everything."[55]

Sarpi's most lasting achievement was his controversial *History of the Council of Trent,* a major contribution to seventeenth-century historiography. It too reflected his preoccupation with dissimulation, since its purpose was to unmask the myths surrounding the famous council in order to expose the abuses of papal power and other corruptions

[55] Quoted in David Wootton, *Paolo Sarpi. Between Renaissance and Enlightenment* (Cambridge: Cambridge University Press, 1983), pp. 37, 112, 119, 128.

that had defeated the reform movement in the Catholic church. The circumstances of the book's publication had their own deceptive features. Impossible to publish anywhere in Italy, the manuscript was smuggled out of Venice with the aid of Dutch merchants and brought to England at the behest of the Calvinist archbishop of Canterbury, George Abbot. It was in Protestant England in 1619 that the first Italian edition appeared under a pseudonym, followed by an English translation the next year.[56]

Hostile observers reported that Sarpi had "more of the philosopher and libertine in him than the monk," and that he was devoid of religion, faith, and belief in the immortality of the soul.[57] Aristotelian and Pomponazzian naturalism were among the major influences in his intellectual development, as was also the political realism of the Machiavellian and Tacitist doctrine of reason-of-state. His private meditations or *Pensieri* on philosophical, religious, and scientific subjects, which remained unpublished till the present century, not only indicate a skepticism toward received beliefs but also suggest that he may have been a materialist and determinist who questioned the existence of God and the immortality of the soul.[58] Some scholars hold that his naturalism and skepticism made him a Christian fideist who placed truth above reason. Others conclude that he was an irenic Catholic reformer or that he subscribed to a form of spiritual religion indifferent to doctrine which trusted solely in God. The latest interpreter of the *Pensieri,* however, perceives him as an atheist. According to this thesis, Sarpi attempted through his political activity and published writings to subvert religion by indirection, and his originality lay in the fact that in his *Pensieri* he anticipated even the skeptic Pierre Bayle as the earliest European thinker to conceive that human society could exist without a belief in God, providence, or an afterlife. Since it was never safe for him to admit to the ideas and aims constituting his real philosophy, he was compelled to become an accomplished dissembler and hypocrite.[59]

Sarpi's own secretiveness and duplicity leave it uncertain how

[56] Ibid., p. 107; see also the introduction to *Istoria del Concilio tridentino,* in Paolo Sarpi, *Opere,* ed. Gaetano and Luisa Cozzi (Milan: Ricciardi Editore, 1969). The London first edition bore the pseudonym Pietro Soave Polano.

[57] Wootton, *Paolo Sarpi,* p. 41 and appendix.

[58] Sarpi's *Pensieri* are printed in *Opere*; see Wootton, *Paolo Sarpi,* chap. 1.

[59] See Wootton, *Paolo Sarpi,* introduction and chap. 1, pp. 46, 64–76, and chap. 4.

valid this interpretation may be. Other authorities, moreover, have dismissed its claims as inaccurate and unfounded.[60] But although the extent of Sarpi's unbelief is debatable, his detachment from essential parts of the Christian creed seems undeniable. We have reason to presume his extreme unorthodoxy from the importance he himself placed upon dissimulation as necessary for survival in Catholic Italy. Whatever the precise character of his ideas, some type of libertinism was probably a vital ingredient of his thought, which he camouflaged by a pretended conformity in accordance with his own precepts.

The split between man and mask, between private conviction and public profession, which marked Sarpi's career finds an even more striking illustration in the case of another philosopher, the Dominican monk Tommaso Campanella (1568–1639), likewise a product of the repressive environment of the Italian Counter-Reformation. It is impossible to do justice to Campanella's sufferings as a victim of oppression. Born a cobbler's son in Calabria in the Spanish-ruled kingdom of Naples, he spent twenty-seven years in the Inquisition's prisons on account of his divagations from orthodoxy. Following earlier collisions with authority, he was arrested in 1593 in Padua by the Holy Office and accused of adhering to the philosophy of Democritus and Epicurus and opposing the doctrines of the church. Three years later he was released after making his abjuration, only to be imprisoned again in Naples as a heretic. Placed in confinement in a monastery, in 1599 he became involved as a prime mover in a futile visionary conspiracy to liberate Calabria from Spanish domination and make it an independent republic. In his own mind this venture was inspired by millenarian prophecies of a new order sustained by a newly purified religion. Charged with heresy and rebellion, he was tried and tortured in separate proceedings for each of these crimes. Informants attributed such blasphemies to him as disbelief in God, Christ, the trinity, miracles, the eucharist, heaven, hell, and the authority of the Roman pontiff. He was alleged to have stated that devils, hell, and paradise were invented to instill fear into men to make them fervent believers, and that the sacraments were not established by God but devised by men as a means of

[60] Boris Ulianich, "Paolo Sarpi 'Riformatore' 'Irenico'? Note sulla ecclesiologia, sulla teologia, sulla sua religione," and Luisa Cozzi, "I *Pensieri* di Fra Paolo Sarpi," both in *Fra Paolo Sarpi. Atti del convegno di studio* (Venice: Comune di Venezia, 1986), esp. pp. 97n, 151n; and the review of Wootton's book by Eric Cochrane, *Journal of Modern History*, 57, no. 1 (1985), 151–153.

social cohesion.[61] It has been generally supposed that, to avoid further torture during his trial by the Inquisition, and facing almost certain execution if found guilty, he pretended madness. To test whether he was lying, his jailers subjected him to *la veglia,* consisting in suspension by the arms, bound behind at the wrists, over a seat studded with spikes. In this posture he could only find relief when the pain became unbearable by sinking onto the spikes, which tore his flesh. Even under this inhuman treatment, though, he maintained his apparent deception. Eventually judged insane, he was sentenced in 1603 to life imprisonment. Having failed in an attempted escape, he was consigned to four years in chains in an underground dungeon. Despite these ordeals, he composed many works while in prison. One of them, written in 1616 and published in 1622 in Frankfurt, was a defense of Galileo arguing that the Copernican cosmology was compatible with scripture. In 1626 through the intervention of Pope Urban VIII he was released in Naples, but after only a few weeks was imprisoned once more in Rome at the order of the Holy Office. The pope, who consulted him eagerly as an astrologer, finally freed him in 1626. Five years later, fearing a plot against himself, he fled Rome for France to seek the favor of Louis XIII and Cardinal Richelieu. He was well received, wrote several works in behalf of French policy, and died in France in 1639.[62]

A man of strong will and ferocious energy, at once duplicitous and rash, Campanella was persistently driven by his sense of mission as an intellectual, religious, and political world reformer. His outlook blended an odd assortment of ideas. One of the strongest influences upon him was a fellow Neapolitan philosopher, Telesio, a naturalist

[61] See Luigi Amabile, *Fra Tommaso Campanella: La sua congiura, i suoi processi, e la sua pazzia* (Naples, 1882), vol. 3, pp. 195–196, cited in Frank E. Manuel and Fritzi Manuel, *Utopian Thought in the Western World* (Cambridge, Mass.: Harvard University Press, 1979), p. 266.

[62] Amabile, *Fra Tommaso Campanella,* is one of the principal authorities for the details of Campanella's life; see also *Enciclopedia italiana,* 36 vols. (Milan: G. Treccani, 1929–1946), s.v.; Romano Amerio's introduction in *Opere di Giordano Bruno e Tommaso Campanella* (Milan: Ricciardi Editore, n.d.). For his philosophy and ideas see Joan Kelly-Gadol, "Tommaso Campanella: The Agony of Political Theory in the Counter-Reformation," in *Philosophy and Humanism: Renaissance Essays in Honor of Paul Oskar Kristeller,* ed. E. P. Mahoney (Leiden: Brill, 1976); Spini, *Ricerca dei libertini,* pt. 2, chaps. 2–3. Also helpful is Joseph Scalzo's "Tommaso Campanella and the Calabrian Conspiracy of 1599: Naturalism, Madness, and Political Thought in Late Renaissance Italy" (M.A. thesis, Syracuse University, 1988).

and empiricist or sensationalist with proclivities toward materialism, noted also for his criticism of Aristotle. Occultism, magic, astrology, messianism, universalistic utopianism, reason-of-state politics, and theocratic doctrines also occupied an important place in his thinking. The changes, contortions, and flat inconsistencies among his writings are so striking that only hypocrisy and outright deceit seem able to explain them. While some students of his work have tried to show that he was basically a genuine Catholic and representative thinker of the Counter-Reformation, others have conceived him as quite the opposite. The latter see him as a *mottegiatrice* or jokester, a put-on artist, and a dissembler of his real beliefs, compelled to assume this posture by the extreme oppression he experienced. In line with this conception he has been characterized as a skilled practitioner of the art of ambiguity, an amphibological personality capable of playing elaborate mental tricks on his adversaries and tormentors, without which he could never have survived the Inquisition's persecution.[63] His feigning madness would be proof of this, if only we could be certain that it was indeed only a pretense.

Soon after the exposure of his anti-Spanish conspiracy, Campanella while in prison wrote the two works for which he remains best known. The first, *The Hispanic Monarchy,* advocated the reign of Spain's universal empire as the will of God and offered practical advice for the advancement of Spanish world rule and the confusion of its enemies. As a political commentator Campanella always claimed to be against Machiavellian deceit or *astuzia* as something distinct from true prudence. Nonetheless, in the counsel it tendered, this work exemplified, even to a crude degree, the reason-of-state analysis we associate with Machiavellianism. He also coupled his vision of Spanish hegemony with the exaltation of the Roman papacy's world primacy, thereby appealing simultaneously to the interests of both.[64] The

[63] Scalzo, "Tommaso Campanella and Calabrian Conspiracy," chap. 1. Scalzo's view is similar to Kelly-Gadol's and ultimately traceable to the judgment of Amabile. B. M. Bonansea, *Tommaso Campanella: Renaissance Pioneer of Modern Thought* (Washington, D.C.: Catholic University Press, 1969), regards his philosophy as fundamentally orthodox. Spini, *Ricerca dei libertini,* pp. 121–122, recognizes his libertinism but considers him as always basically Catholic in his sense of the greatness of the Roman church and its sacerdotal institutions, and questions the view that he was a dissembler.

[64] *De Monarchia Hispanica* (wr. ca. 1600, pub. 1620). I have used the English translation, *Thomas Campanella an Italian Friar and Second Machiavel. His Advice to the King of Spain, for Attaining the Universal Monarchy of the World* (London, 1660).

second of these works was the utopian *City of the Sun,* a dialogue
describing a just and rational society. Ruled by an all-wise monarch,
the Solarian community was based on a deistic natural religion, knew
neither family nor private property, and was dedicated to cultivating
the sciences, practical arts, and education.[65] Some historians have
explained *The Hispanic Monarchy* as reflecting a conversion Campanella experienced in prison under the influence of his confessor.
Others consider *The City of the Sun* the real key to his mind and regard
the works in conflict with it as insincere and deliberate opportunism.
Many of his compositions were undoubtedly produced in the hope of
helping him to regain his freedom. The circumstances of his life and
discordant aspects of his writings make it probable that none of the
latter can be taken at face value. As a victim of the Counter-Reformation, it is very likely that he frequently told those in power what he
considered they wanted to hear.[66]

Among Campanella's principal writings was *Atheism Conquered,*
an antiatheist treatise published first in Rome and five years later in
Paris with a dedication to Louis XIII.[67] Ostensibly aimed at Calvinists,
Machiavellians, and libertines, the work can also be interpreted as
intended instead to promote incredulity. Before its publication
Campanella was obliged to make changes to meet the objection of the
ecclesiastical censors that its arguments cited against the Christian
religion outweighed the replies it made to them. Notwithstanding
these alterations, a noted contemporary German scholar, Herman
Conring, concluded that the treatise should be titled *Atheism Con-*

For Campanella's often-expressed opposition to Machiavelli, see ibid., chap. 5, and
his *Atheismus Triumphatus* (Rome, 1631). Friedrich Meinecke discusses Campanella
as a reason-of-state theorist in *Machiavellism. The Doctrine of Raison d'Etat and Its
Place in Modern History* (London: Routledge & Kegan Paul, 1957), chap. 4; see also
John Headley, "Campanella's Machiavellism," *Journal of the History of Ideas,* 49,
no. 3 (1988).

[65] *Civitas Solis* (wr. ca. 1602; pub. Frankfurt, 1623). See the parallel Italian-
English edition and introduction by Daniel Donno, *The City of the Sun* (Berkeley:
University of California Press, 1981), and the discussion of the work in Manuel
and Manuel, *Utopian Thought,* chap. 10.

[66] See Kelly-Gadol, "Tommaso Campanella"; Scalzo, "Tommaso Campanella
and Calabrian Conspiracy." The former in particular interprets Campanella's political thought as inevitably distorted by the hypocrisy and dissimulation forced upon
him by his persecutors.

[67] *Atheismus Triumphatus seu Reductio ad Religionem . . . contra Antichristianis-
simum Achitophelisticum* (1631) (Paris, 1636).

quering because it seemed to betray rather than defend religion. Campanella's biographer Cyprianus held the same opinion, observing that many passages put the irreligious position, which ought to have been left in the shadows, in a fuller, better light than did the writings of the atheists themselves.[68]

A survey of the work lends support to these comments. The second chapter, for instance, gave arguments against both religion and Christianity along with answers to them. Besides questioning fundamental Christian doctrines, it pointed out the innumerable disagreements of the theologians and the diverse conflicting beliefs among men, indicating that all of them might be deceived. It also raised the problem of the salvation of the uncounted numbers who died before the incarnation and of the many people then alive—Tartars, Japanese, Chinese, Africans, and inhabitants of the Arctic—who never heard of Christ. It stated reasons for the eternity of the world and against an afterlife, noting the opinions of philosophers such as Pomponazzi and Cremonini, who are said to have submitted to theology from fear but otherwise adhered to philosophy. Other chapters posed doubts about miracles and considered the idea that religion was invented by the *politici* to keep men in subjection. They raised perplexing questions such as why God created souls he foreknew to be damned; why an apple brought forth so many evils that God had to be incarnated to redeem men from their crime; and why at present the devil was more powerful than Christ among men. By showing the absurdity of pagan, Jewish, and Muslim superstition, the book permitted the inference that the Christian faith might be no less superstitious. There were also indications in it that Campanella believed in worship of the stars as spiritual intelligences. Moreover, in refuting Machiavelli it allowed ample space for the opinion of his admirers; and although it assailed Machiavellian prescriptions as servile and deceitful, its own treatment of the political utility of religion and of political methods was close to Machiavelli's own.[69]

Atheism Conquered was thus a work of considerable ambiguity. Significantly, the anonymous author of *Theophrastus Redivivus,* one of the most notable libertine treatises of the seventeenth century, drew on it for his attack upon the Christian religion. It is therefore scarcely sur-

[68] G. Ernst, "Campanella 'Libertino'?" in *Ricerche su letteratura libertina.*

[69] *Atheismus Triumphatus,* chaps. 2, 9, 10, 16, 18, 19; D. P. Walker, *Spiritual and Demonic Magic from Ficino to Campanella* (London: Warburg Institute, 1958), pp. 223–227.

prising that Campanella's writings brought him a reputation as a cryptoatheist.[70] Although he may have genuinely intended it as a defense of religion, its susceptibility to a libertine reading forces us to wonder whether he was perhaps employing the method of insinuation Father Garasse and other religious apologists attributed to libertines in spreading their views. All we can conclude is that Campanella remains a profoundly enigmatic thinker, and that as a philosopher of strongly hererodox inclination, he may have been a dissembler whose persecuted language covertly inculcated unbelief while pretending to oppose it.

During the first half of the seventeenth century France replaced Italy as the main intellectual center of European libertinism and irreligion. In his brilliant study of the leading and secondary figures of the French libertinism of this period, René Pintard has repeatedly stressed its split personality, manifested in the dissociation it effected between its true countenance and mask, in its aristocratic esotericism, and in its propensity to conformism and dissimulation.[71] From antiatheist polemicists such as François Garasse we may gather something of this aspect of libertinism. Even though Garasse's obvious prejudice, abusiveness, and wild accusations of atheism make him a less than wholly reliable witness, his *Curious Doctrine* nevertheless affords certain insights into the character of contemporary libertinism which there is no reason to question.[72]

The libertines, according to Garasse, conceived themselves as part of the very few "beaux" and "bons esprits" in the world, who stood far above the fools and the beliefs of the vulgar. Hence they held it necessary to speak of their ideas only in secret to intimates. They spurned the opinions of ordinary people, one of their maxims being that they should not go by the common road or believe common things. In their eyes the denial of God represented the intelligence of an elevated mind, whereas faith was for the feeble populace and

[70] Tullio Gregory, *Theophrastus redivivus. Erudizione e ateismo nel seicento* (Naples: Morano, 1979); Ernst, "Campanella 'Libertino'?" pp. 239–240; Allen, *Doubt's Boundless Sea,* pp. 2n, 10–11, 17, 22–23.

[71] Pintard, *Le libertinage,* pp. 125–126 and passim.

[72] In his anthology of libertine writings, Antoine Adam comments that despite its many faults Garasse's book permits a "probably exact image" of the libertines of this epoch; *Les libertins au XVIIe siècle* (Paris: Buchet/Chastel, 1964), p. 8; Berriot presupposes the same view in *Athéismes,* 2:752–773.

women. Though considering that they should deny nothing to the body or senses in exercising their natural faculties, they took care not to appear impious or abandoned lest they influence the simple and deprive them of their superstition. They treated belief in God solely as a convenience and maxim of state, making an apparent profession of Catholicism and frequenting the sacraments in order to deceive and avoid provoking the simple. They never attacked the Catholic faith directly but sowed their pernicious notions by hidden means. Disguising their true beliefs for fear of exclusion from society, offices, and honors, they declared that one must know how to accommodate oneself to one's surroundings to live in honor.[73]

Duplicity sustained by the sense of constituting an elect minority that disdained religion as a superstition fit only for the vulgar was thus, according to Garasse, a hallmark of the libertine. A major source of the libertine code separating private belief from public posture was the moral philosophy of Pierre Charron (1541–1603), Montaigne's closest disciple and foremost successor as an exponent of philosophical and religious skepticism. Although Charron, a priest, had published an early work opposed to atheism, this did not prevent the antiatheist writers of the 1620s from denouncing him as an unbeliever. They associated him with atheists and deists as an adversary of Christianity and named him as one of the libertine's favorite authors along with Pomponazzi, Machiavelli, Cardan, and Vanini.[74]

The cause of this *odium theologicum* was the critical spirit and extreme skepticism of Charron's great treatise, *On Wisdom* (*De la sagesse,* 1601), which appeared to destroy any rational foundation for certain religious knowledge. In reality, however, like his master, Montaigne, Charron was probably a Christian fideist who, recog-

---

[73] Garasse, *La doctrine curieuse,* maxims 1, 2, 3, 8, and pp. 64, 99, 101, 102, 163, 167, 176, 207, 991, 992.

[74] Pierre Charron, *Les trois veritez contre les athees, idolatres, iuifs, mahumetans, heretiques, & schismatiques* (1593), rev. ed. (Brussels, 1595). See Garasse, *La doctrine curieuse,* pp. 27–31 and passim. Father Marin Mersenne likewise criticized Charron in his *Quaestiones Celeberrimae in Genesim* (Paris, 1623) and *L'impieté des deistes, et des plus subtils libertins découverte* (Paris, 1624). J. B. Sabrié, *De l'humanisme au rationalisme. Pierre Charron* (Paris: Alcan, 1913), chap. 18, and Alan Boase, *The Fortunes of Montaigne* (London: Methuen, 1935), chaps. 13–14, survey the attacks on Charron. Mersenne, an important figure in the history of early modern science, was strongly opposed to Charron's skeptical separation of reason and religion and attempted in his work to defend the cognitive claims of both religion and science and to reconcile science with Christianity.

nizing that religious dogmas were incapable of proof, held that they could be believed only through faith in supernatural revelation. With the revival of Greek skepticism during the sixteenth century and its powerful development by Montaigne and others, fideism became a significant trend in the religious thought of the age. It not only was embraced by some of the finest minds, but also was seized on by a number of Catholic controversialists as a weapon with which to attack the dogmatism of Protestant claims. Skepticism could point in two different directions, however: either toward acceptance of Christian doctrines independently of reason and proof, or toward the rationalistic rejection of supernatural religion and therefore incredulity. The libertine under its influence was more apt to follow the latter than the former course.[75]

Aside from his skeptical, antidogmatic philosophy, Charron also affected libertinism by establishing a profound distinction between the wise man's inner being and outer comportment. He conceived the moral life as independent of religion and based on adherence to nature and reason. Prizing intellectual liberty as an inestimable good, he wrote in *On Wisdom* that "to prevent the freedom of mind is impossible" and "to wish to do so . . . the greatest tyranny that can be." For him, though, this freedom was a purely interior possession that should always remain detached, giving its allegiance to nothing as it examined the reasons of things. Hence the rule of life he recommended to the sage was that the latter accommodate himself in all his external actions to the common view while inwardly preserving his freedom to think and to judge. In keeping with the sentiment of Cicero, which he quoted, the sage would live and speak outwardly as the many, yet think inwardly as the few.[76] It is hardly surprising that these beliefs also led Charron to endorse strongly the principle of reason-of-state as he found it in Machiavelli and Lipsius. As part of the rules of wisdom in politics, he held that the prince might act both the lion and the fox, mingle prudence with justice, and depart from equity and virtue for

[75] Richard Popkin, *The History of Scepticism from Erasmus to Descartes*, rev. ed. (New York: Harper & Row, 1968), has told the story of the revival of Greek skepticism and its issuance in fideism and libertinism, chaps. 1–5; Montaigne and Charron are discussed in chap. 3; see also Henri Busson, *La penseé religieuse française de Charron à Pascal* (Paris: Vrin, 1933), chap. 4 and passim.

[76] *De la sagesse*, 3 vols. (Paris, 1820), 2:33, 37, 39; the quotation ascribed to Cicero, which, according to Charron's editor, is inaccurate, is: "Loquendum et extra vivendum ut multi, sapiendum ut pauci."

the public welfare. "Dissimulation," he declared, "which is vicious in private men, is most necessary to princes" in order to govern and command well. The latter "ought to follow not what is pretty to say, but what is necessary to be done," and if he could not be wholly good, it sufficed that he be half good.[77]

Opposed to bigotry, fanaticism, and dogmatism, Charron sought by his precepts to inculcate an inner freedom and tranquillity of mind involving abstention from any commitment beyond the self. He expressly condemned lying and dissimulation in private life as the vices of a base and cowardly nature. Yet it is not hard to see how his schizophrenic vision of the sage who dissociated his true beliefs from his public performance could also serve as a warrant for dissimulation. Only the thinnest of lines separated the sage's reserve and conformity in speech and external actions to the common opinion from outright duplicity. There can be little doubt that libertine philosophers who practiced the dualism reflected in Charron's teaching often crossed that line.[78]

In addition to its ethic of dissociation, another major theme in libertine thought conducive to dissimulation was its conception of religion as a political imposture. We have already met this idea in Pomponazzi and other authors. Calvin also took critical note of it in his *Institutes of the Christian Religion* when he sought to refute it and prove that the knowledge of God was naturally implanted in men's minds.[79] In essence, this opinion held that supernatural religion originated as a device of rulers and founders of states to keep their people in awe and subjection. With it usually went the corollary notion that the great majority of mankind were not only incapable of enlightenment but should be left in their superstition for the sake of social order and stability. Although both views were indebted to pagan sources such as Lucretius and Cicero, they also owed not a little to Machiavelli, whose works treated religion almost exlcusively from a political standpoint. In *The Three Verities* (*Les trois veritez*), his book against atheism, Charron noted the libertines' opinion that religion was invented by

[77] Ibid., 3:303–307, 312–313.

[78] Ibid., pp. 33–34. On Charron's moral teaching in its relation to libertinism, see Nannerl Keohane, *Philosophy and the State in France* (Princeton: Princeton University Press, 1980), pp. 135–139, 144.

[79] John Calvin, *Institutio Christianae Religionis* (1559), *Institutes of the Christian Religion,* ed. John T. McNeill, trans. Ford L. Battles, 2 vols. (Philadelphia: Westminster Press, 1960), 1:44 (bk. 1, chap 3).

wise princes and founders of commonwealths who taught the people
to believe so as to retain them in fear and reverence. He added that the
libertine, crediting religion only with utility, not with truth, considered that "nothing is more efficacious than superstition for ruling the
multitude." The same view was expressed in a libertine poem, *The
Deist's Quatrains* (*Les quatrains du deiste,* 1624), whose anonymous
author characterized supernatural religion as

> A useful invention to bridle the spirits
> Of insolent men, whose perverse nature
> Contemns the magistrates and their laws
> To live in abandon, without rule or limit.

It was no less common to the "erudite libertines" *(libertins érudits),* as
they came to be known, such as Gabriel Naudé, on whom Machiavelli
exerted a powerful influence. The religious apologists of the earlier
seventeenth century likewise unanimously denounced it as a fundamental libertine position.[80]

The interpretation of religion as a political imposture reinforced the
esoteric side of libertinism and supplied it with a further rationale for
dissimulation. If revealed religion with its superstitious creeds and
rites was essentially a socially necessary lie that kings and priests used
to deceive and terrify the people in order to make them obedient and
law abiding, then reasons of public utility as well as personal safety
might justify the enlightened few in dissembling their incredulity. A
case in point is the doctrine of hell and eternal torment, which theologians and nearly everyone else in the sixteenth and seventeenth centuries deemed an essential deterrent to immorality. As D. P. Walker has
shown, because discussion of the subject was both dangerous and considered likely to undermine the morals of the vulgar, most writers
who doubted the existence of hell veiled their opinion in secrecy and
deception. They held it as an esoteric doctrine reserved for kindred
intellectuals while publicly pretending to believe the opposite.[81]

The linkage between dissimulation and the explanation of religion
as a form of political deceit appears with exceptional clarity in *Theophrastus Redivivus,* one of the most uncompromising expressions of
French libertine thought. This long anonymous Latin treatise dating

[80] See Busson, *La penseé religieuse,* pp. 105–108, 488–492. Adam, *Les libertins,*
pp. 90–108, reprints *Les quatrains du deiste;* the verse quoted is on p. 99.
[81] D. P. Walker, *The Decline of Hell* (Chicago: University of Chicago Press,
1964), pp. 5–6 and chap. 1.

from the mid-seventeenth century was diffused both in manuscript copies and in summaries and occupied a significant place in the clandestine literature of unbelief. Unlike other libertine writers, its unknown author abandoned all Nicodemite precautions and propounded an audacious argument for pure atheism, drawing on both ancient and modern philosophers, among the latter Machiavelli, Pomponazzi, Cardan, Bodin, Campanella, and Vanini. He maintained that the authentic philosophic tradition was atheistic. All the philosophers of antiquity, he claimed, asserted the eternity of the world and denied the existence of God, the immortality of the soul, hell, and an afterlife. All of them, too, conceived religion as a crafty political invention. In his view Plato and Aristotle had both been atheists. Plato created religious myths to avoid the anger of the people and authorities and justified the legislator who utilized lies and fables to teach the people respect for laws through fear of supernatural punishment. Aristotle, like other wise men, also pretended an external acceptance of popular beliefs. To understand the real thoughts of the philosophers, the author said, it was necessary to go behind their façade of adherence to the popular religion to observe how they confirmed its mythical character by indirection. The prime examples of this duplicity among the Latins, he contended, were Cicero and Seneca, both of whom had really been atheists who rejected the common faith.

For him the wise man's dissimulation reflected a dual necessity: first, the need to sustain the people's belief in religious myths as the only means to induce them to obey the laws; second, the need to avoid a conflict with common opinion, which was like a second nature and impossible to overcome. He went on to explain that lawgivers created the gods, who thus were sons of the law. The theologians and poets later elaborated the first religious beliefs until they became a matter of custom stronger than nature itself. The wise man was forced to conform outwardly because it was dangerous not to do so.[82]

There was much else in *Theophrastus Redivivus,* including a philosophic materialism and dismissal of miracles and other supernatural phenomena as things that could deceive only the ignorant plebs but not the "sapientes." In his repudiation of religion the author also adduced the famous theme of the Three Impostors, a heretical concep-

[82] *Theophrastus Redivivus,* ed. G. Canziani and G. Paganini, 2 vols. (Florence: Nuova Italia, 1981). My discussion relies on the detailed summary and analysis in Gregory, *Theophrastus Redivivus*; see pp. 13, 15, 20–34, 46–49, 51–52, 99–100, 114, 161–162.

tion obscurely transmitted in Europe since at least the thirteenth century which portrayed Moses, Jesus, and Muhammad as impostors who had seduced the human race. Religious apologists of the sixteenth and seventeenth centuries were convinced that a clandestine work called *The Three Impostors* was actually in circulation, attributing it to different authors. In fact there seems to be no evidence of the existence of such a book until the eighteenth century. The myth concerning it, however, testifies to the significance of the naturalistic interpretation of religion as a political invention as one of the principal notes of early modern incredulity.[83]

The French *libertins érudits* constituted a few groups in Paris and the provinces whose members gathered together for conversation, exchanged ideas through correspondence, and shared an extraordinarily wide range of interests in philosophy, the sciences, and the most varied kinds of learning. At once both scholars and men of the world, they were naturalists by conviction who set the highest store by their independence of mind and freedom from common prejudices. Among the best-known representative figures of the earlier seventeenth century were the priest, scientist, and philosopher Pierre Gassendi (1592–1655), a critic of Aristotle and Descartes, good friend of Hobbes, and reviver of Epicurean atomism; Gabriel Naudé, man of letters, physician to Louis XIII, and librarian of Cardinal Mazarin's great collections; and François de La Mothe Le Vayer (1588–1672), another polymath and man of letters, magistrate, and tutor to the duke of Orléans and his brother, the young Louis XIV. In certain respects all three thinkers foreshadowed the *philosophes* of the Enlightenment. Averse to all dogmatism, they and their friends had imbibed the Pyrrhonian skepticism of ancient and modern philosophers, although Gassendi devised a mitigated skepticism that based knowledge on appearances without presuming to understand the nature of things in themselves. All were greatly influenced by Montaigne and Charron, whose dissociation between the wise man's inner attitude and public conformism they adopted.[84]

Such men were too circumspect to risk exposing their genuine

[83] Gregory, *Theophrastus Redivivus*, p. 120; Spink, *French Free-Thought*, pp. 68–69, also discusses *Theophrastus Redivivus*; Berriot, *Athéismes*, vol. 1, chap. 3, traces the history of the concept of the Three Impostors.

[84] Pintard, *Le libertinage*, pts. 2–3; Spink, *French Free-Thought*, chaps. 1, 6; Popkin, *The History of Scepticism*, chaps. 5, 7; Boase, *The Fortunes of Montaigne*, chaps. 17–18.

beliefs, which they reserved for their private intercourse with friends. They took as their own Cremonini's maxim "Think inwardly as you like, but conform outwardly to custom," as well as Ovid's motto, "He lives well who conceals himself well" *(bene vixit, qui bene latuit)*. La Mothe Le Vayer expressed his most audaciously skeptical opinions on religion in some early *Dialogues,* which he published under a pseud- onym with a false imprint and date and other precautions. Naudé was a proponent of reason-of-state who in his *Considerations politiques sur les coups d'etats* (1639) accorded priority to the state's and ruler's interests and necessity over the obligations of justice and morality. Like a number of other libertine thinkers, both men were partial to the authoritarian regime constructed by Cardinals Richelieu and Mazarin, and their political approach to religion and contempt for the multi- tude made them prefer expediency to truth when it came to disclosure of their thoughts.[85]

The emancipatory features inherent in libertinism's opposition to religion's domination over philosophy, morals, and culture were blunted in their potential fruitfulness by its aristocratic esotericism and inclination for dissimulation. These traits likewise leave it unclear how radically the skepticism of the *libertins érudits* had detached them from Christian supernaturalism. Nearly all modern scholars have con- sidered most of them to be unbelievers. Thus René Pintard, author of the closest, most penetrating study of their lives and ideas, has noted their "taste for dissimulation" and observance of "the rules of a subtle diplomacy" and their "art of concealed meanings, and double sense" so as to circumvent the censor and avoid accusations. He has described their libertinism as "dissembled," as "reserved, twisted, composed of an interior audacity and practical circumspection," and as "all in nuances." In his view they formed a family of minds "cruelly marked by the stigmata of constraint," minds that suffered from a "malaise of disaccord between themselves and their time" because they were "repositories of a secret." This secret was of course their incredulity.[86]

Richard Popkin, on the other hand, has pointed out that the skep-

---

[85] Pintard, *Le libertinage,* pp. xxxvi, 109, 176, 563; René Pintard, preface to *La Mothe Le Vayer, Gassendi, Guy Patin* (Paris: Boivin, 1949). La Mothe Le Vayer's *Dialogues* appeared under the pseudonym Orasius Tubero and were not included in his posthumously published works. Sections are included in Adam, *Les libertins;* see also François de La Mothe Le Vayer, *Deux dialogues sur la divinité et l'opiniatreté,* ed. Ernest Tisserand (Paris: Editions Bossard, 1922).

[86] *Le libertinage,* pp. 86, 100, 122, 566.

tical outlook of the *libertins érudits* was compatible either with irreligion or with fideism. The fact that their philosophy lends itself to two different interpretations makes it impossible to assess the sincerity of their professions of Christianity and Catholicism. They may have been unbelievers who wanted to make religion ridiculous, or they may have been Christian skeptics who adopted a fideistic solution to the problem of religious certainty. Popkin also suggests that the point of their libertinism may not have been to undermine Christianity, but to serve rather as a buttress for a liberal Catholicism opposed both to superstitious belief and to Protestant dogmatism. Thus Popkin questions the long-standing assumption that duplicity must have underlain the writings and actions of men such as Naudé, La Mothe Le Vayer, and Gassendi.[87]

Other students of libertine thought have not been persuaded by Popkin's arguments. Thus, though acknowledging that Gassendi was probably a fideist who tried to reconcile his philosophical conceptions with religion, they hold that most of the *libertins érudits* used the subtleties of a skeptical philosophy to discredit the truths of Christianity. Pintard has likewise rejected Popkin's argument. He has stressed the need to distinguish a "sincere fideism" from the "tactical fideism" assumed by La Mothe Le Vayer and his friends, and has pointed out that only by situating the libertines in their immediate personal and social context can the real import of their ideas be understood.[88]

A definitive resolution of this problem seems unattainable. It should be noted, though, that in posing the possibility that these libertine philosophers were Christian fideists, Popkin made no mention of their dualistic ethic. This ethic could so easily supply a justification for dissimulation that it alone must provoke suspicion of the genuineness of their religious professions. When we add to this the existence of censorship and the personal danger of freely stating their opinions, our suspicion becomes even greater. Viewed in this light, it is difficult not to interpret the reserve they practiced as motivated in large part by the need to camouflage and dissemble beliefs that were deeply at odds with the doctrines maintained by the ruling powers of their society.

[87] Popkin, *History of Scepticism,* pp. 56, 63, 92–99, 109.

[88] Pintard, *Le libertinage,* pp. xxxiv–xxxv and pt. 3, chap. 2; Adam, *Les libertins,* preface and pp. 121–122, 140–141; R. Zuber, "Libertinage et humanisme: Une rencontre difficile," *XVIIe siècle,* 32, no. 2 (1980), 171, 175; L. T. Sarasohn, "Motion and Morality: Pierre Gassendi, Thomas Hobbes, and the Mechanical World-View," *Journal of the History of Ideas,* 46, no. 3 (1985).

The code of external conformism embraced by French libertines was also recommended by Thomas Hobbes. First as a visitor, then after 1640 as a political exile in France for over a decade, Hobbes had a close association with leading French philosophers and libertine thinkers.[89] Although in his own writings he gave clear expression to his naturalism, materialism, denial of hell and eternal punishment, and other heterodox conceptions that allied him with libertinism, he nonetheless stated a belief in God and in Christ as savior. In accordance with his doctrine of sovereignty, he also held that subjects were obliged to conform to the religion and manner of worship decreed by the sovereign. To support his position he cited one of the classic arguments of Nicodemism, the case of Naaman the Syrian. What should subjects do, he asked, if the ruler commanded them to say with their mouth what they did not believe? They must obey, was his answer; for "profession with the tongue is but an external thing, and no more than any other gesture whereby we signifie our obedience." Thus Naaman, a convert in his heart to the God of Israel, was permitted by the prophet Elisha to accompany his king and bow in the temple of the idol Rimmon. Hobbes approved outward compliance with the sovereign's will in religion not only as the subject's duty but also as necessary to avoid death or a miserable life. Although Hobbes's example had to do with idolatry, it could equally apply to a philosopher's pretended conformity to Christian orthodoxy. Such opinions helped persuade his religious opponents that he was an atheist at heart.[90]

During the seventeenth century, the state's intolerance and its legal penalties against unorthodoxy forced some of the greatest English thinkers to dissimulate their beliefs. Although Hobbes suffered no physical harm, he endured considerable verbal abuse and had to defend himself continually against accusations of heresy and atheism. Another example is Sir Isaac Newton (1642–1727), who, though deeply religious, embraced the Arian heresy. Convinced that the doctrines of the trinity and the deity of Christ had been introduced into the church by fraud and corruption, he could never publish his views because of the danger and his fear of controversy. Newton was understandably secretive and disingenuous about his religious opinions. As a

[89] G. C. Robertson, *Hobbes* (Philadelphia, 1886), chaps. 3, 5.

[90] *Leviathan* (Oxford: Clarendon Press, 1951), pp. 387, 509. Bishop John Bramhall attacked this view in his indictment of Hobbes as an atheist; *The Catching of Leviathan*, in *Works*, ed. A. F. H., 5 vols. (Oxford, 1844), 4:539.

fellow of Trinity College, Cambridge, he swore the required subscription to the Anglican articles and remained a member of the Church of England. Not until this century have historians discovered from his theological manuscripts how widely his true creed diverged from orthodox Christianity.[91]

Similarly, the intolerant times in which he lived gave John Locke (1632–1704) an obsessive concern with secrecy. Till the end of his life he took extreme pains to conceal his authorship of his *Two Treatises of Government* and certain other writings. As a rationalist and independent thinker in religion he rejected trinitarianism like his friend Newton, and was sympathetic to Socinian arguments against the divine sonship of Christ. To escape accusations of Socinianism, however, which its opponents identified with infidelity and unbelief, he denied any knowledge of Socinian books, a claim that was certainly untrue.[92] In politics too he was sometimes less than honest. As a supporter of the Whig cause in the reigns of Charles II and James II, an intimate of the proscribed Whig leader Lord Shaftesbury, and a political exile and conspirator before the revolution of 1688, he prevaricated on various occasions concerning his opinions and conduct.[93] Nothing but a keen and justifiable fear of persecution could have induced Locke, who held strong moral principles, to dissemble any of his convictions.

Another interesting but much lesser English thinker who it has been suggested relied on dissimulation to mask his unbelief was Henry Stubbe (1632–1676). Before the restoration of the Stuart monarchy in 1660, Stubbe was a radical republican, a disciple in some respects of Hobbes, and a fervent advocate of liberty of conscience. Following the

[91] See R. S. Westfall, *Never at Rest. A Biography of Isaac Newton* (Cambridge: Cambridge University Press, 1980), pp. 312–317 and passim, and especially idem, "Newton and Christianity" (Manuscript, 1984), of which he kindly sent me a copy; H. J. McLachlan, *Socianianism in Seventeenth-Century England* (Oxford: Oxford University Press, 1951), pp. 330–331. Newton's Arianism also made him unwilling to be ordained, as the statutes of Trinity College required of nearly all its fellows. Fortunately, he was able to obtain a dispensation from this rule as Lucasian professor of mathematics.

[92] Peter Laslett, "Introduction," in John Locke, *Two Treatises of Government,* 2d ed. (Cambridge: Cambridge University Press, 1967), pp. 5–6. Locke's attraction to Socinianism and his disingenuousness in disavowing his knowledge of Socinian books is demonstrated in a close study of his manuscripts by John Marshall, "John Locke and Socinianism" (Manuscript, 1987), of which he kindly sent me a copy.

[93] See Richard Ashcraft, *Revolutionary Politics and Locke's Two Treatises of Government* (Princeton: Princeton University Press, 1986), pp. 341, 432–439.

Restoration, while practicing as a physician, he engaged in a number of controversies, professing to be a firm royalist and loyal Anglican. A recent study, however, maintains that in reality he never changed his position and remained constantly a republican, pagan naturalist, and deist who propagated his views by subterfuges and deception. In this case, though, the evidence for such an interpretation of Stubbe's writings remains unconvincing.[94] Nonetheless, the seventeenth and early eighteenth centuries, which marked the first phase of the English Enlightenment, undoubtedly saw the development of deism, libertinism, and criticism of revealed religion to a degree that caused the orthodox grave concern. Many more works appeared against atheism than ever before.[95] Yet even in England, where after 1688 speech and the press gradually became freer than in most countries, writers inclined to incredulity still felt compelled to go masked for fear of ostracism and the law. George Berkeley (1685–1755), one of whose principal objects was the refutation of irreligion, pictured the freethinkers of the time as carrying on their work "with much art and industry," concealing their "ultimate" views and acting in secrecy like "moles underground."[96] As we have seen, moreover, John Toland's description of the double doctrine of philosophers in his essay "Clidophorus" testifies to the persistence of dissimulation by thinkers critical of supernatural religion. Although the development of rationalistic attitudes and religious skepticism was one of the major features of English thought in the late seventeenth century, caution and disguise were still deemed necessary by nearly all whose beliefs were antithetical to Christianity.

In his *Tractatus Theologico-Philosophicus* (1670), the reputed atheist Spinoza directly addressed the problem of liberty of thought, conformity, and persecution. Although the work dealt with many basic political questions, its ultimate purpose was to show that the freedom to philosophize and to express dissenting opinions was essential to peace and piety. Its concluding chapter contended that in a free state everyone should be able to think as he pleased and say what he thought. Contrary to Hobbes, who would have placed control of opinion in the

[94] J. R. Jacob, *Henry Stubbe, Radical Protestantism, and the Early Enlightenment* (Cambridge: Cambridge University Press, 1983); see the critical review by Blair Worden, *Times Literary Supplement,* August 5, 1983, p. 837.

[95] John Redwood, *Reason, Ridicule, and Religion: The Age of Enlightenment in England, 1660–1750* (Cambridge, Mass.: Harvard University Press, 1976).

[96] *Alciphron, or The Minute Philosopher* (1732), in *Works,* ed. A. A. Luce and T. E. Jessop, 9 vols. (London: Thomas Nelson, 1948–1957), 3:103.

sovereign, Spinoza defended freedom of expression not only as consistent with the authority of the sovereign and the peace of society, but also as a natural right impossible to surrender or suppress. If its suppression were attempted, so that people feared to whisper a word not prescribed by the sovereign, the inevitable consequence would be hypocrisy. In that case, he predicted, "every day men will be saying one thing and thinking another: belief in another's word . . . will thus be undermined, nauseating sycophancy and deceitfulness encouraged; and hence will come frauds and the destruction of all honest dealing."[97]

The widespread resort of intellectuals to dissimulation in response to repression by states and churches bears out at least a part of Spinoza's statement. He went on to claim, though, that "the assumption that everyone can be made to speak to order is quite impossible." The more government tried to deprive people of freedom of speech, the more it would be opposed by those who, "because of their culture, integrity, and ability, have some independence of mind."[98] Here Spinoza was assuredly too sanguine. The experience of early modern Europe shows how powerful were the agencies for enforcing conformity. The currency of doctrines that legitimated dissimulation provides one of the strongest proofs of this fact. The Protestants, Catholics, sectarians, Jews, intellectuals, writers, and philosophers who took refuge in pretended conformity and secrecy to conceal their true religious convictions or their incredulity far outnumbered the advocates of religious toleration and liberty of thought and conscience. Montaigne went to the heart of the matter in his essay "Of Profit and Honesty" when he said of the hatreds and hypocrisy of the Wars of Religion that "innocence itself in these times is unable to negotiate among us without dissimulation."[99] We have tried to see through the masks and disguises certain thinkers used to dissemble their ideas, but we can hardly doubt that there were numerous others who adopted the same practice in self-protection.

The sixteenth and earlier seventeenth centuries have long been known primarily as the Age of the Reformation and Counter-Reformation. The results of our inquiries here indicate that we might add to this designation a further title and also name this era the Age of Dissimulation.

[97] Benedictus de Spinoza, *Tractatus Theologico-Philosophicus,* in *The Political Works,* ed. and trans. A. G. Wernham (Oxford: Clarendon Press, 1958), p. 227.
[98] Ibid., pp. 235, 237.
[99] "Of Profit and Honesty," in *Essays,* trans. John Florio, 3 vols. (London: Dent, 1910), 3:13.

Index

Abbot, George, 198, 312
Abbot, Robert, 203
Abraham, example of, 23, 24, 27, 30, 69, 113, 172
achrist, 296, 299
Agrippa, Henry Cornelius, 266–271, 274, 299
Alciati, Andrea, 178
Alexander VI, pope, 263
Alexander VII, pope, 217
Allen, William, 137, 138, 140, 187, 192, 207
Alsted, Johann, 221
alumbrados, 47, 62, 83–84
Ames, William, 160, 240–242
amphibology, 170–171, 178, 180, 183, 184, 201, 208, 209
anabaptists, 94, 107, 111–112, 113, 115, 117, 127
Ananias, example of, 212, 238
Appellants, 198–200, 208
Aquaviva, Claudio, 189, 190, 202
Aquinas, Thomas, 5, 6, 28–31, 161, 176, 177–178, 182, 184, 209, 302
Arias Montano, Benito, 125–127, 280
Aristotelianism, 301, 302, 306, 312
Aristotle, 295, 302, 324
Arnauld, Antoine, 154–155, 216
Athanasius, 64
atheism, 257, 289, 290, 293–294, 296, 298, 299, 300, 302, 304, 308–310, 312–313, 316–318, 329; nature of, 291–292
atheists, 107, 296, 299, 304
Augustine, 5, 15, 17–25, 26–27, 28, 30–31, 34, 35, 147, 176, 180, 214

Averroës, 302
Averroism, 44
Azor, Juan, 159, 181–182, 200, 210, 241
Azpilcueta, Martín de. See Navarrus

Bacon, Francis, 11, 256, 267, 271–274, 291
Bacon, Sir Nicholas, 108
Bagshaw, Christopher, 198–199
Bancroft, Richard, 227
Bañes, Domingo, 210
Barnabas, 16–22
Barnes, John, 213–215
Barrefelt, Hendrik van, 118, 120, 126, 127
Baruch, example of, 73, 284
Baudouin, François, 80–81
Bauduinus, Frederick, 221
Bauny, Father, 154
Baxter, Richard, 160, 240, 248, 251–254
Bayle, Pierre, 124, 312
Bell, Thomas, 146, 149, 150
Bellamy, Anne, 190
Bellarmine, Robert, cardinal, 206
Berkeley, George, 329
Berman, David, 293–294
Berriot, François, 290
Beza, Theodore, 71, 95, 107
Bible, Polyglot, 121, 125, 279, 280
biblical precedents cited for dissimulation: John 3:1–2, 12, 68; Galatians 2:11–14, 15, 147; Acts 16:3, 17, 19; Acts 18:8, 17; 1 Corinthians 9:20, 17, 18; 1 Corinthians 10:22, 17; 2 Kings 10:18–28, 17, 110, 147; 1 Samuel 21:12–13, 17, 23, 110; Exodus 1:17–20, 21, 23; Genesis 27:19, 21, 23; 1

biblical precedents (*cont.*)
Corinthians 9:22, 22; Genesis 12:11–13, 23; Luke 24:28, 23, 97, 187; 1 Corinthians 10:4, 23; Revelation 5:5, 23; Job 35:2, 25; Judith 15, 30; 2 Kings 5:17–19, 32; Deuteronomy 5:33, 57; Baruch 6:5, 60; Esther 2:10, 61; Matthew 6:24, 63; Matthew 10:23, 64, 90; John 3:4–5, 76; Matthew 10:16, 79; Revelation 2:3, 114; Matthew 7:6, 129, 262; Luke 9:26, 136; Mark 13:32, 170; Matthew 24:36, 170; Psalms 1:5, 170; John 7:8–10, 183; John 2:19–22, 209; John 1:21, 210; John 8:15, 210; Acts 5:3–10, 212; Matthew 5:33–37, 224, 234; Acts 23:6, 238
Biel, Gabriel, 177, 181
Blackwell, George, 196, 198, 206
Bodin, Jean, 281–288, 323
Borne, Dirk van den, 118
Borromeo, Carlo, 166
Bostocke, Robert, 271
Bradford, John, 108
Brémond, Henri, 216
Brunfels, Otto, 12, 13, 68–69
Bruno, Giordano, 257
Bucer, Martin, 67, 72, 86, 301
Bullinger, Henry, 95–86, 109
Burton, Robert, 292
Busson, Henri, 290, 303

cabala, 260, 262, 263, 264, 269, 270, 277, 280, 282
Cajetan (Thomas De Vio), Cardinal, 210
Calvin, John, 12, 35–36, 68–82, 83, 86, 89, 92, 93, 95, 100, 106, 112–113, 116, 140, 253, 296–298, –299, 321
Campanella, Tommaso, 257, 313–318, 323
Campion, Edmund, 141, 192, 207
Cano, Melchior, 161
Cantimori, Delio, 12, 85, 98
Cardan, Jerome, 271, 305, 319, 323
Cardoso, Fernando, 46
Carli Piccolimini, Bartolomeo, 93–94
Carlson, Leland, 232, 233
Carnesecchi, Pietro, 85, 86
Caro Baroja, Julio, 40
Carranza, Bartolomé de, 165–166
Carter, William, 138
Cartwright, Thomas, 228
Casaubon, Isaac, 203–204
Cassander, George, 80
Cassirer, Ernst, 302

Castellio, Sebastian, 95, 116, 279–280
Castiglione, Baldassare, 7–8
casuistry, 57, 139–141, 153–185, 187–188, 217–220, 221–254
Cecil, Sir William, 108
Celsus, 301, 304
Chaldean oracles, 259
Chapman, George, 255
Charles I, 244, 245
Charles V, 80, 165, 179
Charron, Pierre, 319–321, 324
Chrysostom, John, 24
Cicero, 295, 304, 321, 323
Ciudad Real, *conversos* in, 49–52
Clement of Alexandria, 24
Clement VIII, pope, 198
Coke, Sir Edward, 133, 190, 191, 196–197, 202, 203, 309
Collins, Anthony, 293
Colonna, Vittoria, 85, 87
confessional, 158, 171
Conring, Herman, 316
Contarini, Gasparo, cardinal, 86
conversos, 38–62, 83, 84
Coornhert, Dirck, 79–80, 124
Cosin, Richard, 229–230
Coton, Father, 202
Council: of Trent, 87, 136, 165, 169; Fourth Lateran, 158; Fifth Lateran, 202
courtier, 7–8
Court of High Commission, 225, 226–231, 243
Crane, Elizabeth, 232
Cremonini, Cesare, 305–306, 325
cryptography, 265–266, 272
Cudworth, Ralph, 292
Curione, Celio Secundo, 102–103
Cyprian, 63–64, 158

David, example of, 18, 20, 23, 27, 31, 69, 110, 171
Decretum (Gratian), 25–28, 29
Dee, John, 11, 97, 271, 274–276
deist, 298, 299
Des Périers, Bonaventure, 299–301
Descartes, René, 10, 324
d'Holbach, Paul Henri Dietrich, baron, 293
Diana, Antonio, 159
dissimulatio, 3
Dolet, Etienne, 257, 299–300
dolus, 110, 172, 238

Donne, John, 203, 240n1
Douai seminary, 137, 138, 186
Du Chemin, Nicholas, 71

Edward VI, 222
Egyptian midwives, example of, 21, 23, 27, 30, 31, 69, 238–239
Elizabeth I, 131, 223, 274; excommunication of, 132, 133, 149
Engagement, case of, 245–248
English College in Rome, 186, 187, 207
epicureans, 77, 107, 298, 299
Epicurean sources, 306
equivocation, doctrine and practice of, 58, 64, 65, 66, 110, 148, 149, 157, 163, 187, 191, 193–197, 204–205, 206, 207, 208, 209, 210, 211, 212, 213, 214, 233, 237, 241, 243, 244, 246, 247, 249, 252
Erasmus, Desiderius, 34–35, 83–84, 156, 264, 278, 289–290, 301
Esau, example of, 21, 23, 24, 38
Escobar y Mendoza, Antonio, 154
esotericism, 11, 259–260, 261, 265, 269, 271, 272–278, 282, 286, 287, 294–296, 304, 310–311, 322
Espina, Alonso de, 48–49
Esther, example of, 69, 103
Eudaemon-Ioannis, Andreas, 202
evangelism, Catholic, 83–88
Eymerich, Nicholas, 65

Family of Love, 117–130, 279, 280
Farel, Guillaume, 37, 67, 75
Febvre, Lucien, 289–291, 296
Ferdinand of Aragon, 38–42
Ficino, Marsilio, 11, 259, 260–262, 263, 268, 276
fideism, 319–320, 326
Flaminio, Marcantonio, 85, 86
flight, question of, 64, 75, 82, 90–93, 105–107, 111
Francis I, 276
Francis of Assisi, 168
Franck, Sebastian, 114–115, 117
Fuller, Thomas, 221, 235

Galatians, epistle to the, 15–20, 22, 23, 27, 28, 33–37, 130, 147, 151, 238
Galileo, 314
Garasse, François, 306, 307, 318–319
Garnet, Henry, 135, 136, 146–151, 188, 189–190, 193–197, 202, 204, 208

Gassendi, Pierre, 324, 326
Gerard, John, 191
Ginzburg, Carlo, 12, 13, 68–69
Gohory, Jacques, 271
Gonzaga, Giulia, 85, 87
Gracián, Balthasar, 8
Granvelle, Antoine Perrenot, cardinal de, 121
Gratian, 25–28, 168, 169, 245
Greene, Robert, 308
Gregory I, the Great, pope, 25, 26, 27, 169, 177, 180, 245
Gregory XIII, pope, 167, 169
Guicciardini, Francesco, 7
Gunpowder Plot, 193, 196–197, 202, 205, 207, 225

Halevi, Solomon, 44
Hall, Joseph, 240, 242–244
Halorki, Joshua, 44
Hammond, Henry, 155
Harding, Thomas, 137
Harriot, Thomas, 308, 309
Henri III, 283
Henri IV, 202
Henry VIII, 225
Hermes Trismegistus, 259, 262
hermeticism, 259, 272, 275, 282, 310
Hieronymites, 53, 126, 127
Hobbes, Thomas, 10, 292, 293, 324, 327, 328, 329
Homem, Antonio, 60–61
"Humanae aures" (Gregory the Great), 25, 26, 168, 169, 177, 178, 181, 184, 194
Hutten, Ulrich von, 35

immortality of the soul, 301–304, 305, 311, 323
Innocent VIII, pope, 263
Innocent X, pope, 217
Innocent XI, pope, 218
Inquisition: Spanish, 38–39, 45, 46, 47–48, 49, 52–53, 54, 165, 175; Portuguese, 43; Venetian, 54–55, 277, 280, 313; medieval, 64–65; Roman, 65, 87, 88, 98, 135, 217, 218; Neapolitan, 314
inquisitorial manuals, 64–66
Interim, 88, 100
Ironside, Ralph, 309–310
Isaac, example of, 113, 172
Isabella of Castile, 38, 42

Jacob, example of, 21, 23, 24, 30, 172
James, Thomas, 203
James I, 131, 193, 206, 227
Jansenism, 216–217
Jehu, example of, 17, 27, 31, 118, 147, 151
Jerome, 16–17, 19, 27, 28, 31, 34, 35, 36,
    147, 171, 174, 177
Jesuits, 181, 186, 194, 207, 212, 230, 231,
    250, 276; and dissimulation, 13, 155,
    163–164, 176, 187, 208–209; and probabi-
    lism, 162, 201; opposition to, 154–155,
    198–199, 201–202, 203–204, 215–217,
    229, 243
Jesus, example of, 21, 23, 24, 27, 31, 36, 90,
    91, 97, 110, 157, 170, 183, 191, 201, 209,
    210, 215, 219, 235, 239, 242, 295
Job, example of, 25
John the Baptist, example of, 210
Joris, Davis, 113–116, 117, 118, 128, 130
Joseph, example of, 172
Joshua, example of, 204
Judith, example of, 30, 69
Julian the Apostate, 304

Kant, Immanuel, 5
Kelley, Edward, 275
Kepler, Johannes, 308
Kingsley, Charles, 156–157
Koran, 3, 4
Kristeller, Paul Oskar, 303
Kuntz, M. L., 278
Kyd, Thomas, 308

La Mothe Le Vayer, François de, 324–325,
    326
La Rochefoucauld, François, duc de, 256
Langdale, Alban, 145–146, 149
Lea, Henry Charles, 160
Lefèvre d'Etaples, Jacques, 36–37, 68,
    69–70, 71, 264, 278
Lefranc, Abel, 289
Lessius, Leonard, 184, 187, 214, 215, 306
libertines, 78–79, 107, 110, 112–113, 296,
    298, 299, 306, 318–319, 322–323,
    324–327
libertinism, 11, 257–258, 291, 301, 303,
    305, 306, 310, 313, 318–319, 320,
    321–322
Liguori, Alfonso, 156, 157, 220
limpieza de sangre, 41–42
Lipsius, Justus, 122–125, 320
Locke, John, 9–10, 320

Lollards, 67–68
Lombard, Peter, 27–28, 176, 177
Lopez, Luis, 210
Louis XI, 174
Louis XIII, 314, 316, 324
Louis XIV, 324
Lucian, 301, 304
Lucianists, 77, 297, 299, 305
Lucretius, 321
Luther, Martin, 33–34, 85, 86, 117, 301

Machiavelli, Niccolò, 6, 7, 94, 124, 214,
    238, 256, 271, 306, 319, 320
Machiavellianism, 6, 7, 8, 315, 317
magic, 259–266, 267–270, 272, 274–276
Maimonides, 57–59
Major, John, 177
Margaret of Navarre, 76–79, 300
Mariana, Juan de, 202
Marlowe, Christopher, 255, 267, 308
Marprelate tracts, 230, 231–233
Marranos, 13, 38–62, 284
Martin, Gregory, 134–135, 136, 138–139,
    150
Martinengo, Celso, 83
martyrdom, 64, 82, 105, 119
Mary I, 87, 108, 109, 119, 129, 222
Mason, Henry, 204–205
Maximilian II, 276
Mazarin, Jules, cardinal, 324, 325
Medina, Bartolomé de, 161–162
Melanchthon, Philipp, 72, 80
mental reservation, doctrine and practice
    of, 163–185, 186–220, 237, 243, 244, 249,
    252, 259
Milton, John, 240n1
moderatores, 80
Molière, 311
Molina, Luis, 154, 210
Montague, Anthony Browne, viscount,
    133, 145
Montaigne, Michel de, 257, 319, 320, 324,
    330
Morice, James, 230, 231
Moriscos, 41n5
Morton, Thomas, 200–201, 203, 208, 209,
    211, 212
moyenneurs, 80–81
Musculus, Wolfgang, 100–102, 223

Naaman, example of, 32–33, 69, 73, 102,
    104, 109, 110–111, 136, 138, 139, 140,

144–145, 146, 147, 151, 223, 237, 244, 284, 327
Naudé, Gabriel, 305–306, 322, 324, 325, 326
Nauert, C. G., 268
Navarrus, Dr. (Martín de Azpilcueta), 164–185, 186, 187, 194, 195, 201, 204, 211, 212, 215, 219, 239, 243
Nescit vivere qui nescit dissimulare, 8
New Christians, 38–62
Newman, John Henry, 156–158
Newton, Sir Isaac, 327–328
Nicholas of Lyra, 32–33
Niclaes, Hendrik, 117–120, 127–128
Nicodemism, 12–13, 68–82, 83–99, 100–130, 132, 134, 146, 151–152, 156, 222–223, 237, 244, 253, 259, 275, 283, 284, 297, 298, 327
Nicodemites, 68, 75, 77, 78, 102, 109, 110, 111
Nicodemus, example of, 12, 68, 76, 78, 102, 104, 146, 223
Northumberland, Henry Percy, ninth earl of, 308

oath: of allegiance, 205–207, 225, 246; *ex officio,* 225–226, 228–231, 232, 243; of supremacy, 225, 246
occultism, 257–288
Ochino, Bernardino, 85, 87, 90
Oecolampadius, Johannes, 67
Olivares, Gaspar de Guzman, count-duke of, 54
Olivétan, Pierre, 300
Oporinus, Johannes, 279
Ordinance of 1643, 212
Origen, 19, 24, 258, 262
Orobio de Castro, Isaac, 56
Orphic hymns, 259
Ortelius, Abraham, 122, 279
Orwell, George, 301
Ovid, 325

Palingenio, Marcello, 256
Paludanus, Petrus, 210, 215
Paracelsus, 11, 271
Pareus, David, 221
Parmenides, 295
Parsons, Robert, 133–134, 136, 140, 141–144, 145, 187, 198, 200
Pascal, Blaise, 6, 63, 154–155, 156, 217
Pasquier, Etienne, 201–202

Paul, example of, 16–17, 18–20, 22, 23, 28, 34–35, 36–37, 69, 73, 74, 79, 90, 104, 109, 115, 209, 223, 238, 239
Paul III, pope, 86
Paul V, pope, 206, 311
Peña, Francisco, 65–66
penance, 158, 159, 167, 222
Pérez, Luis, 126
Perkins, William, 160, 221, 235–240, 242, 253
Peter, example of, 16–17, 18–20, 22, 23, 28, 34, 36, 239
Philip II, 47, 120–121, 125, 126, 165, 166, 167, 174, 207
Philip IV, 54
Pico della Mirandola, Giovanni, 260, 262–263, 268
Pintard, René, 291, 318, 325, 326
Pius IV, pope, 135
Pius V, pope, 87, 132, 166, 167
Plantin, Christophe, 119–127, 279
Plato, 295, 302
Pole, Reginald, 85, 86–88
Pomponazzi, Pietro, 302–304, 312, 319, 321, 323
Pontano, Giovanni, 94
Popkin, Richard, 325–326
Postel, Guillaume, 276–281, 283, 287
Poullain, Valerand, 75
Prideaux, John, 203
Prierias, Sylvester, 154, 159, 177–178, 210
prisca theologia, 259, 264
Priscillianists, 22–23, 79, 214
probabilism, 161–163, 195–200, 218, 249
Pucci, Francesco, 97–99, 257
Puritans, 223–233, 240, 242
Pyrrhonian skepticism, 304, 320, 324
Pythagoras, 295

Quadra, Alvaro de, bishop, 134
Qui nescit dissimulare nescit regnare, 174

rabbinical *responsa,* 45, 59, 60
Rabelais, François, 289–290
Raleigh, Sir Walter, 204, 308, 311
Ranters, 129
Raymond of Peñafort, 159, 177
Raynaud, Théophile, 215
reason of state, 6, 123–124, 174, 176, 312, 315, 320–321, 325
recusancy, 132–152, 197
Regensburg, conference of, 86

religion as political imposture, 304, 306, 321–323, 324
Richelieu, Armand du Plessis, duc de (cardinal), 314, 325
Ridley, Nicholas, 223
Rogers, John, 128
Rosicrucians, 278–279
Roussel, Gérard, 71, 75–76
Rovere, Giulio Delle, 91–92
Rudolf II, 275
Rutherford, Samuel, 130

Sa, Emanuel, 154, 200, 210
St. Bartholomew's Day massacre, 107–108
Saint-Cyran, abbé de, 216
Sanchez, Tomás, 154, 164
Sander, Nicholas, 137–138
Sanderson, Robert, 240, 244–248, 253
Sarah, example of, 23, 24, 27, 30, 69
Saravia, Hadrian, 121, 124
Sarpi, Paolo, 311–313
Schneider, Gerhard, 290
Schwenkfeld, Caspar, 279
Scotus, Duns, 177
Secret, François, 281
Seneca, 323
Seneor, Abraham, 44
Sepúlveda, Juan Ginés, 179–181, 201, 204, 211, 215
Servetus, Michael, 95, 96, 116, 257, 280, 299
Shakespeare, William, 193–194, 255–256
Shi'ites, 3–5
Siculo, Giorgio, 89–90
Sigüenza, Jose de, 127
Silvius, Willem, 276
simulation/*simulatio*, 3
Sixtus IV, pope, 38
Soto, Domingo de, 159, 161, 178–179, 195, 200, 201, 204, 211
Southwell, Robert, 186, 187, 188, 190–191, 193, 209
Sozzini, Fausto, 94, 96–97
Sozzini, Lelio, 94–96
Spedding, James, 273
Spiera, Francisco, 88–90
Spinoza, Benedict de, 293, 329–330
spiritualism, 78, 112–113, 298, 299
spiritualists, 94, 107, 111–130, 298–299
statutes: Act of Supremacy, 131; Act of Uniformity, 131; against recusancy,
131–132; oath of allegiance, 205, 225; Test Act, 212, 225
Strauss, Leo, 9–11
Stubbe, Henry, 328–329
Suarez, Francisco, 154, 182–184, 210
subscription, 224–228, 237, 250, 251, 252
Swift, Jonathan, 301
Sybilline prophecies, 254

Tacitus, 6–7, 123
taqiyah, 4–5
Taylor, Jeremy, 160, 222, 240, 248–251
Telesio, Bernardino, 314
temporizer, 80–81, 101–103
Ten Commandments, 167, 181–182
Tertullian, 64
Theophrastus Redivivus, 317, 322–324
Thorndike, Lynn, 268
Three Impostors, 323–324
Throckmorton, Job, 232–233
Timothy, example of, 19
Tindal, Matthew, 293
Toland, John, 10, 293, 294–295, 329
Toletus, Franciscus, cardinal, 210
Torquemada, Tomás de, 42
Tresham, Francis, 196, 197
Trithemius, Johannes, 264–266, 267, 269, 274
Tyndale, William, 234

Udall, John, 230
Urban VIII, pope, 314

Valdés, Fernando de, 165
Valdés, Juan de, 62, 83–87, 130
Valencia, *conversos* in, 52–53
Valencia, Gregory de, 154, 159, 184, 210
Vanini, Lucilio, 257, 306–307, 319, 323
Varro, 295
Vaudois, 64–67
Vaux, Lawrence, 136–137
Vazquez, Gabriel, 154, 162
Vergerio, Pier Paolo, 85, 87, 89, 90–91
Vermigli, Peter Martyr, 72, 85, 87, 90, 109–111, 223, 234–235
Viret, Pierre, 81, 103–107, 298–299
Vitel, Christopher, 127
Vitoria, Francisco, 161, 243
Vives, Juan Luis, 52–53
Voetius, Gisbertus, 292, 304–305

Waldensians. *See* Vaudois

Walker, D. P., 261, 266, 270, 322
Watson, William, 199
Webster, John, 255
Whichcote, Benjamin, 292
Whitgift, John, 224, 226, 227
William of Orange, 121

Yates, Frances, 268, 270

Zayas, Gabriel de, 121, 126
Zoroaster, 295